SAN FRANCISCO

The Virago Woman's Travel Guides

Series Editor: Ros Belford

Amsterdam
New York
Paris
Rome
London
San Francisco

forthcoming:

Athens and The Greek Islands
Great Britain

YOLO COUNTY LIBRARY
226 BUCKEYE STREET
WOODLAND, CA 95695-2600

The Virago Woman's Travel Guide to

SAN FRANCISCO

917.9461
SWI

HARRIET SWIFT

BOOK PASSAGE PRESS a division of RDR Books

Berkeley, California

Published by BOOK PASSAGE PRESS, a division of RDR Books 1994
P.O. Box 5212, Berkeley, CA 94705

Copyright © Harriet Swift 1994

All rights reserved

Printed in Hong Kong by Twin Age Limited

First published in the United Kingdom by Virago Press LTD, 1994

ISBN   1-57143-015-6
Library of Congress Catalog Card Number: 94-70040

Virago Cover Design: The Senate
U.S. Cover Design: Bonnie Smetts Design
U.S. Editor: Wendy Ann Logsdon
Editorial Associate: Deborah Dunn

CONTENTS

ACKNOWLEDGEMENTS

This book is dedicated to the memory of four dear friends who made San Francisco such a great adventure: Bill Critchfield, Bruce Grant, Bethany Korwin-Pawlowska and Lacey Fosburgh.

First of all, thanks to my patient and skilful editors at Virago, Lennie Goodings and Ruth Petrie, and to my US publisher, Roger Rapoport.

Special thanks for sharing insider knowledge and awesome research skills to Julie Bourland, Carla Dole, David Gere, Carol Harper (in London), Rosemarie McMichael and Karen Sulkis.

For their help in ways too diverse to list, thank you to Yasmin Anwar, Christine and Jerry Barnes, Cynthia Bowman, Jane Ellen Cason, Gray Brechin, Lonnice Brittenum, Morton and Jean Cathro, Janet Fletcher, Colleen Gallagher, John Glodow, Sara Hare, Mary Ann Hogan and Eric Newton, Dean and Judith Morgan Jennings, Rachel Kaplan, Larry Kelp, Diana Ketcham, Andrew Hoyem, Marilyn King, Rod Kiracofe, Garth Korwin, Steve LaVoie, Cathy Meyer and her son Gregory, Peggy Moffett, Mike McMichael, Muriel Parenteau, Brenda Payton, Jill Pickerell, Sarah Pollock, Patric Powell, Jon Rochmis, Sharon Rooney of the SF Convention and Visitors Bureau, Janet Rudolph and Perry Marker, Patti Saik, Lynda Seaver, Pauline Scholten and Sylvia Allen, Peter Shifter, Gordy Slack, Martin Snapp, Susan Stern, Bob and Decca Treuhaft.

Thank you for turning your San Francisco vacations into experiments in tourism to my cousin, Mary Leslie Rutherford, Gulf Shores, Alabama; Marguerite (Miss Rusty) Mitchell, Colorado Springs, Colorado; Jim and Teresa Beardsley and their children, Rachel and Noah, Wilcox County, Alabama; Sylvia Smith Isabel and her son, Duran, Long Island, New York.

A special thanks to my mother, Lall Hybart Swift, for her encouragement. And finally, thank you to Pat Brown and Robin Orme for introducing to me to San Francisco during that long-ago magical summer of 1971.

Disclaimer
The author and publisher have made every effort to ensure the accuracy of information contained in the *Virago Woman's Guide to San Francisco*, but can accept no liability for any loss, injury or inconvenience sustained by any traveller as a result of information or advice contained in this guide.

BAY AREA OVERVIEW

PACIFIC OCEAN

FORESTVILLE

SEBASTAPOL

TO THE REDWOOD EMPIRE

SANTA ROSA

CALISTOGA

(29) **ST HELENS**

RUTHERFORD

(12)

(101) **SONOMA COUNTY**

OAKVILLE

YOUNTVILLE

(1)

PETALUMA

(116) **SONOMA**

(29) **NAPA COUNTY**

POINT REYES NATIONAL SEASHORE **INVERNESS**

POINT REYES

(121)

(12) **NAPA**

MARIN COUNTY

NOVATO

(29)

(37)

VACAVILLE

(80)

(1)

(101) **SAN RAFAEL**

SAN PABLO BAY

FAIRFIELD

SELANO COUNTY

STENSON BEACH

VALLEJO

(680)

(780)

MUIR WOODS

MARIN CITY

(580)

(80)

RICHMOND

SAN FRANCISCO

GOLDEN GATE BRIDGE

SAUSALITO

UNIVERSITY OF CALIFORNIA

BERKELEY

(4)

LAFAYETTE

(680)

BAY BRIDGE

(280)

(80)

CONCORD

DALY CITY

(101)

ALAMEDA

OAKLAND

WALNUT CREEK

CONTRA COSTA COUNTY

(4)

PACIFICA

SOUTH SAN FRANCISCO

(580)

DANVILLE

(280)

SAN FRANCISCO INTERNATIONAL AIRPORT

SAN FRANCISCO BAY

(880)

MOUNT DIABLO 3849

(680)

HALF MOON BAY

(92)

BURLINGAME

(92)

HAYWARD

(580)

BELMONT

PLEASANTON

(101)

REDWOOD CITY

(880)

MENLO PARK

(84)

FREMONT

STANFORD UNIVERSITY

(680)

LIVERMORE

(580)

PALO ALTO

NEWARK

(35)

MOUNTAIN VIEW

ALAMEDA COUNTY

(280)

SAN MATEO COUNTY

(101)

(1)

SANTA CLARA

BIG BASIN REDWOOD STATE PARK

SARATOGA

SAN JOSE

SANTA CLARA COUNTY

SANTA CRUZ COUNTY

BOULDER CREEK

(17)

LOS GATOS

(101)

N

0   20 MILES

0   20 KILOMETRES   40 KILOMETRES

INTRODUCTION

San Francisco has been called 'the city that knows how' for more than a century and shows no signs of losing its magic touch. Everyone raves about the city's physical beauty, set on a peninsula of undulating hills framed by the Pacific Ocean and San Francisco Bay, but it is San Francisco's absolute genius for having a good time that endears it to residents and brings back visitors time after time.

The city sprang up almost overnight in 1849, after gold was discovered in the nearby Sierra Mountains, and developed because all those instant millionaires needed some place to spend their money. The habit of putting fun first never left San Francisco which is fairly bursting with restaurants, clubs, coffee houses, arcane celebrations, parties, silly contests, parades, street fairs, concerts and merrymaking of every kind. Even better, San Francisco's legendary atmosphere of tolerance and experimentation means that everyone, absolutely everyone, will find fun of her or his liking here.

San Francisco is a city with a capital 'C', cosmopolitan, diverse, sophisticated and energetic. But even better, it is a manageable, user-friendly place. Alas, it is not problem free, but its degree of crime, chaos, traffic, homelessness and congestion pale alongside Los Angeles, New York or Chicago. People walk in San Francisco; day and night you will find them walking from home to office, bus stop to café, bar to bar. This is a sociable, outgoing city where women blend in easily and partake of the excitement. As with everywhere in the world, there is need for caution and a certain urban guardedness, but women don't feel they have to dress up in protective armour to enjoy San Francisco.

In small-scale San Francisco (only 49 square miles – roughly seven miles in depth and breadth) one of the greatest joys is the uncomplicated sampling of urban life at its best.

And there's tons more. San Francisco has excellent museums and world-class opera, symphony and ballet. Architecturally the city is a treasure trove, from the nineteenth-century Victorians to the palatial Beaux-Arts buildings of government and commerce to Post Modern highrises with genuine style. You can also stay in the city limits and have a glorious time outdoors. Golden Gate Park has more than 1000 acres of trails, lakes, gardens and bridle paths. Soon the Presidio, the oldest military installation in the US, will be converted to a national park adding another 1000-acre preserve.

Chinatown, Japantown and the Mission are lively ethnic neighbourhoods while the clubs and bohemian cafés South of Market are the province of another high-profile minority group, the 'twenty something' generation. The Castro, too, counts as kind of an ethnic neighbourhood. As the most out-front gay quarter in the world, the several blocks of shops, cafés, bars, clubs, offices and businesses make up a world unto itself. Visitors are welcome to see where gay is the norm and heterosexuality is marginal.

Women have always had a big place in San Francisco life. In the early days when the Gold Rush made the city almost entirely male, women were idolised, firmly placed on a pedestal whether they wanted one or not. Many of the early San Francisco women were prostitutes and madams. A fierce mystique has grown up about these women which pretty much continues to the present. Actually, it is a kind of affirmative action. Many of the city's nineteenth-century male leaders were rogues of the first degree; San Francisco has raised its harlots to an equal legendary status in city folklore.

Since the 1970s, tourism has become San Francisco's number one industry. The city is always in danger of becoming a caricature of itself, a kind of Disneyland of Urbania. San Francisco has always been able to reinvent itself, from a sleepy outpost of colonial Spain to an instant city, from the rubble of the 1906 earthquake and fire to the most beautiful city in North America, from a city of prosperous trade unionists to a city of over-educated service industry workers. The engines of the tourist industry are often several beats behind what is really happening. Instead of the tickytacky at Fisherman's Wharf, walk the Golden Gate Promenade from Aquatic Park to the Golden Gate Bridge. Skip the bus and walk up to Coit Tower through the dense little neighbourhoods and the community flower gardens. Avoid anything chain. Stay at one of the historical hotels, such as the elegant Palace to the incredibly funky Phoenix Motel in the Tenderloin. Go on a studio tour of artists' lofts, visit one of the great churches, Grace Cathedral, Saints Peter and Paul or the Swedenborgian Church and visit the herbalists in Chinatown instead of the souvenir markets. Ride the cable cars before 8 a.m. when it will be just you and the gripman zinging up and down hills through a just-waking city.

'At the ends of our streets, stars!' gushed one forgotten poet over San Francisco. Yes. Look for them.

PRACTICALITIES

WHEN TO GO

Autumn is the best time to visit San Francisco. While the vast majority of tourists flood the town during summer, autumn offers the best weather and off-season prices and pace.

Despite Mark Twain's much quoted (and apocryphal) observation that, 'The coldest winter I ever spent was one summer in San Francisco,' an unending number of non-Californians insist on believing that the Bay Area is somehow connected to the semi-tropical beaches of Southern California. They come dressed for the sun in shorts and tank tops, only to come face to face with the fog-shrouded summer months which require at least a long-sleeved jacket and frequently several more layers.

June through September, the cold currents of the Pacific Ocean churn up a mass of fog which gravitates towards land, only to be repelled by California's unbroken chain of coastal mountains. One of the few breaks is Golden Gate, opening onto San Francisco Bay. The fog pours through, blanketing San Francisco with cooling white fogbanks. But come mid-September to early November and you'll find mild, sunny days with little rain and only a touch of fog.

San Francisco's weather is mild all year around, with the temperature hovering between 54 to 65 degrees in summer and 49 to 59 degrees in winter. The rainy season – December to March – returned last year (1992–93), after several worrisome drought years. The wet months are the least pleasant times to visit, being both damp and chilly, but hold a certain cosy charm for San Franciscans.

The second prime time to visit is spring, from March to May. Drenching rains are not unknown in spring, but there are enough sunny, clear days to make up for the occasional wet ones.

There's never a completely non-tourist season in San Francisco, which regularly tops national and international polls as everyone's 'favourite city'. A vigorous convention and trade show industry (the city's No. 1 business) keeps a steady stream of visitors in the city.

PUBLIC HOLIDAYS

Major holidays, when you'll find all government offices closed, practically all shops, cafés and businesses shut and only the bare bones of public transport operating:

New Year's Day 1 January

Easter (Not a government holiday, but most businesses close.)

Independence Day 4 July

Labor Day first Monday in September

Thanksgiving Day fourth Thursday in November

Christmas Day 25 December

Minor holidays, when government offices are closed but a significant number of businesses and activities continue:

Martin Luther King's Birthday third Monday of January

President's Day second Monday of February

Memorial Day last Monday of May

Columbus Day 12 October or second Monday in that month

FESTIVALS

San Francisco is a party-mad city, happy to drop everything for an event. Oddly, for such a pleasure-oriented town, it doesn't have a signature event such as New Orleans's Mardi Gras or New York's Thanksgiving Parade, or even Washington's quadriennial Inaugural celebrations. Events pop up, become all the rage, then fade away – and sometimes resurge. The daily newspapers have large entertainment sections that eagerly herald what's happening, and the weekly papers (*Bay Guardian*, *SF Weekly*, *Bay Area Reporter*) are highly attuned to local celebrations, if sometimes over-stating their importance and/or entertainment value. For exact dates and times, call the **San Francisco Convention and Visitors Bureau** (tel. 974 6900), and check the papers.

JANUARY **Chinese New Year**, which falls on the first full moon after 19 January, usually runs through early February and includes free outdoor activities, non-stop firecrackers all over the Chinatown area and the anachronistic Miss Chinatown USA pageant, culminating in the Golden Dragon parade on the final night.

MARCH The **Bay Area Music Awards**, or Bammies, San Francisco's version of the Grammy Awards, are held early in the month. You can usually count on seeing a clutch of local stars such as the Grateful Dead, Jefferson Starship, Bonnie Raitt and Journey. **St Patrick's Day** is celebrated with a cheerfully boozy parade on the weekend before the 17th.

APRIL The **baseball season** starts with big opening day ceremonies on both sides of the bay. The San Francisco Giants at chilly Candlestick Park and the Oakland Athletics at the Oakland Coliseum in the East Bay. Japantown celebrates all things Japanese with the **Cherry Blossom Festival** on two consecutive weekends with dancing, flower shows, and a parade. The last Sunday of the month is **Opening Day of Yachting Season** when everyone who owns or can rent a sailboat heads out on the bay for parties afloat. It's a spectacular panorama from shore, too, with the Navy and Coast Guard joining in.

MAY On the 5th, **Cinco de Mayo**, Mexican Independence Day takes over the largely Hispanic Mission district for a weekend. At the end of the month, the Mission hosts a curious carnival celebration. It was inspired by Rio's famous pre-Lenten bacchanal, but as the timing coincides with the Bay Area's cold and wet season, this ersatz Carnival was relocated to a better weather month. San Francisco is at its absolute wackiest with the **Bay to Breakers Race**. The 7.4-mile race draws a handful of world-class runners and about 75,000 amateurs, many of whom are in costume. On odd-numbered years the **Black and White Ball** takes over the Civic Centre for one Friday night in May, drawing upwards of 10,000 revellers in formal dress.

JUNE The exuberant, colourful **Lesbian-Gay Freedom Day Parade** is the final Sunday of the month, but a solid schedule of events and merrymaking leads up to the day. June is also the major month for weekend **street fairs**. The fairs can usually be counted on to offer crafts for sale, food booths and children's events. First among equals is the **North Beach Fair**, the city's oldest.

JULY **American Independence Day**, the 4th of July, is celebrated with fireworks over the bay. Traditionally families and friends gather at Crissy Field for a ringside view. Many take to the bay in boats for an even better look.

SEPTEMBER The **Renaissance Pleasure Faire** in Marin opens on Labour Day (first Monday in September) weekend. This recreation of merry olde England in the redwoods is a big favourite with families. For blues fans, the outdoor **San Francisco Blues Festival** in the Fort Mason meadow is a must. Relaxed and good-natured, it's a throwback to the early days of outdoor concerts before big bucks and attitude took over.

OCTOBER and **NOVEMBER** **Columbus Day**, 12 October, is enthusiastically celebrated in North Beach, the traditional Italian quarter. In the 1990s, Native American activists began holding counter celebrations, villifying Columbus as a white male imperialist oppressor – this makes for the kind of cultural tension that San Franciscans adore. **Halloween** is lustily celebrated by the male gay community as a drag paradise. It is slightly less absorbing for lesbians. The once racy **Exotic Erotic Halloween Ball** has disintegrated into a photo opportunity for tabloid TV and press. Mexican American artists have jettisoned Halloween for Dia de los Muertos or **Day of the Dead**, the old Mexican celebration for All Saints' Eve and Day. There's usually a wildly costumed procession through the Mission.

DECEMBER The downtown stores go crazy over Christmas, from the elaborate window decorations at I. Magnin, Gump's and Saks, to a two-storey tree in the Neiman-Marcus lobby. *The Nutcracker*, which was retrieved from obscurity by the San Francisco Ballet more than fifty years ago, is an extremely popular family event.

Getting There

The best way for domestic and international travellers to get to San Francisco is a direct, nonstop flight into SFO (the airline and popular shorthand for San Francisco International Airport).

Most airlines provide service to SFO so have your travel agent search out the least expensive fare. Prices vary according to the season, your point of origin and comfort tastes.

For European and Pacific Rim travellers, there are only a few nonstop flights to San Francisco, meaning that you do not have to change planes at least once in the US before arriving at SFO. You'll be in the air a minimum of eleven hours no matter what, and the plane change in New York, St Louis, Chicago, Hawaii, Los Angeles or wherever, comes as a jarring and unwelcome interval for many travellers. **United Airlines** is a good bet for nonstop flights. Check with your travel agent for others. Carriers such as TWA, American Airlines, Northwest Airlines and Virgin Atlantic offer comparable service in terms of price and amenities, but break their route with stopovers on the East Coast or in Hawaii and Los Angeles.

Domestic travellers may chose to book a flight into either the **Oakland** or **San José** airports. Because of their smaller size, the hassle factor is alleviated. If you plan to visit the Silicon Valley or Santa Cruz mountains during your stay you might chose to fly into San José. If your primary destinations is solely San Francisco then San José (50 miles south) may be a little far. The Oakland Airport is especially convenient, however, because BART (Bay Area Rapid Transit) provides a quick and inexpensive connection from the airport to downtown San Francisco and other East Bay locations.

If travelling with **children** aged two to eleven, expect to pay 50 to 75 per cent of the adult price. Infants and toddlers up to two may be carried on your lap, but you will still be charged 10 per cent of your ticket price. **Pregnant women** should quiz airlines carefully about their policies. The specifics vary, but in general you will be accepted without any question up to seven months pregnant. After that, restrictions range from a doctor's written approval to being accompanied by a nurse at your expense.

There are cheaper ways to travel, as any bucket shop client knows; **low-budget** especially **student** agencies offer some excellent values. Council Travel, one of the most well known student travel service with over 60 offices nationwide and overseas has an excellent track record for delivering what they promise. With other budget agencies that you're not sure about, it is always wise to take a steely-eyed, investigative approach to discounted tickets, getting the offer in writing as well as refund procedures for cancelled flights. Be vigilant about extra charges, too, which are unnecessary and expensive.

Package tours are another option to look into, especially if you are a first-time visitor to San Francisco with any qualms about travelling on your own. Typically, a package tour will provide hotel rooms, airfare and a rental car for one price, usually a little cheaper than if you booked everything yourself. In a city of hotels madly competing to be the cutest, trendiest, smartest, cosiest or most San Franciscan, the packages book their clients into same-old-same-old chain hotels, often near Fisherman's Wharf which even the heartiest Mid-western naif tires of after a day and a half.

If you have time to spare, other options for travelling to San Francisco include **Amtrak** or **Greyhound** services. The train, leisurly and scenic, is becoming a popular way to travel, while the bus, although not as comfortable, is unbeatable if you're trying to cut costs.

A word of advice about **renting a car** for your stay, either through a package tour or on your own: don't. San Francisco is a compact city with good public transport. Parking a car in the city is time-consuming, frustrating and costly. While you may want to hire one for a day's outing to the Wine Country or to explore the further reaches of the Bay Area, don't burden yourself with the unending hassle of having a car in the city.

HELPFUL NUMBERS

Airports
San Francisco Airport (SFO), tel. 876 7809
Oakland Airport, tel. (510) 577 4000
San José Airport, tel. (408) 277 4759

Low cost flights
Council Travel, Student travel agency with over 60 offices worldwide. Look in the Yellow Pages for the office nearest to you.

Alternate Transportation
AMTRAK, tel. 1 800 872 7245
San Francisco Greyhound Terminal, tel. 558 6789

Regulations

For foreign tourists, visiting regulations vary. We advise you contact your American Consul for exact details. Citizens of the UK, for example, need a valid passport and must show a roundtrip, non-refundable ticket. With this, you will be free to stay in the country for 90 days. Your stay may be extended through petitioning the Immigration and Naturalisation Service (INS) which oversees foreign visitors.

Among young travellers who have the time and energy, a popular way to extend the stay is to pop up to Canada or down to Mexico for a few days. When you cross back into the states – Eureka! – you have another ninety days at your disposal.

If you have ideas about working in the US it is a different matter. Student visas and short-term, temporary work visas for summer camps, universities and hospitals are a fairly simple matter to obtain (again check with your US Embassy or Consulate). Anyone being transferred to work in the United States or taking jobs offered by American firms will face a bureaucratic maze to obtain a Green Card, a permit for non-citizens to work in the country. It is extremely difficult to obtain permanent or open-ended working papers for non-citizens. Your company will have to be a full partner in this process, petitioning the government for your admission and submitting documentation to show that the job cannot be filled by an American citizen. Start your research with the INS office in your country.

If you are coming over on a short-term business trip, conditions are the same as for a tourist stay: 90 days.

Under the table work, of course, is far from unknown. It is rare, however, to find undocumented jobs that pay more than the minimum wage ($4.25 an hour) and aren't of the domestic or back-breaking variety, i.e. babysitting, moving furniture, gardening or dog walking. Businesses, even very small ones, are reluctant to bend the rules for undocumented workers because of the huge fines and possible prison time mandated by the harsh federal laws of the last few years.

Going through Customs, you may or may not be asked a number of questions and required to open your bags. Don't bring in anything giftwrapped; it is axiomatic that the agents will insist you take it apart. On the plane you will be given an INS form that will be collected and turned over to Customs on arrival. You will be expected to give some indication of where you're staying, listing a hotel or a friend's address.

You may also be asked to demonstrate you have enough money to get by on. The minimum to satisfy a picky Customs official is around $150. Should you land on a particularly busy day, you might find the Customs agents brusque and borderline rude. Assume a cool and correct attitude, answer questions fully and keep a lid on your annoyance. You will get through much quicker.

Insurance

Travellers' insurance is crucial for foreign visitors in the United States. National health insurance does not exist and people without insurance have been known to die in emergency waiting rooms where hospitals have refused to admit them.

If you have to see a doctor, dentist or visit a hospital during your stay, they will probably be hesitant to take your insurance as immediate payment. A visit to a doctor for a minor complaint, such as a cold, will start at $35. A dental emergency, for instance replacing a filling is rarely less than $75. Hospitalisation is easily $5000 a week.

Because doctors and hospitals are used to trying to work out a payment deal, most will probably agree to a down payment with the idea that you can have your insurer reimburse you. Doctors in small practices will usually accept a partial payment and the larger establishments, such as medical testing labs and hospitals, will take credit cards (Visa and Mastercharge being the most widely accepted). See also p. 32.

Your travel agent is the best place to start looking for a policy. Many Access and Visa cards will provide insurance if you purchase your plane tickets under their auspices.

Money

The basic denomination of American currency is the dollar ($1). Based on the principle of ten, $1 is 100 cents, called pennies. Coins come in 5c, 10c and 25c denominations. The 50c and $1 coins were discarded several years ago.

Feminist leader, Susan B. Anthony, was the only woman ever to appear on US currency when the Treasury Department tried to re-introduce the one-dollar coin in the 70s. Heavy and odd-shaped (octagonal), the Anthony dollar never found favour with the public. Even women's groups eventually gave up pushing its use. Note denominations are $1, $5, $10, $20, $50 and $100.

Foreign visitors should have some American currency in your pocket when you land in the US. All international airports have a currency exchange office somewhere, but it is not necessarily next door to the Customs section. Be sure to have quarters and dollar bills. At San Francisco International Airport luggage carts are provided free for international visitors, but everything else requires American cash, from porters to help with your bags to paying for a taxi or shuttle into the city.

DENOMINATIONS

All coins are round, but vary in size and thickness. Pennies are copper and brownish; all others are silver.

1c: penny
5c: nickel
10c: dime
25c: quarter (sometimes 'two bits')
100c: Susan B. Anthony dollar, very rarely used

All bills are green, whatever their value. Denominations are prominently written on all four corners, both sides. Remind yourself to look carefully at your bills when spending money.

Changing Money

For the international visitor, San Francisco is something of a backwater when it comes to money changing. You won't find the easy access and competitive currency offices of other European cities. Taking care of money will require some thought and planning, but it's not an overwhelming task.

The biggest favour you can do yourself is to get your travellers cheques in dollars instead of your own currency. Travellers cheques are truly the coin of the realm for most San Francisco businesses which are heavily dependent on tourism. It is also useful to get cheques most familiar to Americans – **Visa** or **American Express**. Thomas Cook is accepted grudgingly and Eurocheques practically not at all outside of currency offices.

To change your own money or travellers cheques, the easiest place to go is a **Thomas Cook** office (downtown), American Express (four offices) or **Bank of America** (only currency exchange in San Francisco International Airport) which offers more exchange offices than any other San Francisco bank.

It is best not to carry too much cash. Muggings are a fact of life in urban America and no matter how hard you try to avoid it, you'll probably be labelled a tourist before you even open your mouth in most parts of San Francisco. If you should ever be accosted, give up your cash and valuables immediately and without a hassle. Most robbers, even when armed, are quite businesslike about the whole ordeal. They want your money, no mess, no fuss, and a quick getaway.

A credit card is close to a necessity of life in the US. It will make transactions much easier to pay bills by credit card, reducing the amount of cash or travellers cheques you'll need. A credit card is also seen as a key ID, next to your passport. Also, the cash advance system solves most problems about how to have ready access to cash without the drawbacks of carrying it around.

Visa, Mastercard and American Express are the most recognised and trusted cards. They also hook up with the pervasive cash dispensing machines that cover American cities. You should check with your credit card company beforehand to ensure that your card and access code will translate to American bank machines. Even easier than taking chances with a machine is to simply visit a bank during hours and get a cash withdrawal. Show a teller your credit card, ID and tell her or him how much you want, in what denominations. The teller writes out a credit slip as if you were buying an item, you sign and the cash is handed over. While malfunctions are not a common problem among Bay Area bank machines, the last thing you want to deal with on holiday is a mangled or erroneously repossessed credit card.

EXCHANGE OFFICES

Here are some easy to find, foreign visitor-friendly currency offices. Check under 'Foreign Exchange' in the telephone directory Yellow Pages for more information.

American Express, 237 Post St, tel. 981 5533, open 9 a.m.–6 p.m. Mon–Fri, 10 a.m.–5 p.m. Sat. Off Union Square, this office has a reputation for briskness bordering on rudeness. Amex checks are cashed free; $3 charge for exchanging currency.

Bank of America. Most US banks are clueless about foreign money. B of A offers currency service at four offices: 345 Montgomery St in the Financial District, tel. 622 2451; 1 Powell St (at Hallidie Plaza) downtown, tel. 622 4097; 420 Post St. on Union Square, tel. 622 2379; and at SFO, International Terminal, tel. 742 8079.

Thomas Cook, 75 Geary St, tel. 362 3452, open 9 a.m.–5 p.m. Mon–Fri, 10 a.m.– 4 p.m. Sat. Free cashing of Thomas Cook, MasterCard Travellers cheques; $3.50 charge for changing foreign currency into dollars. Office will hold emergency cash wires sent from abroad for a $25 charge.

Cost of Living

The Bay Area is one of America's most expensive cities – the prices only look good compared to New York. Because San Francisco is a tourist mecca, there is a concentrated interest in presenting visitors with as much stuff as they can buy, eat, tour or consume at top dollar rates. Distance yourself from the tourist circuit and your money will go much further.

A very careful traveller can have a perfectly pleasant time in San Francisco for under $55 a day. With a room at a hostel ($12) or a hotel with hall bathrooms ($31) as a starting point, you can have a bagel and juice for breakfast ($2), a sandwich and soft drink for lunch ($5) and splurge at an ethnic restaurant for dinner ($10). Drinks and/or snacks along the way add another $5.

The more typical visitor won't watch her pennies quite so hawkishly and will average more like $190 a day. A comfortable, modern hotel room can be had for $90, a full breakfast is $10, while lunch in one of the city's excellent restaurants is $15 and dinner in a good place with wine will be $35. Add $15 for drinks at an upscale bar and/or treats like designer ice cream and cappuccinos with pastry. Two cab rides and a cable car roundtrip will cost a further $13.

For those who have even more financial latitude, San Francisco is eager to help you out. A visitor may easily drop $500 a day in the city without even approaching conspicuous consumption. A room in one of the luxury hotels will be at least $250. Breakfast from room service or an upscale hotel dining room checks in at $15, lunch at a haute cuisine restaurant at $30 and dinner in one of the city's world-class restaurants can easily cost $100. Drinks and little treats along the way add up to at least $25 and taxi rides all over the city add another $30.

PRICES

HOTEL ROOMS
Modest hotels and out-of-the-way motels, $50–$80.
Boutique and mid-range chain hotels, bed and breakfasts, $90–$150.
Luxury and full-service hotels, $175–$500.

MEALS
Ethnic and fast food, $10 and under.
Upscale ethnic restaurants, California cuisine cafés, $12–$20.
Notable and world-class restaurants, $30–$100.

MUSEUMS
Most history and art museums cost $3–$6, with discounts for children (under 12) and seniors (over 60). Most museums have at least one free day a month.

CLUBS, MUSIC AND COMEDY
Expect $3–$10 cover charge for smaller clubs, $12–$20 for the bigger houses when they have name acts. Most clubs have a two-drink minimum, but it's rarely enforced.

THEATRE
Fringe, week nights at mainstream theatres, $5–$15.
Touring Broadway shows and major theatres, $15–$60.

CONCERTS
Major ballet, symphony, opera can range from $10 to $55.
Smaller classical groups, $5–$25.
Stadium rock shows, $20–$30.
Concert hall rock and jazz, $15–$35.

What to Pack

Come prepared for several kinds of weather. Having warm clothes in summer is the key to enjoying your visit to San Francisco.

- Sturdy walking shoes.
- Sweatshirts or sweater pullovers that you can add as the temperature drops.
- Long trousers for daytime wear; shorts are not adequate on most days.
- A presentable dress or smart trousers ensemble for the opera, sym-

phony, dinner parties or dining out at one of the upscale restaurants.
- Raincoat and umbrella if you are coming during the rainy season, November–March.
- Prescription drugs; non-US doctor's orders can't be filled by American pharmacists.
- Credit cards.

Information

San Francisco, as one of the world's major tourist destinations, is easy to research before you go. There is a huge body of literature about the city, ranging from Allen Ginsberg's poetry to guidebooks as specific as how to tour with your dog.

For detailed information before you arrive, you may write or call San Francisco's vigorous **Convention and Visitors' Bureau**, P.O. Box 42907, San Francisco, Calif. 94142-9097, tel. (415) 391 2000. They can send you an information package with extensive lodging, dining and shopping listings. Maps of the city are also included in the two booklets they provide.

Once you arrive in San Francisco, you will find the Convention and Visitors' downtown information centre a helpful source of information and guidance. Don't be put off by its dingy surroundings in Hallidie Plaza, adjacent to a BART station. The homeless panhandlers are aggressive, but not prone to crime. The information centre offers hundreds of brochures and advertisements that range from hotels and restaurants to walking tours and limousine services.

The staff, positioned behind an enormous counter like airline check-in clerks answer questions quickly and knowledgeably, even if the service is more assembly line than personal. This is a particularly good place to find help about San Francisco's sometimes confusing public transport system. Staffers are brisk, but generally patient, in explaining how the buses, trolleys, cable cars and ferries operate and their complicated tie-ins. A pay phone is available for you to make room reservations or other calls; the staff advise, but don't make the calls themselves.

One overlooked repository of easy-access, thoroughly reliable information about the city and various services is the telephone directory. The Yellow Pages (commercial and institutional listings) are prefaced by an amazingly thorough compendium of information that includes post office listings and postal regulations, a guide to tourist sites, maps of public transport, a calendar of Bay Area events and copious listings of consumer groups. If you know specifically what you are looking for, the business section of the White Pages will help you find that information more quickly.

Maps
A good map will be invaluable in making the most of your San

Francisco visit. Like most American cities, San Francisco was planned to some extent, with its nineteenth-century settlers laying out a grid based on right angles. The city's unusual geographical features combined with the disastrous 1906 earthquake and fire to render the city less than completely rational in its layout. Two radically different grids come together at Market Street, which bisects the city. Streets south of Market do not cross above it. Further, the hilly terrain means that the shortest route between two points is often not a direct one, if going from A to B involves, say, walking up Russian Hill (a 31 per cent grade) in the process.

When picking up a map, keep in mind the smaller and more unobtrusive the better. You don't want to advertise yourself as a clueless tourist by standing in the middle of a sidewalk unfolding a map the size of a poster. Rand McNally's City Flash series includes a San Francisco map, available in most travel sections of bookshops. *City Flash: San Francisco* is plasticised and folds up neatly while offering a good visual layout and useful information such as subway and bus routes. The map that the Visitors' Bureau sends out is not as sturdy, being paper, but the three-dimensional map drawings give a much better sense of the city's topography.

On arrival you might also check out *Streetwise San Francisco* (Streetwise Maps, $4.95) or *Fastmap: San Francisco* (H.M. Gousha, $4.95). Both are plastic fold-ups that fit easily in the bag or backpack and offer comprehensive information about transport and major sites.

Unfortunately, there isn't a map as comprehensive and easy to use as the London A–Z series for San Francisco. The *San Francisco CrossStreet Directory* handbook (Rand McNally, $4.95) is a reasonable substitute, breaking down the city into two-page map grids. It is small – the size of a paperback book – making it easy to carry around and handle for quick reference.

More detailed is the *Regional Transit Guide* (Metropolitan Transportation Commission, $3.95), a small book that has more public transit info than anyone could ever absorb. Yet it is a how-to-get-anywhere manual for the Bay Area, complete in one place.

Keep in mind that many maps are still catching up with changes dictated by the 1989 Loma Prieta Earthquake. The Embarcadero Freeway, which once dominated part of the waterfront, was ordered to be demolished after the quake, experts warning that it might not withstand another big shake. Because the Freeway's future was in doubt for more than a year, even newer maps sometimes retain it.

Communications

Post   The US Postal Service, often a favourite target of American comedians for bureaucratic indifference and carelessness, is actually quite efficient, especially if you go to post offices at off-peak hours (avoid the opening hour, noon lunch break and closing time). In general, you'll find post offices open 8.30 a.m. to 5.30 p.m. or 9 a.m. to 5 p.m. Monday through Friday. Saturday openings are selective, and have shorter hours, usually 9 a.m. to 2 p.m.

To insure, register or send letters or packages express, you'll have to complete some simple paperwork. Typically a clerk will give you a form, tell you to fill it out and return to the head of the queue when finished. Packages must be completely wrapped and sealed before the Postal Service will accept them. Regulations are displayed. Although the larger offices sell supplies such as padded envelopes, boxes and tape, postal employees are adamant about not lending a hand (or handing over a piece of tape).

If you have anything larger than a big envelope to send home, you might consider using one of the increasingly popular 'packing stores' which will wrap and ship anything from a box of handkerchiefs to a computer terminal. The packers prepare your items for shipping, then send them via parcel delivery, air freight or even surface mail. It's pricey, but you get a cheerful, can-do attitude and prompt service.

Stamps are most easily and cheaply bought at post offices which also have stamp-dispensing machines. Postcards to Europe take 40c stamps; letters to Europe are 50c for the first half-ounce, 45c for the next. Most letters are typically 95c to mail. It will take a letter or postcard five to seven days to get from San Francisco to Western Europe. Your mail will move quicker if you drop it off at a post office rather than at a hotel or even a street corner post box, which usually see only one pick-up a day.

An overnight courier service is available for delivery almost anywhere, within the United States or abroad. The Postal Service has reliable overnight and second-day delivery services. Most businesses tend to prefer Federal Express for domestic overnights. In fact, the term 'fed ex' has become slang for express delivery in the way that 'Xerox' means copies, not the company, to most Americans. For international overnights, however, DHL is the preferred service.

If you want to receive mail while in San Francisco, the best plan is to have it sent to your hotel or even better, a friend's home. Poste restante (called general delivery in the US) is not much used these days. The post office only accepts poste restante through one branch, so ask your correspondents to address your mail in the name that appears on your passport to: General Delivery, Hyde Street Station, San Francisco, Calif. 94142. The post office branch is located at 101 Hyde St in the Civic Centre area.

You will need two IDs to claim your mail, and one must be a photo identification. Mail not claimed after thirty days is returned.

COMMUNICATIONS

PRACTICALITIES

USEFUL ADDRESSES
Post Offices
There are more than 35 post offices within the San Francisco city limits; the following three are easy to find and have good hours. Consult the Yellow Pages for the complete list.
Macy's Station, on the ground floor of Macys department store on Union Square, Stockton and O'Farrell streets, open 9.30 a.m.–5.30 p.m., Mon–Sat and 11 a.m.–5 p.m. on Sun (extremely rare).
City Hall Station, on the first floor of City Hall in the Civic Center Plaza, Van Ness and McAllister streets, open 8.30 a.m. to 4.30 p.m. Mon–Fri.
Rincon Annex Station, off the Embarcadero, 180 Steuart St (at Howard), open 7 a.m. – 6 p.m., Mon–Fri and 9 a.m.–2 p.m., Sat. Be sure to take in the wonderful Anton Refregier murals that dominate the 1940s lobby in the old part of the building.
Packaging Stores
Handle With Care Packaging in the Financial District, 200 Pine St (between Sansome and Battery), tel. 986 5568, open 9 a.m.– 6 p.m., Mon–Fri, 10 a.m. –2 p.m. Sat. A pick-up service is available.
Supermail International is in Building 4 of the Embarcadero Center, Clay and Battery streets, tel. 392 7788.
Courier Services:
DHL, tel. 1 800 225 5345 to make arrangements for pickup or delivery.
Federal Express, best to call its local number, tel. 877 9000, to arrange for services.
Faxes have almost replaced San Francisco's famous bike couriers, male and female daredevils who covered the town like grunged-up offspring of Mercury. But there are still a few services that use the bikers, including **Aero Delivery**, a full-service messenger service, tel. 989 9707.

Telephones To make an international call dial 011, then the country code, then the city code and phone number.

When making domestic long-distance calls you will always dial '1' first, even when calling toll-free 800 numbers.

An '800' prefix means that the caller will not be charged for the call. A '900' prefix means that the caller pays for the call, often at exorbitant rates. A '976' long-distance code alerts you that this is a sexually-oriented phone service, and the rates are sky-high, starting at $2 per minute.

For local calls, simply dial the seven-digit number. To call out of your area code – 415 for San Francisco – you must dial 1-area code-phone number. At pay phones a local call is 20c. The machines will also work with 25c (a quarter), which many callers use for the simplicity of using one coin.

If you're staying in a hotel, be sure and check the house policy on phone calls. Some hotel corporations have installed the appalling practice of charging for local calls, even when the guest is doing all the dialling. Worse are the extras added to long distance calls. Even though you'll have to take a fistful of change into the booth, it is often cheaper to make your calls from a pay phone. On pay phones, you will deal with an operator who will ask you for payment at three-minute intervals. A three-minute call to the Europe at the lowest rate time is $5.50.

Keep in mind that calling time rates for international calls are different than domestic calls, both on private phones and pay phones. Prime time, highest rate for calls abroad is 7 a.m. to 1 p.m.; 1 p.m. to 6 p.m. is lower and 6 p.m. to 7 a.m. is the lowest rate. For domestic calls, prime time is 8 a.m. to 5 p.m., with lower rates 5 to 11 p.m. and lowest from 11 p.m. to 8 a.m. Rates also drop on weekends.

Pay phones are in abundance all over the city and generally in good working order. Hotel lobbies and the women's toilets of restaurants are always good bets for finding a quiet phone. For information about phone numbers within the 415 area code, call 411 (just those three digits). If you want a number out of the 415 area code, dial 1-area code desired-555-1212. Along with 911 for life-and-death emergencies, these three numbers are now standard all over the United States.

AREA CODES FOR THE BAY AREA

San Francisco: 415
Marin: 415
East Bay (Oakland and Berkeley): 510
San Jose: 408
Napa: 707

Faxing

Faxes are almost as thick on the ground as telephones in San Francisco. You'll find faxes at copy shops, department stores, hotels and stationery stores. Upmarket hotels, such as the Clift and the Ritz-Carlton, will arrange to have them placed in your room (or suite), but almost all hotels have fax services available for guests.

Copymat, a well-known chain of copy shops, has a reliable fax service at all of its sixteen San Francisco stores. Check the telephone directory for one nearest you.

Media

Television   American television is the decisive cultural influence in US society. The debate since the 1950s about whether TV has a major impact on its viewers has reconfigured itself in the last decade to attempts, usually futile, to harness or direct its power. TV has no single consciousness; it sprawls and spreads, acting as a mirror rather than an arbiter of the society.

Television is a bellwether to the culture, but offers almost nothing in the way of genuinely entertaining or provocative programming. The news programmes are quick updates on the day's most pressing stories and/or the most filmable ones. Nothing terrifies a TV news director more than the prospect of 'talking heads', people explaining what is going on. Of course, that's when television is usually at its best: film of current events put into context by a knowledgeable reporter. Bay Area TV has been exemplary in times of crisis. During the 1989 Loma Prieta earthquake and the 1991 Oaklands Hills firestorm, local stations went to a total news format, keeping citizens up to the minute on developments and keeping down the panic factor by a symbolic restoration of order.

American TV comes in two forms: **free broadcast TV**, supported by advertising revenues, and **subscription cable** television, available through monthly fees. What you'll see in San Francisco is basically what every American sees: the three main networks, ABC, CBS, NBC, filtered through their local stations, and the new Fox network which is available over independent stations. There are three Public Broadcasting System outlets in the Bay Area, that provide some of the best public television around. With cable you can see literally hundreds of channels, ranging from other American cities' TV channels and CNN's 24-hour news channel to soft-core porn and old movies.

Public access cable, of the sort so deftly lampooned in the film *Wayne's World*, exists but is limited in the Bay Area. Only a few cable subscribers receive the public access channels and there's nothing like the devoted cult followings for shows in the New York City area.

You'll find reliable, up-to-date information on both the network and local news shows, if light on depth and analysis. Because of the Bay Area's changeable and quirky weather, news shows place heavy emphasis on weather predictions. You'll find this information useful in planning your activities. For national and international news, *The McNeil-Lehrer Report* on PBS is the choice of most well-informed people over the network news broadcasts. For local news, independent station KTVU (Channel 2), has a very grounded, if somewhat stately, handle on the Bay Area scene.

The most widely received outlets in San Francisco are **KTVU**, Channel 2 (independent and Fox), **KRON**, Channel 4 (NBC), **KPIX**, Channel 5 (CBS), **KGO**, Channel 7 (ABC), **KQED**, Channel 9 (PBS), Channel 20, **KOFY** (independent), Channel 44, and **KBHK** (independent).

Radio Radio is primarily a background noise in the United States, used in times of crisis for a headline service, but rarely providing any thoughtful programming. In the Bay Area, however, you will

find one of America's few radio hotspots, where stations and programmes run the gamut from sterile Top 40 to sizzling intellectual
debates to politicised pop music.

Like commercial television, most radio is ad-driven, but the Bay
Area has several important alternative stations that scrape by on lis-
tener donations and grants. The key station is **KPFA** (94.1 FM), the
country's oldest listener-supported radio station. Its jammed schedule leaps from world beat music to Caribbean politics to women's
issues and everything in between. The station's leftist, affirmative
action, feminist perspective almost guarantees that it is in a constant
battle with itself over political correctness, but turning on KPFA
provides a quick, instructive tour of Bay Area leftist politics and
issues. There are several women's programmes, but the schedule is
always changing, so it's best to check the station for times and
topics (tel. 510-848-6767).

KQED (89.1 FM) is the local National Public Radio outlet, the
audio sister of PBS television. Most of the programming is national
and international – you can catch the BBC news hour live, beginning at 12 midnight. National news broadcasts from **NPR** in
Washington are uniformly excellent. While there's no 'women's
programme' on either local or national public radio, this is probably
the medium most attuned to women's issues. **KALW** (90.1 FM) is
also allied with NPR but, as a project of the San Francisco School
Board, it is obliged to broadcast long, tedious board meetings without interruption.

On commercial radio, **KGO**'s (81 on AM) all talk programming is a San Francisco staple, with a good representation of
women guests and women's issues.

Other unusual stations include **KKHI** (102.1 FM), an all-classi-
cal music station, **KCBS** (74 AM), an all-news station, **KJAZ** (92.7
FM), an all-jazz station and **KALX** (90.7 FM), the University of
California at Berkeley student station, where you'll get a crash
course in what's hot musically among the twentysomethings, served
up with a sometimes impenetrable youth narrative laced with all the
newest slang.

Newspapers The *San Francisco Chronicle*, (50c daily), the
700,000-circulation morning paper, owns the city. Residents fume
over and belittle the Chron's trend-happy reporting and decry the
lack of 'serious' news, but in fact no San Franciscan dares to let
more than a day or two go by without at least skimming the paper
for local news and updates. Politically the newspaper is liberal
Democratic, but in the Bay Area's frequently overheated leftist
roller derby it is seen as woefully conservative, if not reactionary.

Key to the *Chronicle*'s dominance is daily columnist Herb Caen
(pronounced cane), a local institution with no known equivalent

anywhere. His three dot column, which has appeared since 1942, is a witty gumbo of gossip, innuendo, anecdotes and tart town scold (rudeness to tourists receives much of Caen's indignation). He not only writes about local lore and folkways, he creates it. Rival newspapers all have their columnists, but no one has Caen's audience and impact. He reduces San Francisco to a charming if somewhat daffy small town, taking readers with him to boozy luncheons with local politicians and swapping catty *bons mots* at the Opera opening. It may be a fantasy town, but it is one that most of the inhabitants believe in. Reading Herb Caen is a vivid illustration of San Francisco's collective consciousness.

The afternoon *San Francisco Examiner* (50c daily), the flagship of the Hearst publishing empire, has a radically smaller circulation, but as No. 2 goes after the Chron tooth and nail. The editorial pages are middlingly liberal, but the paper's true religion is doing anything to increase its measly market share.

The *Chronicle* and *Examiner* co-publish a Sunday paper ($1.75) in the manner of many large US dailies, which are steadily losing their readers to TV. The Chron's Sunday entertainment section, the 'Datebook', is the best single guide to entertainment available. Called 'the pink book' for the hideous paper it is printed on, the Datebook has not just listings but advertisements from all the major presenters of upcoming events.

Both dailies have a well-developed sense of women as equal partners to men in American life. Women's issues are covered as fully and sensitively as in any major American newspaper. The kinky side of San Francisco life also gets a full hearing. The Examiner in particular delights in turning up the volume on 'only in San Francisco stories'. An Examiner piece on the emerging lesbian sex clubs had gays and straights buzzing for weeks.

The free weekly papers around the Bay Area are the liveliest and most revealing reading. Most began as sixties' alternative publications, full of hippie liberation and anti-war energy. Those that have grown to middle age have retained their angry politics, but tacitly acknowledged their real mission as covering music, theatre, comedy and lifestyle. While none of the weeklies are women's publications, they are highly sensitised to feminism. The *Bay Guardian* and the *SF Weekly* appear in street boxes, bookstores, cafés and clubs every Wednesday. In addition to their thorough and reliable listings, the weeklies devote most of their space to stories-behind-the-story coverage of local politics and the cutting edge arts and entertainment.

The *East Bay Express*, which concentrates on Oakland and Berkeley, has the same strong listings, but is particularly good on publishing long pieces about political issues and puts a heavy emphasis on women.

The gay community has a thriving alternative press, but no strictly lesbian publication. The two largest gay newspapers, the *San Francisco Sentinel* and the *Bay Area Reporter* (usually called the B-A-R), make token efforts to include lesbian stories but have an essentially male orientation. The newer *Bay Times*, published every other week, is very plugged into the lesbian scene. Its advertisements and listings are the single best guide to not only lesbian, but woman-only events in the Bay Area.

Magazines   There are only a few magazines published specifically for the Bay Area. *San Francisco Focus* ($2.50), a big, glossy magazine published by KQED, is the largest and best known. Like public television itself, the magazine has an agenda of unhurried progressive politics, liberally interspersed with celebrity profiles, wine tastings, travel stories and restaurant reviews. It also contains a detailed listing of KQED TV and radio schedules.

Several magazines have recently gone under, but *SOMA* ($2.95), a quirky monthly devoted to 'Left Coast Culture', throws together an erratic but often entertaining mixture of music, grunge fashion. It is an authentic insider's view of the SoMa (meaning South of Market) scene.

Two lesbian magazines published for a national audience from San Francisco are more reflective of their hometown than America. *On Our Backs* ($5.95) is a bi-monthly, originally started by a group that included lesbian sex priestess Susie Bright. Often unapologetically vulgar, OOB is the party girl of lesbian periodicals. *Deneuve* ($4, six times a year), a new slick publication, aims for a more elevated tone with stories about lesbian attorneys, dating by computer, record reviews and mild humour.

Language

San Franciscans speak an easily understood dialect of American English. The San Francisco accent, in fact, is no accent to American ears, having none of the colourful exaggerations of Southerners nor the broad pronunciations of New Yorkers and New Englanders.

In some parts of the city English is definitely the second language. Spanish rules the Mission and various Chinese dialects are spoken in Chinatown, but everyone, particularly in the shops and cafés, can communicate in English.

Everyone is heartily sick of the phrase 'politically correct', but the Bay Area is one of its strongholds. Women are women, blacks are African-Americans, the disabled are physically challenged and manifestations of cultural imperialism are sternly dealt with in letters to the newspapers.

SOME USEFUL PHRASES, ABBREVIATIONS AND COMMONLY USED SLANG

Like any region, especially one so self-conscious, San Francisco has little language cul-de-sacs and localisms you will find handy to know about. Included here too are common Americanisms that sometimes cause confusion to British visitors.

Asian People, places, culture. Use the term 'Oriental' for rugs only.

The Avenues Lower middle-class residential area on the numbered avenue streets, generally considered a metaphor for dreariness.

Bad Hair Day The ultimate in bad karma.

BART Bay Area Rapid Transit, the subway system.

Bay Area Backup Traffic congestion, especially on the bridges.

Bay Bridge San Francisco–Oakland Bay Bridge, the little-known sister to the Golden Gate.

The Big One Like death, every San Franciscan confidently expects it to come along: the inevitable 8.0 earthquake that will shake everything into the Pacific (see p. 51).

Bohos Bohemians of the nineties, usually college age or just past.

Bow Heads Young women, usually of college or novice careerist age whose Laura Ashley-Young Republican conservative chic ensembles inevitably include a bow adornment for the hair.

'Burbs Suburbs. Not complimentary.

Cable Cars The cable-driven cars that you know from the movies – not the electric trolleys that run on flat streets. San Franciscans are very particular about the nomenclature of their street cars.

Cal Nickname for the University of California at Berkeley.

Californian Noun only, meaning a resident of California. The unfamiliar use of 'Californian' as an adjective confuses locals who say 'California state of mind' or 'California girl' rather than 'Californian state of mind', etc.

Calistoga Generic term for bottled mineral water; San Franciscans favour the bubbly bottled water from the small Napa Valley town of Calistoga.

Channel Surfing Constant TV channel switching with the remote control. Considered a peculiarly male obsession.

Chron San Francisco Chronicle.

Dope Really "cool."

East Bay Geographically means everything on the opposite shore of San Francisco Bay; in practical terms translates to Berkeley and Oakland.

Ex *San Francisco Examiner.*

411 Gossip, as in the information number you get 'the 411 on her new date'.

Femi-Nazis Rightwing insult aimed at aggressive feminists or any woman found unusually annoying.

Foodie Culinary groupie; not necessarily a cook herself (or himself), the San Francisco foodie is actually aware of what restaurants are in, who the hot chefs are and what the dish of the minute is.

Grunge Fashion statement of the younger set, involving loose clothes, ugly shoes and an unwashed look.

Hella Slang for "very."

Loopy Drunk.

LAX Los Angeles International Airport.

Marin Pronounced Mah-Rin (not marren). Refers to not just the cute woodsy county north of the Golden Gate Bridge, but a mindset of zen-flavoured, go-with-the-flow California life.

Multi-Culti Multi-culturalism, can be a put-down or insider shorthand, depending on who's talking.

Muni San Francisco Municipal Railway, the San Francisco public transit system of buses, streetcars and cablecars.

Noe Valley A charming residential neighbourhood full of Victorians and coffee houses. Pronounced NO EE (rhymes with Zoe).

Patchy Coastal Fog San Francisco's habitual weather forecast.

Pissed Angry, not drunk.

Po Mo Post modern – anything from bands to attitudes.

Ride Bareback Unprotected sex.

Scenester One who makes the scene; very hip until there are too many scenesters then 'nouveau scenester' sets in.

SFO San Francisco International Airport.

Slackers The twentysomething generation, the languid young women and men you will see reading Camille Paglia books in cafés during working hours. Also called 'Generation X'.

Slammin' Fabulous, absolutely the coolest music, club, ensemble, attitude, whatever going.

SoMa South of Market, usually used for ironic effect to tacitly condemn the trendification of the warehouse-industrial-low rent district.

The City San Francisco's preferred term for herself. The *San Francisco Examiner* goes so far as to use 'the city' for all second references for SF, capitalised, no less.

The Park San Francisco's preferred term for Golden Gate Park.

Yuppie Still the reigning pejorative term of young urban professionals for other young urban professionals they dislike. (A term coined, by the way, by Berkeley writer Alice Kahn in the *East Bay Express*.)

Police and Crime

San Francisco, like all American cities, is plagued by crime. And, more unfortunately, like all big tourist meccas, has spawned a more specialised set of crime aimed at tourists. While the city hasn't seen anything as deadly as Miami's infamous 'bump and jump' robberies (where armed thugs spot tourist cars, ram them, then rob the visitors when they get out to discuss what seems to be a minor accident), visitors are seen as an especially rich resource by criminals.

The San Francisco Police Department is the city's primary law enforcement agency although different crimes can bring out the BART police and SF sheriff's department. San Francisco's police officers have a good reputation for dealing with crimes against women. The SFPD ranks include women, minorities and gays at every level, from cops on the beat to the upper ranks.

San Francisco's crime rates are not the highest for an American city or even for California, but there is enough random and tourist-targeted crime to warrant constant caution in moving about the city. Armed robbery is the most prevalent and the diciest crime to come up against. The standard and best advice is to give an assailant whatever he (it's almost always he) wants without complaint or hassle. 'Nothing is worth your life', advises Sgt Richard Frost of the North Beach station which sees many unhappy tourists reporting stolen cameras, cash, watches and handbags.

Suggestions from Sgt Frost and other safety experts boil down to common sense. 'Any time you feel the least bit uncomfortable, leave', says Frost. Official San Francisco, acutely aware of tourism as its No. 1 industry, refuses to acknowledge that one place is more dangerous than another in the city. Residents, though, can name the trouble spots at the drop of a hat: public housing neighbourhoods, Hunter's Point, Bayview, the Tenderloin, Western Addition, parts of the Mission and the Richmond district, and anywhere you find yourself alone on the streets after dark.

Even this list can be misleading. The Mission has a high crime rate, but has busy, bustling streets full of families with young children and women alone. The Western Addition blends almost imperceptibly into Pacific Heights, the city's most stylish neighbourhood. San Francisco is a remarkably compact city which makes even the dodgy parts of town cheek by jowl with the most fashionable.

Take a preventative attitude towards crime. Don't advertise yourself as a tourist. Even when you aren't sure where you're going, walk and act purposefully. When you need to consult your map step into a shop or find a quiet corner. By all means ask for directions, but follow your instincts.

Dress to fit into the San Francisco milieu and keep walking-around luggage to a minimum. Handbags, always the thief's favourite accessory, should be small and easily obscured. Consider a bum bag or a small traveller's bag that you can wear like a big necklace. Backpacks too, have become a target of the criminal element who sometimes slit them with knives, grab what they can and flee. Don't take anything with you that you cannot do without. Carry a minimal amount of cash and only one credit card or ID.

The homeless who clog several prime tourist areas are not exactly a crime problem. Scruffy, smelly and full of despair, they ask for money by thrusting paper cups at passersby or lounge in doorways, often surrounded by pets and their worldly goods crammed into a shopping cart. If you're not used to seeing homeless people, the first look at this depressing urban problem can be unnerving. In the last decade women and families have become increasingly visible among the homeless. While San Francisco has devoted far more energy and compassion to the dilemma of the homeless than most American cities, its very tolerance fuels the problem. The mild climate, lack of harassment and more resources than most areas all make San Francisco the favourite city of the homeless, too. And, for the homeless people who panhandle, tourist gathering points are a natural hangout spot. A firm, 'No, not today', will usually discourage most of the begging. Be especially direct with the people who ask 'for a minute' to tell you long, drawn-out tales of woe. If you are not comfortable saying no, keep some change handy in your pockets to hand out. Don't stop to dig money out from your bag or wallet which always puts you in a vulnerable position.

If you are robbed or assaulted contact the police immediately. Dial 911 (pay phones don't require money for this call) which puts you through to the police. Typically, the officer will ask for a description of your attacker so all officers and patrol cars in the vicinity can immediately be on the lookout. For non-emergency calls, such as discovering that something has been stolen from you, call 553-0123. Remember you will need to have police documentation for insurance claims, so don't just shrug a crime off, even if it is low-impact.

Hotels are loath to make it an issue, but armed robberies and rapes have been a problem, even in the best hotels. One of the most common ploys has been a person coming to the door and identifying himself as a repairman. If you haven't asked the desk to send anyone to your room, don't admit the person without calling to check first.

Sexual Crimes

The increase in sexual crimes has caused American women not only fear for their safety but spurred a fierce philosophical debate about what constitutes rape (the date rape debate) and whether the increase is in crimes committed or crimes reported.

For the woman facing a possible attack these concerns fade completely. The key thing is to *think*. One study of rape reports found that most women were paralysed thinking over and over, 'I can't believe this is happening to me'. Many attackers rely on just that sense of shock and confusion. If you can fight back or escape do it immediately; hesitation gives the attacker a stronger hand. Screaming, calling attention to yourself is very effective. Yell at the attacker to leave you alone, scream for someone to dial 911.

While a woman has the choice of reporting a sexual assault or not, the SFPD gets high marks from women's groups for its compassionate treatment of victims and careful investigation of rapes. Call 911 for emergency police response or, if you want to talk to someone, call the San Francisco **Rape Treatment Center Hotline** at 206 3222. San Francisco **Women Against Rape** also have a 24-hour hotline, tel. 647 7273, and offer counsellors who will go to the hospital and through the police investigation with you.

The Rape Treatment Center is part of San Francisco General Hospital at 995 Potrero St. Another contact is the SFPD's **Sex Crimes Unit**, tel. 553 1361.

EMERGENCIES

For all **emergencies**, medical, fire, ambulance or criminal call 911.

San Francisco Police Department, non-emergency calls, tel. 553 0123. The person you talk to will direct you to the nearest police station or send a police officer to you.

SFPD Sex Crimes Unit, tel. 553 1361

San Francisco Rape Treatment Center, tel. 206 3222 (24-hour hotline)

Sexual Harassment

In terms of late-twentieth century, post-industrial urban life, San Francisco is probably the best that can be hoped for on the public sexual harassment barometer.

Ogling, touching, pinching, whistling and yelling at women by men who are strangers to them is just not done. Even in social situations with women who are dressed to kill, the initial response is covert glances and mumbling approval rather than a round of Hollywood va-va-vooms.

Brasher approaches are not unknown, but in general women visitors to San Francisco don't have to steel themselves to deal with public displays of male testosterone.

There are some differences, however, particularly among people of colour. In the black community where recognition is a key factor to self-esteem, black women report that it is usually wiser to make some kind of response to street talk, especially if it comes from a group of men. A brief nod without breaking stride acknowledges that you have heard the putative compliments without encouraging any follow-up. If ignored, a man easily becomes a target of ridicule by his friends, which in turn can be turned on the woman with unhappy results if alcohol is involved.

Latinas have similar problems and responses in dealing with Latino men. To completely ignore men's flirty chatter sometimes invites trouble, but it is crucial not to encourage it. Every woman alive has discovered this thin line at some point and struggled to walk it. In San Francisco, with its tolerant nature and devotion to progressive politics, you will find the line easier to negotiate than many cities.

Dress

How a woman dresses only enters into the sexual harassment arena obliquely. While San Francisco has a history of being a dress-up town with emphasis on public display of fashion, there are no hard-line taboos. Halter tops, cleavage, shorts, bare legs and arms don't invite censure, but can make you look out of place. Because of the city's changeable, chilly weather almost everyone dresses in layers with a sweater or jeans close at hand to slip on when the fog rolls in.

Especially in summer, tourists are seen all over the city in thin clothes meant for the beach, instantly marking them as outsiders. The dress-for-Southern-California *faux pas* is a boon for T-shirt shops which do a brisk business in sweatshirts.

If you want to minimise your tourist status, avoid the tourist uniform of stonewashed jeans (usually brand new), white running shoes and T-shirts with some kind of San Francisco or California insignia.

To blend into the San Francisco landscape remember that this is a city, not an amusement park. In the Financial District you will find women and men carefully dressed up in suits and ties, but over the rest of the city most people are dressed casually but are in no way scruffy (except the Grunge element but that's a very scrupulously nurtured look). San Francisco women are fairly style conscious so you will see plenty of jeans, but accented with well-designed jackets and interesting shirts. The hippie legacy is still visible in the many cotton weave skirts and Birkenstock sandals all over the city, but they are balanced by the Magnin's (see p. 343) legacy of chic women who have devoted their lives to dressing well. You can wear jeans and comfortable shoes and look native, just forgo the 'Alcatraz Swim Team' sweatshirts and too-new stonewashed denims.

The sign of a true San Franciscan is to *never* wear white shoes. In a local exaggeration of the old etiquette custom that dictated white shoes were for summer and worn only between Easter and Labor Day, San Franciscans reasoned that their fog-shrouded summer months were not truly summer weather so it was inappropriate to wear white shoes during the traditional white shoe season. And, as it was also inappropriate to wear white shoes during non-summer months, white shoes were effectively banned from SF wardrobes. It is a fading custom, but you can still catch San Franciscans glancing at footwear and exchanging smirks at the sight of white shoes.

At the Workplace

In business settings sexual harassment is generally subtle, but nonetheless present as the increasing number of lawsuits show. There are serious penalties for sexual harassment in the workplace, both from federal law and career derailment for the harasser. Your own sense of propriety will dictate if you want to take up a colleague on that post-conference drink, but corporate and public law can put a quick stop to unwanted attentions or pressures at the office.

Racism

San Francisco has a longstanding reputation as a haven for diversity and racial tolerance. The successive settlements of Spanish colonists,

Mexican revolutionaries, Russian trappers, American entrepreneurs, Chinese labourers, Japanese farmers and European immigrants made San Francisco a centre of multiculturalism before the word was invented.

On closer scrutiny the racial history of San Francisco isn't quite so uplifting as the legend holds. Yet neither is it as loathsome as revisionist historians have said. Within the context of history, San Francisco has always been an oasis of possibility.

Under the Spanish, who claimed the California coast in 1542 but didn't settle it for another 230-odd years, the unwarlike Native Americans were rather easily persuaded to accept the military and religious authority of Spain. Herded into the missions to be 'civilised' by Catholicism, European-style peasant farming and patriarchy, the tribes were decimated by disease and cultural upheaval in a matter of generations. From an estimated high of 300,000 before Spanish settlement to 150,000 by 1845, the population of California's natives dropped to less than 16,000 by 1900.

Unlike most of the Spanish colonies in the Americas, the natives did not much intermarry with the California conquerers. The Californios, the Mexican land-owning families who made up most of the state's population until American takeover in 1846, were inordinately proud of the fact that they were of 'pure' Spanish descent. Without a *mestizo* (mixed Native American and white) class that blended race lines, as in Central and South America, California developed a more rigid racial consciousness.

The Americans, in turn, were contemptuous of the Californios as layabouts and wastrels for leaving California largely undeveloped. Able to live comfortable, amusing lives on their vast *rancheros* with ridiculously little effort, the Mexicans saw no reason to upgrade their happy world.

The pattern of displacement, subjugation and superficially peaceful co-existence continued through the twentieth century. While there were usually economic reasons at the root of most conflict and accommodation, there was also a struggle to come to grips with the democratic promise of the American dream and the age-old baggage of ethnic, gender and nationalist prejudice. Slavery was outlawed in California while it was still a territory, the flashpoint being the fury of the mining camps over Southerners who showed up with crews of slaves to do their gold digging for them. The white miners were outraged on a number of levels, foremost being the advantage that the slaveowners had for greater productivity, but the issue of simple human fairness was also at work.

Discrimination against people of colour was amazingly straightforward in nineteenth-century California. Until the 1870s, African and Native Americans could not testify in courts of law. The ban was extended to the Chinese because, reasoned a California Supreme

Court justice in 1852, Native Americans and Chinese were probably descended from the same Asiatic stock which made the Chinese Indian in legal terms.

Anti-Chinese sentiment took root early and extracted a heavy toll from the Chinese. Chinese miners were forced to pay special taxes; mob violence and personal humiliations were constant threats. Eventually this California prejudice was ensconced in federal law with the Chinese Exclusion Act of 1882, which halted all immigration from China. The Japanese, who began to come in serious numbers in the early twentieth century, were subjected to the same sort of unreflective racism, but like the Chinese quickly adopted behaviours and strategies to combat the bigotry. Prohibited from owning land, Japanese immigrants would sign over their land to Chinese Americans in carefully worked out legal arrangements. Curiously, it was during the disgraceful removal of West Coast Japanese Americans during World War II when the Chinese Exclusion Act was finally deleted from the lawbooks.

The World War II mass immigration of African Americans from the rural South changed the complexion of the Bay Area dramatically. San Francisco has had black citizens even from Spanish times. With the terminus of the railroad in Oakland, a thriving bourgeois black community based on railway conductors, cooks and stewards, developed in Oakland and Berkeley in the late nineteenth century, but the huge numbers who came to work in the war industries was a major change. African Americans settled in decaying Victorian neighbourhoods (Fillmore) and industrial fringe areas (Hunter's Point), wherever they could get housing. It was again a case of resistance and accommodation, with African Americans eventually working their way into the political power structure.

Despite its frequent xenophobic and racist assumptions, San Francisco has nonetheless taken a hearty civil pride in its mixed citizenry, proudly pointing out the achievements of non-white San Franciscans and eagerly showing off Chinatown, Mission Dolores and other landmarks of its ethnic communities.

The place of non-white women was of course complicated by the generally confused attitudes toward race. Prostitution, seen as a necessity in a primarily male society, has been a particular sinkhole for minority women. Native women were drawn in by the Spanish and Mexican soldiers. The Chinese, extending the customs of home, imported young women bought from their poor families for the most degrading kind of sexual slavery. During the Gold Rush and beyond, the brothels of San Francisco were widely – and proudly – reported to be stocked with women of every ethnic background.

Women had some leverage in nineteenth-century San Francisco just by their scarcity. Marriage, as a career choice, offered more latitude here than other places of the time.

A South American visitor to San Francisco in 1849 wrote home that several Chilean women 'from the red light district of Valpraiso have married here and even enjoyed the luxury of choosing among their suitors'.

Immigration is again a charged topic in California with the worldwide upheavals that have sent new waves of Southeast Asians and Latin Americans surging into California and especially San Francisco. The influx has overwhelmed many of the public institutions such as schools and hospitals, but created a perplexing moral dilemma. Any number of professional working women in the Bay Area guiltily employ undocumented Mexican, Asian, Guatemalan, Peruvian or (increasingly) African women to take care of their children and homes.

San Francisco today struggles to finally live up to its democratic ideals, but often loses its perspective in the over-heated politics of correctness that engulf every public forum. What outsiders see is not the broken promises of the nineteenth century, but a city of remarkable racial and cultural diversity. The rough edges don't negate the city's cross-cultural allure. Women of colour who come as visitors find it a simple matter to blend into the San Francisco parade and enjoy the city from one end to the other, top to bottom.

Disabilities

The Bay Area is home to a vigorous disabled rights community, making the region one of the most user-friendly areas for disabled people in the world.

Visitors in wheelchairs will find almost all public buildings accessible. Implementation of comprehensive federal laws to make the entire country barrier free to the disabled have been fully applied in the Bay Area. Only a handful of older buildings that cannot be remodelled without damaging their historic significance have been allowed to skirt the strict laws.

Disabled travellers will find that their situation compares favourably with able-bodied visitors in San Francisco and surrounding areas. The barrier-free environment campaign has flattened street curbsides, rebuilt building entrances for ramps, installed wheelchair-accessible toilets and mandated wheelchair lifts for buses.

Berkeley's **Center for Independent Living** has been a pioneer in the disabled rights movement. A significant number of disabled men and women have been drawn to the Bay Area because of this activism, forming a potent nucleus. It is not at all unusual to see women in wheelchairs travelling around by themselves, getting on and off public transport, attending theatre and concerts or going to the parks.

Many performances make arrangements for signers or headsets

for the hearing impaired. It's always a good idea to call ahead to make arrangements as every theatre, concert hall and arena has a different procedure and/or accommodation for disabled clients.

DISABLED RESOURCES

The **Center for Independent Living**, 2539 Telegraph Ave, Berkeley, has a helpful, friendly staff who will suggest resources to visitors by phone. To visit the world-famous locus of disabled rights, make an appointment at least two days in advance, tel. (510) 841 4776.

The **Independent Living Resources Council** of San Francisco will help travellers with problems such as how to use the transit system, finding deaf interpreters and referrals. For the best help, write in advance requesting specific advice to the Council, 70 Tenth St, SF 94103, tel. (415) 863 0581.

The **Bay Area Outreach Recreation Program** is a nonprofit agency that organises recreation and classes for people with disabilities, offering everything from white water rafting to tennis. BORP, 830 Bancroft Way, Berkeley, Calif. 94710, tel. (510) 849 4663.

Travel Agents Specialising in Disabled Needs

Bonnie Lewkowicz of **Escape Artists Travel**, P.O. Box 11031, Oakland, Calif. 94611, tel. (510) 652 1700 and fax (510) 652 6510.

Miller Travel (Marin County) Donna Miller, 101 Casa Buena Drive, Corte Madera, Calif. 94925, tel. (415) 924 1080 and fax (415) 924 1092.

Health and Sex

Health insurance is an absolute necessity for travellers to San Francisco. US health costs have escalated out of all control and the resultant byzantine maze of insurance and payments have made going to the doctor a major investment of time and emotion.

If you have a medical problem or emergency the best response is to ask a friend or colleague to refer you to her or his doctor. The personal goes a long way in cutting through the unbelievable layers of medical bureaucracy. If you don't have friends in San Francisco, ask your hotel for help. On your own you can call the **San Francisco Medical Society** at 567 6234 for a referral, or look through the Yellow Pages in the phone directory under Physicians.

There are clinics that provide free care or determine charges by ability to pay, but they are few in number and crowded. Be prepared to wait and deal with all the problems of an overworked staff. The famous **Haight-Ashbury Free Clinic** is still in business, welcoming all comers. The University of California at San Francisco's **Medical School** clinic is the freebie of choice for most locals, where they can be ministered to by one of the nation's best training hospitals. The city's Public Health Department is also an option for checkups, STD testing and baby care.

Because of the Bay Area's huge number of foreign tourists and business travellers, most doctors, dentists and institutions have some experience dealing with non-US payment. The most typical practice is for the doctor's office to ask you to pay for all services at the time. The doctor or dentist will prepare a full statement for you to submit to your insurance company upon your return. Some doctors have been known to accept partial payment until the insurance company at home can be dealt with. Hospitals and some clinics accept credit cards (see p. 9 for more details).

For small problems such as colds and upset tummies check a drugstore for over-the-counter (non-prescription) remedies. Pharmacists are knowledgeable and helpful about commercial preparations and will usually give quite good advice. If you're inclined toward holistic medicine, health food stores are well-stocked with vitamins and a variety of herbs and mixtures. Acupuncture, massage, chiropractors and herb doctors are an accepted part of life in San Francisco. You won't have to look far to find a non-traditional healer.

Tampons and pads are easily found at drugstores and supermarkets.

Contraception and STD

As an epicentre of the AIDS epidemic, San Francisco is hugely sensitised to sexually transmitted diseases and the consequences of sex. Safe sex is practically a religion in the Bay Area, male to male, female to female, male to female, whatever. Condoms are demanded and expected by everyone who engages in sex.

Condoms have become something of an obsession in San Francisco, spawning new products and not completely tongue-in-cheek missionaries. Safe Sex Sluts, Captain Condom and Lady Latex with their 'condom people' retinues descend on clubs, parties and large public gatherings to hand out condoms and perform songs and skits encouraging safe sex. A shop called **Condomainia** (two locations) offers a stunning variety of condoms and novelties. Condoms are also available at drugstores, grocery stores, handed out in nightclubs and sold in dispensers in the men's and women's bathrooms in clubs. Some hotels include condoms in their room supplies.

Other contraceptives are also easy to come by. **Planned Parenthood** clinics prescribe birth control pills while alternative methods such as the sponge can be located with a little looking. The morning after pill still isn't universally embraced in the US, but can be obtained. Planned Parenthood, the most obvious dispenser for a traveller with no local doctor, reluctantly administers the morning after treatment. A full gynaecological exam is required. Persistence is called for, as well as decisiveness as one must be seen by a doctor within 72 hours of intercourse.

AIDS is a major San Francisco topic even among the people furthest from the gay community. At this point, everyone knows some one, usually a good friend, who has died of this horrible disease. T-cells, AZT, pneumocystis, positive and negative are all terms you'll hear in casual conversation. In fact, the language of AIDS has entered the general domain in some amusing ways. A person's HIV status, positive (sick) or negative (well) has become a shorthand of 'he's negative' or 'I'm positive', which in turn has given the term's usual meaning a twist. It's not unusual to hear someone described as, 'She's such a positive person – good positive, that is', or, 'He's so negative, and not in a good way'.

San Francisco's gay community has been the world's leader in dealing with AIDS and has provided a shining example of what group cohesiveness and determination can do. A saturation educational approach to the problem had an immediate impact once the depth of the threat was known.

In San Francisco new AIDS cases among young gay men dropped off sharply after 1988. Women, more than gay men, are now seen as the group most at risk in the US. More women are infected through heterosexual sex than through intravenous drug use, formerly the leading cause of HIV among women.

If you think you have come in contact with AIDS (which can only be transmitted through an exchange of body fluids) or another STD, it is vital to be tested immediately so treatment can begin as soon as possible. Planned Parenthood, Lyon-Martin Women's Health Services, Berkeley Free Clinic and the Women's Needs Center (see box below) are all good places to start, for testing, counselling and sensible talk.

Pregnancy and Abortion

Any woman pregnant in San Francisco has the widest possible range of resources available to her. Pregnancy can be determined through safe, simple at-home kits available at every drugstore and supermarket, or through free or low-cost tests at public clinics.

The renewed American debate over abortion was never in question in the Bay Area where the commitment to reproductive rights is an article of faith among women – and men. Operation Rescue, the religious right group that targets abortion clinics and brutally harasses women entering them, has never ventured into San Francisco or the East Bay. The group has made tentative appearances in the suburbs of San José and Contra Costa (east of Berkeley), but a broad umbrella of groups under the Bay Area Coalition for Reproductive Rights have mounted counter-offensives, organising escorts for women and staff into the besieged clinics and confronting the Bible-thumping (many male) demonstrators.

Abortion in San Francisco, and all of California, is almost unrestricted, safe and available through low-cost clinics, private hospitals and a wide range of other medical institutions. The California law is among the most liberal in the US: abortion up to the 24th week of pregnancy, no age requirements or parental permissions required.

Abortion: a Brief History

Abortion was practised quite openly in San Francisco in the nineteenth century. Visitors to the thriving city were shocked to see abortionists advertising in local newspapers, albeit through euphemisms. While only prostitutes and the well-off could afford the services of these doctors and midwives (or even knew such a thing existed), the city took a casual attitude toward Victorian mores. As long as the unconventional was done tastefully, San Francisco could accommodate almost everyone.

In 1872 California passed its first abortion law, making abortion a crime for the woman having it, anyone arranging it and the person performing the abortion. The California law was modelled on similar state laws being enacted all over the US as part of a general codification and regulation of the professions. Abortion was not a passionate issue in San Francisco or most of California where the Catholic Church's colonial roots gave it a certain avuncular eminence, but it had nothing like the hegemony the Church exercised in the East or other deeply Catholic enclaves of the Midwest and Southwest.

Beginning in 1967, California began easing legal restrictions on abortion, first with the Therapeutic Abortion Act which allowed abortion if pregnancy posed a risk to a woman's physical or mental health. Many doctors chose to interpret mental health quite liberally, making legal abortion much more accessible. Still, it was a matter of knowing and manipulating the system, which meant abortion was primarily used by middle- and upper-class white women.

By the time the Supreme Court had ruled that women have a right to abortion (the famous 1973 Roe vs. Wade case), California had already substantially loosened up its laws on the issue. California feminists had worked hard for legal abortion, but ironically, it only became the focus of women's groups in the wake of Roe v. Wade when the abortion backlash began to build. Reproductive rights is the rallying cry and single most motivating factor among local feminist and women's organisations.

The state budget has become a battleground over abortion, with the pro and anti forces zeroing in on Medi-Cal (the state health insurance for the poor) and whether abortion will be included in healthcare. The battles shift from court to legislature and back again, but in recent years public funding for abortions has been restored, both in California and in the federal public health budget.

USEFUL RESOURCES

Bay Area Coalition for Reproductive Rights (BACORR), 750 La Playa, tel. 252 0750. Aggressive umbrella organisation that trains and deploys volunteers to keep abortion clinics open and confront right-wing demonstrators.

Berkeley Free Clinic, 2339 Durant St, Berkeley, tel. (510) 548 2745. Some drop-in, full women's care.

Condomainia, 541 Castro St, tel. 552 6851; and 1969 Union St, tel. 346 9984. Everything you can imagine (and some you can't) associated with condoms.

Haight-Ashbury Free Clinic, 558 Clayton St, tel. 431 1714. All services; appointment suggested; donations gratefully accepted.

Lyon-Martin Women's Health Services, 1748 Market St, tel. 565 7667. Open to all women, but emphasises lesbian care and issues. Children's health, HIV, testing, counselling.

Planned Parenthood, 815 Eddy St, Suite 200, tel. 441 5454. (There are seven PP clinics in the Bay Area; this is headquarters and can refer you to the others.) Pregnancy tests, STD diagnosis, abortions, HIV testing, exams.

Pregnancy Consultation Center, 1801 Bush St, tel. 567 8757. Free pregnancy tests, diaphragm fittings, birth control pills prescribed, STD testing. Also has an Oakland office.

Quan Yin Healing Arts Center, 1748 Market St, tel 861 4964. An acupuncture and Chinese herbal therapy centre. Not only for women, but offers many women-oriented programmes, such as PMS and menopause counselling.

San Francisco **Department of Public Health** has seven neighbourhood clinics. Try **Potrero Hill Health Center**, 1050 Wisconsin St, tel. 648 3022. STD testings and care, women's healthcare, physical check-up, immunisation shots.

University of California at San Francisco **Screening and Acute Care Clinic**, 400 Parnassus Ave, tel. 476 4602. Drop-in clinic; clients are referred to other UCSF departments after an examination.

University of California at **San Francisco Dental Clinic** 100 Buchanan St, tel. 476 5608. Teaching clinic; treatment by faculty and dental students. Reduced fees.

University of the Pacific School of Dentistry, 2155 Webster St, tel. 929 6501. Drop-in programme, treatment by faculty and dental students; fees are much lower than practising dentists.

Women's Choice Clinic, 2930 McClure St, Oakland, tel. (510) 444 5676. A woman-run centre that offers the full range of women's health needs. Fees are on a sliding scale according to income.

Women's Needs Center, 1825 Haight St, tel. 221 7371. Birth control, HIV testings, gynaecological exams.

PHARMACIES

Walgreens, 498 Castro St, tel. 861 6276. Full service drugstore open 24 hours, with a pharmacist on duty.

Walgreens, 135 Powell St, tel. 391 4433. Located near the cable car turnaround.

One Market Plaza Pharmacy, 1 Market Plaza (at the foot of Market St downtown), tel. 777 0404. Open weekdays, 7.30 a.m. – 5.30 p.m.

Women and Feminism

San Francisco bristles with female energy. It starts at the top and throbs all through the city. A majority of the eleven-member Board of Supervisors (city council) are women, including two lesbians. Women patrol the streets as police officers, run major theatres, manage hotels, direct multi-million dollar banking deals, preside in the courts, own world-class restaurants, hold prestigious chairs in the colleges, make up a significant proportion of doctors, head museums and even excel in that age-old female role of adornment, with a crop of gregarious socialites who are almost as famous locally as sports stars.

There's a powerful feminist consciousness in San Francisco, which shows up in everything from making childcare a major issue in corporate boardrooms to a still potent coterie of radicals who prod the public discourse from a variety of soap-boxes. Feminism has been a mostly comfortable fit with San Francisco's historically progressive personality. It has fit so well, in fact, that there is some fretting going on that the women's community is losing its identity through assimilation. At the time of writing there is only one feminist bookstore in the city (Old Wives' Tales) and it has almost gone under several times, competing against general bookstores which make women's feminist/gay sections a priority. The Women's Building is a cultural landmark, but doesn't exude a power buzz. There are legions of self-described feminists who have never set foot in the rambling old building in the Mission. Even lesbians worry that their cohesiveness is being siphoned off by women opting for more individualistic lives. There are no exclusively lesbian bars or clubs in San Francisco – or the entire Bay Area – with the closing of Amelia's in 1992.

Yet, San Francisco is a city of joiners, agitators and doers so there is no shortage of women's groups to keep the cause alive. Struggling back to full steam after the 'I'm-for-equal-pay-but-I'm-not-a-feminist' years of Reagan and Bush, San Francisco women were early and enthusiastic supporters of Bill Clinton's quest for the presidency. Hillary Clinton became something of a local icon, visiting a number of times during the campaign to pump up the troops and discreetly remind deep pocketed contributors of the high cost of presidential campaigns. Concern over the increasing clout of the anti-abortion forces and a rise in crimes against women have contributed to a renewed commitment to women's issues.

SUSAN FALUDI

Susan Faludi recognises that people are startled by her appearance when they come to hear the fiery, sardonic feminist writer. So slender that she could qualify as a Victorian wraith, she favours little-girl ballet slippers and wears her dark hair long and loose. Her huge doe-like eyes complete a look that suggests a Jane Austen character rather than the woman who unveiled the second wave of contemporary American feminism.

Faludi confounds expectations in more than one way. Her nimble sense of humour keeps her burgeoning celebrityhood in focus. 'I am woman, hear me whisper,' she tells adoring audiences in her tiny soprano.

Who would not like this bright, thoughtful, self-deprecating woman? Non-fan No. 1 is the cretinish Rush Limbaugh, the rightwing DJ whose syndicated TV show has become a depressing thermometer of American yahooism.

Faludi, whom Limbaugh lambasts as a 'femi-nazi' at every opportunity, is unimpressed by her detractors. She has only recently left newspaper work after a distinguished career that included a Pulitzer Prize while at the *Wall Street Journal*. Faludi is unusual for an American journalist in her lack of interest in establishing her credentials as a completely neutral observer. She calls herself a feminist and defines her work as part of a feminist worldview, leaving it to her readers to make up their minds if she's the propagandist that Limbaugh and his ilk claim.

This new wave of feminism was encouraged and articulated by Susan Faludi, a San Francisco journalist. Her book, *Backlash: The Undeclared War Against American Women*, shot to the top of the bestseller list and stayed there for almost all of 1992. Although vilified as feminist paranoia in some corners, *Backlash* crystallised the unsettling sense of things gone awry among American women. Citing an avalanche of scholarly studies, media coverage, TV images, books and public policy, Faludi adroitly pointed out that whatever gains women had made in the last decade, the subtext was always: 'Look at the cost! Women suffer when they move out of their old roles! Is it worth it, ladies?'

'Yes, and get out of my face', retort San Francisco women who are active on an astonishing range of issues. Women over forty, abortion rights, rape, daycare for children, black women, Asian women, Pacific Islander women, women in recovery, lesbian mothers, professional women and dozens and dozens of others have their own organisations, networks and agendas. This wide-ranging activity involving women in a multitude of political and social issues has paid off handsomely. In 1992, California elected two women to both its US Senate seats, an unprecedented phenomenon in American history. Dianne Feinstein, former San Francisco mayor, and Barbara Boxer, a member of the US House of Representatives from Marin, were elected after uphill battles. Despite weak Republican opposition, the two had to fight their way through the Democratic Party primary to win their nominations, then contend with the inviolate California tradition that dictates one senator is from the southern part of the state and one from the northern. This almost always means one Republican and one Democratic.

Dianne Feinstein

It is an image that no one who saw it ever forgot: stricken Dianne Feinstein, her natural self-assurance shattered, standing woodenly atop a City Hall staircase, announcing to a frantic crowd that San Francisco mayor, George Moscone, and Supervisor Harvey Milk had just been assassinated by an embittered former supervisor, Dan White.

From that tragic and unlikely pulpit, Feinstein was propelled into the mayor's chair by the laws of legal succession in 1978. Viewed as a smart doctor's wife who had unaccountably chosen politics instead of bridge as her avocation, Feinstein won grudging respect on the Board of Supervisors as a hard-working public servant. No one was prepared for the way that she so fully embraced the mayor's job and made it her own. Calling herself 'tough but compassionate', she went on to win two mayoral elections on her own and make a national reputation as a high-profile, effective mayor.

Savvy and ambitious, Feinstein was emblematic of the new woman politician. Tall, well-tailored and forceful, she made a striking impression without overly intimidating men. She came of age in the fifties when the only way to power was through male patronage. By the eighties she was building bridges to women's groups and actively currying gay support. Narrowly defeated for governor in 1990, Feinstein bounced back to win a senate seat. In a whimsical twist, she defeated a Republican appointee for the unfinished senatorial term of her gubernatorial opponent, sitting governor Pete Wilson.

Although Barbara Boxer won the full term and was already a Washington insider from her years in the House of Representatives, Feinstein has emerged as a Senate star, capturing the media spotlight and the eye of the Clinton Administration. Women senators are no longer a novelty at Washington, but Feinstein, striding through the corridors of power in her primary colour suits and getting big play in the network news, is poised to become, if not the most powerful female senator, then certainly the most famous.

The San Francisco political training ground produced another 1992 election breakthrough when President Clinton named Roberta Achtenberg, an openly gay city supervisor, to a high federal post in Washington, that of assistant secretary of Housing and Urban Development. Achtenberg and her partner, Judge Mary Morgan, and their young son moved to Washington like any other ambitious, accomplished young couple moving up in the world.

The ascension of Achtenberg was particularly sweet for San Francisco lesbians who have laboured in the shadow of the gay men's movement for many years. Invisibility is a very sore subject with Bay Area lesbians who feel that the male drive to dominate whatever stage is available, coupled with the AIDS crisis, have significantly minimised the gay women's community and agenda.

Lesbians had begun to settle in San Francisco in substantial numbers after World War II for the same reasons that gay men did. After serving in the military, working in the war industries or just being caught up in the frenetic excitement of the war, they didn't want to go back to Cleveland or Chattanooga or Bakersfield and a full-time closet. San Francisco offered friends, community, tolerance and romance. Rosie Riveters and girlfriends stayed on.

In 1955, Phyllis Lyon and Del Martin founded Daughters of Bilitis, a social club that would provide an alternative to the bars and the first openly lesbian organisation ever. Lyon and Martin suffered through police raids, humiliating publicity and constant suspicion, but outlasted it all to become the grand dames of San Francisco lesbianism. Today the Lyon-Martin Women's Health Services agency is a living memorial to their courage and perseverance.

The sex positive versus anti-pornography debate has been waged in San Francisco, but without the vigour or stamina of other parts of the country. Feminist theoreticians Catharine MacKinnon and Andrea Dworkin (both based in the East) have established a fierce legal and philosophical attack on pornography as violence to women. One of the first feminist anti-porn groups, Women Against Violence in Pornography in the Media, was established during the 1970s in the Bay Area and initiated Take Back the Night actions and consciousness-raising tours of porn areas on Broadway and in the Tenderloin. WAVPM has passed from the scene and while leaving followers, the San Francisco habit of *laissez faire* and pleasure-seeking at all costs is a powerful counterforce. SF lesbians have been in the forefront of the sex positive movement, throwing off the flannel shirts and overalls of the seventies for high heels, leather and makeup. 'Lipstick lesbian' isn't even a current term any more, the feminine look having become such an integral part of gay life. Go-go girls decorate the dance clubs, lesbian-made erotic movies are easy to rent and the emergence of women-only sex clubs has given the gay scene a whole new cachet.

It isn't an unexpected development, given San Francisco's obsession with the sensual. The curious re-romanticisation of prostitution first emerged in San Francisco in the seventies under the aegis of avowed hooker Margo St James and her advocacy group, COYOTE (Call Off Your Old, Tired Ethics).

Prostitutes have a firm place in San Francisco mythology. The legends of the Gold Rush era are as much concerned with the luxurious whorehouses of San Francisco as with the actual mining of gold. As the old ditty goes:

'The miners came in '49,
The whores in '51;
And when they got together
They produced the native son.'

This cherished legend of a city founded by adventurers and outlaws, male and female, has produced a strange interaction with the genuine Western tradition of rugged individualism which offered women far more opportunities and possibilities than they had in Europe, Asia or America east of the Mississippi.

Women often gained ground because it was expedient and convenient for the new society. In a first for an American state, women's property rights were written into the state constitution in 1849. In California, a wife's property was separate from her husband's whether acquired before or during the marriage, a radical advancement in American jurisprudence. This was a continuation of Mexican law, but raised a few eyebrows among the all-male constitutional delegates. What carried the day was not the argument of equal rights or even fairness, but the need to attract more women to the territory. The law's champion pointed out to his lonely fellow delegates that property rights would lure not just ordinary potential wives but even better, wealthy potential wives.

In that same vein of pragmatism, California developed workable divorce laws in the nineteenth century.

Women's right to vote was a major issue from the early days of statehood. An organised suffrage movement was at work from 1869 on. The Western states were light years ahead of the East on women's rights. Wyoming gave women the vote in 1869, while it was still a territory. California was poised to do the same in 1896 when suffrage was put on a statewide ballot. It was defeated by a substantial margin, led by San Francisco. The suffragists' intertwined relationship with the temperance movement put off fun-loving San Franciscans in a big way. California women won the vote in 1911, far in advance of the passage of the Nineteenth Amendment in 1920, but even firebrand San Francisco suffragists remained ambivalent about temperance.

WOMEN'S GROUPS AND ORGANISATIONS

Lesbian Avengers, tel. 267 6195. Direct action group in the mode of ACT UP but dedicated to lesbian issues, weekly meetings.

National Organisation for Women, 3543 18th St, tel. 861 8880. The largest and most well-known American feminist group; the SF chapter works on a variety of issues and holds regular meetings and forums.

National Women's Political Caucus, P. O. Box 190055, SF 94119, tel. 922 5004. SF branch of the nationwide group working to put progressive women in public office, regular meetings with well-known political figures as speakers.

Options for Women Over Forty, the Women's Building, 3543 18th St, tel. 431 6944. Resource, counselling organisation that offers drop-in socialising and training groups.

Pacific Center, 2712 Telegraph Ave, Berkeley, tel. (510) 548 8283. Twenty-year-old switchboard, referral service, counselling centre for 'sexual minorities', lesbians, gay men, bisexuals, transsexuals and transvestites.

San Francisco Commission on the Status of Women, 25 Van Ness Avenue, tel. 252 2570. City clearing house agency on job discrimination, domestic violence, job search.

Women's Action Coalition, 3543 18th St, tel. 431 1180. A new manifestation of nineties' feminism, this loose-knit group takes on whatever issue looms largest, from abortion clinic defence to striking women airline workers.

Women's Alliance, P. O. Box 21454, Oakland, CA 94620, tel. (510) 658 2949. Fosters inner growth, spirituality and sponsors very popular summer camps for women-only in the mountains.

Women's Building, 3543 18th St (at Valencia), tel. 431 1180. Centre for many women's organisations, meetings, classes; open daily, 9 a.m. – 8 p.m., Mon – Fri; 12 noon to 5 p.m. weekends.

Directory

AIDS
See p. 32.

AIRLINES
American Airlines, St Francis Hotel lobby, Post & Powell, tel. 1 800 433 7300; **British Airways**, 51 O'Farrell St, tel. 1 800 247 9297; **Delta Air Lines**, 287 Geary St, tel. 552 5700; **United Airlines**, 400 Post St, tel. 397 2100.

AIRPORTS
San Francisco International Airport, 14 miles south of SF on Highway 101 – continual bus and cab service; **Oakland Airport** on the eastern side of SF Bay – bus, taxi and BART service to the city; **San José Airport**, 50 miles south of SF, taxi, bus, train service to the city. Call airlines for flight information; shuttle and taxi companies for transportation.

AIRPORT SHUTTLE
SFO Airporter, tel. 673 2432; **Super Shuttle**, tel. 558 8500; **Quake City Shuttle**, tel. 777 4899 (particularly

good on private home and residential neighbourhood pick-up and drop-off).

BABYSITTERS
The informal rate is $3 an hour for a teenager from the neighbourhood to look after your child for an evening. Be prepared to pay substantially more for these professional agencies.

- **Bay Area Babysitters**, 758 San Diego Ave, Daly City, tel. 991 7474. A 46-year-old agency that will send out carefully screened sitters to private homes or hotels, wherever requested.
- **Second Mom**, 535 Geary St, tel. 474 8084. In business for eight years, has a variety of sitter and nanny services.
- **Temporary Tot Tending**, tel. 355 7377. Operates several centres for drop-in care in San Mateo County, just south of San Francisco. Temp Tots take infants to age 12 on short notice, 7 a.m.–6 p.m. with plans to expand to 24 hours.

BICYCLE RENTALS

Park Cyclery, 1865 Haight St, tel. 751 7368 – No. 1 with the local bike aficionados; **Velo City,** 638 Stanyan St, tel. 221 2453; **Presidio Bicycle Shop,** 5335 Geary Blvd, tel. 752 2453.

BUS INFORMATION

San Francisco, MUNI, tel. 673 MUNI; East Bay, **AC Transit,** tel. 1 800 559 INFO; San Mateo, **SamTrans,** tel. 1 800 660 4BUS; Marin and Sonoma, **Golden Gate Transit,** tel. 332 6600; beyond the Bay Area, **Greyhound,** tel. 558 6789.

CABLE CAR INFORMATION

San Francisco Municipal Railway (MUNI), tel. 673 MUNI.

CAR PROBLEMS

Auto Motion, full-service, woman-owned car service and repair, 185 Bayshore, SF, tel. 550 2400; **Phoenix Auto,** 4200-A East 14th St, Oakland, tel. (510) 533 3356. Also woman-owned, specialises in Japanese cars, some American, and will cheerfully give referrals; **Gooch Towing,** 265 30th St, Oakland, tel. 893 9466.

CAR RENTAL

Alamo, 656 Geary St, tel. 673 9696; **Budget Rent A Car,** 321 Mason St, tel. 775 5800; **Hertz,** 433 Mason St, tel. 771 220.

CAR AND DRIVER

Associated Limousines, 1398 Bryant St, tel. 563 1000; **Ishi Limousine,** 718 Masonic Ave, tel. 567 4700 (favourite of rock stars and visiting celebrities).

CHILDREN'S DAY CARE, CAMPS AND PLAY GROUPS

Drop-in day care centres are the fastest growing segment of the childcare industry. San Francisco and the Bay Area are blanketed with day camps in the summer months and after-school classes and enrichment programmes throughout the school year (September-May).

- **Bananas,** a non-profit Berkeley-based referral and counselling agency, is the best local resource for children. The switchboard is jammed, but extremely helpful once you get through, tel. (510) 658 0381; drop-in visits welcome, 5232 Claremont Ave, Berkeley.

- **Bippidy-Bop Preschool,** tel. 543 4595. Financial District private day care centre accepts drop-ins 2½ to 5 years, in the Rincorn Center, Mission and Spear. Expensive.

- **Children's Switchboard,** tel. 243 0111. Part of the non-profit Children's Council of San Francisco. Offers referrals and resources at no charge, drop-in visits welcomed, 1 Second St, between Mission and Market, 4th floor.

- **The Jungle,** 555 9th St, tel. 552 4FUN. A three-level indoor playground in the South of Market area, offers games, a foam forest, slides, nets, tunnels. No drop-offs, but a big staff oversees the children once they are at play. Costs $5.95 for the first hour, $1 each additional hour; open daily.

- **Temporary Tot summer day camp,** 2217 Delvin Way, South San Francisco 94080, tel. 355 7377. June through September, structured daily programmes of games, field trips, sports. Various rates, but expensive.

- A number of popular museums and agencies hold summer camp and weekend/after school classes for children as young as three or four up to age 15 or 16. Call for more information: **California Academy of Sciences** in Golden Gate Park's Junior Academy, tel. 750 7100; art classes with the **San Francisco Children's Art Center** in Fort Mason, tel. 771 0292; **Slide Ranch** in the Marin Headlands offers overnight campouts, hands-on projects with animals and ranch life, tel. 381 6155; **San Francisco Zoo** sponsors the Zoo Club which offers nature walks, wildlife programmes and evening tours of the zoo, tel. 753 7080.

- Safe, well-equipped neighbourhood playgrounds for children include pocket-sized **Huntington Park**, atop Nob Hill across from Grace Cathedral, at California and Taylor; **Michelangelo Park** on Russian Hill – walk in through a stairwell off Greenwich St while the kids slide through tunnels, between Leavenworth and Jones; **Cow Hollow Playground**, just outside the Presidio and an easy walk to the Exploritorium and **Marina Green**, full of kid-tested play stuff such as slides, swings and even a baby cable car, on Baker St, between Greenwich and Filbert. **The Children's Playground** in Golden Gate Park is equipped with slides, swings, sandpits, things to crawl through and during the summer and weekends, a gorgeous restored carousel (near the park's eastern border, near Stanyan St, off Kezar Way in the park).

CIGARETTES AND SMOKING

Smoking is out. Most public places in the Bay Area, from restaurants to government buildings, forbid smoking. Smokers are regulated to some outside spot, where they huddle together like POWs. In offices, cafés, hotels and especially in private homes, always ask before lighting up and be prepared for a shocked, 'No! Of course not!' Cigarettes are still widely available in vending machines, supermarkets and convenience stores.

CONTRACEPTION

See p. 32.

CONSULATES

British Consulate General, 1 Sansome St, Suite 850, SF 94104, tel. 981 3030. Offices are open weekdays 9 a.m.–4 p.m., closed for lunch, 1–2 p.m. **Australian Consulate General**, 1 Bush St., SF 94110, tel. 362 6160. Offices open weekdays, 10 a.m.–4 p.m.

DENTISTS

California Dental Society referral service, tel. 421 1435; **Gay Medical & Dental** referral service, tel. 673 3189.

DOCTORS

Life-threatening illness, call 911; **San Francisco Medical Society** referral service, tel. 567 6234.

DRINKING

Not as outre as smoking, but on that same track. Legal drinking age is 21 for all types of alcohol. Many bars and stores will 'card' (check ID) of anyone buying alcohol, even women and men who are obviously long past their twenties. Always keep a photo ID handy when you plan to do any drinking.

Concerns about foetal alcohol syndrome have led to a massive public education programme that requires every store or restaurant which sells or serves alcohol to post signs warning that drinking alcohol while pregnant can result in birth defects. If you are visibly pregnant and have even a small glass of wine in public be prepared for shocked expressions and disapproving glares.

Drunk driving has become a high visibility crime; even hard-drinking macho types routinely pick a 'designated driver' on party evenings, meaning that person stays completely sober and does all the driving. Bartenders don't hesitate to cut off heavy drinking patrons and send them home in taxis. Complete strangers will press Alcoholics Anonymous phone numbers to you if you appear at all tipsy. To Americans, alcoholism has replaced first marriages as the seminal coming of age experience that everyone must experience and survive before evolving into a fully responsible adult. If you find this neo-temperanceism intrusive and rude, just smile and nod to discourage advice and/or help. You will only be accused of being in denial if you refuse to admit you need a twelve-Step programme.

Dry Cleaning
Mack's Valet Cleaners, 766 Post St, tel. 474 3090; **Ray's French Cleaners,** 1205 Union St, tel. 885 4171.

Emergencies
Call 911 for police or health emergencies.

English Expatriates
In spite of the Mission, North Beach, China and Japan towns, San Francisco doesn't have a significant Anglo expatriate community. The lack of language barriers and the comparatively few British, Scots and Irish who emigrate or come as long-term residents work against the development of a well-organised, high-visibility expat community. Traces of San Francisco's substantial Irish community are visible, primarily in bars which feature posters of IRA martyrs and/or quaint scenes from Eire. Organisations tend toward older memberships with conservative inclinations: **British American**

Chamber of Commerce, 41 Sutter St, SF 94104, tel. 296 8645; **Daughters of the British Empire in California,** 631 O'Farrell St, SF 94109, tel. 673 7858; **English Speaking Union,** SF chapter, 465 California St, Suite 739, SF 94104, tel. 362 6985; **St Andrew's Society of San Francisco,** 41 Sutter St, SF 94104, tel. 391 8652; **Welsh American Society of Northern California,** 32 Ocean Ave, SF 94112, tel. 587 1100.

Finding a Job
For foreigners this is difficult without a Green Card (work permit). For off-the-books work, check listings in the weeklies such as the *Bay Guardian, East Bay Express, SF Weekly,* and look on bulletin boards in cafés or bookstores. You can place your own newspaper ad for your services, but if you give any hint that you are not a US citizen you could be visited by the Immigration and Naturalization Service.

Faxing
A fax on almost every corner. Check the telephone directory Yellow Pages for the most convenient place. See also p. 17.

Feminist Organisations
p. 40.

Flowers
Flower carts are numerous around Union Square and cut flowers are available at many supermarkets and grocery stores. For more formal presentations, especially for business and social courtesies: **Rosebowl Florist and Wine Shop,** 601 Van Ness Ave (in Opera Plaza), tel. 474 1114; **Bloomers Florist,** 2975 Washington St (Pacific Heights), tel. 563 3266.

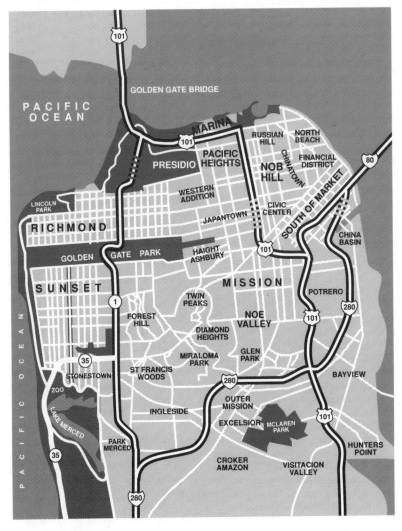

PACIFIC OCEAN

GOLDEN GATE BRIDGE

101

MARINA

RUSSIAN HILL

NORTH BEACH

101

PACIFIC HEIGHTS

PRESIDIO

CHINATOWN

NOB HILL

FINANCIAL DISTRICT

80

WESTERN ADDITION

CIVIC CENTER

SOUTH OF MARKET

LINCOLN PARK

JAPANTOWN

RICHMOND

CHINA BASIN

GOLDEN GATE PARK

HAIGHT ASHBURY

101

SUNSET

MISSION

POTRERO

TWIN PEAKS

1

NOE VALLEY

280

FOREST HILL

101

DIAMOND HEIGHTS

MIRALOMA PARK

GLEN PARK

35

ST FRANCIS WOODS

STONESTOWN

BAYVIEW

ZOO

280

INGLESIDE

OUTER MISSION

LAKE MERCED

EXCELSIOR

MCLAREN PARK

101

35

PARK MERCED

HUNTERS POINT

CROKER AMAZON

VISITACION VALLEY

280

PACIFIC OCEAN

N

0   10 MILES

0   10 KILOMETRES   20 KILOMETRES

HAIRCUTS

St Tropez, 1980 Union St, tel. 563 3514, pricey but super-professional full service salon; **Mr Lee Beauty Hair & Health Spa**, 834 Jones St, tel. 474 6002, socialite and visiting celeb world headquarters – get your roots done and eavesdrop on haute gossip. For budget cuts try the **Nice Cut** shops which start at $10, 2187 Union St, tel. 929 7744, 1508 Haight St, tel. 255 4570, 2224 Chesnut St, tel. 441 1235; or one of the hairdresser's schools, **International Academy of Precision Haircutting**, 1702 Washington St, tel. 474 1133 or **Miss Marty's School of Beauty & Hairstyling**, 278 Post St, tel. 781 7950. For experts in dealing with black women's hair, try the upscale **Rafiki Salon**, where many of San Francisco's African American TV personalities have their hair done, 111 Maiden Lane, tel. 398 6644, or Sheila Head's funky and friendly **Head Design**, 6522 Telegraph Ave, Oakland, tel. (510) 658 3942.

HEALTH CLUBS/GYMS

Aerobics classes are a way of life in the Bay Area. You will find classes for large women, pregnant women, Christian women (who prefer gospel music to pop for their workouts) and literally dozens of subsets. For drop-in aerobics classes check out **André's Body Shop** in the Civic Center area, 371 Hayes St, tel. 241 0203, or **Jazzercise classes**, more than a dozen sites in the city, tel. 561 9300. **Dierdra Roger's Fitness Break** is a favourite with the Financial District set, 30 Hotaling Place, tel. 788 1681. **YMCAs** offer a wider range of activities, Stonestown (tel. 759 9622) and Buchanan (tel. 931 9622) being local favourites. Short-term memberships and drop-in visitors are

welcomed at the 24-Hour **Nautilus Fitness Center**, 1335 Sutter St, tel. 776 2200 and San Francisco **Bay Club** (best place to meet a stockbroker or attorney), 150 Greenwich St, tel. 433 2200.

HELPLINES

Haight-Ashbury Switchboard, problem-solving, information, tel. 621 6211; **Alcoholics Anonymous**, tel. 661 1828; **Consumer Action Line**, tel. 777 9635; **Pacific Center Lesbian & Gay Switchboard**, tel. 841 6224; **Drug Crisis Line**, tel. 752 3400; **Shanti Foundation**, AIDS information and counselling, tel. 777 2273; **Suicide Prevention Hotline**, tel. 221 1423; **Travelers Aid Society**, tel. 255 2252; **San Francisco Sex Information Switchboard**, for basic sex information, tel. 621 7300.

HOSPITALS AND FIRST AID

Go to a 24-hour emergency room for immediate healthcare: **California Pacific Hospital**, 2333 Buchanan St, tel. 563 4321, helpline, 923 3333; **Children's Hospital of San Francisco**, 3773 Sacramento St, tel. 386 7000, helpline, 750 6031; **University of California San Francisco Medical Center**, 505 Parnassus Ave, tel. 476 1000, helpline, 476 1037.

LAUNDERETTES

Do-it-yourself laundromats are easy to find all over San Francisco. Many are staffed by attendants who will do your laundry for a modest fee. Laundromats with cafés are a new entertainment form in the Bay Area. **Brainwash**, a South of Market hot spot, offers clean facilities, a café and live music many nights, 1122 Folsom St, tel. 431 WASH. **Duds 'n' Suds** is a franchise laundro-ent shop with tons of video games and TV monitors showing quite good movies. Duds is found in North Beach, 817 Columbus Ave, tel. 885 1222.

LEFT LUGGAGE
Most hotels will keep your bags before or after checkout at no charge other than tipping the bellman ($1 per bag). **Amlock** at SFO, tel. 877 0422, **International Terminal** (near Air France), lockers, $2–$10 per 24 hours, depending on size of bags; do-it-yourself lockers are in the **Greyhound Bus station** (part of the Transbay Bus Terminal), First and Mission streets, $1.50 for 24 hours.

LESBIAN ORGANISATIONS
National Gay & Lesbian Task Force, local chapter of largest US gay activist group, weekly meetings at the Women's Building, tel. (510) 653 2571; **Lesbian Avengers,** new direct action group, weekly meetings, tel. 267 6195; **Lesbian Uprising!** calls for a return to radicalism, tel. 441 6238; **Women's Professional Network,** social and business group, tel. (510) 482 8583; **Lesbians of Color,** meetings at the Pacific Center in Berkeley, tel. (510) 548 8283. Check the Resources listings in *Bay Times* for the most complete round-up of lesbian and gay-lesbian organisations in the Bay Area.

LIBRARIES
Main library is in the Civic Center, Larkin and Fulton streets, tel. 558 2638; **San Francisco Performing Arts Library and Museum,** 399 Grove St, tel. 255 4800; **Gay and Lesbian Historical Society of Northern California,** call or write for hours, P.O. Box 424280, San Francisco 94142, tel. 626 0980; **Alliance Française,** 1345 Bush St, tel. 775

7755; **Goethe Institut,** 530 Bush St, tel. 391 0428.

PARKING
Parking is at a premium in San Francisco. Street meters are strictly monitored and expensive tickets freely written, making parking garages your safest bet. Downtown, look for public garages under Union Square (entrance across from Macys on Geary) and the Sutter-Stockton garage a block away from Union Square at Sutter and Stockton streets.

Towing away is a constant threat; read all signs carefully before leaving your car on the street, being especially observant of street cleaning times and rush hour regulations, when parking lanes become traffic lanes. Colour-coded street parking is another area to watch closely. Red curbs mean no parking at any time; green is for quick stops of no more than ten minutes; yellow curbs are loading zones for commercial vehicles only; white curbs are five-minute drop off/pick up of passengers; blue curb is for the disabled (vehicles must show a state-issued disabled ID). Bus zones and fire hydrants are also forbidden parking slots, although you'll see desperate motorists risking it.

PHARMACIES
See p. 35.

PHOTOCOPYING
Copy shops are all over the city, in every neighbourhood. Shops open seven days a week include **Copymat,** 705 Market St, tel. 882 7377 and **Copy Central,** 2404 California St, tel. 567 5888. The only 24-hour copying office is **Kinko's,** 555 Buckingham Way (at Stonestown Galleria), tel. 566 0572.

POLICE

For emergencies, dial 911. Non-emergencies and general, tel. 553 0123; medical, tel. 431 2800.

TRAFFIC LAWS

California accepts a valid driver's licence from any Western nation for short-term visitors. A peculiarity of local driving laws to be aware of, for both walkers and drivers, is the right-of-way given to pedestrians. At clearly marked crossings without traffic lights, walkers have right of way. All cars and trucks must stop.

SWIMMING

Beaches in Northern California tend toward damp sand, rocky coastline and cold, cold water. **Ocean Beach** in SF and **Muir Beach** and **Stinson Beach** in Marin are the best bets for ocean swimming.

The **SF Parks and Recreation Department** maintains a number of public pools, call 753 7026 for a full listing. Two well-maintained pools with easy access to public transport are the **North Beach Pool**, Lombard and Mason, tel. 274 0201, and **Rossi Pool,** near the University of San Francisco, Arguello Blvd and Anza St, tel. 666 7014.

TAXIS

Yellow Cab, tel. 626 2345; **DeSoto Cab Co.,** tel. 673 1017; **Luxor Cab Co.,** tel. 282 4141.

TIPPING

In restaurants, 15 to 20 per cent of the pre-tax total is the norm. Taxi drivers get 10–20 per cent of the fare. For porters, skycaps and doormen, $1 per bag. Valet parking is $1–$5; masseuses, hairstylists and manicurists get $2–$20 depending on the size of your bill and your inclination; hotel maids $2 per night.

TOILETS

Public toilets are not nearly as plentiful as they should be in San Francisco. You'll find good 'rest room' facilities in museums, department stores, fast-food outlets and the better hotel lobbies. Upscale restaurants are almost always a good bet. If you're adult, decently dressed and self-confident you can use any rest room in the city – just walk briskly toward the facilities with an air of belonging. Unfortunately, efforts to keep the homeless and street people at arm's length have resulted in a less than open door policy on toilets in many shops, cafés and small hotels.

TRAIN INFORMATION

CalTrain, train service from SF south through the Peninsula to San José and Gilroy, tel. 1 800 660 4287; **Amtrak,** the US railway system, tel. 1 800 USA RAIL. The train station is in Oakland, with bus service to SF.

ARRIVAL AND GETTING AROUND

Arrival

Three airports service the Bay Area, but all direct international flights come into San Francisco International Airport, called **SFO.**

International travellers may fly into one of the smaller Bay Area airports, Oakland or San José, upon request. A number of airlines have international passengers fly into New York, Chicago or even Los Angeles where they clear Customs before connecting to a domestic flight into the Bay Area.

Foreigners landing at SFO will be directed through a claim area for luggage. In the Customs section, luggage carts are made available at no charge for international passengers. After leaving the Customs area follow signs to 'Ground Transportation' where you have several options for the fourteen-mile trip north to downtown San Francisco. (The airport is located on a desolate stretch of bayside wetlands in neighbouring San Mateo County.)

The airport, seventh busiest in the world, handling upwards of 32 million passengers a year, is big and confusing. It is made up of eight terminals on two levels arranged in a semi-circle, with the International, or North, Terminal in the centre. Flights are frequently delayed, re-routed and rescheduled because of the weather: fog in the summer, rain in the winter. If you're marooned at SFO with children ask to use the nursery, a big playroom with toys opened by custodians on request. There is also a fully-staffed medical office open 24 hours a day.

SFO is in the process of re-evaluating the hoardes of van **shuttles** that compete for airline passengers. Currently there are two types, the set route companies that pick up and drop off travellers at major hotels in downtown and the Fisherman's Wharf area, and the gypsy vans that offer door-to-door service, but run on an erratic schedule as they need a full van (ten people) to make a run. Beginning in 1994, the airport is expected to rule that only two established shuttles will serve the airport on a regular basis while the others will work on an advance reservation basis.

Shuttle vans stop on the curb outside the airport baggage area. Follow the signs outside and look for signs identifying the various companies' collection points. You don't have to worry about tickets; passengers pay the driver directly.

Super Shuttle, Yellow Airport Service and SFO Airporter are all reliable services, charging $8 one way, $14 roundtrip. Buses depart every twenty minutes on different routes. If you're not staying at one of the drop-off hotels, ask the driver what route you need to take. Most drivers are knowledgeable and helpful, though not with bags. The shuttles are on a tight schedule and expect their passengers to step lively.

Taxi service is expensive, but worth it if you have tons of bags and/or have your hands full with children. The trip takes 20–40 minutes and one way fares average $27. On a bad traffic day it could be $32. A 15 per cent tip is expected, 20 per cent appreciated.

Businessmen make a practice of searching one another out and sharing cabs into the city. It is an efficient and cost-effective way to make the trip as SF cabs charge for the ride, not per person. Because women are wary about either approaching or being approached by strangers it's not as common among businesswomen, but if you look executive-ish don't be surprised to be invited to hire a taxi. If you feel the least bit uncomfortable say no.

Porters, called skycaps, are available to help with your baggage. They are easy to spot, wearing pilot-type caps and wielding big carts. Tip them $1 per bag.

SFO SERVICES

Currency exchange

Bank of America, International Terminal, near United Airlines, open 7 a.m.–11 p.m. daily, tel. 742 8079.

Information

Travellers Aid Society, International Terminal, near British Airways ticket desk, upstairs from Customs arrival area, 9 a.m.–9 p.m. daily, tel. 7 0118 on the ubiquitous white courtesy telephones in all terminals. Volunteers, usually retired men and women, answer questions, dispense brochures and provide information and directions to in-airport services.
Airport Police, call 6 2424.

Medical

Medical station, fully staffed, open 24 hours, is near the Customs area in the International Terminal. Call 7 0444.

Nursery

In the International Terminal, not staffed; opened by the custodial staff on request only, tel. 6 2359.

For the budget traveller, the cheapest way into the city is the SamTrans **bus** service (the San Mateo transit line). The bus stop is on the upper level of the airport, near the Delta-United areas. Look for Bus 7-B. Other buses cover the same ground, but only 7-B allows luggage. The fare is 85c. You will need exact change as the driver doesn't have access to change (typical of American bus systems to discourage robberies). He or she will, naturally, accept $1 in lieu of the exact amount. This is definitely the no-frills route to town. The bus stop is a long haul from the International terminal, there are a number of stops en route and you disembark finally at the Transbay Bus Terminal, a grimy meeting point of the various regional bus services that converge in San Francisco. The Transbay is dreary in daytime and borderline dangerous at night. After dark don't chance walking to your destination. Take a taxi or a city bus.

Oakland Airport

The great advantage of using the Oakland Airport is its manageable size and **BART** connection. An amazing and depressing history of bureaucratic stalemates have left SFO without a subway service. Many San Franciscans routinely use Oakland for quicker access to downtown.

Shuttle and **taxi** services are available, though slower paced than SFO. Shuttle vans charge $15 a person from the airport to Union Square in downtown SF. There are white courtesy phones to call for service if no van is on site. Taxi service runs about $40–$45 one way.

The nearby BART station, open until midnight, is reached by a bus service called AirBART which costs $2 per person (exact change required). The BART fare from the Airport/Coliseum station to one of the downtown SF stops will be $1.90; again, exact change needed for the ticketing machines in the station.

San José Airport

San José is also popular with local travellers who prize its easy accessibility and modest scale. However, being fifty miles south of San Francisco and having no BART connection, it doesn't get the kind of use by SF-bound travellers that Oakland does. It is, however, ideal for visitors heading to Silicon Valley, the American computer capital. Connections to San Francisco by **bus** and **train** (CalTrain) are not terribly difficult to make.

EARTHQUAKES

Earthquakes are a fact of life for San Franciscans who have lost a bit of their jauntiness about awaiting 'the big one' since the destructive 1989 quake that closed the Bay Bridge and turned part of the Marina into a war zone. Called the Loma Prieta earthquake for its epicentre located near Santa Cruz, the quake registered 7.1 on the Richter scale and was one of California's biggest shakers since the monumental 1906 quake (8.2). Geologists predict the Bay Area has a 67 per cent chance of hosting another big earthquake in the next thirty years. If your trip should happen to coincide with an earthquake, there are several important points to remember; key among them is that you have an excellent chance of emerging completely unscathed, even in a major quake. California's rigorous and strictly enforced building code means that not just new structures are earthquake resistant, but old buildings must be brought up to code or be torn down. During Loma Prieta, for instance, the only buildings to completely crash were the residences built on the turn-of-the-century landfills that make up the pricey Marina district. Even on the huge Bay Bridge, only one small section gave way, causing one death. Four other bridges span San Francisco Bay and all of them held firm: Golden Gate, Richmond–San Rafael, Dumbarton and San Mateo.

A section of an ageing freeway called the Cypress collapsed in Oakland which was responsible for the most deaths. Similar freeways all over California are being rein-

EARTHQUAKES

forced or demolished. The Embarcadero Freeway on the San Francisco waterfront didn't fall down, but as it was almost identical to the Cypress, it was demolished. Californians don't dally when it comes to earthquake safety.

The watchwords for earthquake safety are 'Duck, Cover and Hold', which are drilled into the children of California before they can walk. Most injuries and deaths from quakes result from falling objects and collapsing buildings, so it is essential to shield yourself as much as possible. As soon as you feel the tiniest motion dive under a strong table or desk or run into the nearest doorway. Hold on to the table or door-frame while covering your head and face as best you can. Windows, mirrors and tall furniture can be lethal in a quake so try to dive in the opposite direction of any of these potential hazards. DO NOT MOVE UNTIL THE SHAKING STOPS. If you are indoors do not go out of the building unless your life is in danger; there will be small aftershocks that will send more debris or objects tumbling downward. If you are driving, move over to the side of the road and stop your car. Bridges, overpasses and powerlines are to be avoided. If on foot outdoors, move quickly to the most open space you can find, away from buildings, trees and powerlines.

Stay calm, especially if you have children with you. Ask people around you for help or information. Traditionally, Californians have been at their best in earthquake crises. When the Cypress freeway collapsed, some of the first and most valiant rescuers were the neighbourhood junkies.

Orientation

As late twentieth-century life takes us deeper into urban dilemmas and cities seem increasingly unliveable, San Francisco's appeal has increased because it continues to be human-scale, manageable and breathtakingly beautiful. Of course there are all the problems of cities to be found here, but there are also intimate neighbourhoods, wonderful parks and a seemingly unextinguishable *joie de vivre*. If the end of the world were announced for 5 p.m. Friday, San Francisco would throw itself into organising the most fantastic farewell party.

Tidily arranged at the tip of a peninsula bordered by the Pacific Ocean and San Francisco Bay, the city's compact forty-nine square miles are easily traversed on foot, cable car, BART, bus and street-car. Public transport is a way of life in San Francisco and you can adapt to its systemic quirkiness with a little concentration. A good way to start a San Francisco visit for first-timers is to take a **bus tour** to get a sense of dimension and sample the highlights. Grayline has extensive tours or there are the open buses decorated to look like cable cars that give a basic look-see in an hour.

After an overview tour, book a **walking tour** (see p. 60) into the areas or sights that appeal to you the most. San Francisco, a superb walker's city, has masses of walking tours, both private and non-profit, that investigate every corner of the city. There are also numerous guidebooks devoted to step-by-step walking tours, but save these for your follow-up forays. The people who lead the organised tours are knowledgeable, thorough and a few are celebrities in their own right such as Don Herron, who leads the Dashiell Hammett tour, and Shirley Fong-Torres, Chinatown's tireless champion.

San Francisco is dotted with museums, monuments, historic sites and endless 'must dos' listed on tourist brochures. Don't be seduced into seeing the sights at the cost of missing the city's soul. Buy a morning paper and go to a small café and read it over espresso and sticky buns. Sitting in the Café de la Presse outside the Chinatown gate or Caffe Trieste in North Beach or La Bohème Café in the Mission – you'll see a fascinating parade of people and begin to know San Francisco at ground level.

Wander over to Union Square and catch the 30 Stockton **bus**, locally called the Orient Express, and ride through the teeming streets of Chinatown and finally the upscale Mariña. Working people, from executives to seamstresses, crowd on the bus. You'll hear Cantonese, Spanish, even a little English. Hop off at the Marina and walk along the Marina Green where children fly their kites in the shadow of the Golden Gate Bridge.

San Francisco is a fairly easy city to learn because of its diminutive size and distinct neighbourhoods. Chinatown, North Beach, the Mission, South of Market, Russian Hill, the Castro, Noe Valley, Telegraph Hill and the Financial District are unmistakable after one visit. Market Street, the diagonal artery that runs southwesterly from the waterfront to Twin Peaks, is the city's most important landmark. Everything else is described in its relationship to Market.

North of Market (sometimes called Above Market) is the heart of the city, the nucleus of nineteenth-century San Francisco, which includes the Financial District and the old ethnic neighbourhoods such as Chinatown and North Beach.

South of Market is the old warehouse and industrial district, now rapidly being transformed into 'SoMa', a popular blend of clubs, galleries, artists' lofts, cafés and discount shopping. Further west are Mission Dolores, the 1776 landmark that launched San Francisco and its surrounding Mission district, a Latino enclave that blends into the Castro, stronghold of gay San Francisco and beyond that Noe Valley, perhaps the quintessential residential neighbourhood.

For most of the early years, Divisadero Street was the city's western boundary, marking off the Presidio, the military outpost and the acres of windswept sand dunes that led to the Pacific. West of Divisadero is now fully developed, of course, but is yet another San Francisco of closely-built single family houses in the Sunset and the Avenues. Golden Gate Park, one of the city's greatest achievements, is there prefaced by the Haight-Ashbury, once the capital of hippiedom, now a pricey, upscale neighbourhood. Beyond the park is Ocean Beach and miles of rocky coastline. The Presidio, now being transferred from military to park use as part of the peace dividend, may soon join Golden Gate Park as a crown jewel.

Past the city limits, the East Bay and Marin are inextricably linked to San Francisco. They are part of the San Francisco continuum, hewing to the patterns of progressive politics, offbeat lifestyles and intriguing landscapes. Marin is a little dream world of charming bayside villages and farther afield, unusual art centres and museums, and breathtaking coastline. In the East Bay, you'll find several important museums, the world-within-a-world of the University of California in Berkeley, and some thriving women's enterprises, including Alice Waters's *Chez Panisse* and Mama Bear's, a woman-only coffee house-book-store-community centre.

OPENING HOURS

The general pattern among **museums** is a Wednesday through Sunday schedule in order to be accessible all weekend and closed on Monday and Tuesday. Some of the smaller museums are open fewer days. Hours of operation are usually 10 a.m. to 5 p.m. with the larger institutions setting aside one evening a week for late hours, ordinarily to 7 p.m.

Historically significant **churches** such as Grace Cathedral and Saints Peter and Paul are open every day by virtue of their large parishes and ongoing schedule of programmes. Visitors are provided for with brochures and information displays. Smaller churches that attract visitors either for architectural or historic significance will typically have one or two days a month for public tours, but welcome visitors to regularly scheduled worship services.

San Francisco is highly attuned to the needs of tourism and you will find that schedules are often adjusted for the high season, April through September. It is a good idea to call ahead or check the local newspaper listings for exact hours and days before setting out.

The commercial attractions of **Fisherman's Wharf** and **Pier 39** are open every day. A handful of other spots such as the **San Francisco Zoo, Alcatraz** and **Maritime Museum and Park** are also open daily.

Monday is traditionally the day off for Bay Area **restaurants**. Sunday you'll find many of the major restaurants operating on a shorter schedule, usually concentrating on brunch.

Getting Around

San Francisco is one of the world's great **walking** cities. The private automobile does not reign supreme in San Francisco. Indeed, a car is a liability most of the time because of the density of traffic and scarcity of parking.

The city is hospitable to walkers. Even the perpendicular hills are walker friendly with stairways substituting for public streets in

some quarters and steps built into some of the more ski-jumpish
sidewalks.

Public transport is plentiful, reasonably reliable and inexpensive. The San Francisco Municipal Railway, called Muni, is made up of the world-famous cable cars, buses, streetcars and connects with BART (Bay Area Rapid Transit), the **subway** system. Muni and BART in turn make fitful connections with the **ferries** that ply the bay, CalTrain, the **train** service that runs south to San José and a clutch of regional **bus** services to Marin, the East Bay, Sonoma and Napa counties to the north.

BART is clean, safe and dependable, but sadly limited in scope. It has only one line in the city (it crosses the bay and services Oakland, Berkeley and suburban Contra Costa County), from the Financial District downtown through Civic Center, the Mission, and southern residential districts ending in the commuter town of Daly City. You will be using buses and streetcars more than BART to criss-cross San Francisco. At the Tourist Information Center in Hallidie Plaza you may pick up a free brochure called 'BART & Buses' that explains how to use BART, Muni and the East Bay bus system, AC Transit. Take some time to study the instructions and keep it handy to refer to routes, especially BART-bus tie-ins which you will need to know to make full use of public transport.

Smoking and eating are prohibited on all public transport. The eating ban is casually enforced but the smoking ban is absolute.

Bus, Streetcar, Light Rail Muni is baseline reliable, but the buses are a citywide sore point, as they are often dirty, late and crowded. Yet they are widely used by every segment of the population.

Most Muni transport is by bus, but there are also some light rail cars which travel underground on some routes.

Bus fares are $1. Children under five are free and discount fares of 25c are given to seniors (over 65), youth (5–17) and the disabled. Carry exact change as drivers have no money.

Avoid the morning and evening rush hours if at all possible, 8 to 9 a.m. and 5 to 6 p.m. The service is scaled back at night, though some buses run 24 hours. Choose your nighttime bus with care. Sit near the driver and be aware of what's going on around you. Don't exit at lonely spots. Often passengers will band together leaving the bus. If they look dependable join them.

BART In contrast to Muni, BART trains are clean, spacious and timely. Unfortunately, the subway system doesn't go to nearly enough places. In addition to the SFO, BART will not take you to Golden Gate Park, the Golden Gate Bridge, the Pacific Ocean, Candlestick Park, the San Francisco Zoo, the Haight and numerous other city highlights.

Realising that BART won't be nearly as useful as a subway should be, plan to use it whenever you can. It will take you to several central points within the city and makes the East Bay tremendously accessible to the non-driving visitor. It is also very safe, being constantly patrolled by its own police force. BART runs from 4 a.m. to 12 midnight with some adjustment for weekends and special events.

Fares vary according to your destination, ranging from 80c to $3. Children under four ride free and discounts are available for seniors, children from five to twelve and disabled people. Tickets are dispensed from elaborate ticketing machines in each station. Although BART staff are everywhere, no one can help you with money. The machines take paper money, but coins are always better. Large multi-coloured wall charts near the ticket machines spell out fares and show routes. If you can't figure out what you need on your own, ask a BART employee for help.

Tickets are fed into an electronic turnstile on entering and exiting the station. It will calculate your trip and return your ticket if you have any fare remaining, which you may use on your next trip.

FRIEDEL KLUSSMANN

Years after her battles with city hall to save the cable cars, Friedel Klussmann never ceased to wonder that she had actually won the war.

'It was a miracle,' she recalled in a 1984 interview at the age of ninety, just a few months before her death. 'They had bought the buses to replace the cable cars. They thought we were just a bunch of flighty old ladies.'

Klussmann, a nurse who lived on Telegraph Hill with her doctor husband, Hans, was horrified when she heard that the mayor and board of supervisors had summarily decided to close down the cable cars in 1947. Mayor Roger Lapham and his bean counters dismissed the system as a creaky old antique, calling it 'dangerous, expensive and inefficient'.

Klussmann rallied a grassroots campaign and doggedly took on city hall on its own turf – with facts and figures. While the cable cars had an undeniable emotional and sentimental appeal to San Franciscans, Klussmann and her 'little old lady' comrades went beyond tear-jerker campaigns. Digging into the official records and amassing an impressive cable car archive of her own, Klussmann built a powerful defence for the cable cars as an efficient and durable public transport system whose main ailment was bureaucratic indifference and incompetence.

In 1947, the retention of the cable cars was put to the voters and won by a three-to-one margin. Still the forces of so-called progress chipped away at the system, reducing the six lines to three by 1954. In 1971 the supervisors had targeted the California Street line for demolition, but the Klussmann coalition held again and the cable cars were written into the city charter as untouchable by the board of supes. In 1964 the US made the cable cars a historic landmark, further placing them out of harm's way.

Women have had an odd relationship with the cable cars in some respects. Klussmann saved them from oblivion, even as the system enforced the prim Victorian edict forbidding women from standing on the running boards. In 1964, the cable cars were sued for nymphomania when a 29-year-old former dance instructor insisted that the trauma of a cable car accident transformed her into a sex addict. Sixty-two red-faced, mumbling men were called to the witness stand to substantiate her claim and the court awarded her $50,000 in damages.

There are only a handful of women cable car operators, the plum jobs requiring years and years of Muni seniority. Yet when the cable cars were reopened in 1984 after a $58 million, twenty-month overhaul, many women presided over the big day, including Dianne Feinstein, San Francisco's first woman mayor, and the ever-vigilant Friedel Klussmann.

'The only ones who wanted the cable cars were the people,' Klussmann once said. Lucky for the people that they had Friedel Klussmann as their champion.

Cable Cars   Don't call them trolleys or streetcars. San Franciscans are obsessive about their cable cars and rightfully so, having snatched them from the jaws of ersatz 'progress'.

Developed by Andrew Hallidie, a Scots mining engineer who had been working in the gold fields with cable transport systems for moving ore, supplies and dirt, the passenger-carrying cable cars made their debut in 1873 on Clay Street, climbing the western side of Nob Hill. The cable cars conquered San Francisco's hills and opened the entire city to development.

Much of the cable car system was destroyed in the 1906 earthquake and fire. The lines serving the steepest hills were rebuilt, other cable car lines being turned over to the increasingly powerful electric trolleys. In 1947 the city decided that the cable cars were a ridiculous anachronism in a modern American city and began phasing them out. An indignant citizen named Friedel Klussmann led a grassroots revolt that ultimately resulted in the cable cars being incorporated into the city charter in 1955. In 1964 the cable cars were named a National Historic Landmark, the first one on wheels.

The cable car routes will take you to Nob Hill, Fisherman's Wharf, the Financial District and North Beach. The system runs from 6 a.m. to 1.30 a.m. During high tourist times there are long waits to board, especially at the Powell Street turnaround and at Fisherman's Wharf. Ticket machines are located at the end of the routes and at a few major stops. Fares are $3 for adults, $1 youth (5–17), seniors and the disabled. You don't have to have a ticket to board. Cable cars are the last vestige of hands-on human operation in American transit. A gripman operates the car through manipulating an enormous tiller-like 'grip' in the centre of the car. A conductor takes fares, makes change and jokes with the passengers.

Cable cars slow at intersections for riders to board and disembark. It is a very casual system so don't wait to be asked to get

PRACTICALITIES

on. If the car is too full the conductor will wave you off, but most likely he will make the people onboard crunch together and pull you on.

Women were prohibited from riding on the cable car running boards until 1964 when an exasperated University of California student finally sued Muni (see box). The 'law' that kept her and her sisters seated demurely on board the cars was discovered to be an unwritten tradition whereby 'ladies are not permitted to hang on the outside', a genuine anachronism of nineteenth-century ideas about propriety.

Ferries Ferries, which swiftly faded after the Bay Bridge and Golden Gate Bridge opened in 1936 and 1937, respectively, have made a comeback on San Francisco Bay.

A ferry commuter system from Marin to San Francisco was restored in 1970 in an effort to alleviate some of the traffic on Golden Gate. In the aftermath of the 1989 Loma Prieta earthquake, which closed the Bay Bridge for more than a month, an East Bay commuter ferry system was organised. Neither system is financially robust, but both contribute to keeping the bridge traffic just short of gridlock.

The routes are divided among several ferry companies. Marin County commuters ride the Golden Gate Transit (tel. 332 6600) ferries from Larkspur Landing and Sausalito to the Ferry Building at the foot of Market Street, roughly 6 a.m. to 9 p.m. weekdays, 9.30 a.m. to 7.30 p.m. on weekends. The East Bay ferries, run by the Blue & Gold Fleet (tel. 522 3300), travel between Oakland and Alameda to the Ferry Building and Pier 39, from 6 a.m. to 9 p.m. weekdays and 10 a.m. to 8 p.m. on weekends. All the schedules make seasonal adjustments. The Red & White Fleet (tel. 546 BOAT) operates a regular service between the Ferry Building and Tiburon and Vallejo. Fares at $3.50 each way, children under age five riding free.

Ferries compare with cable cars as an only in San Francisco transit pleasure. The boats are big, oafish things but safe, comfortable and equipped with bars.

Sightseeing ferries are far more numerous, but don't put passengers ashore, instead offering a tour bus afloat, often with pre-recorded narrative to point out the sights.

Fast Pass

If you're a high-energy, gotta-see-it-all traveller who is out on the streets all day, every day, you would do well to buy one of the Muni passes which give unlimited travel on all Muni transit, including cable cars. Muni Passports are one, three and seven-day passes ($6, $10, $15) aimed at short-term visitors.

For a longer San Francisco stay, the Fast Pass at $32 is a bargain for anyone making daily use of public transport. For casual use of bus, BART, etc., you'll be better off buying one ticket at a time. Passports and Fast Passes are available at the Visitor Information Center in Hallidie Plaza, the Cable Car Museum and dozens of hotels, shops and other venues. Call 673 MUNI for a complete list.

Taxis and Limousines   Taxi cabs are carefully regulated in San Francisco with a set number of licences or medallions issued. Gypsy cabs are not part of the scene. The meter begins when you get in the cab and you'll be charged for the ride, not the number of passengers or distance. The basic charge is $2.90 for the first mile, $1.50 thereafter. Because of San Francisco's intimate scale, taxis aren't a big expense. Nob Hill to North Beach or the Financial District is about $5, for instance.

Taxis are easy to come by in the Downtown-high tourist areas North of Market. Wave for them from the curb. Major hotels, Union Square, the Ferry Building and Moscone Convention Center usually have lines of taxis waiting for customers.

Businesswomen sometimes find having a car and driver at their disposal useful for work and entertaining. These are, of course, executives with very big expense accounts. Limousine rates generally begin at $40 an hour with a three hour minimum. If you do hire a limousine, insist on a dark-coloured sedan. Showing up anywhere in a 'stretch limo' instantly brands you as a complete beginner. A white car compounds the error.

USEFUL NUMBERS
De Soto Cab Co., tel. 673 1414
Luxor Cab Co., tel. 282 4141
Yellow Cab, tel. 626 2345
Associated Limousines, tel. 563 1000
Ishi Limousine, tel. 567 4700

Tours

Gray Line has a large selection of half-day and daylong tours in the city and further afield, 558 9400; Cable Car Charters, quick overviews via open buses designed to look like cable cars, departures every half-hour at Fisherman's Wharf, 922 2425; Quality Tours & Superior Travel Services, small scale (six people) excursions in the city and day trips, gay-oriented tours available, 994 5054; Tower Tours is noted for its mini-van tours of the Napa and

Sonoma Wine Country, 434 8687; 3 Babes and a Bus escorts small groups on a zany, hip club crawl of nighttime SF, 522 CLUB; San Francisco Jewish Landmarks Tours visits homes, historic sites, art collections and synagogues, 921 0461; A Day in Nature is led by a naturalist and limited to four for trips to the Marin Headlands, Muir Woods or Napa, 673 0548.

Walking Tours

San Francisco sometimes appears to be one big walking tour. It's not unusual to see two or more groups converge on the same Must See Tourist Sight at once, prompting the guides to manoeuvre their charges around like infantry captains. But these tours flourish because of their high entertainment value and relevance to the San Francisco experience. Check the Sunday Pink Book (Chronicle entertainment section) and Friday *Examiner* arts section for new listings and updates.

CITY GUIDES NEIGHBORHOOD WALKS

Free history and architecture tours sponsored by the Friends of the San Francisco Library. Pick up schedules at the city library or call 557 4266 for a recorded announcement. (The all-volunteer guide corps has a patchy reputation for reliability so have a Plan B in case your tour doesn't take off.)

CRUISIN' THE CASTRO

A much-praised historical and cultural walk of gay SF led by the ebullient Trevor Hailey, a pioneer lesbian activist; $30 includes brunch, tel. 550 8110.

MARK GORDON'S FRISCO PRODUCTIONS.

A tour conglomerate with walking tours, bus tours, productions for your convention. One favourite is the 'Film and Fiction' walking tour which visits the spots filmed and suggested in the movies, from *Dirty Harry* to *Vertigo*. Prices are $15 and up, depending on the tour, tel. 681 5555.

DASHIELL HAMMETT TOUR

The granddaddy of US walking tours, escorted by Hammett/mystery/SFiana expert Don Herron, meets every Saturday at 12 noon, May–August, on the front steps of the main library, Larkin & McAllister. Reservations aren't necessary but call Herron at (707) 939 1214 for more info if you want. Cost $10.

GLORIOUS FOOD

This tour takes walkers through Italian North Beach and/or Chinatown for shopping, eating and storytelling. Chef Ruby Tom includes a meal, tel. 441 5637. Cost $30.

MISSION MURALS

Covers the outdoor murals of the Mission District with a slide lecture, tel. 285 2287. Cost $1–$3.

San Francisco Strolls

These come in a variety of themes. Folklorist Jim Riggs loves all SF stories, but leavens them with a historian's sense of proportion. The Brothel Stroll is excellent, a lively but harrowing history of San Francisco prostitutes, tel. 282 7924. Cost $20.

Wok Whiz

Shirley Fong-Torres's 3½-hour walk through Chinatown is a combination of history, culture and food, culminating in a dim sum lunch, tel. 355 9657. Cost $33.

NORTH OF MARKET

The heart of the city is nineteenth-century San Francisco, the brawling, bustling waterfront village that transformed itself from Gold Rush boomtown to the 'Paris of the Pacific' in a generation. In modern day terms, the area north of Market Street, bounded by San Francisco Bay to the east and Divisadero Street to the west, is scarcely a tenth of the official municipality of San Francisco, but it includes many of San Francisco's most famous landmarks: Chinatown, North Beach, Nob Hill, Fisherman's Wharf, Telegraph Hill, Russian Hill, Pacific Heights, City Hall and Union Square.

This is where you will spend the great majority of your time, especially if it is your first trip to San Francisco. As well as celebrated landmarks, many famous restaurants and the most popular entertainments are here.

The colourful neighbourhoods above (north) Market defined San Francisco during its turbulent beginnings and in many ways still do. Founded, in 1776, as one of Spain's northernmost colonies and first called Yerba Buena, the little settlement never truly thrived, being maintained more as a half-hearted attempt to stymie Russian, British and French encroachment on the Northern California coast rather than to build a genuine outpost of Spain.

California passed to Mexico from Spain in 1822 as part of Mexican independence, but it remained a backwater. When the Americans brazenly annexed California in 1846, San Francisco didn't seem much of a prize. The military installation, the Presidio, was barely manned and Mission Dolores, the mission established by the Franciscans to convert the Native American peoples, was practically in ruins. There were still a few shacks on Yerba Buena cove that made up a shambling maritime business community. Whalers, navy vessels from various nations and trading ships sailed into the bay, all marvelling at the stunning natural harbour and belittling the lack of enterprise among the Californios, the native Spanish-Mexican residents.

In 1848, gold was discovered at Sutter's Mill, in the Sierra foothills ninety miles east of San Francisco, and everything changed. The population rocketed from 457 (138 of whom were women) to

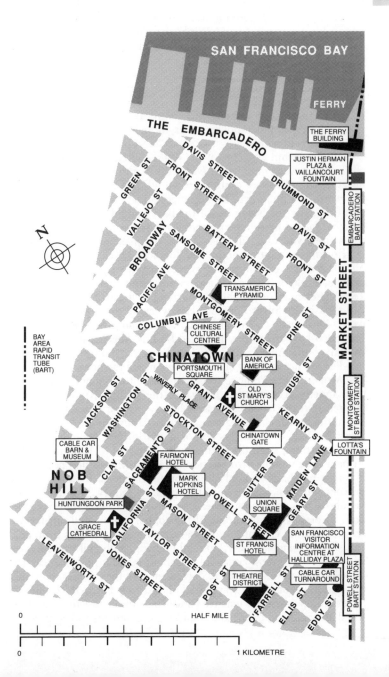

SAN FRANCISCO BAY

FERRY

THE EMBARCADERO

THE FERRY BUILDING

JUSTIN HERMAN PLAZA & VAILLANCOURT FOUNTAIN

GREEN ST

DAVIS STREET

FRONT STREET

DRUMMOND ST

EMBARCADERO BART STATION

VALLEJO ST

BATTERY STREET

DAVIS ST

BROADWAY

SANSOME STREET

FRONT ST

PACIFIC AVE

MONTGOMERY STREET

TRANSAMERICA PYRAMID

MARKET STREET

COLUMBUS AVE

CHINESE CULTURAL CENTRE

PINE ST

CHINATOWN

BANK OF AMERICA

PORTSMOUTH SQUARE

BUSH ST

BAY AREA RAPID TRANSIT TUBE (BART)

JACKSON ST

WASHINGTON ST

WAVERLY PLACE

GRANT AVENUE

OLD ST MARY'S CHURCH

KEARNY ST

MONTGOMERY ST BART STATION

STOCKTON STREET

CHINATOWN GATE

LOTTA'S FOUNTAIN

CABLE CAR BARN & MUSEUM

CLAY ST

SACRAMENTO ST

FAIRMONT HOTEL

SUTTER ST

NOB HILL

MARK HOPKINS HOTEL

POWELL STREET

MAIDEN LANE

GEARY ST

HUNTUNGDON PARK

MASON STREET

UNION SQUARE

GRACE CATHEDRAL

CALIFORNIA ST

TAYLOR STREET

SAN FRANCISCO VISITOR INFORMATION CENTRE AT HALLIDAY PLAZA

ST FRANCIS HOTEL

LEAVENWORTH ST

JONES STREET

POST ST

THEATRE DISTRICT

CABLE CAR TURNAROUND

POWELL STREET BART STATION

O'FARRELL ST

ELLIS ST

EDDY ST

0   HALF MILE

0   1 KILOMETRE

6000 by August. Gold seekers poured into the recently renamed San Francisco on ships and overland, en route to the gold fields. When the cold and rainy autumn weather set in, making mining work impossible, the miners would drift back to San Francisco, rich or not.

The city developed at a fantastic rate, telescoping cycles of urban growth into a few frantic years. A series of disastrous fires were an ironic impetus to San Francisco's shaping of itself. With money pouring in from the gold fields, frantic demand for goods and a seemingly unlimited potential for making money, business-men and speculators rebuilt with frenzy after each fire, putting up bigger stores, grander houses, ever more elaborate opera houses, saloons and churches.

While certain elements of the town shifted, the locus remained close to the waterfront, with Nob Hill marking the outer limits of development. The very centre of town was Portsmouth Square, now the centre of Chinatown. Montgomery Street, one block to the east, was originally the beginning of the bay. Landfill has now extended the city a good half-mile into the bay. Even with landfill and disas-trous fires, you can still trace its development and identity in the interlocking neighbourhoods. The Financial District, with its tower-ing glass office buildings and armies of pin-striped bankers, deal-makers, brokers, attorneys, accountants and their support troops, keep the engines of capitalism churning, a linear descendant of the Gold Rush and Silver Bonanza days when all those fabulous profits were sent directly to San Francisco banks and profiteers. While San Francisco has lately been displaced by Los Angeles as the financial capital of the American West, San Francisco bankers and money handlers do not give any sign they have heard the news.

Money, a San Francisco landmark since the beginning, has never been quietly accumulated. Early on, the visiting Rudyard Kipling marvelled at the city's 'aggressive luxury'. It is a characteristic that has not dimmed. Union Square, an easy walk from the Pacific Coast Stock Exchange, is the anchor of a world-class shopping district with everything from the home-grown elegance of I. Magnin to an Armani store with its own espresso bar and a Macy's that needs three different buildings to hold all its consumer goods. If Union Square mirrors San Francisco's genius for spending money, Nob Hill loom-ing above it is an almost too-easy symbol of its passion for conspic-uous display. Once the home of the robber barons and nineteenth-century venture capitalists who harvested massive profits from gold and silver mining and later, railroad building, Nob Hill was crowned with some of the most godawful over-built mansions in America. The 1906 earthquake and fire cleared away most of the excesses, but other manifestations of wealth reappeared immediately to cap the California Street hilltop where the massive Grace Cathedral and Fairmont Hotel stand as witness to the need to build big monuments to big money.

In a northerly direction, the Financial District's businesslike bustle blends easily into North Beach and Chinatown, two of the city's most famous districts which are becoming more and more one neighbourhood. Actually, they are similar case studies of San Francisco's multi-cultural personality. Italian immigrants settled in North Beach, Chinese in Chinatown. North Beach retains a heavy Italian sensibility in its restaurants, coffee houses, bakeries and churches, but it is no longer an immigrant neighbourhood. Families grew up, found some measure of prosperity and relocated to the suburbs.

Chinatown, however, still a magnet for new waves of Asian immigrants from mainland China, Hong Kong and Southeast Asia, remains an intensely immigrant-ethnic enclave. It is a complete town in itself with a thriving industry (tourists) and shops, services and residents.

Fisherman's Wharf, once the province of the Italian fishermen who lived in North Beach, sprawls along the waterfront with its huckster attraction. The working fishing boats have long since decamped, leaving T-shirt shops, festival market places, bad restaurants and an unapologetic air of carnival. Further along the waterfront is the Marina, with its kite-flying green, yacht club and funky Fort Mason, headquarters of off-beat theatre, art and non-profit causes.

Behind the Marina rise up some of San Francisco's most formidable hills, home to the lucky elite who can afford to live in Pacific Heights, a select coterie that includes pop star Linda Rondstadt, millionaire Gordon Getty, most of the city's socialites and other rich people. Among the Victorians and designer houses are too-darling-to-believe shopping and eating pockets where knick-knacks cost a week's salary and no meal is complete without an unpronounceable cheese.

Japantown, a sleek collection of shops, cafés, cinemas and offices in a mall-like setting, is the dividing line between Pacific Heights and the Western Addition. The Addition is a tough neighbourhood that gives way to the gentrification of Hayes Valley and the grand Beaux Arts Civic Center plaza of City Hall, and its stately sisters, San Francisco Opera, Louise M. Davies Symphony Hall, San Francisco Museum of Modern Art, the Main Library and attendant government buildings and offices.

FINANCIAL DISTRICT

'I have seen purer liquors, better seegars, finer tobacco, truer guns and pistols, larger dirks [daggers] and bowie knives and prettier cortezans, here in San Francisco than any place I have ever visited,' wrote Hinton Helper in his well-known 1855 book about Gold Rush California. 'It is my unbiased opinion that California can and does furnish the best bad things that are obtainable in America.'

Helper's happy discovery of a wide open city that revelled in its exuberant lust for pleasure was a discovery made over and over in San Francisco's history as one incredulous (and often disapproving) traveller after another wrote letters or books or newspaper reports of the frontier capital that was more European than American.

The essential ingredient in the quick and cohesive crystallisation of San Francisco's character was big, big money. In the American scheme of things, the development of San Francisco Bay was inevitable, its superb natural seaport being unmatched on the West Coast of the American continent. But many historians think a non-Gold Rush, non-Silver Bonanza development would have put the major city at Oakland, on the warmer, more temperate eastern shore of the bay. Further, it would have been a slower, more stable settlement driven by families and conventional businesses. Instead there was the Gold Rush of 1849, closely followed by the discovery of enormous silver deposits in the Sierra Nevada in 1859. San Francisco was the fulcrum for these fabulously rich finds, hurriedly growing into a city to accommodate the supplying of the mines, providing entertainment and most importantly, handling the money.

The Financial District has been in place since the earliest days of the Gold Rush and neither fire nor earthquake, nor the increasing clout of Los Angeles, has displaced it. Montgomery Street now, as in the nineteenth century, is called 'The Wall Street of the West' and the business of capitalism is practised with fervour and skill. To begin your examination of San Francisco with the Financial District is to begin at the beginning.

It's an area of indistinct boundaries, but think of Montgomery as the high street and the Transamerica Pyramid (600 Montgomery), the Bank of America Building (555 California St) and the Ferry Building as gateways to an imperial walled city. The day begins early in many quarters of the Financial District, where brokers and bankers have to get a pre-dawn start to monitor the New York stock market which opens at 6 a.m. on California's Pacific Standard Time (9 a.m. in New York).

You don't have to start that early to see the Financial District at its more interesting, but the place does hum on weekdays and early evenings when the office corps repair to the many bars, restaurants and even lectures to exorcise the tension and tedium of making money. It's a happy area of town to find yourself in around lunchtime because of the quite good little cafés, salad bars, street carts and other eateries that cater to the office crowd. This being San Francisco, even fast food has to have some standards.

Much of this classic downtown is unfortunately high rise office buildings of the modern period – glass boxes that San Franciscans condemn as 'Manhattanising' their beautiful landscape. An uneasy compromise between the powerful monied forces of development and the dedicated protectors of historic San Francisco and slow growth emerged in the 1985 Downtown Plan that keeps a lid on development without squelching it altogether. San Francisco's insistence on its individuality, coupled with the architectural trend away from detail-phobic modern design towards the smaller scale and whimsy of post-modernism, has been very good for the city's dense downtown. Parks and open spaces are mandated in new designs which guarantees wonderful little pockets of greenery and space for relaxation. Inspired by the 1975 Transamerica Pyramid, corporate and business structures aim for eye-catching design rather than the biggest phallic symbol.

Where the Money Came From Fantastic tales of endless gold deposits had been floating around California since the first days of the Spanish Conquest. By the mid-1800s the discovery of gold was a stock rumour in the West. The stories had quickened in 1848, then exploded on 12 May when Sam Brannan, a wily Mormon businessman, returned from a foray into the Sierra foothills. Holding aloft a small bottle filled with nuggets, Brannan shouted the news as he ran down Montgomery Street, 'Gold! Gold! Gold from the American River!'

Of course, Brannan had prudently bought up all the picks, shovels, blankets, shirts, boots, beans and other supplies for his stores in the Sierra foothills and San Francisco before sharing the good news.

In 1847, a Swiss entrepreneur named Johann Augustus Sutter had mounted a massive operation in the Sacramento Valley. Sutter's Fort was a busy trading centre surrounded by his fields and orchards. By the beginning of 1848 Sutter had another venture in full swing. Forty-five miles away Sutter's lieutenant, James Marshall, was overseeing the construction of a sawmill at Coloma. In January Marshall noticed golden looking nuggets and flakes in the streambed. Some of the workers had also commented on the same goldish bits, but no one could quite believe this might be GOLD. Jenny Wimmer, the camp cook, soon established that it was indeed gold and Marshall took his news back to Sutter.

JENNY WIMMER

Jenny Wimmer, wife of a foreman and the camp cook and laundress, was the only one among the crew who knew what unrefined gold looked like. When she was a girl back in Georgia, there had been a modest gold discovery in the north Georgia hills. Jenny remembered how the gold had been panned from streams and how difficult it was to tell the real thing from ordinary rock. She also knew how to find out what was real gold and what wasn't. She took Marshall's nuggets and soaked them in vinegar. Then she boiled them in her lye soap vat all night. The next morning Jenny poured out the soap as everyone gathered around. At the bottom of the post was a lump of potash.

Jenny lifted it out and, '… there was my gold as bright as could be,' she remembered years later.

A nugget about the size of a peanut is now on display at the Bancroft Library at the University of California at Berkeley and is reputed to be the very rock that James Marshall saw in the stream on 24 January 1848 and Jenny Wimmer boiled in her lye vat. There is some dispute over whether this little rock is the very one, but it is completely accepted as one of the first nuggets identified as gold. It is called the Wimmer Nugget.

Although the word had to get out sooner or later, Wimmer is sometimes blamed for it being sooner. The sawmill camp agreed to keep the find secret until Marshall could confer with Sutter and decide on some kind of plan. In the meantime, Martin Wimmer, Jenny's little boy, shared the secret with his great friend Jacob Wittmer, another Swiss emigré who drove the supply wagon up to camp. When Wittmer called little Martin a liar, this child of the frontier was enraged. His mother was brought forth as his witness. Swearing Wittmer to their pact, Jenny Wimmer told him the story to defend her son. Wittmer blabbed as soon as he could get back to town.

The Gold Rush descended on California like an avalanche on an innocent Alpine village. After Sam Brannan's bizarre announcement in San Francisco, the city emptied. By 27 May the editor of the *California Star* lamented, 'The stores are closed and places of business vacated, a large number of houses tenantless, various kinds of mechanical labor suspended or given up entirely, and nowhere the pleasant hum of industry salutes the ear as of late … everything is dull, monotonous, dead.' Having had his say, the editor then closed his shop and headed for the gold fields.

Word gradually spread through California, then south to Mexico and South America. Chile, which had gone through a gold boom of its own, responded quickly. But all this migration was just a prelude to December, when President James K. Polk included the news of gold in his annual message to Congress. Polk was eager to add glory to his policies that had led to the war with Mexico (1846–8) and acquisition of Mexican territories. Gold certainly put a new shine on California.

Polk's confirmation of gold was like an electric starting bell being rung at the races. Thousands upon thousands of Americans dropped everything and raced for California. As many as 25,000 came overland in 1849, walking, riding and in wagon trains. Others came by sea. Sailing ships, or anything that could float, left New York, Boston, Baltimore, New Orleans and set off for San Francisco. Called Argonauts, as a nod to Jason's arduous search for the golden fleece, the gold seekers came from every possible direction. Some sailed as far as Panama or Nicaragua, hiked through the jungles to the Pacific and caught another overloaded, barely seaworthy boat to California. Some sailed the whole distance, all the way round dangerous Cape Horn.

Once in California they bought incredibly over-priced supplies in San Francisco (often from wildly prosperous Mr Brannan) and headed for 'the diggings'. The mines were, in fact, just that – shallow diggings into dry streambeds, ravines and other places where the gold had sunk after a prehistoric glacier had melted and left its minerals behind. The first gold seekers literally picked up the gold as Marshall had. The easy stuff was snapped up fast and soon followed by hard, frustrating work with pickaxes, shovels and sweat.

By the time the Gold Rush had peaked in the mid-1850s, an estimated 250,000 people had poured into California and extracted upwards of $400 million in gold. A lucky few became rich; a fortunate handful made a nice profit and went back to Maine or Kentucky to become prosperous burghers and talk endlessly about their adventures in California. But the great majority of the gold seekers made nothing and stayed in California. Many settled in San Francisco or the Bay Area. Most importantly, however, the Gold Rush had remade the Americans in its image rather than the other way around. Kevin Starr, the pre-eminent scholar of California history and culture, says that the 'habit of the Gold Rush' established speculation, money-making and thrill-seeking as the norm for San Francisco, rather than peak experiences that come once or twice in a lifetime.

Fortunes were made and lost overnight, but there was little significance attached to how one made money or whether one lost it. 'The sand-shoveler and the millionaire may change places tomorrow and they know it,' observed Gold Rush journalist John Hittell, 'so the former does not cringe nor the other strut when they meet'. A prostitute who was said to have made $50,000 in one year among the miners was proudly cited in many letters and articles of the time as yet another example of what hard work could accomplish.

This belief in what has been called the 'jackpot mentality' of San Francisco was only reinforced by the discovery of silver on the California-Nevada border in 1859. The Comstock Lode proved every bit as rich as the Gold Rush, yielding more than $400 million before petering out in 1880. Even bigger individual fortunes were made in the silver mines which required capital investments for heavy machinery and organised work crews. There was no place for the solitary digger in the quest for the deeply entrenched silver. San Francisco, with its Gold Rush experience, was ready for the silver boom and again became banker, entertainer and home base. Among those making their fortunes off the Comstock were George Hearst, a midwestern mining engineer whose son William Randolph would become a California legend. But at the top of the heap were the so-called Silver Kings, James G. Fair, James C. Flood, John W. Mackay and William S. O'Brien, who with their families would set new standards of nouveau riche gaucherie that would make even other American parvenus reel.

Today's Financial District   It is not just the spirit of the Gold Rush that survives in today's San Francisco. A surprising number of businesses from that era continue to have a presence in the city. Levi Strauss (1850), the blue jean conglomerate is probably the most famous, but several more important firms continue, including Wells Fargo Bank (1835), the jewellers, Shreve & Co. (1852), and Gump's (1861), dealers of art and antiquities.

The most unlikely Gold Rush merchant to survive into the late twentieth century is undoubtedly Robison's Pets, 135 Maiden Lane. In 1849 David Neely Robison bought up green bananas as he passed through Panama, having been told that anything would sell in merchandise-hungry San Francisco. His bananas ripened nicely and sold at a hefty profit. Robison saw his future as a greengrocer and opened Robison's Produce. The shop was a favourite with sailors, starved for fresh fruit and vegetables after long voyages. Robison fell to bartering with the sailors and ended up not with just oddities and curios from faraway place, but exotic animals brought back from Asia and other ports. Eventually the animals took over and today Robison's stocks everything from darling puppies to rhinestone collars to pet food.

The rough egalitarianism of the Gold Rush has vague echoes in the place that women have carved for themselves in the San Francisco business world. Women lawyers, bankers and executives have achieved a critical mass in San Francisco that has put them beyond being mistaken for secretaries, but not yet cracked the final heights of power. Business is conducted in an affable, civilised tone where gender and race are rarely acknowledged. While issues of the glass ceiling and sexual harassment are major concerns among the women who work in the Financial District's highrises, the prevailing attitude is a projection of the Californian's self-image of easy-going tolerance, fairness and sophistication. In fact, nothing riles a San Franciscan, male or female, so much as to be called biased, bigoted or unfair. A current status symbol among downtown offices is hiring gay male secretaries which silently broadcasts the messages: (1) We straight men here are completely secure in our sexuality; (2) We are an open-minded, equal opportunity enterprise; and (3) We are a very cool kinda place.

Women coming to San Francisco to do business will do well to regard the laid-back attitude with some scepticism. Although long, leisurely lunches and after-work drinks at high profile spots such as Postrio and Jack's (lunch) and the London Wine Bar and Gordon Biersch Brewery (drinks) are touted as an integral part of the biz life, they are also a part of the San Francisco self-image which abhors showing strain. San Francisco wheeler-dealers work as hard and as long as their peers anywhere in the world, but are loath to be perceived as workaholic grinds.

In other financial districts of the world points are awarded to whomever is working the longest and hardest, practically living at the office. In San Francisco, the most admired people in the office are those who show up with bulging briefcases in one hand and their evening clothes in the other. After polishing off a day of high finance and gruelling trial work, these life-to-the-fullest types change into black tie and shimmery dresses in the office restroom and rush off to the opera, a fund-raiser or the Black & White Ball.

The reality, as always, is a little different. Many of the *bons vivants* will slip back to the office and spend long, long hours catching up and getting ahead, but you won't hear about it. Wearing one's success lightly is crucial to one's standing. The nasty toe-to-toe confrontationalism of New York isn't found in most San Francisco boardrooms, but don't be misled. Just because the boys don't break a sweat in the warm-ups doesn't mean they aren't playing hardball. Work hard, play hard and always keep a slightly ironic smile about the lips and you are playing the San Francisco game.

DINING THE OLD WAY

Part of playing the game is dining out at one of these grills. Before there was California Cuisine there was John's Grill (1908), and before John's, there was Sam's Grill (1867) and Jack's (1864) and before them all, the Tadich Grill (1849). San Francisco abounds in these genuine, old-fashioned steak and seafood houses. The food is good, the panelling is dark, polished wood and the waiters are grown-ups who do not introduce themselves. Even if you're not much interested in restaurants (which begs the question why are you in San Francisco?), taking a meal at one of these delightful anachronisms makes you a San Franciscan for a day. Be prepared for a certain amount of gruffness. At Tadich, for instance, there are no reservations, no matter how big your corporate title is. Strictly first come, first served, just as they have been doing it since 1849.

Walking the Financial District is a visual delight, especially for anyone with an interest in architecture. The great drama between the imposing modern skyscrapers and the smaller, usually more interesting buildings makes for a varied canvas. Ride the California Street cable car from the Embarcadero (get on at the end of Market Street, outside the Hyatt Hotel) for a cinematic view of the area. When you get to the end of the line, ride the car back for the double experience of climbing and descending the steep California Street hill to the bay. An architectural walking tour is always a good idea or pick up a handy foldup map called *The Map of San Francisco Architecture* (Woodbridge Publications, $4.50) for quick reference. The map, which concentrates on downtown, is a distillation of Sally Woodbridge's and John Woodbridge's superb architectural guidebooks of the Bay Area.

The area is full of corporate museums which usually translate into a room of memorabilia or half-hearted displays. With the exception of the Wells Fargo History Room you will be better off saving your museum hours for SF's more important institutions.

Wells Fargo History Museum

420 Montgomery St (at Sacramento), tel. 396 2619. Open Mon–Fri, 9 a.m.–5 p.m.; free.

A fully restored 1865 Concord stagecoach is the centrepiece here. Even though there's no touching, much less stepping inside the incredibly small interior, the stagecoach brings the old West to vivid life. Established in 1852, Wells Fargo delivered passengers, mail, gold and merchandise by stagecoach, wagon and even ran a branch of the Pony Express. The company flourished in Gold Rush California because of its reputation for stodgy dependability. 'Pay no more for gold dust than it is worth,' a Wells Fargo superintendent admonished his agents, 'nor pay any less. This is the only true motto to do any kind of business on'. The history room recreates a telegraph office of the era and has even imported a set of doors from a Gold Country Wells Fargo office that has bullet holes from an 1800s' robbery.

A far corner is devoted to women, noting that women were often Wells agents, ran stagecoach stops and post offices and were even stagecoach drivers, although this was very rare. The woman's corner also pays homage to the first woman to break through the executive barrier, becoming a vice president in 1964.

There's no guide nor even very many written materials, but the little museum does have perhaps the best concentration of Gold Rush artefacts in one space. The tools used by the miners are interesting. Be sure to notice the Vigilante Committee medallion in one of the display cases. The Vigilantes were a well-mannered mob that formed in 1851 and again in 1856 to 'clean up' lawless San Francisco through hangings and floggings. It was a matter of great pride among San Franciscans to have a Vigilante in the family. Each member was given a number according to when he signed the membership book and the lower the number, the higher the prestige.

Transamerica Pyramid

600 Montgomery St (at Washington). Observation area open Mon–Fri during business hours; free.

Heartily vilified at its inception in 1970, even old, old San Franciscans now take some pride in the Pyramid, one of the world's most recognisable buildings. It's the tallest building in the city (853 feet) and dominates the skyline. Visitors are directed to an enclosed observation area on the 27th floor (there are 48 floors altogether).

The views are impressive, but not really any better than you can see from Coit Tower or other strategic points. Like many icons up close, the Pyramid isn't terribly interesting. The best thing about the building is the charming park behind it. Redwood Park is a half-acre of green lawns and fully grown redwoods. Concerts and musical performances are a regular noon-hour feature during the summer.

Pacific Coast Stock Exchange and City Club

Sansome and Pine streets. Closed to the public.

This gloomy 1915 pile is only truly interesting on the inside. The mausoleum-like building houses the West Coast equivalent of the New York Stock Exchange, created in 1957 when the San Francisco Stock Exchange (1882) and the Los Angeles Exchange merged. Although the exchange itself, facing Pine Street, is closed to the public, you can arrange to visit a balcony to see the frantic display of business in action.

The exchange's original building is around the corner on Sansome, the upper floor's now a private business club, the City Club of San Francisco. During a 1930 remodelling, Mexican muralist Diego Rivera was hired to paint murals inside. No one has completely explained why it was thought a good idea to have a Mexican communist decorate the inner sanctum of California capitalism, but there it is. Rivera was accompanied to San Francisco by his wife, Frida Kahlo, and the two became the toast of the town. Kahlo joined Rivera on his scaffolding as he painted to keep him company. Kahlo's first public notice as a painter came in San Francisco. 'Mrs Diego Rivera Revealed as Portrait Artist in Own Right' was the headline on a newspaper story of the time which indulgently explained, 'Diego beams as he tells you of his wife's work' and 'Mrs Rivera' was painting a portrait of a young San Francisco society woman who had befriended them. The reporter, eager to show he was hip to the essential nuttiness of modern art, added that Kahlo 'has also done a mystical painting portraying Luther Burbank arising from his grave beneath a growing tree'.

Viewing the Rivera murals is available to non-club members only through regularly scheduled tours by the Mexican Museum. Call 441 0404.

Bank of America Headquarters

555 California St (between Montgomery and Kearny).

This forbidding tower is no longer owned by B of A which leases it back from a holding company in yet another strange twist of contemporary business. Built in 1969, of dark red carnelian marble, the tower is not the tallest SF building but it is the tallest building one can go to the top of, the Pyramid not having access beyond the 48th floor. At the B of A's 52nd floor is the Carnelian Room, a gaudy, overpriced restaurant that is a local favourite for Sunday brunch (see listings p. 239). However much you're paying for your scrambled eggs it's still worth the price to watch the fog roll in and slowly obliterate everything below you, transforming the dining room into a space ship above the earth. Sunset is another prime time event from the Carnelian Room. Go for drinks around sunset time.

The plaza in front of the tower is decorated by a black marble sculpture of no particular significance save its popular nickname: 'The Banker's Heart' (real title, 'Transcendence', by Masayuki Nagari). The little joke is a sad summation of B of A's history from immigrant triumph to corporate confusion. A.P. Giannini, the son of Italian immigrants, parlayed a family produce business into a small bank, the Bank of Italy. After the 1906 earthquake Giannini saved the assets of his bank from the fire by loading everything from his vault into a produce wagon and covering it with smelly fruit and vegetables. When the smoke cleared, he opened for business with a table and chair set up among the rubble.

And Keep in Mind Crocker Galleria is an upscale, three-level open mall covered by a skylight at 50 Post St, between Montgomery and Kearny. Not quite as upscale as it sells itself, the real star here is Nicole Miller, the witty young designer whose ties and scarves are neo-fifties theme cartoons. Dresses and other clothes, too – all expensive but possessed of genuine style.

Exit on the Sutter Street side of the Galleria and admire one of downtown's most gorgeous buildings, the 1917 Hallidie Building. Its elaborate cast-iron framing sets off an all-glass front, the first use of the 'glass curtain wall' design.

A couple of blocks away at the junction of Market, Kearny and Geary there's a small pie-shaped concrete island dominated by a soaring cast iron column. Popularly called Lotta's Fountain, it was given to the city in 1875 by the Gold Rush entertainer, Lotta Crabtree. Once it was truly a fountain, with heavy tin cups chained to the base for communal use. Crabtree was so intertwined in local memory with the Gold Rush and saloons that a small riot broke out when the monument was dedicated; a huge crowd had trooped over from the Barbary Coast expecting the fountain to pump beer. They were outraged when it spewed mere water.

The fountain became a gathering spot after the 1906 earthquake, being one fixed landmark to remain intact. Every year, on 18 April, an informal memorial is held at the fountain when the dwindling group of 1906 survivors, friends, family and the curious place wreaths on the fountain and observe a moment of silence at 5.12 a.m.

LOTTA CRABTREE

There were many ways to make a fortune in Gold Rush California and in 1857 nine-year-old Lotta Crabtree was well on her way to making hers on the stage.

Called 'California's Pet' or 'California's Diamond', the red-haired, dark-eyed tyke was a favourite on the mining camp entertainment circuit, singing, dancing and donning black face to do a heart-tugging mini version of *Uncle Tom's Cabin* that consisted entirely of her portrayal of Topsy, the child slave.

It wasn't an easy climb to the top, even for this prototypical Shirley Temple. Entertainment was big business in the mining camps and San Francisco and the competition was fierce. Miners were particularly fond of child performers, most of them being either bachelors or men living apart from their families. Lotta, guided by a stage mother with a will of iron, managed to outshine them all, even a three-year-old bareback rider, three singing sisters and numerous other kiddie acts.

Surprisingly, she seems to have thrived on the attention despite the unsavoury nature of many of her venues (her accompanist accidently shot his best friend one night during her run at San Francisco's Bella Union, a popular and raucous music hall). Her protective, controlling mother, Mary Ann, fiercely discouraged suitors, but the teenage Lotta was a mascot for San Francisco's firemen and taken up by the Bohemians such as Bret Harte and the infamous dancer Adah Issacs Menken. Photos of Lotta show a startlingly attractive young woman who resembles a nineteenth-century Meg Ryan with her small, sensual mouth and shoulder-length, wavy hair.

At seventeen Lotta left for New York in a blaze of glory and after a few false starts, became a major stage star on Broadway. Her persona as the spunky Western girl who sings and dances her way into everyone's heart found its way into everything from adaptations of Dickens (*The Old Curiosity Shop*) to plays written just for her.

Lotta returned to San Francisco several times to perform and gave the city the peculiar fountain that has become a landmark. She retired from the stage at 45, never married, lived quietly in the East and died in her sleep in 1924. 'California's Pet' left a fortune of $4 million which went to various charities.

Head down Market Street towards the bay to make a loop of the Financial District, some of which dips across Market Street. The Palace Hotel, 639 Market St, at New Montgomery, was first built in 1875 by one of the silver millionaires, William C. Ralston. The hotel was gutted in the 1906 fires and rebuilt, in both instances a ridiculously overdecorated, oversized (800 rooms) folly. Of course it was a success. Now officially the Sheraton Palace and refurbished in the late 1980s, the hotel is still popular and inordinately plush. The Palm Court Garden, an elegant glassed-over Victorian dining room, is a must-see. Also, the Pied Piper Bar, with its Maxfield Parrish mural, is one of the most romantically cosmopolitan bars imaginable.

The US Federal Reserve Bank, 100 Market St, at Spear Street, offers tours and films about money and how it goes about being the bank for bankers. Bankers' hours, 9 a.m. to 4 p.m., Monday through Friday, tel. 974 3242.

Continue down Spear Street and you'll come to Rincon Center, a truly worthy redevelopment project. The 1940 building that housed the main post office annexe has been reworked into a multi-use centre. The post office's striking California history murals (Anton Refregier, 1946–8) have been retained and a new atrium is built around a fountain called the Rain Column, a ninety-foot freefall of water. One of the most interesting features of the complex is the Bippidy-Bop Pre-School, a comprehensive daycare agency. Situated in bright, cheerful rooms that open onto a courtyard, Bippidy-Bop is part of the new thrust in American childcare, placing children near their parents in downtown business districts.

From here head directly towards the bay and walk along the newly liberated Embarcadero, as the waterfront is called. Until 1992 it was obscured by the Embarcadero Freeway, a spur off the Bay Bridge that was originally planned to span the entire waterfront to Golden Gate Bridge. Outraged San Franciscans managed to get construction stopped at Broadway. The year was 1958, the dawn of citizen activism. After the 1989 earthquake, the freeway was closed, owing to engineers' concern that it could not withstand another jolt. To the delight and joy of most citizens it was later completely torn down, opening up the marvellous vistas of the bay. It's difficult for anyone seeing this waterfront for the first time to realise what a tremendous gift it is – one of the few times that so-called progress has been properly and completely rescinded.

The Ferry Building, which dates from 1896, was modelled on the Cathedral Tower of Seville by architect A. Page Brown. It now houses the World Trade Center, a grandiose title for a nonentity that mostly sponsors art shows. The regular Saturday farmer's market is the highlight of the week for the Ferry Building which was the gateway to San Francisco until the Golden Gate and Bay Bridges were built in the late thirties. Before the bridges, thousands of workers commuted by ferry every day from the East Bay and Marin.

Cross back to Market Street and walk through Justin Herman Plaza, the site of midday concerts during the week and the haunt of feral skateboarders on the evenings and weekends. The Vaillancourt Fountain (1971) is another controversial SF landmark, widely condemned when it first opened but now such a part of the landscape that no one except Herb Caen (see p. 19) seriously objects to it. The towering concrete tubes of water drown out traffic and can be walked through, or near. The fountain is equipped with a network of stairs and catwalks that allow you to walk into its centre without getting drenched. Children adore exploring the Vaillancourt.

The Embarcadero Center towering over the plaza is a set of four highrises by architect John Portman (1971–82) that mix shops, restaurants, parking garages and offices. This is an excellent place to rest, find a clean bathroom and get a snack. The shops can be fun, but there's nothing here worth a special visit.

LEARNING TO NETWORK

The crucial importance of networking to one's career is an article of faith among American businesspeople. Women in particular have embraced this idea of connections equal access with an ardour that borders on fanaticism. There are any number of groups that cater to the different professions or specialities, but three large civic groups are the key forums which set the tone and involve almost every serious-minded businessman or woman in the Bay Area at some point. The Commonwealth Club, World Affairs Council and SF Chamber of Commerce are all membership groups but visitors, especially out-of-towners, are usually welcomed.

If so inclined, you may attend meetings morning, noon and night and hear everyone from Vice-President Al Gore to experts on gardening and Asian cosmetics markets. For the most up-to-date listings and networking news, look through San Francisco *Downtown*, a free monthly tabloid that covers the Financial District.

Meetings to check into:
Bay Area Career Women, tel. 863 0538. Social and networking group for lesbians. Their Friday cocktail parties are famous for pulling together the Top Girls.
Commonwealth Club of California, tel. 597 6705. Organised in 1903, the club now has more than 16,000 members and a full calendar of talks, luncheons and get-togethers. The large scale makes it easy for newcomers to drop in.
San Francisco Chamber of Commerce, tel. 392 4511. This is the city's biggest booster and sponsor of an endless stream of business-oriented events.
World Affairs Council of Northern California, tel. 434 5112. Another Big Picture group which hosts diplomats, ambassadors, Washington bureaucrats and authors.
On a lighter note, the **Center for Creative Work** is dedicated to bringing creativity, art and inspiration to the Financial District and schedules a varied selection of noontime events, ranging from poetry readings to bookbinding classes to an after-work salon for women artists. Most of the programmes are free or have a modest charge. Contact the centre at 425 Bush St, Suite 425, SF 94108, tel. 989 9809 or fax 296 8780 for information and current schedules.

UNION SQUARE

Union Square is San Francisco's centre and its triumph. While most of America has vacated its centre for the mall, San Francisco retains an honest-to-god downtown with a vital, pulsating retail district that is the goal and envy of every American city, town and village.

The 2.6-acre park bordered by Geary, Powell, Post and Stockton streets is more of a focal point than an actual park, but gives the downtown a specific point of reference and a face. Centred around a soaring ninety-foot statue of a female symbol of victory commemorating Admiral Dewey's Manila triumph in the Spanish-American War of 1898, Union Square is a severely formal garden. The flowers are sometimes quite lovely, especially if the gardens have been dressed for a big civic event such as the opening ceremonies for Chinese New Year.

The on-going, all-star event around Union Square is shopping. Immediately around the square are Neiman-Marcus, Saks Fifth Avenue, Macy's and I. Magnin. Within a five-minute walk are Emporium-Capwell, Nordstrom's, Bally, Brooks Brothers, Chanel, FAO Schwarz, Gump's, Burberry's, Gucci, Tiffany, Louis Vuitton, Wedgwood, Gianni Versace, Polo-Ralph Lauren, Mark Cross, Pierre Deux, Laura Ashley, Cartier, Hermes and an ever-changing parade of little shops and boutiques that are gambling on breaking into the retail big-time.

Christmas is actually the square's best time, even though it is the height of San Francisco's drizzly-to-miserable rainy season. It never snows in San Francisco, but Union Square is one of the most Christmas-intensive spots imaginable. The square has a huge Christmas tree and menorah and twinkles with coloured lights. The big stores compete with one another for the most elaborate window decorations, but Gump's usually wins with its cosy little scenes starring heart-melting puppies and kittens from the San Francisco Society for the Prevention of Cruelty to Animals. Starting the day after Thanksgiving (the fourth Thursday in November) shoppers clog the streets and the stores, but their holiday energy takes the edge off the usual I-hate-how-commercialised-Christmas-is grumbling.

And is it commercial! The first shopping day after Christmas produces a human crush that is reminiscent of newsreels of the liberation of Paris. Part of the success of the Union Square shopping is that there is truly something for everyone. At the very top are rarefied corners of Magnin's, Saks, Neiman and the other top-of-the-line shops where the saleswomen know their customers by name, have their likes and dislikes on file and call them when something comes in that, 'I know you would love', never mind the four- or five-figure price tag.

Bargain hunters, however, are not out of place around Union Square. The recession of the last few years has held all retailers' feet to the fire, making sales a regular feature in every shop. Emporium and Macy's, two of the great old department stores, are the best in that category, with rotating '30 per cent off!' specials and bargain basements to boot, but even the toney shops such as Wedgwood and the little linen specialist places like Kris Kelly offer sale tables and mark-downs. Nobody expects to pay full price in today's economy.

The Union Square area is the crossroads for San Francisco, where locals and tourists share the turf. The cable cars clang up and down Powell Street; the St Francis Hotel, whose rich and racy history mirrors the city's, looms over the square, while the theatre district is a block away, at Geary and Mason. Art Galleries are another entertainment close at hand, many of them offering undiluted schlock, but there are a handful of worthwhile galleries. To the north a new pocket of interest is developing across from the Chinatown Gate at Bush and Grant, where a Euro Quarter is becoming more visible around the Café de la Presse.

Union Square has been a public space since 1850, but only slowly displaced Portsmouth Square as the town centre. Its name comes from the days just before the Civil War when the square was a rallying point for the unionists who decried both slavery and the break-up of the US through Southern secession. 'The union and nothing but the union!' declared the huge banners that festooned the square. California, despite some after-the-fact hyperbole, was never in serious contention to leave the union. The slavery issue had been disposed of early on and there was really no advantage for the state in throwing its lot with the Confederates. While there were many Southerners in California and more than a few of those in powerful positions, their agitation for slavery and the Confederacy never amounted to a serious challenge to California's statehood.

JESSIE BENTON FRÉMONT

'Oh, if my husband had only been more positive!' Jessie Benton Frémont confided to a family friend in the twilight of her life. 'But he never did assert himself enough. That was his great fault.'

Historians, on the other hand, charge John C. Frémont (1813–90) with asserting himself all too much. An ambitious young army officer, he led overland expeditions to California in the 1840s as topographical missions to map the interior. These treks would have been just more interesting frontier reports without the literary talents of his wife Jessie. She transformed Frémont's sprawling and self-congratulatory memories into a riveting bestseller that established him as 'The Pathfinder'.

The daughter of a powerful senator, Thomas Hart Benton of Missouri, Jessie Benton fell in love with the dashing young Frémont when he visited her father in Washington. She was 16, he was 27. A precocious intellectual trained by her father in logic, languages and discourse, Jessie eloped with Frémont and eventually won her father over to the marriage. Together, the Bentons relentlessly and ruthlessly promoted Frémont as a new American hero.

In his 1846 expedition to California, Frémont later insisted he was under secret orders to bring California into the US. Leading a column of tested soldiers, Frémont engaged in confrontational meetings with the Mexican authorities and ignited rumours of war among the growing numbers of American settlers. Frémont's sabre-rattling led to the Bear Flag Revolt, a brief and ragged rebellion by American settlers, declaring California an independent republic. (To 'raise the Bear Flag' is an old-fashioned term in California for fighting city hall.) Frémont quickly put himself at the head of the rebels.

The Mexican-American war had been declared and the California altercations were simply added to the bubbling pot of intercontinental politics. Frémont was briefly military governor of California – or so he thought, having pushed aside a brigadier general. Recalled to Washington, Frémont was court-martialled despite the best efforts of Jessie and her father.

The Frémonts settled in California where they were briefly very rich and powerful. Frémont inadvertently bought land with gold near Yosemite where they had a great estate. They also had a home in San Francisco, Black Point, on what is now Fort Mason, where Jessie was regarded as the epitomy of California ladyhood. Frémont was elected one of California's first senators and ran for the presidency in 1856.

The money was lost through Frémont's always erratic business dealings, the political position faded and even being recalled to the army for the Civil War came to naught. Through it all Jessie moved from coast to coast and tended her husband's reputation and fame, gritting her teeth over his spotty political and financial judgement. She began writing under her own name at the age of fifty and supported the family through her earnings. Praised as the perfect wife in her lifetime and afterwards (*Immortal Wife* is the title of one fictionalised account) in retrospect it seems clear that The Pathfinder was in fact a great fictional character that was equal parts Jessie's powerful intelligence and John's unbridled physical courage. It was an illusion that could not endure, to Jessie's eternal consternation.

Their collective bluster, in fact, suggests that like fellow San Franciscan Mark Twain, many of the white Southerners were fleeing the overwhelming questions of morality, loyalty and responsibility raised by slavery. The Southerners paid lip service to the Southern cause, but the vast majority of them stayed put in San Francisco when the war finally erupted in 1860. Mark Twain 'lit out for the territories' after a brief, unhappy stint as a Confederate soldier under his real name Samuel Clemens, landing in silver-mad Nevada, then moving on to San Francisco.

The Union Square rabblerousing was symptomatic of the San Francisco appetite for theatre, the more public and dramatic, the better. The primary actor in the drama of saving California for the union was a pint-sized Unitarian preacher named Thomas Starr King, a Boston transplant. A fiery orator, King came to the pulpit of San Francisco's Unitarian Church in 1860, the city's richest and most socially prominent congregation. Encouraged by Jessie Benton Frémont, the shrewd and influential wife of Col. John C. Frémont, King made unionism a crusade. He travelled all over the state exhorting his new fellow Californians to support Abraham Lincoln and the union, becoming one of the first statewide heroes. He died in 1864 at age 39, primarily from exhaustion.

Maiden Lane

Across Stockton Street from Union Square, in the gap between Bally of Switzerland and Athur Beren Shoes, is Maiden Lane. A charming little alley that only runs for two blocks, crossing Grant and ending at Kearny Street, Maiden Lane is one of those folklore landmarks of female degradation that always seem to become jokes.

Now an incredibly swish shopping artery with its own brass gates to close off traffic for street fairs, Maiden Lane was Morton Street for most of its existence, a hellish place of brothels and violence.

The houses of prostitution on Morton Street weren't even houses but 'cribs', flimsy structures built to be brothels or older buildings haphazardly hacked into the smallest possible space that would accommodate a bed and a window open to the street for solicitation.

'Not only were the Morton Street cribs the lowest in San Francisco's red light district,' according to Herbert Asbury, a 1920s' chronicler of San Francisco's lurid past, 'they were also the most popular, partly because of the great variety and extraordinary depravity of the women to be found there, and partly because the police seldom entered the street unless compelled to do so by a murder or a serious shooting or stabbing affray. Ordinary fights and assaults were ignored.'

In Morton Street's late nineteenth-century heyday, women, naked to the waist, would sit in window seats hawking themselves to the men parading up and down the alley. Morton Street, as the nadir of the San Francisco prostitution market, was bargain basement: passersby could fondle one breast for 10c, the pair for 15c or come inside for further services ranging from 25c to a dollar. This was a stark contrast to the more stable bordellos where $20 was the standard charge for sex.

There is nothing left of the old Morton Street. It was completely devoured in the 1906 fires. It was the fires, in fact, that finally ended the alley's infamy, with city fathers taking care to rebuild *sans* cribs. It was a while, however, before the name disappeared. The street was renamed several times, but nothing seemed to dislodge 'Morton Street' from the public vocabulary. In the 1920s, jeweller Alfred Samuels, whose shop was once there, suggested Maiden Lane after streets in London and New York (centre of that city's diamond trade). Finally the new name took and it has been Maiden Lane ever since, with decades of bad jokes contrasting the little street's swank present and bawdy past with plenty of nudges and winks about what fun those girls were having.

The non-shopping standout in the lane is Circle Gallery, 140 Maiden Lane, a visual gem designed by Frank Lloyd Wright in 1949. The sweeping spiral design of the interior would seem to be a test pattern for Wright's later work in New York's acclaimed Guggenheim Museum. The artwork now sold and displayed by the gallery is pseudo-avant garde, but is thoughtfully arranged so as not to detract from the interior.

St Francis Hotel

335 Powell Street
(between Geary and Post).

Across the square from Maiden Lane this is one of the city's legendary hotels. Built in 1904 by the Crocker family, the St Francis surpassed the Palace as the city's society hotel. It survived the 1906 earthquake with minor damage, only to burn in the fires that followed. The St Francis was later rebuilt, as grand as ever, and quickly enlarged. The ugly tower that rises behind it was added in 1969 by William Pereira Associates, designers of the Transamerica Pyramid.

Officially called the Westin St Francis these days, to include its current corporate ownership, the hotel remains big, plush and self-satisfied. Business travellers predominate but the place still conjures up its old magic. Queen Elizabeth II and Prince Philip stayed here in 1983 during their American tour. The Compass Rose bar off the lobby is a favourite meeting place for businesspeople and theatre-goers.

From its earliest days San Francisco has been a public city where hotels and restaurants played an unusually high profile role. Victorian mores on both sides of the Atlantic deemed hotels far too public for women to visit except when absolutely necessary. In San Francisco, as with many other social strictures, women simply rewrote the social rulebook. Certain hotels were judged perfectly acceptable for 'respectable' women. The St Francis, for instance, had the double seal of the Crocker (silver fortune) name and the arbiter of society, Mrs Eleanor Martin. After inspecting the new building during its lavish opening night party in 1904, she announced she would have her niece's coming out party at the hotel, making it as socially sanctioned as a church.

The St Francis figures heavily in one of the first big Hollywood scandals, the Fatty Arbuckle story. In 1921 Arbuckle was the king of Hollywood, better known than Charlie Chaplin and making something like $3 million a year. To celebrate a new contract and the completion of several movies (the silents were made back-to-back in those days) Arbuckle drove up to San Francisco, rented three rooms at the St Francis and hosted a nonstop party.

At one point a pretty but withdrawn young woman named Virginia Rappe seemed to spin out of control; she was feeling sick, she was feverish, she began tearing at her clothes, moaning that she was dying. A slightly tipsy Arbuckle and his equally liquored up friends tried a variety of cures including one gent holding Rappe upside down by her ankles. Nothing seemed to help. They put her to bed in one of the three rooms and carried on. Arbuckle returned to Hollywood the next day. He was dumbfounded to be charged with her murder the next week. Rappe had died in a clinic several days after Arbuckle left the city and a shady friend who brought her to the party, Maude Delmont, told police that the enormous (21 stone) Arbuckle had raped and abused the aspiring actress, causing her death from vague internal injuries.

HOLLYWOOD NORTH

Even though *The Maltese Falcon*, perhaps San Francisco's signature film, was filmed in Hollywood, the city itself has had a powerful on-screen history from the first days of motion pictures. Filmmakers love to get San Francisco on film, even if the increasingly stringent filming regulations make it harder and harder to do. Here's a selective list of some of the best made-in-SF movies:

Fog Over Frisco (1933) An absolute howler, with a hard-boiled Bette Davis. Makes no sense at all but great background shots of the bay without bridges.

The Barbary Coast (1935) Howard Hawks's bare-knuckled take on the wide-open city, with Miriam Hopkins.

Dark Passage (1946) Humphrey Bogart escapes from San Quentin and takes refuge with Lauren Bacall in her gorgeous apartment at 1360 Montgomery St, a landmark Moderne building on Telegraph Hill.

Out of the Past (1947) Robert Mitchum is a gumshoe set up for a frame. He saunters around night-time SF trying to figure out if Jane Greer is devil or angel. Maybe the best film noir ever.

I Remember Mama (1948) Greer Garson is the perfect mama and wife, a loving compassionate, naive Norwegian emigrant in turn-of-the-century San Francisco.

Vertigo (1958) Wonderful feel for the city as besotted James Stewart falls in love with suicidal Madeleine, then tries to remake working-class Kathy in her image (both played by Kim Novak).

Petulia (1968) Julie Christie as the emblematic free spirit of the sixties – so why in hell does she chase after repressed, controlling surgeon George C. Scott?

Bullitt (1968) Cop Steve McQueen's barely suppressed rage finally gets its fullest expression in a hair-raising car chase over SF hills, which led the city to ban that kind of shooting.

Dirty Harry (1972) Oakland-born Clint Eastwood brings all back home with his nihilistic cop hero, Harry Callahan.

The Laughing Policeman (1973) Walter Matthau in a much-underrated police procedural based on the characters of a popular Swedish series of detective books, unaccountably transposed to SF.

The Conversation (1974) Maybe Francis Ford Coppola's best film; professional eavesdropper Gene Hackman is profoundly disturbed by his work and its consequences.

Tell Me a Riddle (1980) Lee Grant's sensitive retelling of Tillie Olsen's novel.

Chan is Missing (1982) Wayne Wang's first film, an insider's tour of Chinatown.

The Presidio (1987) Sean Connery, Mark Harmon and Meg Ryan try their darnedest to find a story here. Notable for its beautiful rendering of the Presidio, full of mist and melancholy.

Sister Act (1991) Las Vegas lounge singer Whoopi Goldberg hides out in a San Francisco convent and teaches the nuns how to boogie.

TV movies and series, as well as commercials and rock videos, are also filmed in San Francisco so the chances of running across a shoot-in-progress are quite good. If you want to make sure you see some filming, call the San Francisco Film and Video Arts Commission. The 'extra hotline' at 554 4004 lists features being filmed at the moment and gives the number of the company production office for anyone who wants to apply for work as an extra. You could sign on and spend your holiday finding out for yourself what stars are always complaining about – that film work means endless sitting around and waiting for something to happen.

Three trials later, Arbuckle was declared innocent with the judge apologising for the injustices that had been heaped upon him by an opportunistic district attorney and the scandalmongering Hearst press. It was too late. His career was completely ruined. Arbuckle died of a heart attack at 46, still hoping for a comeback.

Cintra Wilson, a hot young San Francisco actress and writer who is the uncrowned queen of SoMa, turned the Arbuckle story into a play a few years ago, getting quite good reviews with the American-turned-English TV star Micheal (correct spelling) McShane as Fatty. Wilson, part of the post-feminist generation, reclaimed the story not just from the puffed-up moralists of the time, but feminists who had appropriated the story as another example of Hollywood's macho sense of entitlement to women.

Wilson, drawing on the voluminous court records and newspaper reports of the time, saw the Arbuckle-Rappe story as an American tragedy. Rappe was a sometime prostitute, suffering from the effects of messy abortions and the late stages of syphilis. Her appearance at the party was a last bit of wish fulfilment about getting to Hollywood. Arbuckle probably never even noticed her until she became ill. A classic case of an anything-to-please fat boy, Arbuckle was in fact very uneasy about his new-found attraction for women. Arbuckle's fame and Rappe's pathetic life were a surprise concoction of fire and gasoline; their brief meeting became a framework for the American love-hate relationship with Hollywood.

AROUND UNION SQUARE

Cintra Wilson's take on the case was actually the same as a private detective's who worked for Arbuckle's lawyers – Dashiell Hammett. Before he wrote his way to fame with *The Maltese Falcon* and the rest of his classic mysteries, Hammett worked as a detective for the Pinkerton Agency in San Francisco. He later said the Arbuckle case was a frame-up 'by some of the corrupt local newspaper boys'.

Hammett worshippers have carefully collated the locations described in his novels and the real San Francisco. The longest-running US guided walking tour is Don Herron's Dashiell Hammett Tour, now available in book form (see p. 60). The St Francis is the model for the St Mark in *The Maltese Falcon*, and either the Sir Francis Drake up Powell or the Clift on Geary is the model for the Alexandria, the hotel of the mysterious fat man seeking Brigid O'Shaughnessy, detective Sam Spade's equally enigmatic client.

This prototypical hard-boiled mystery is commemorated in a brass plaque in Burritt Alley, a tiny dead-end street a block north of Union Square off Bush Street, hard by the Stockton Street Tunnel.

If you haven't read *The Maltese Falcon* and don't want to know whodunnit, avert your eyes from the plaque which untangles

the mystery of detective Sam Spade, his mysterious client Brigid
O'Shaughnessy and his partner, Miles Archer.

The 1941 film version, with John Huston directing Humphrey
Bogart and Mary Astor, is a perfect match for Hammett's elegant
novel. Both perfectly catch the city's texture and allure, although
the film was completely shot in Hollywood.

Beyond Burritt Alley, the other significant Hammett presence in
San Francisco is at John's Grill, 63 Ellis St, two blocks south of
Union Square off Powell. The restaurant is mentioned by name in
The Maltese Falcon as a place Spade frequents. With its dark interior and no-nonsense menu John's effortlessly retains the atmosphere that endeared it to Hammett (a regular customer). The
restaurant has a small collection of memorabilia connected to the
book, Hammett and San Francisco at the time.

There is also a Dashiell Hammett Lane off Bush Street, between
Powell and Stockton. The little street has no connection with
Hammett, but reflects the rather successful campaign led by poet
Lawrence Ferlinghetti to get the city to honour its literary heroes
and heritage.

Hammett's famous liaison with playwright and memorist
Lillian Hellman came after he left San Francisco, permanently as it
turned out, for Hollywood. Hellman had no part in Hammett's San
Francisco life, where he produced all of his best work. In fact,
Hellman battled furiously with San Francisco writer Diane Johnson
over the 1983 Hammett biography she had authorised Johnson to
write when she learned that the novelist was devoting at least half
the book to Hammett's San Francisco (non-Hellman) life.

'As Pascal said, "I came into it long before I came into it,"'
Hellman said to Johnson by way of argument for being included in
the first half of Hammett's life story.

About those Cable Cars The main cable car turnaround or station is a short walk from Union Square at Powell and Market. This
stop is best avoided during the high tourist season and on weekends. The queues to get on the cars fill most of Powell Street and a
depressing array of street people and self-proclaimed entertainers
work the crowd (see p. 57). If your purpose is simply to ride a cable
car, not necessarily to get anywhere, the best plan is to take the
California Street line which is much less used. The line ends at the
Embarcadero, next to the Hyatt Hotel where Market Street and
California converge. Even if there is a wait to get on, it will be much
shorter than Powell Street.

The other plan of attack is to ride early in the morning before
8 a.m., or in the evening, after 10 p.m., when the crowds fall off
sharply. Two lines run from Powell Street – the Powell-Mason and
the Powell-Hyde lines – which take you towards Fisherman's

Wharf. Powell-Mason will take you through North Beach while Powell-Hyde takes you over the dramatic Russian Hill terrain, ending at Aquatic Park, next to Ghiradelli Square.

Theatre District

The American Conservatory Theater, universally called ACT, is the anchor of San Francisco's vigorous theatre community. Now more than 25 years old, it has been praised as the model American repertory company, mixing Shakespeare, Broadway hits, revivals of forgotten classics and brash new works. It is unusual among US theatre companies in having a full-fledged conservatory, or training programme, with its professional company.

Occasionally big name stars such as William Hurt join productions and the company has seen a number of its members and students go on to Hollywood success, including Annette Bening, Don Johnson, Nicholas Cage and Winona Rider. But ACT is even more notable for the superb acting company that stays in residence.

ACT's home, the historic Geary Theater, 415 Geary St, was seriously damaged during the 1989 earthquake and isn't expected to be back in service until 1994, if then. The company makes do with other venues, such as the equally opulent Curran, next door at 445 Geary or the Stage Door up Mason Street. There are several other small theatres and cabarets in the Mason-Geary area, usually with musical revues or bawdy comedy aimed at the tourist trade. The touring Broadway shows are more often a little farther afield, in the larger Golden Gate Theater at the corners of Market, Golden Gate and Taylor, or the Orpheum at Market and Grove, both close to Civic Center and on the edge of the sordid Tenderloin, San Francisco's porn-drug zone.

The Divine Isadora   Fittingly, Isadora Duncan was born a stone's throw from the current Theatre District. The site of her birthplace at 601 Taylor St (between Post and Geary) is marked by a plaque and an alley nearby has been renamed Isadora Duncan Place in her honour.

The plaque was dedicated in 1973, 95 years after her birth. It was a moment Duncan would have loved. Amid the roar of traffic, a huge crowd gathered for speeches and tributes. A large number of young women appeared in Isadoraesque white tunics and danced barefoot on the rough pavement to recordings of Schubert.

This was in stark contrast to Duncan's return to San Francisco after World War I. As famous for her chaotic and unconventional love life as her dancing, Duncan's indifference to the war and her European life made her less than welcome in San Francisco which, after all, did have to draw a line somewhere in the propriety business.

Duncan was hurt but not upended by her hometown's hostility to her. She had violently rejected conformity early on. Her banker father had deserted her mother and their three other children just before Isadora's birth. Instead of a comfortable upper middle-class childhood, the Duncans were forced to make do, cut corners and scrimp. Duncan's mother embraced the San Francisco bohemianism of the late 1800s and raised her children in complete freedom. Isadora revelled in her freedom, which she pushed to the limit. She burned her parents' marriage certificate so she could declare herself a 'love child'.

Guided by poet Ina Coolbrith (see p. 130), who used her post as Oakland's head librarian (the Duncans lived for long stretches in the East Bay) to cultivate and educate promising youngsters (including Jack London), young Isadora read widely and became enamoured of Walt Whitman, declaring herself his 'spiritual daughter'.

Eschewing the ballet, Duncan began inventing her own dance steps and movements to parallel what she saw in nature. In 1895, at 17, she presented herself to dance impresario Augustin Daly and insisted he put her onstage. 'I bring you the dance,' she told the astonished man. 'Where have I discovered it? By the Pacific Ocean, by the waving pine forests of the Sierra Nevada ... For the children of America I will create a new dance that will express America. I bring to your theatre the vital soul that it lacks, the soul of the dancer!' Whether or not the dancer used these exact words (as she later put them down in her autobiography), Duncan did bring a new soul to dance with natural movements, loose, free garments, and a Western grace that looked to other masters than classical music and dance.

Duncan continued her free, anti-bourgeois life in New York and later in Paris. She had two children by different fathers and watched them both drown in a swimming mishap, to her unending grief. She married a young Russian poet, separated from him and continued her peripatetic European life. She was killed in 1927 in a fantastically improbable automobile accident when one of her signature long scarves caught in the wheels of the car she was riding in and she was strangled. Duncan is buried in Paris.

You Gotta Have Art   Union Square is glutted with art galleries, many of which would better be called interior design shops as the work on display is cynically pretty, obviously created to sell rather than express. The genuinely interesting galleries tend to be a bit removed from the square itself and on upper floors where the rents are cheaper.

Several buildings have multiple galleries which is convenient for everybody. The building at 251 Post has a number of galleries of which Bomani, 6th floor, is the most famous, for being owned, at this point, by celebrities, Asake Bomani and her husband, actor Danny Glover, but Bomani is taking her work seriously and is particularly dedicated to women and artists of colour.

Gallery Paule Anglim, 14 Geary St, is good for young California artists and John Berggruen, 228 Grant Ave, is one of the city's most prominent galleries. Photography galleries are clustered together at 49 Geary St. The Fraenkel Gallery is particularly outstanding, featuring nineteenth- and twentieth-century photographers. Robert Koch and Scott Nichols, in the same building, are also good.

Nob Hill

Nob Hill, according to the older San Francisco guidebooks, derived its name from one of two sources. It was either an abbreviation of 'Knob Hill', which referred to the hill's knobby-knollish appearance. Or, given the sophistication of the rapidly maturing city, 'nob' was a nineteenth-century borrowing from the English colonial term for the rich, 'nabob', which was shortened.

Any San Franciscan will tell you without hesitation: it is Snob Hill.

Even in these high-rise times Nob Hill still stands out on the San Francisco grid, 376 feet at its tip and easily identifiable by its landmark buildings: Grace Cathedral, Fairmont Hotel, Mark Hopkins Hotel and Pacific Union Club.

In the earliest Gold Rush years, San Francisco's newly affluent had to settle for Rincon Hill, a gentle rise slightly south of the business district where the anchorage for the Oakland Bay Bridge now rests. With the advent of cable cars in 1873, Nob Hill (first called California Street Hill) was available for settlement, the limits of horse and mule horsepower having been circumvented.

The nabobs quickly bought lots and began to compete with each other for the biggest, most ostentatious dwelling. The hands-down champion was Mark Hopkins, one of the Big Four of railroad development fame, whose house was a nightmare of turrets, gothic spires, gingerbread ornamentation and demented proportions. His wife Mary, a childless devotee of romantic novels, was the overseer of the house, apparently pouring a lifetime of longing into the 'hallucination', as one horrified architect called it.

Mark Hopkins, a mild-mannered Sacramento storekeeper, had made his millions by a fortuitous alliance with three fellow small businessmen, Leland Stanford, Charles Crocker and Collis P. Huntington. In 1860 they had hesitantly invested in a plan for a transcontinental railroad. The idealistic young engineer who planned and lobbied for the railroad, Theodore Judah, died and the shopkeepers took over. With a lucrative government subsidy, they began building the railroad. To ensure their profit margin, the associates, as they liked to call themselves, formed a number of other businesses that supplied all the railroad's needs. The Big Four made obscene amounts of money, soon abandoning all pretence that they were mere businessmen. 'The Octopus', as their Southern Pacific Railroad came to be called, was a controlling, menacing cartel that held sway over California and the West for decades.

Also staking claims on Nob Hill were the four Silver Kings, a quartet of Irishmen who had struck lucky with a massive silver find, in Nevada's Comstock Lode. Laughingly called the 'Irish-tocracy', James G. Fair, James C. Flood, John W. Mackay and William S. O'Brien, were not as powerful as the Big Four, but their money was every bit as big.

The houses that they built were monstrous. Only the brown-stone Flood mansion survives today in any form, but the stories of the hideous houses continue to be one of San Francisco's favourite themes. In most of the telling, the wives of these working-class and lower middle-class surprise potentates are ridiculed for their excesses. Jumped-up bar maids and seamstresses, the Mesdames Flood, Crocker, Fair, Mackay, Hopkins and their ilk have been disparaged as greedy, tasteless social climbers for whom no price was too big for status. What most of these stories omit is the utter impossibility of these women spending their husband's ill-gotten gains without their permission and indeed, their urging. Wives were public barometers of a man's success. Whatever grumblng about 'she who must be obeyed' was done by the millionaires among friends, they underwrote the ostentatious displays and expected them.

Today Nob Hill is more famous for its luxury hotels than private homes, but it remains an impressive address. Several exclusive apartment buildings ring the crown of the hill, including the Brocklebank Apartments, 1000 Mason St (at Sacramento). Built in 1926 by businesswoman Mrs M. V. B. MacAdam, who invested her entire fortune in the building and lost it in the Depression, the elegant, swell-egant Brocklebank is a cult landmark courtesy of Alfred Hitchcock. The building was prominently featured in his 1958 film *Vertigo*, as the presumed home of the enigmatic heroine played by Kim Novak.

At the Top

A walk around Nob Hill offers a number of pleasures. Getting there (if you're staying elsewhere) is a brisk ride on the California Street cable car. None of the stately apartment buildings are open to the public in any way, but the hotels are worth a visit for themselves. Grace Cathedral, mother church to Northern California Episcopalians (American Anglicans), is one of the great American churches.

The 'hill of palaces,' as Robert Louis Stevenson called Nob Hill, was swept clean by the 1906 fires. All the sprawling houses except Flood's were built of redwood and burned in the blink of an eye. The nabobs, perhaps embarrassed by their early nouveau riche efforts, abandoned Nob Hill. The Crockers, who owned two houses, deeded their property to the Episcopal Church. The Stanford home had already been given over to fledgling Stanford University and the hideous Hopkins manse was an art school. The Flood house, whose outer stone walls survived the fire, became the exclusive Pacific Union Club for men. The Collis P. Huntington site was given to the city by Huntington's widow, Arabella, and is now Huntington Park, an inviting green space.

Stately apartment houses began to appear where the mansions had been. Two of these have been restructured into luxury hotels, the Stanford Court at California and Powell and the Huntington Hotel at California and Taylor. The Huntington is the least known of the Nob Hill Hotels, but is a particular favourite with British celebrities who prize its quiet elegance and reserve. Jilly Cooper, Princess Margaret, Alastair Cooke and lesser English royals have been quiet and repeated guests over the years.

The intimate landscape of the English-influenced Huntington, the high church Grace Cathedral, lovingly maintained Huntington Park and defiantly all-male Pacific Union Club have caused the hill-top to be designated 'that corner of San Francisco which is forever England'.

Fairmont Hotel

950 Mason St (between California and Sacramento).

Familiar around the world through the American TV series, 'Hotel', the Fairmont has been locked in a not-always friendly rivalry with the St Francis for primacy as *the* San Francisco hotel. Begun by the Fair family of Silver Bonanza fame, the Fairmont dates its beginnings to 1902, but didn't open until five years later. The hotel project had been sold by the Fair family and was on the eve of its opening in April of 1906, the furniture sitting in crates, the workers putting the finishing touches on the building. The exterior of the hotel withstood the earthquake, but the fire completely gutted the interor. Tessie Fair Oelrichs, the determined daughter of 'Slippery Jim' Fair, took the hotel back from its ruined owners and launched a rebuilding. Working night and day, Fair Oelrichs was able to open the Fairmont a year to the day after the earthquake with an extravagant celebration.

James Fair had planned to build a huge private home here, but his acrimonious divorce from Tessie's mother in 1883 had halted his plans although a foundation had been laid. Fair died in 1894 without building the house.

Entering the Fairmont today is to visit a grand hotel of the old school, a complete village in itself with shops, restaurants, night-clubs, laundry, health club, gardens and a permanent population (staff) of several hundred. The Fairmont is popular with Japanese and German tour groups who don't mind paying top dollar rates to stay in the hotel they think they know from TV's 'Hotel', which seems to be in perpetual reruns in Germany. (Actually, the 1964 Arthur Hailey novel *Hotel* was set in New Orleans; TV magnate Aaron Spelling switched the setting to San Francisco and his fave hotel, the Fairmont.)

One of the best rides in the city is the glass elevator from the Fairmont's ground floor to the 22nd floor of the Fairmont Tower, added in 1962. Positioned at the back (Powell Street side) of the building, the slow-moving elevator provides a marvellous pano-ramic view of the city. When you reach the Crown Room at the top, come back down. The buffet serves indifferent food, the bar makes sloppy drinks and it is all overpriced.

The hotel's famous supper club, the **Venetian Room**, closed a few years ago but its small bar, the **New Orleans Room**, has lately emerged as San Francisco's surprise hot club, booking the insider's (as opposed to merely big name) who's who of jazz and R&B musicians.

Not overlooked but not as easy to get to, the Fairmont's Presidential Suite is famous for its opulence. There is a private ter-race, circular library and a tiled billiards room right out of the Arabian Nights. The penthouse rents for $5000 a night, comes with its own staff and is frequently booked for weeks at a time by Saudi princes. During World War II it was the meeting place of top-rank-ing diplomats hammering out the United Nations. The World War II Big Four: Britain's Anthony Eden, US Secretary of State Edward Stettnius, USSR Minister V.M. Molotov and China's Premier T.V. Soong came to terms here in late-night and, frequently, all-night ses-sions after the official meetings at the San Francisco Opera House. It's also reported to be the spot for several assignations by John F. Kennedy during his presidency.

Mark Hopkins Hotel

999 California St (at Mason).

Built on the site of Mary and Mark Hopkins' frightful mansion, the 1925 hotel has no connection with the family. After her death Mary Hopkins' second husband, a much younger interior decorator she met while building new estates on the East Coast, made a gift of her house to the University of California's art school. After the earthquake and fire, the school sold the lot and rebuilt on Russian Hill. The Hopkins Institute of Art became a separate entity from UC and is now the well-regarded San Francisco Institute of Art.

The Mark (never the Hopkins) is best known for its glassed-in bar at the top of the hotel. A sensation when it opened in 1939, the Top of the Mark became an international watering hole during World War II when San Francisco was the headquarters of the war in the Pacific. Top of the Mark was a favourite meeting place for couples and was often the site of poignant last meetings before the soldier or sailor shipped out for the front. Wives and girlfriends often retreated to the bar to watch their beloved's ship sail out of the bay and the westward corner was dubbed 'weepers' corner'.

The views are still spectacular, but as with the Crown Room, the drinks are silly and expensive.

Outside the hotel, notice the retaining wall along California Street. It is all that is left of Mary Hopkins' dream house. It was shared with the Leland Stanford house downhill on California, where the Stanford Court Hotel now sits. Foundations and walls for both houses were supplied by a Southern Pacific quarry and, of course, the work of SP labourers.

Grace Cathedral

1051 Taylor St (Between California and Sacramento).
Open every day; visitors' hours dependent upon services.

Grace Cathedral is an interesting amalgam of social gospel and society Christianity. The favoured setting for old money weddings, christenings and funerals, the huge Gothic inspired church is beautifully dressed with stained glass, memorials, exquisite craftsmanship and even a set of doors cast from the moulds of Ghiberti's 'Gates of Paradise' doors for the Baptistry in Florence. Yet the church sponsors serious programmes for the homeless, runs a school and welcomes projects by a wide array of social and cultural activists. Often several services and meetings will be going on at once in the enormous interior.

Constructions   The Crocker (railroad money) family donated its block of land to the Episcopal church after the 1906 fires. Until then Charles Crocker lived in an ornate Second Empire style house (1877) and his son William occupied an equally lavish Queen Anne style mansion (1888). The site was not particularly promising as Christian attitudes go, being most famous for Crocker Senior's 'spite fence'. When German undertaker Nicholas Yung would not sell Crocker his tiny lot at the multimillionaire's low price to complete Crocker's block, the two men declared war. Crocker built a thirty-foot fence around the undertaker's modest two-storey house, making it uninhabitable. Yung retaliated with a ten-foot coffin, painted with skull and bones, aimed at the Crocker house.

Denis Kearney, briefly San Francisco's leading demagogue during the unsettled 1870s, sparked a riot over Crocker's fence. He led a mob of angry, out-of-work men up Nob Hill to put the Crockers *et al.* in their place. Kearney's followers were only turned back after a violent battle with the police. The Crockers were able to buy the 25-foot lot after both Charles Crocker and Nicholas Yung were dead.

Despite all this, the church gratefully accepted the square block of land and made plans to build the West's Episcopalian seat, based on Notre Dame. It was a long haul. The corner-stone was laid in 1910 and construction didn't begin until 1928, soon halted by the Depression. Building went on fitfully, with segments being completed in 1941 and again in 1961. The cathedral was finally consecrated in 1964.

In 1993 the crumbling parish hall facing Taylor Street was demolished, opening up the front of the church to full view for the first time. A new parish hall is under construction along Sacramento Street.

The Visit   The further you walk into the church, the more its serene spirit envelops you. As with most of the world's famous churches, there is a gift shop and a constant to-and-fro of tourists, yet the church exudes the kind of reverential peacefulness that makes it appealing to everyone, even the 'unchurched', as the staff politely calls non-religious visitors.

The Ghiberti doors are the first treasure you will see. They came to Grace Cathedral in 1964 – a socialite's gift. The original doors underwent a painstaking restoration in Florence after being hidden from Nazi plunderers during the Second World War. An identical pair were cast to hang at the Baptistry during the work – these doors, now at the cathedral, are the substitutes, identical in every detail to the 1452 Ghiberti doors.

Old treasures decorate the church interior, including a Flemish altar dating from 1430 in the Chapel of Grace at the rear of the sanctuary, a thirteenth-century Catalonian crucifix and a sixteenth-century Brussels Gobelin tapestry. Newer treasures are just as elaborate, particularly the stained-glass windows. The more traditional windows (Christ as the light of the world) date from the 1930s, from Charles Jay Connick. The newer windows, from the sixties, reinforce the cathedral's commitment to social justice. The Willet Windows, a series of stained-glass windows in the nave, installed in 1966, celebrate the idea of renewal with leaders ranging from Moses and Martin Luther to Albert Einstein and Franklin Delano Roosevelt. The imagery among all eras is noticeably short on women.

In the chapel, another Crocker gift, the kneelers are sweetly decorated with needlepoint done by the women of the parish. Designed by Mona Spoor, they show California wildflowers and symbols of California Episcopalianism.

Services with the famous Grace Cathedral men and boys' choir make for a very special experience in the church.

San Francisco Clubs

The Pacific Union Club, 1000 California St, is the 1886 Flood mansion, redone by architect Willis Polk in 1912 for the club, which traces its history to 1852. In recent years the P-U (it's really called that) has become the unwilling centre of a legal storm over sexism.

Women's advocates, arguing that private men's clubs are in fact extensions of the office where deals are hatched and careers are made, have launched serious challenges to them. The Pacific Union, as the most visible and most exclusive, has been a particular target. Today only this club and the even more famous Bohemian Club remain all-male enclaves.

The clubs, modelled on English and East Coast men's clubs, are clustered between Nob Hill and Union Square. By virtue of its hill-top clubhouse, the Pacific Union is the most visible. The Bohemian Club, 625 Taylor St, is perhaps more famous because of its anarchistic summer 'encampment' in Bohemian Grove, a 2700-acre retreat on the Russian River, north of the city. Presidents, cabinet-ministers, captains of industry, movie stars and ordinary rich men attend the summer camp which mixes elaborate pageants with lectures by world leaders. After several years of tense demonstrations at the Grove gates by women protesting sexism as well as elitist shadow governments, the activists have pretty much gone away.

'I mean, none of us really want to get into this geeky club,' said one of the former activists explaining why she had moved on to more meaningful social protest.

The mighty Olympic Club, 524 Post St, has only recently agreed to admit women. Also falling into line with a maximum amount of grumbling was the University Club, 800 Powell St, at California, built on the site of Leland Stanford's lavish stables. The Family Club, 545 Powell St (ironic name), and the Jewish Concordia-Argonaut Club, 1142 Van Ness Ave, complied quietly.

Most of the private clubs have been brought to heel through punitive tax laws which allow no business-related deductions for either club membership or expenses connected with the clubs. The Pacific Union and Bohemian have resisted, coming up with new ploys. Also, these clubs have members who can afford the steep annual fees without declaring them business expenses.

A quirky side-effect of the anti-discrimination laws has been to rob women's clubs of their new cachet. The Metropolitan Club, 640 Sutter St, had recast itself as a power centre for businesswomen. In order to keep its designation as a private club, the Metropolitan, like the Pacific Union, was obliged to discourage all types of open business dealings and discussion, making even an exchange of business cards *verboten*.

The Francisca Club, 595 Sutter St, and Town and Country, 218 Stockton St, two exclusive women-only clubs, have never aspired to be more than social clubs. The membership ranks have felt the effects of working women, however, as many members or potential members, don't have the time for leisurely lunches and recuperative teas after long days of shopping at nearby Union Square.

Whatever the complications of changing the women-only and men-only rules, the leading advocate of desegregation remains steadfast.

'Everyone knows that some of the most lucrative and important business in the city is conducted in those clubs,' says Drucilla Ramey, executive director of the San Francisco Bar Association and a former civil rights attorney. 'By excluding certain people, you exclude them from these transactions.'

Huntington Park

1000 block of California Street (next to Pacific Union Club).

Less than two acres, this little pocket park is a perfect urban resting spot. If you have children with you, they will adore the sturdy sand-covered playground with swings, tunnels and monkey bars.

The park is kept up by the Nob Hill Association which employs a part-time gardener in addition to the city's maintenance. There are two attractive fountains, both gifts from women. The larger fountain, newly restored, is *Fontana della Tartaruge*, or 'Fountain of the Turtles', a nineteenth-century replica of a 1585 work. It was discovered in Rome in the 1930s just as it was about to be discarded by workmen making way for Mussolini apartment houses by Mrs William H. Crocker, whose home once stood next door on the Grace Cathedral site. She brought it back to her Peninsula estate, later donating it to the city.

Nearby is 'Dancing Sprites', a charming ode to childhood in bronze by French sculptor, Henri Greves. It was given to the city in 1942 by 'Mrs James L. Flood Donor', according to the inscription. That would be Maud Fritz Flood, the second wife and widow of Jimmy Flood, the unremarkable only son of silver king James C. Flood.

DOWN THE HILL

Because the name Nob Hill is still magic, you will hear any number of places downtown placing themselves on Nob Hill. In reality, the area is rather small and once you leave the summit, the neighbourhood becomes residential, still upscale but not especially prestigious. Pacific Heights is the four-star address in San Francisco, with Russian Hill and Sea Cliff close behind.

Amusingly, one of the city's great industrial sights is on the lower slopes of Nob Hill, the Cable Car Barn at Washington and Mason streets. Open daily from 10 a.m. to 5 p.m., free, this is the nerve centre of the cable car system. A video explains how it all works; then you can look at the vintage cable cars on display, as well as a photographic history. Through a window, you can also see the cables at work. The three-storey redbrick building dates from 1887. It was rebuilt after 1906 and weathered the 1989 quake nicely.

Leaving the tip of Nob Hill in the westerly direction, you'll descend to Polk Gulch, the offbeat commercial strip along Polk Street, parallel to Van Ness Avenue, the borderline between downtown and the neighbourhoods.

In the 1970s Polk was the centre of gay life in San Francisco. The colourful, madcap street life of preening male peacocks and the first wave of openly gay businesses has since faded. Once Castro Street supplanted Polk Gulch as the gay neighbourhood, the area seemed to lose its way, turning into a dispiriting pickup scene. There are a handful of funky shops and restaurants along Polk.

Women of Nob Hill

The lack of a significant memorial/monument to the tragedy of the earthquake of 1906 is periodically raised and debated in San Francisco. An equally egregious oversight is the complete omission of public recognition for Theresa Rooney Fair, a one-time boarding house proprietor who became one of the richest women in America by divorcing her disgusting husband, silver king James Fair.

In her sensational 1883 divorce, Theresa Fair firmly established that a man's money, property and assets were common property and must be shared with his spouse. A devout Catholic and obsessive mother, Mrs Fair is an unlikely feminist heroine and would no doubt resist being called one, but her divorce on the grounds of her husband's 'habitual adultery' went a long way towards encouraging women to make use of California's relatively liberal divorce law to end untenable marriages. By all accounts, the poor woman had been driven past her limits by the boorish Fair, who liked to boast that early in his capitalist career he had duped his own wife in a stock deal, manipulating her into investing her money in a failing enterprise, which others would read as Fair's seal of approval. Everyone but Mr Fair was bankrupted.

Fair's silver partners, Flood and Mackay (O'Brien had died) sided with Mrs Fair in the divorce, even guiding her lawyers through the mazes of Fair's far-flung wealth. In the end, Theresa Fair emerged with more than $4 million outright as well as their San Francisco house and other properties.

Mrs Fair was awarded custody of the two daughters, Tessie and Birdie, both of whom married into families of the Eastern elite, the Oelrichs and Vanderbilts. The two Fair sons, Charley and Jim, were consigned to the father, both becoming uncontrollable alcoholics and dying young. Charley married Maud Nelson, a well-known San Francisco madam several years his senior. Actually, it was the best thing that ever happened to Charley, a caricature of the second-generation weakling son. Nelson managed to help him sober up for long stretches before he killed them both in a car crash in France.

Jennie Flood, the high-spirited daughter of Fair's partner, also had aspirations to a bigger stage and was tentatively engaged to Ulysses S. Grant Jr, son of the ex-president. 'Buck' Grant, however, dallied too long and the beautiful Jennie broke the engagement. After a half-dozen or so further fiancés, she retired from the marital derby and became San Francisco's most popular unmarried belle, dying a grande dame.

The wives and daughters of the San Francisco capitalists were the popular entertainers of their time. Like today's rock stars and the royal family, the public couldn't get enough of their money, clothes, love lives, foibles and occasionally, their successes. Marie Hungerford Mackay, the wife of taciturn John Mackay, the brains of the Comstock silver partners, was allowed to be the 'good' rich wife, even though she decamped for Europe with her three children. Perhaps her success in Paris and London was seen as a legitimisation of San Francisco's success. Queenly and shrewd, the one-time seamstress made her way with a generous pocketbook and excellent manners, even winning over the Prince of Wales, who was particularly taken with her husband, calling Mackay, 'the most unassuming American I have ever met'.

Childless Mary Hopkins, of course, was the 'bad' wife, nagging her poor husband into building her goofy fairytale house.

And then there was Ellen Colton, who was wife as avenger, a role not much appreciated at the time. Her husband, David D. Colton, was the ultimate slick lawyer. He handled so much dirty work for the Big Four's railroad empire that the newspapers began referring to the 'Big Four and a Half'. After Colton died suddenly in 1878, Mrs Colton came to question the paltry half million dollars settled on her and her two daughters by Colton's associates. When her inquiries about stocks and so on were met with contempt, she sued for $4 million. The railroad barons set out to crush her, but Mrs Colton introduced hundreds of letters from Collis Huntington

to Colton into the case. The letters were amazingly blunt, instruct-
ing Colton on who and how to pay off among government officials
and agencies.

The 'Colton Letters' caused a sensation, but didn't win Mrs
Colton any more money. The state supreme court turned down her
suit, but her letters were the beginning of the end for the Big Four.
They also constitute one of the most valuable historical archives of
American history. The letters tell a humiliating story, but provide
one of the few as-it-happened records of pre-twentieth-century corporate malfeasance.

Of all the Nob Hill women, Jane Stanford is the only one
to make a contribution of lasting importance. Mrs Stanford was a
full partner with her husband, Leland, in establishing one of
America's great universities, Leland Stanford Junior University, on
the peninsula.

The Stanfords' only child, Leland Jr, born after eighteen years
of marriage, died at the age of fifteen. 'The children of California
shall be our children,' father said to mother at their son's death and
they set about building a memorial to him. Reportedly, their first
idea was to double the size of Yale or Harvard, but the Ivy League
princelings were cool to the idea. Instead the Stanfords decided to
build their own school on the site of their vast horse farm at Palo
Alto. Leland Sr, who had been California's governor and senator,
died in 1893. Jane Stanford – a loving if autocratic mother –
devoted the rest of her life to the university. She poured her entire
fortune into the university which encountered unforeseen problems
owing to death taxes on her husband's estate. Stanford was
designed as a co-educational university and almost half of the first
class (1891) were women.

CHINATOWN

Everyone wants to go to Chinatown. Even world-weary Rudyard
Kipling was avid to visit 'the Chinese quarter' when he passed
through San Francisco in 1889, en route home to England from India.
He pronounced Chinatown 'a ward of the city of Canton set down
in the most eligible business quarter of the place' and went on to
describe a highly suspect tale of barely escaping alive from a shoot-
out in a Chinatown gambling den three storeys beneath street level.

Chinatown has changed substantially since Kipling's day (it
burned to the ground in 1906), but it is still an object of intense
curiosity from outsiders. Visiting Chinatown you will see a densely-
packed community not unlike Hong Kong. Street life is loud, busy
and varied. Shops and restaurants are open every day, usually all
day long and into the evening (9 a.m. to 9 p.m. is typical with even
longer hours in the summer) and Chinatown's streets are lively and
relatively safe, making it a very attractive urban scene.

Most visitors enter through the ornate Chinatown Gate at Bush and Grant streets and march straight down Grant to Broadway, emerging into North Beach. 'Done,' they congratulate themselves, and take Chinatown off their 'to do' list – but the loss is entirely theirs. For a fuller experience of the district, vary your route and spend some time away from Grant Avenue which is mainly populated by tourists.

Pay particular attention to the alleys off the main streets where you'll find not only tightly-packed apartment buildings, but the beautiful association buildings which are painstakingly decorated with historic Asian architectural motifs, bright colours and an impressive amount of detailing. The associations are groups dating from the nineteenth century that now serve as a kind of neighbourhood-family-religious-civic clubhouse.

Waverly Place, running parallel to Grant between Sacramento and Washington streets, is particularly rich in association buildings. Some of the associations welcome visitors to their temples. A donation is usually requested. The Sue Hing Benevolent Association building, 123–9 Waverly Place, dates from 1911 and has the Tien Hau Temple on its top floor. Open 10 a.m. – 5 p.m. daily, the temple was founded in 1852 and is dedicated to Tien Hau, the Goddess of Heaven and Sea who ministers to prostitutes, wanderers, sailors, fishermen and performers. Some artefacts from vanished temples of Northern California are incorporated into the temple, recalling how the Chinese were driven out of most smaller towns in the late nineteenth century.

Another temple to visit on Waverly is Norras Temple in the Lee Family Association building at 109–11. The temple, on the third floor, is open 9 a.m. – 4 p.m. every day. More visible to outsiders are the Christian churches which seem to be on every Chinatown corner, such as the First Chinese Baptist Church, 15 Waverly Place, founded in 1880. Nineteenth-century Protestants were particularly enamoured of China and poured huge resources into missions there. That evangelical fervour extended to the Chinese in America. Because the churches were often their only advocates and protectors in the white world, many Chinese Americans embraced Christianity.

The Chinese immigrants, despite their large numbers and devotion to hard work, were in need of protection. A virulent anti-Chinese movement welled up in the 1870s in the wake of a massive depression. California's economy was ironically fuelled by the opening of the transcontinental railroad in 1869 which had been hailed as a new era for the West. Instead, it temporarily lowered prices on goods and opened the way for a stampede of new settlers from the East Coast. Working-class and middle-class discontent found an easy answer to these problems in the Chinese, who had just finished building the railroad faster and cheaper than the white crews they had replaced.

Chinese labourers were derided as 'Crocker's Pets', although the supposedly magnanimous Charles Crocker paid them $31 a month – $14 less than whites – made them work in blizzard conditions in the Sierra, enforced prison camp conditions and mercilessly crushed any signs of discontent.

DONALDINA CAMERON

Born in New Zealand of Scottish parents and raised on a ranch in Southern California, Donaldina Cameron (1869–1968) became the most famous woman in Chinatown through her relentless campaign against the forced prostitution of Chinese women.

Superintendent of the Presbyterian mission for women at 920 Sacramento St, Cameron became a legend in her own time as she rescued young women by climbing through skylights, breaking down doors, liberating underground prisons and snatching young women out of the hands of well-known gangsters in broad daylight. A dedicated Presbyteriaan with a no-nonsense attitude, Cameron never married but was called *Lo Mo* or 'The Mother' by her charges and admirers in Chinatown. In her work she didn't trouble herself with constitutional rights, cultural sensitivity or the big picture. Cameron was thoroughly Eurocentric in her outlook, never learning more than a few words of Cantonese and looking upon her flock as children to be nurtured into obedient, Christianised, English-speaking, second-class American citizens. She had nothing to say about the Chinese Exclusion Act nor the rampant anti-Asian prejudice of the time. She was relentlessly small picture in her approach, focusing on one enslaved girl at a time, prying her out of the hands of her brothel or keeper and rehabilitating her. In retrospect, it was probably Cameron's one-dimensional outlook that made her so effective. She was definitely a doer rather than a thinker and unquestionably eased the lives of thousands of Chinese women, even if she was acting out of cultural imperialism.

A high-spirited tomboy as a girl, Cameron also seems to have chanced upon one of the few socially acceptable outlets for a woman as adventurer in her time. She was always taking the midnight train to San José, jumping into cars with armed policemen and matching wits with the Chinese and white men who controlled prostitution. 'I am simply doing the work that I most enjoy,' she modestly told a gushing interviewer in 1914. 'There is no self-sacrifice in that.' She was, of course, too well-bred to elaborate. And, she probably wouldn't even admit to her Presbyterian soul that she was having one hell of a good time.

The Presbyterian mission, now called the Donaldina Cameron House, was rebuilt on the same spot after burning in 1906. Julia Morgan, another magnificent work-obsessed spinster, was the architect.

By 1880 there were more than 25,000 Chinese in San Francisco, a quarter of all Chinese men and women in the US. Only a few thousand were women. Most of the immigrants had come to America ('Gold Mountain') to make their fortune and go home – a common dream among European immigrants as well. The idea of a temporary sojourn, along with the traditional strictures imposed on

Chinese women that kept them very close to home, made the Chinese American community overwhelmingly male. Gambling, prostitution, drug use, minor arguments escalating into violence were endemic among the Chinese, as they were among the pioneer Western communities in general.

Vice was disproportionately ferreted out and prosecuted in Chinatown. The so-called tong wars, assassinations and campaigns of retribution, were decried and criticised even as white San Franciscans challenged each other to duels, shot one another down in the street and engaged in all manner of gambling, prostitution and destructive drinking. But nothing so shocked and titillated non-Chinese as the slave girl trade.

Lurid stories about kidnapped upper-class Chinese maidens who were shipped to San Francisco as sex slaves were a standard sob story in the press. They followed the same outline of the white slave trade mythology of a worldwide network of evil overlords working day and night to destroy Christian decency and virtuous womanhood. As with the white slave trade, the Chinese slave girl stories are so drenched in sexual repression and misogyny that it is difficult not to dismiss them as male magical thinking. However, there was a very real and sordid trafficking in women, sometimes as young as eleven or twelve, unwillingly forced into prostitution. But even the most dedicated reformers, such as Presbyterian lay worker Donaldina Cameron, could not fully shed their cultural and racial biases and see that the American colour line and discrimination against the Chinese engendered and perpetuated most of the crime and 'perversity' in Chinatown. The 1882 Chinese Exclusion Act, a shameful triumph of xenophobia, stopped all Chinese immigration to the US and made bringing over wives or wives-to-be impossible.

AH TOY

Donaldina Cameron's exact opposite was Ah Toy, a Chinese prostitute and madam who achieved legendary status among San Francisco's male population.

Reportedly born in Hong Kong in 1828, she arrived in Gold Rush San Francisco in 1849, said to be the second Chinese woman to set foot in California and the first Chinese prostitute. Ah Toy, whose name was spelled various ways, is known today because of the attention she attracted from individual men who recorded their impressions in diaries and journals and through her famous court appearances.

Albert Benard, a French would-be Gold Rush millionaire who was largely contemptuous of everything he found in California, rhapsodised over 'the strangely alluring Achoy, with her slender body and laughing eyes'. Another Argonaut years later departed from a bout of anti-Chinese invective to recall Ah Toy as 'a tall well-built woman. In fact, she was the finest-looking woman I have ever seen.'

Part of Ah Toy's fame was her pioneer status, as the first Asian woman ever seen by many whites. Further, she was the first to answer the enduring white male question about Asian female physiognomy. In one of her first court appearances, a curious judge asked Ah Toy why her house was so popular with the Gold Country miners who lined up at her door. Her answer, sanitised by a newspaper reporter of the time, was that the miners 'came to gaze upon the countenance of the charming Ah Toy'. The court-room apparently dissolved into hysteria over this. Translated, it meant that the miners didn't necessarily pay for sex, but just to see her genitals and discover for themselves if they were 'normal' like those of caucasian women, or as rumour had it, slanted like Asian eyes.

San Francisco, of course, laughed at Ah Toy rather than the men she serviced, in typical nineteenth-century fashion. Her achievements, however, are far more remark-able than any of the chortling city fathers'. Whatever obstacles the early pioneers overcame to reach San Francisco and eventually prosper pale beside the struggle of a young Chinese woman in nineteenth-century California who escaped early death, obscurity, poverty and male oppression to achieve financial and personal indepen-dence. The stories about Ah Toy vary, but she is said to have been high-born, as she had bound feet. In California she bought her independence from her first master and set up on her own as a prostitute, quickly becoming prosperous enough to have a large house on Pike Street (now Waverly Place). When the first Vigilante Committee of 1851 turned its Old Testament wrath on Chinatown, Ah Toy side-stepped deporta-tion or worse by taking the Vigilante brothel inspector, John Clark, as her lover.

San Francisco newspapers announced the departure of Ah Toy several times, to be married in Sonoma, to return in triumph to China, but her name continued to appear on the police blotter until the 1860s, then dropped from sight.

In 1928 the San José papers announced the death of a local woman known as 'China Mary', widow of a prosperous Chinese merchant. She was also known as Mrs Ah Toy, but the reports seemed most interested in the fact she had died a few weeks before her hundredth birthday. Perhaps the 'strangely alluring' Ah Toy had the best revenge after all, living well and long.

In 1905 a group formed to buy all the land parcels in Chinatown and force the Chinese out of the downtown district. Not unaware of the power of Chinatown's local colour, the United States Improvement and Investment Co. planned to relocate the Chinese community in Hunter's Point or San Mateo County where it would be a kind of amusement park for tourists. This incredible idea was knocked out by the 1906 earthquake. The Chinese did not wait for civic funds or encouragement to rebuild; the handful of Chinese landowners began reconstruction immediately, completely circumventing the huffing machinery of government. The Chinese community, did, however, seem to take some hints from the Improvement Co., putting the unmistakable stamp of Asia on its buildings with pagoda roofs, railings and even streetlights. Chinatown had learned that its exotica was an asset, if carefully managed.

The Chinese-American population dwindled dramatically through the first part of the twentieth-century. World War II was an unlikely agent of change for the Chinese community when, owing to the wartime alliance with China, the federal exclusion act was repealed. As with other minorities, wartime emergencies allowed Chinese Americans entry to jobs and opportunities denied to them before. Many college educated Chinese Americans were able to find work in their field for the first time, even as Japanese Americans on the West Coast were sent to detention camps, in one of the more bizarre side-by-side contrasts of the illogic of racism.

The final vestiges of anti-Asian immigration didn't disappear until 1964 when US immigration laws were completely revamped. In the early 1960s Chinatown was an ageing, if not dying, community. With the advent of civil rights laws and the removal of residential 'covenant laws' (these were a nasty American institution that weren't laws but exclusionary provisions written into sales contracts for houses, with new owners pledged to sell only to other whites) Chinese Americans were able to move out of Chinatown to the suburbs and the neighbourhoods. When US immigration laws changed, new Asian immigrants began pouring into Chinatown. The area is so crowded that other little Chinatowns have sprung up. The Vietnamese, for instance, have gathered around the seedy Tenderloin near Civic Center. The most recent wave of immigrants are from Hong Kong, fleeing the uncertainty of turnover to the People's Republic of China.

Despite its colourful overlay of pagoda architecture Chinatown is a genuine ethnic ghetto. Most residents are foreign-born with little or no English, living in cramped quarters and working in dead-end jobs. Women often turn to the semi-legal garment sweatshops where they sew for terrible wages, but their lack of English is not a handicap and frequently they are able to bring their babies and small children to work with them.

Chinese Historical Society of America

650 Commercial St (between Kearny and Montgomery), tel. 391 1188. Open 12–4 p.m. Tues–Sat; free.

The story of the Chinese in America is told through displays, artefacts and photographs in this absorbing little museum. Captions are in English and Chinese.

While you are on Commercial Street, visit the Pacific Heritage Museum, 608 Commercial St, Mon – Fri 10 a.m. – 4 p.m., free. On the site of San Francisco's first mint, the museum today presents changing exhibitions on the Pacific Basin culture along with a permanent display on the old building, a partial survivor of the 1906 earthquake and fires, together with its $13 million in silver and gold.

The Chinese Cultural Center

750 Kearny St (third floor of the Chinatown Holiday Inn), tel. 986 1822. Open 10 a.m. – 4 p.m., Tues–Sat; free.

The Chinese Cultural Center offers a busy schedule of programmes, art shows and community events. The gallery mixes contemporary and historical art, Chinese American and Chinese artists. The centre's walking tours of Chinatown (free) are some of the best in the city. The centre is a handy resource if you have general or specific questions about Chinatown.

The Holiday Inn that houses the centre was built after a fierce and angry community debate in the late sixties. The hotel overshadows everything around it, most importantly Portsmouth Square, Chinatown's unofficial town hall and social centre. The unlovely pedestrian bridge and the Cultural Center floor were compromise efforts to soothe community feelings.

Portsmouth Square

700 block of Kearny (bordered by Clay, Washington and Walter Lum Place).

Portsmouth Square is a magnet for Chinatown residents. Retirees meet to play checkers; grandmothers with little children in tow gather to chat. The park sits over a four-storey underground car park (similar to the one underneath Union Square).

There is a lovely memorial to writer Robert Louis Stevenson in one corner of the park, a model of the galleon Hispañola from *Treasure Island* atop a podium with excerpts of Stevenson's famous *Christmas Sermon*, much of it written in the park. Stevenson spent many long hours here during his brief tenure in San Francisco, as he courted the married Fanny Van de Grift Osbourne. Stevenson had met Osbourne in France. She was separated from her husband and vowed to get a divorce. In 1879, Stevenson followed her back to California and took a room at 608 Bush St while Osbourne, at home in Oakland, began divorce proceedings. The writer spent most of his days in the park, getting to know some of the Chinese residents and working on his stories. Stevenson and Osbourne were eventually married in San Francisco in May 1880, soon leaving for Scotland and eventually settling in Samoa, an idea, by the way, that Stevenson imbibed from a San Francisco writer, C.W. Stoddard, who had lived in Hawaii and travelled the South Pacific.

Portsmouth Square was the centre of old San Francisco. In Spanish times it was the plaza, adjacent to the village's first street, *Calle de la Fundación*, now Grant Avenue. The first permanent structure, the home of Englishman-turned-Californian William Richardson, was at roughly 827 Grant Ave. The street was renamed Dupont for a US Navy officer, and later named for President Ulysses S. Grant. The Chinese community continued to call the artery Dupont *Gai* (street). There is no 'R' in the Cantonese dialect and the new name (which they had not been consulted about) was not pronounceable.

Originally, the plaza was almost on the waterfront. During the Gold Rush so many ships were abandoned in the harbour that they were deliberately sunk. The next step was landfill, which added another half mile to downtown. The plaza was renamed Portsmouth, after the ship that the American authorities sailed in on in 1846, when they pronounced California a US possession. Portsmouth Square was the site of the first city hall, jail (where the Holiday Inn now sits) and US custom house, making it the nerve centre of official San Francisco. Gradually, however, the centre began to shift towards Market Street and Portsmouth Square and its neighbourhood fell behind. The Chinese, who were regrouping in San Francisco from the mining fields and railroad work in the 1870s, gravitated towards Portsmouth Square and by the 1880s the area was called the Chinese Quarter.

Among themselves, the Chinese referred to San Francisco as 'the safest place', a poignant rubric considering the humiliations they suffered here. The Chinese community was tightly organised and firmly hierarchical. In the 1850s Chinese immigrants banded together in tongs or associations based on where they came from in China. Eventually these groups became very formalised and formed a kind of shadow government among the Chinese. The associations in turn were governed by a coordinating body which acted as agent for the Imperial Chinese government in the US until late in the nineteenth century. Called the Six Companies (although there were sometimes as many as eight associations), this body funded legal battles, arbitrated disputes and handled relations with white San Francisco. The Six Companies still exists, with headquarters at 843 Stockton St, but is much diminished from its old eminence.

Bank of Canton

743 Washington St.

Originally built in 1909 as the Chinese telephone exchange, the bank is an excellent example of the fantasy architecture model used for the rebuilding of Chinatown.

The telephone exchange was a marvel. It was staffed by women operators who were not only fluent in English and five dialects of Chinese, but had to memorise every client's phone number as many

Chinese felt it was rude to refer to a person as a number, so would simply ask to be connected with say, Bill Wong. The exchange was finally closed in 1949 and replaced by rotary dialling phones.

This was also the site of San Francisco's first newspaper, the *California Star* (1847–9), published by Sam Brannan, the Mormon businessman who dominated early San Francisco.

Old St Mary's Church

600 California St, St Mary's Square. Across from the church on California, between Grant and Kearny.

St Mary's was once the city's most fashionable Catholic church, the first Roman Catholic cathedral on the West Coast. The redbrick church was built in 1854 with brick brought round the horn from Boston and a foundation of granite from China.

Old St Mary's is a quiet Paulist community parish today, with a sweet little bookstore tucked behind on Grant Avenue. The church ignored its proximity to Chinatown for years. American Catholics (particularly Irish parishes, such as this one) didn't have the same evangelical fire about converting the Chinese as their fellow Christians, the Protestants did.

The church hosts noontime concerts every Tuesday at 12.30 p.m. that are popular with Financial District workers who take the cable car up the hill for soothing chamber music.

The church tower proclaims an oddly stern message from Ecclesiastes, 'Son, Observe the Time and Fly from Evil'. Years ago the church faced St Mary's Alley, a prime spot for brothels. The brothels have been replaced by St Mary's Square and a handsome Beniamino Bufano statue of Dr Sun Yat Sen (1938) (exiled as a revolutionary before the overthrow of the Manchu Dynasty in 1911, Sun Yat Sen spent several years in San Francisco), but the admonishment remains.

A new St Mary's was built in 1893 on Van Ness (since replaced with the stark new New St Mary's on Geary). This church was gutted by fire and rebuilt after 1906 and again in 1969.

Shopping in Chinatown   Chinatown is about shopping. Little shops and multi-level stores are crammed with everything from children's toys to first-class jade jewellery. If you are a shopper you'll thoroughly enjoy yourself. If you find shopping a tedious bore, keep moving. When you do find something you want, especially if it's on the expensive side, prepare to make a deal. If you aren't comfortable bargaining, then definitely take time to compare prices since the Chinatown shops have made underselling one another a matter of honour. If you have children in tow, try to convince them of the wisdom of this as the same items crop up over and over at wildly varying prices. The prices are usually more expensive the closer you are to the entryways to Chinatown, where merchants are counting on that first gotta-have-it impulse to buy before you see other merchandise.

There are plenty of cheap knick-knacks for yourself, the kids and friends back home, but there are also some worthwhile items to be had, depending on your preferences and pocket-book. Linens are a major commodity in Chinatown. In recent years quilts made in Asian sweatshops, based on traditional American quilt patterns, have also entered the market. The provenance makes them politically incorrect, but the prices make these quilts irresistible to some shoppers.

On the high end of goods, you will find silk, jade, jewellery, cameras, porcelain and cloisonné. Don't buy big if you don't know the field, but look carefully because there are some great deals for the knowledgeable. A plus for non-US visitors is the Chinatown shops' familiarity with international shipping; you don't have to lug it home yourself.

Some specialist shops worth keeping an eye out for include the Chinatown Kite Shop, 717 Grant Ave, the Ten Ren Tea Shop, 949 Grant Ave, for wonderful teapots and more than fifty types of tea, and the Golden Gate Fortune Cookie Factory, 56 Ross Alley (between Washington and Jackson), where you can watch cookies being made and sample the product.

Chinese herbal shops are a staple in Chinatown, although it is still a mystery how they functioned during the darkest days of the Cold War when all trade with mainland China was forbidden. The shops are concentrated on Jackson and Washington streets and despite the New Age mania for Chinese medicine, these places remain resolutely Old World. Herbalists will suggest herbs or teas for mild ailments but a Chinese doctor (healer) sometimes in a back room, will be consulted for major problems.

Stockton Street, parallel to Grant, is Chinatown's genuine main street, home to the shops and businesses that the residents use. You will find most of the foodstores and grocery shops here.

AMY TAN

The huge success of Amy Tan's rich, engrossing first novel, *The Joy Luck Club*, in 1989 had repercussions beyond a talented writer finding her voice. With her multi-generational story of Chinese-American mothers and daughters, Tan significantly added to the American literary discourse, bringing the Asian American experience into the mainstream.

Born in Oakland to immigrant Chinese parents, her father a Baptist minister and her mother a homemaker, Tan was raised all around the Bay Area. She married her college sweetheart (who comes from an Italian American background) and was working as a freelance technical writer when a publisher jumped at the chance to publish *The Joy Luck Club*.

Tan and her husband have continued to live in San Francisco. They bought a new apartment in Pacific Heights, but Tan's indulgences from her newfound wealth have been lavished on her mother with trips to China and a condominium.

Tan has become a literary star in the mode of sister San Franciscan, Alice Walker (*The Color Purple*), writing fiction firmly rooted in an ethnic millieu but accessible to outsiders through masterful storytelling.

The enormous success of *The Joy Luck Club* and the boom in Asian American writers was a movement building for years. Chinese Americans particularly longed for new voices to replace the assimilation fantasies of *Flower Drum Song* (based on San Francisco immigrant C.Y. Lee's novel). Jade Snow Wong, another San Franciscan, had a big success with her bestselling autobiography of 1950, *Fifth Chinese Daughter*, but it was also in the vein of second-generation immigrant problems, focusing on her father's domination of her life rather than the ambivalence of white America to native-born Americans of colour.

Maxine Hong Kingston, who now lives in Berkeley, signalled the changing consciousness with her pivotal book, *Woman Warrior* in 1976. Tan solidified her reputation with the success of her second novel, *The Kitchen God's Wife*, in 1993. (Meanwhile critical mass was reached with Gish Jen's 'Typical American,' Gus Lee's autobiographical 'China Boy' and the plays of David Henry Hwang, Philip Kan Gotanda and Frank Chin, as well as scholarly and nonfiction work such as UC professor Ronald Takaki's history of Asian Americans, 'Strangers From a Different Shore' (1989).

Tan, at work on her third novel, took a detour in 1993 and immersed herself in the film version of *The Joy Luck Club* with San Francisco director Wayne Wang. In fact, Tan has been so successful she has to contend with a reactionary effect. The Tan revisionist school is led by playwright Frank Chin who suggests that Tan, like African American women writers, has been embraced by the white majority because she writes acceptable, non-threatening books. Tan doesn't reply. She keeps writing.

NORTH BEACH

San Franciscans and visitors have a long-standing affection for the neighbourhood that the old bohemian praised. There have been several names for this district, as well as complete shifts of population. Despite being so destroyed (see p. 217) by fire, in 1906 however, the area of the city north of Chinatown, south of Fisherman's Wharf, and roughly bordered by Telegraph Hill to the east and Russian Hill to the west, has always been a place of excitement and great fun.

Sometimes the fun wasn't so good as with the down and dirty Barbary Coast (see p. 117) where the verb 'to shanghai' was invented. But North Beach and its environs has been home to several generations of San Francisco bohemians, beginning with Mark Twain and Bret Harte to the Beats of the 1950s, and continuing. The first genuinely hip comedy clubs flourished in North Beach with

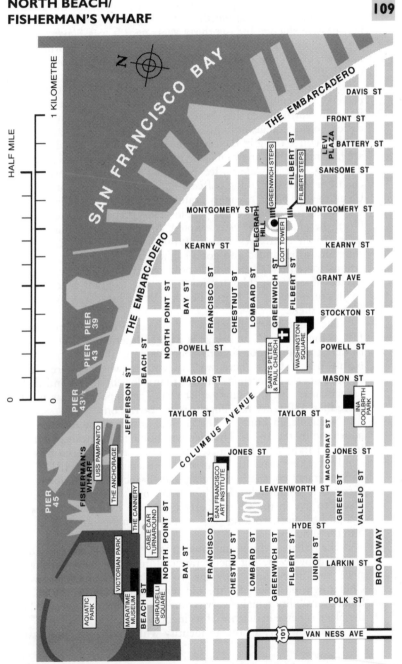

SAN FRANCISCO BAY

THE EMBARCADERO

1 KILOMETRE

HALF MILE

DAVIS ST

FRONT ST

LEVI PLAZA

BATTERY ST

SANSOME ST

MONTGOMERY ST

GREENWICH STEPS

FILBERT STEPS

FILBERT ST

MONTGOMERY ST

TELEGRAPH HILL

COIT TOWER

KEARNY ST

KEARNY ST

GRANT AVE

FRANCISCO ST

CHESTNUT ST

LOMBARD ST

GREENWICH ST

FILBERT ST

BAY ST

NORTH POINT ST

STOCKTON ST

WASHINGTON SQUARE

POWELL ST

POWELL ST

BEACH ST

SAINT'S PETER & PAUL CHURCH

THE EMBARCADERO

MASON ST

MASON ST

INA COOLBRITH PARK

JEFFERSON ST

TAYLOR ST

TAYLOR ST

PIER 39

PIER 43

PIER 43½

COLUMBUS AVENUE

JONES ST

JONES ST

MACONDRAY ST

USS PAMPANITO

SAN FRANCISCO ART INSTITUTE

LEAVENWORTH ST

GREEN ST

VALLEJO ST

THE ANCHORAGE

FISHERMAN'S WHARF

THE CANNERY

HYDE ST

BROADWAY

PIER 45

CABLE CAR TURNAROUND

NORTH POINT ST

FRANCISCO ST

CHESTNUT ST

LOMBARD ST

GREENWICH ST

FILBERT ST

UNION ST

LARKIN ST

VICTORIAN PARK

BAY ST

AQUATIC PARK

MARITIME MUSEUM

BEACH ST

GHIRADELLI SQUARE

POLK ST

VAN NESS AVE

101

Lenny Bruce and his hipster brothers. The sixties gentrification of stripteasing was born in North Beach, too, when Carol Doda bared her massive silicone breasts thirty years ago. It was *Playboy* magazine acted out, called topless dancing and accepted as a form of sexual liberation. Punk rock moved into many of the tired old clubs in the 1980s, giving North Beach another new wave, now fizzled.

It's not exactly a novel entertainment form, but coffee has become the latest North Beach *cause célèbre*. Courtesy of the Italians, North Beach has been home to glorious neighbourhood coffee houses for generations. The rest of America began to tune into the coffee thing in the early nineties. Cities that couldn't generate first-rate coffee and ambience on their own were presented with charming little upscale coffee boutiques from one of several new chains devoted to making coffee a major new consumer item. Most US cities were embarrassingly grateful to them for this amenity.

When the chain coffee people made preparations to open in North Beach, however, war erupted. Amidst dark rumblings about 'going to the mattresses' and 'cultural chernobyls', the North Beach community demanded and got a slight change in the licensing regulations for coffee shops which now require a public hearing. No elected official or public employee is going to grant a licence to a chain coffee house in North Beach. His or her career would end then and there.

The name North Beach is one of San Francisco's misnomers. Just as the Golden Gate Bridge is painted International Orange and Union Street does not lead to Union Square, there is no beach in North Beach. Once there was, of course, when Nature was in charge of the shoreline rather than development-minded San Franciscans. The little sandy inlet near Telegraph Hill was filled in more than 120 years ago, but the name carries on.

North Beach built up quickly and was a dense, urban neighbourhood by the 1870s. The area was home to Mexicans, Germans, Irish and Italians in the nineteenth century and has been predominantly working class for most of its existence. However, like most of San Francisco, that's changing. San Francisco, with nowhere to expand, is completely developed. As one of the most desirable places to live in the US, property prices are extremely high which has pushed most working-class, middle-income people and families into the suburbs.

The Italians, who began moving into the area in the mid-1880s, owned it by 1915. But their grandchildren have been moving out since the fifties and the new Asian immigration has swollen Chinatown, pushing back the old boundaries to North Beach. The Italian sensibility remains very strong, and, as the coffee wars show, the place is fierce in defence of its identity.

It is, however, a protean identity which welcomes and assimilates differences. The Beatniks, like the nineteenth-century Bohemians who preceded them, were initially drawn by the cheap rents and inexpensive restaurants. The exuberant street life and *laissez faire* attitude of North Beach were bonuses. The cheap rents are a memory approaching mythic status, but the good food, lively street scene and engaging ambience continue.

In fact, North Beach seems to have a special genius for making the best things last. In the 1906 inferno, the fires destroyed everything from the bay to Van Ness Street and the Mission, except three little islands within the North Beach sphere on Telegraph Hill, Russian Hill and Jackson Square. Similarly, a half century later, the Beatniks moved on, but City Lights Bookstore at 261 Columbus Ave, the Beat word made flesh, endures even though it has reluctantly given up anarchy and now co-operates with authority figures to the extent of allowing shoplifters to be arrested. Vesuvio, 255 Columbus Ave, the archetypal 'fifties' San Francisco bar, likewise continues its eccentric course, oblivious to the changes around it. Tosca, at No. 242, another North Beach bar cum institution, where Puccini dominates the jukebox and Mikhail Baryshnikov and Sam Shepard drop in to play pool, remains a graceful old style hangout neither selling T-shirts nor installing a doorman to screen the hoi polloi. (See listings, p. 313, for details.) The coffee houses are intact, *Beach Blanket Babylon*, the madcap cabaret show plays to packed houses and masses in Italian proceed as they always have at Saints Peter and Paul. The details of North Beach may change, but the essence remains the same.

North Beach is particularly attractive for the traveller who likes to soak up a place by osmosis. Sitting in cafés, dropping by a poetry reading at City Lights, walking through the quirky shops on Upper Grant Street or having a drink at the old working-class bars are increments that build into a complete North Beach experience.

Women feel secure if a bit wary in the district. The sense of North Beach being an Italian male place is still strong. A couple of years ago an affronted Italian husband shot his estranged wife's lover in broad daylight on Columbus Avenue. The husband was further affronted to be arrested and charged with murder, indignantly pointing out that this was a matter of honour between men. The testosterone level is also pumped up by the vestiges of sex club sleaze along Broadway. Sailors on leave still roam the streets in packs, looking for Carol Doda but often seeming to take refuge in neighbourhood ice cream shops, where they cast longing glances at teenagers on dates.

For women, alone or in a group, it is not so much dangerous as uncomfortable to venture into some of the smoky, dark bars, such as Gino and Carlo's at 548 Green St – the kind of male neighbourhood preserve where everyone is on a first-name basis and the regulars feel they own certain barstools. Depending on your affinity for the seamy corners of life, North Beach's non-tourist bars can be intriguing and gritty or brain-dead male bonding pits.

North Beach blends seamlessly into Telegraph Hill and Russian Hill, two of the city's most alluring residential areas. Telegraph Hill is instantly recognisable, topped by Coit Tower, a phallic white column overlooking the bay. It's a mandatory tourist stop, but many visitors miss the charming steps, winding streets and cottages around the tower. Russian Hill is even more unknown to outsiders. It is almost entirely residential without any major tourbus stops. In addition, the hilly terrain discourages many walkers. Russian Hill offers lovely vistas and several little-known but captivating landmarks, largely architectural and literary.

Washington Square

Columbus Avenue (bounded by Filbert, Stockton and Union streets).

There's a pleasantly off-kilter quality about North Beach that Herb Caen once summed up as follows: 'This is North Beach, which isn't a beach. Its heart is Washington Square, which isn't on Washington Street, isn't a square, doesn't contain a statue of Washington but of Benjamin Franklin.'

The vaguely rectangular park is undistinguished but friendly, with the imperial Church of Saints Peter and Paul dominating the north side and busy Columbus Avenue providing a ceaseless soundtrack of car horns and squealing brakes to the west. The square is a good orientation spot for North Beach. Columbus Avenue is the district's main street, running from downtown to the bay.

Cafés, bakeries and delis are close at home if you want to make an impromptu picnic. Early spring to early autumn you can also have a front-row seat for the non-stop weddings that march through Peter and Paul, the Italian National Church of Northern California. Often during the high wedding season (May and June) florists, limousines, bridesmaids and guests will be stacked up like airport traffic as the tightly scheduled nuptials shuttle in and out.

In the park itself, there is that odd statue of Benjamin Franklin, early American patriot and statesman who never travelled west of Pennsylvania and died before California was even heard of among Americans. The Franklin memorial was the gift of a teetotalling Dr Henry Cogswell, who was always trying to raise the moral standards of San Francisco. Another statue in the square is more coherent, a memorial to SF firefighters from Lillie Hitchcock Coit, another local eccentric. Coit Tower, atop Telegraph Hill, is her major achievement (see p. 121).

During the 1980s Washington Square had an international

resonance through a neighbourhood restaurant, the Washington Square Bar and Grill, 1707 Union St, which was the favoured stopping place of American and European journalists, film stars, rock and jazz musicians and *bons vivants*. The 'Washbag' is still going strong but its founder, ex-reporter Ed Moose, has come out of retirement to open a new eatery across the square, Moose's, at 1652 Stockton St, trying to recreate the magic again. This has caused a certain amount of friction and questions of loyalty among Washbag fans and Moose fans. Like the coffee wars, it has churned up the kind of mini-tempest that San Francisco adores, mixing up some of the city's favourite themes: personalities, gossip and food.

Saints Peter and Paul Church

666 Filbert St (between Powell and Stockton). Open daily, 7.30 a.m. to 6 p.m.

An Italianesque Gothic Revival design, perhaps based on the cathedral in Orvieto, Italy, Saints Peter and Paul was built in 1922–4 from funds that had been raised for years among Italians up and down the Pacific Coast.

It was once called the church of the Ten Commandments for its starring role in Cecil B. DeMille's 1923 epic of the same name. While the church continues to be known as the Italian National Church for San Francisco, Peter and Paul changes with the times. A large part of the local parish is Chinese American so in addition to the daily Italian masses, there is also a mass in Chinese on Sunday. The church programme is printed in English, Italian and Chinese.

Following the 'big tent' theory of political parties, the Catholic Church in San Francisco is trying to solidify Catholics into larger, more viable congregations and closing smaller churches. Saints Peter and Paul now administers St Francis of Assisi, a much older congregation, at Vallejo and Columbus, a source of much friction within the Catholic community.

If the old Italian ways are slipping away, homage is still paid to Peter and Paul where every Italian family wants to have its daughters' weddings, babies' baptisms and grandparents' funerals. The annual Columbus Day Parade (early October) grew out of a parish celebration and makes a ceremonial pass before the church reviewing stand. Another October festival, the Blessing of the Fleet, emanates from Saints Peter and Paul with all the pomp and circumstance of Rome. (See pp. 4–5 for festival dates.)

The exterior of the structure is only interesting for the very front, facing Washington Square. The 191-foot twin spires are heavily embellished. A ribbon of Dante across the facade, over the front doors, greets the visitor: *La gloria di colui che tutto muove per l'universo penetra e risplende* ('The glory of Him who moves all things penetrates and glows throughout the universe').

Inside the church, you are further transported to Italy. Every inch of the interior is decorated or devoted to a saint or celestial. The altar area alone is worthy of a five-act melodrama with a full-size replica of the 'Pieta', two minor marble altars, and a soaring hand-carved pulpit.

There are more than half a dozen life-size statues of saints, the majority of them women. St Rita, St Mary Mazzarelli, St Gemma Galgani, St Francesca Cabrini, as well as the Virgin, are all represented in great detail. Peter and Paul has an altogether feminine feel.

ALONG COLUMBUS AVENUE

Columbus Avenue connects Washington Square and Broadway, the two distinct centres of North Beach. It is a pleasant walk either up or down Columbus, especially if you zigzag through the area.

If you're lucky, you'll hear a tinkling piano, either during the afternoon or in the evening and follow it to the corner of Columbus, Green and Stockton, where 'The Piano Man', Tim McLeroy, is holding forth. McLeroy pulls his piano out of its storage spot at the New Pisa, 550 Green St, sets up beside a bank (Bayview Federal) and plays whatever anyone wants to hear. He used to leave his piano outside, but to his everlasting chagrin, it was stolen. The neighbourhood raised money for a new one and now The Piano Man is resigned to locking it up.

To get a full idea of North Beach history, there's the North Beach Museum, on the mezzanine of the Eureka Bank, 1435 Stockton St. Photographs and other memorabilia are on display during banking hours, Mon – Fri, 9 a.m. – 4 p.m.; free.

Around the block is Club Fugazi, 678 Green St, an Italian American social hall that is the more or less permanent home to *Beach Blanket Babylon*, a dizzy cabaret show that combines outrageous costumes, five-foot high headdresses, rock music and topical humour (see p. 333). When Queen Elizabeth visited San Francisco in 1983, a special performance was staged for her with the frenzied finale including a singer wearing a headdress that included Buckingham Palace (instead of the traditional City Hall). Newspaper photos the next day showed a very amused royal box with Prince Philip guffawing and pointing out the subtleties (a tiny mechanised changing of the guard) to the Queen.

Around the next corner is another landmark, Capp's Corner, 1600 Powell St, an Italian family restaurant and bar where you'll find socialites in hand-made white motorcycle jackets happily rubbing shoulders with old Italian guys from the neighbourhood in flannel shirts.

Recrossing Columbus, head for Grant Avenue, home to an ever

changing variety of shops and boutiques. Some are junky beyond belief, but that's part of their charm. Quantity Postcards, 1441 Grant Avenue, must have a copy of every postcard ever printed. At night, there's a pretty hot club scene around Green and Grant, shifting among three bars: the Lost & Found Saloon, The Saloon, at Fresno Alley, and the Savoy Tivoli, all on Grant Avenue. The first two places, which are frequently confused, have been called the original grunge scene – not grunge in its stylised dirt pedlar look, but unaffected biker cum slob milieu, where nothing matters but the music. Women who are self-confident and practised at staring down unwanted advances can have a good time at the saloons. The Tivoli is a milder, younger scene, with a bar, recorded music and no dancing. The crowd is dismissed by some locals as 'Eurotrash on the make, or at least someone to buy their drinks', but as it is jammed most nights, some people must like it a lot.

At the corner of Columbus and Broadway you have come to the other centre of North Beach, where the ghosts of Jack Kerouac, Lenny Bruce and the denizens of the Barbary Coast still hold sway.

City Lights Bookstore

261 Columbus Ave (between Broadway and Pacific), tel. 362 8193. Open daily, 10 a.m. – 11.30 p.m., Mon–Fri, to 12.30 a.m. Sat and Sun.

Poet Lawrence Ferlinghetti decided to open this bookstore in 1953 with the idea that it would support a fledgling literary journal called *City Lights*. The journal nosedived soon after but the bookstore, the first all-paperback store in the US, flourished. It became the West Coast touchstone for the Beats, a group of bohemian, nonconformist, alienated youth who had found each other in postwar New York City, principally through Columbia University. Poet Allen Ginsberg, novelist Jack Kerouac and all-round wild man Neal Cassady regrouped in San Francisco in the early 1950s. Other friends drifted out to the coast while Ginsberg *et al.* forged new relationships in the Bay Area.

They called themselves Beats either for being worn and beaten down or a sense of beatification. Herb Caen immediately zeroed in on this ripe target and flippantly called them beatniks, a name they despised but could not shake off. The poets, writers, musicians and camp followers were into drugs, multiple sexual partners, of both sexes and apolitical rebelliousness. Remarkably, they also found time to work and produced serious, if not always memorable, work. Ginsberg read *Howl* for the first time in San Francisco and Ferlinghetti decided to publish it. An obscenity trial ensued in 1957, becoming a typical San Francisco circus.

'The Cops Don't Allow No Renaissance Here,' announced the *Chronicle* as poets and critics shoved and elbowed one another to get into court and testify that Ginsberg's work was the dawn of a new era in American letters and to condemn American yahooism.

The dawn did break, reshaping outmoded US obscenity laws and launching a new American literary boom. Ferlinghetti continued to publish poetry and prose he thought important and the store expanded from a storefront to most of the pie-shaped block it occupies.

The bookstore is run collectively and while Ferlinghetti is comfortably well off, he's far from being the rich man he could have been. 'We were never here to make money,' said Ferlinghetti, celebrating the bookstore's fortieth anniversary in 1993, 'the business side of the bookstore is secondary. This isn't a business, it's a way of life.'

City Lights is not the best stocked bookstore in San Francisco, but it is one of the most interesting. Women, minority and Third World writers are sought out and imaginatively displayed. The staff is remarkably well-read and passionate, even for a world-class bookstore which can lead to exchanges that are as interesting as the books. Ferlinghetti himself can be glimpsed around the store, although at 73, he spends most of his time on his writing and painting.

After City Lights you could drop in for a drink at Vesuvio's (see p. 313).

ALONG BROADWAY

For almost three decades the Broadway symbol was a three-storey neon sign of a busty woman with blinking red lights for nipples. This was the sign of the Condor Club, on Columbus and Broadway, where Carol Doda started dancing topless in 1964. Doda finally put her clothes back on in the 1980s, the sign was changed to merely say Condor and the club has become a bistro.

Despite Take Back the Night protests in the seventies, a declining market for nudie shows, owing to the availability of porn-at-home through VCRs and the falling off of San Francisco's traditional market of hordes of homesick and horny military guys, the porn stage shows continue on. Broadway is the high end of the market, luring in tourists, also out for a laugh. The Tenderloin near Civic Center, and lower Market Street are home to the bottom line raunchy hardcore movie theatres and sex shows.

As the sex positive versus anti-porn debate among feminists bounces around the halls of academe and within women-only conferences, the debate is acted out on Broadway. Take, for instance, the Lusty Lady Theater at 1033 Kearny St, which proudly advertises itself as 'owned and managed by women'. The theatre is clean (a major innovation in the field) and emphasises that employees are treated respectfully. The Lusty Lady is a working model of the argument which insists that women are going to be sexually exploited in this society, so the only truly honest response is for women to make a profit. Women sometimes venture into the LL where they are not hassled but are far more objects of curiosity than the naked dancers. 'So whaddaya think?' is not a come-on, but a genuine expression of curiosity.

THE OLD BARBARY COAST

No one has ever condemned and vilified the Barbary Coast as completely and vehemently as Eastern Journalist B.E. Lloyd after his 1874 fact-finding mission to San Francisco.

'Barbary Coast is the haunt of the low and vile of every kind,' he wrote in his 1876 exposé, *Lights and Shades of San Francisco*.

The petty thief, the house burglar, the tramp, the whoremonger, lewd women, cut-throats and murderers, all are found there. Dance-houses and concert saloons, where blear-eyed men and faded women drink vile liquor, smoke offensive tobacco, engage in vulgar conduct, sing obscene songs, and say and do everything to heap upon themselves more degradation, unrest and misery, are numerous. Low gambling houses thronged with riot-loving rowdies in all stages of intoxication are there. Opium dens, where heathen Chinese and God-forsaken women and men are completely overcome by inhaling the vapors of the nauseous narcotic, are there. Licentiousness, debauchery, pollution, loathsome disease, insanity from dissipation, misery, poverty, wealth, profanity, blasphemy and death, are there. And Hell, yawning to receive the putrid mass, is there also.'

Lloyd's account probably increased the numbers of visitors to 'the Coast' by the thousands. Another visitor, San Franciscan Clarence E. Edwords [correct spelling], took a different view, saying that 'Up to the time of the closing Barbary Coast molestation of women on the streets of San Francisco was almost unheard of,' he insisted. 'Since its closing it is becoming more and more hazardous for women to walk alone at night …' While Edwords's view of unmolested women is questionable, his opinion that the Coast absorbed and quarantined crime was widely held in San Francisco, which only reluctantly joined in national crusades against vice.

The Barbary Coast dates from Gold Rush days when the saloon and red light district was as close to the waterfront as possible. Named after the private hideout in North Africa, the Coast was home to dance halls, brothels, cribs, gambling dens, rooming houses, theatres, saloons, and even legitimate businesses. By the time of Lloyd's visit, the Coast was well-defined, centred around Broadway and Pacific from the waterfront to Chinatown. Later its boundaries were even more tightly drawn at Montgomery, Pacific, Washington and Kearny. The prostitutes were concentrated on Pacific, dubbed 'Terrific Pacific' by visiting sailors.

While many cities had red light districts with unsavoury reputations, none seemed to approach the Barbary Coast's infamy. A memorable Los Angeles headline immediately after the 1906 earthquake and fires proclaimed 'San Francisco Punished', echoing a pervasive opinion of the day. When it was discovered that one of the few buildings to survive was the Hoatling wholesale liquor warehouse in the Jackson Square area, poet Charles Field issued this retort on the city's behalf:

If, as they say, God spanked the town
For being over-frisky;
Why did He burn the churches down
And spare Hoatling's whisky?

The Barbary Coast's particularly nasty reputation is partially explained by the Shanghai scoundrels who operated with seeming impunity in San Francisco. The very real and extremely vicious practices of kidnapping men to work on ships was a danger in every seaport, but seemed to be unusually professional in San Francisco, where the very term 'shanghaiing' originated. There was no way out for victims once the ships were under way and the transitory nature of the sea life made retribution, legal or otherwise, difficult.

San Francisco, a major shipping centre after the Gold Rush, was always full of ships needing crews. The ships were hellholes afloat, where brutality and filthy living conditions were the rule. Instead of improving any of these problems, the captains turned to recruitment specialists such as Shanghai Kelly, whose infamous bar at 33 Pacific had custom-made trapdoors for quick delivery to waiting ships. Shanghaiing seems to have been an equal-opportunity line of exploitation; the names of Mother Bronson and Miss Piggott can still send shivers up spines. Shanghaiers, also called crimps, ran bars and boarding houses where whisky laced with opium were the specialities of the house. The Sailors Union of the Pacific was founded in 1885 in San Francisco to fight the abuses. In 1904 Congress at last granted some relief with the 'Act to Prohibit Shanghaiing in the United States'.

The sleazy clubs on Broadway have been called a continuation of the Barbary Coast, but that old devil was well and truly killed in 1917 by the sweeping reforms under what were called the red light abatement laws. The Coast had burned down in 1906 and quickly reappeared in makeshift housing and tents. The dens of iniquity never regained their earlier sense of invincibility.

The total defanging of the old Barbary Coast can be summed up in one example: In 1985 the Barbary Coast National Bank was established on Sansome Street. No one seemed to find anything scandalous about the name at all.

Less ambiguous but more puzzling is Centerfolds, at Montgomery and Broadway, a 'classy' strip place where the dancers are reputed to be former *Playboy* and *Penthouse* models. The club recently opened in a renovated restaurant, Del Vecchio's, that had once been part of the Barbary Coast.

Centerfolds is a full-service restaurant and bar, both entirely unremarkable. The beautiful women dancing, shedding their clothes and talking to the customers like old friends (no touching allowed) is of course the key. In San Francisco's hotly competitive restaurant scene this place would normally sink without a ripple. Who needs an expensive strip joint? The answer isn't clear yet. When the Playboy club finally wheezed its last in the seventies, it seemed to close the door on the whole idea of men's bars with near-naked waitresses. Now this.

The only controversy really over Centerfolds was a never-acted-upon plan to picket the place. The women who almost went into action were upset to learn that the dancers not only don't make a salary, they have to pay a 'stage fee' to dance. Their income is strictly from tips. When the groups discovered that the 'stage fee' stratagem is standard for most clubs the idea was dropped.

TELEGRAPH HILL

When she died in 1929, Lillie Hitchcock Coit left the city of San Francisco $118,000 for the purpose of 'adding to the beauty of the city which I have always loved'. The result of her vague gift was Coit Tower, a decisive white column atop Telegraph Hill near the waterfront, giving San Francisco another one of its unlikely, unforgettable landmarks.

Telegraph Hill has been an important San Francisco landmark from the earliest days. The Spanish called it *Loma Alta* and grazed goats and cows there. As the tallest hill nearest the bay (248 feet), it became a prime lookout point as harbour traffic grew. A signalling station was erected in 1849 with huge arm-like apparatuses. Specific positions of the arms alerted the waterfront, and the eager public, to the arrival of different ships. Most popular in the early days were the side-wheel steamers which carried passengers and mail, both precious commodities to the isolated locals.

Everyone knew the ship signals by heart. The story is told of a travelling production of Sheridan's *The Hunchback*, in 1850, which included a scene where an actor rushed onstage during an argument, threw out his arms and demanded, 'What does this mean?' to which the audience roared back, 'Side-wheel steamer!'.

In 1853 an electric telegraph system was installed on top of the hill and the name Telegraph Hill came into general usage.

The first Telegraph Hill dwellers were Chileans who came for the Gold Rush. Their encampment on the west side of the hill, called Little Chile, was the site of San Francisco's first mass attack of xenophobia. The Chileans, like the Chinese and the Mexicans in days to come, were labelled 'foreign' and harassed by thugs who had early on banded into informal gangs. The nasties became formalised under the name of the Hounds when they were contracted by ship's captains to hunt down runaway sailors. The Hounds' ranks were soon swelled by the arrival of more experienced felons from the Australian penal colony, dubbed the Sydney Ducks.

The Hounds soon spun out of control, collecting 'taxes' from the vulnerable non-American miners and merchants, stealing from the better established. In July 1849, one of the head Hounds was incensed to discover that his favourite Chilean prostitute was doing business with a German emigré. After beating up the customer, the drunk Hound returned to headquarters (a tent bar on Portsmouth Square) and rounded up his fellows to attack Chiletown, which seemed to be a fitting punishment for his sexual humiliation by a

Chilean. The Hounds went on a looting, burning, raping, beating rampage around Telegraph Hill, shouting, 'California for the Californians!', which must have had an odd ring to it in an Australian accent.

San Francisco was outraged by the riot. Donations were raised for the Chileans and a 'Citizen's Safety Committee' of 230 men volunteered to hunt down the Hounds. This was the precursor of the Vigilantes, organised in 1851. The Hounds who weren't quick enough to slip out of town were tried and convicted, but as there was no real jail, state prison or permanent police force (one part-time constable constituted the peace-keeping force in 1849) the criminals were banished from San Francisco.

The Chileans rebuilt on Telegraph Hill which soon had a large Irish population as well. By 1900 the Italians were the predominant residents. Writers, artists, poets and their fellow travellers were quick to see the charm of the hill as well. Newspapermen and women were the core group of bohemians, living in the little shacks and cabins that often seemed in danger of falling off the side.

Until the 1920s Telegraph Hill was a rural patch in the heart of the city, with most houses accessible only by footpath. A cable car line briefly ran up to the top of the hill where a public park was established in 1876, but generally it was tough going (the cable car line shut down after several people were killed when a runaway car careened off the tracks). It wasn't until the 1930s, with the blanket public works programmes of the Depression, that the dirt roads around the hill were graded, paved, maintained and made easily accessible to cars. That, of course, changed everything. The hill became seriously chic and its fabulous views persuaded the well-off to either move in and redo the little cottages or build their own houses. A 1935 newspaper story succinctly explained the shift: 'Bohemians Edged Out'.

Today even with the high rents, zero parking and deluge of tourists, Telegraph Hill is still ardently sought after by San Franciscans of all races, backgrounds and incomes. The Hill is perhaps as close-knit an urban neighbourhood as exists anywhere, but there are spats now and then. In the 1970s, the late socialite Whitney Warren was entertaining Princess Margaret at his villa on Telegraph Hill Boulevard, right below Coit Tower. Warren and the police began parking the cars of the royal entourage in neighbours' tiny driveways, Warren assuring the security people that his neighbours were honoured to have royalty on Telegraph Hill. Warren overlooked his next door neighbour Bill Bailey, retired longshoreman, ex-communist and Spanish Civil War veteran, who occupied one of the Hill's 1906 earthquake cottages (115 Telegraph Hill Blvd). Bailey, the grandson of Irish rebels executed by British soldiers, marched out of his tiny house and ordered the 'parasites of the working man and woman' off his place. Warren was equally adamant that they stay. After a heated exchange, cars were moved and the princess got to have lunch on Telegraph Hill, Bailey having registered his power to the people protest and Warren getting to forge ahead with the social coup of the year.

The easiest, most comfortable way up the hill is to catch the 39 Muni bus at Washington Square. They run every twenty minutes and take passengers to Coit Tower on the top of Telegraph Hill. Dress comfortably for walking and range around the Hill after exploring the tower.

Coit Tower

Top of Telegraph Hill Boulevard (tel. 362 0808). Open daily, 10 a.m.–5 p.m.; $3 admission, $2 for seniors, $1 children, 12 and under.

LILLIE COIT

Lillie Hitchcock Coit (1843–1929) is one of San Francisco's favourite eccentrics. As a child she became obsessed with fires and firemen, attaching herself to the Knickerbocker Hose Company No. 5 as their mascot. She had her own fireman's uniform and distinctive helmet, often dropping everything to swoop down on a fire to cheer on her firemen.

Lillie dressed in men's clothes, smoked, drank bourbon, rode astride and played poker with the boys. It is not clear exactly how she was able to stand convention on its head and remain a beloved local eccentric rather than a pariah, but she managed. Further, Lillie was the only daughter of protective, indulgent Southerners who openly supported the Confederate cause in a Union stronghold. The wealthy Hitchcocks did, however, choose to live in Paris for a good deal of the time when the war raged, avoiding sticky social stituations.

After numerous engagements, some broken because she was forever flying out the door to visit fires, Lillie Hitchcock fell in love and married mining engineer Howard Coit in 1863. The marriage foundered on the interference of Lillie's mother and they informally separated. He died in 1885. There were no children. Lillie continued with her unladylike pursuits and globetrotting ways.

Contemporary lesbians have claimed Lillie as one of their hidden sisters, but many historians aren't so sure. Transvestite seems a better definition. Lillie identified so completely with men that she wanted to be one; more to the point she certainly seems to have had erotic feelings towards them.

Construction When she died in 1929, dividing her fortune among the city of San Francisco, the University of California and the University of Maryland (state of her birth), the city wasn't quite sure what to do with the bequest. Initially, it looked as though the $118,000 would be blended into the overall city budget for parks. Lillie's friends, however, protested and a commission was set up to find an appropriate beautification scheme for the money.

The committee decided on the public park on Telegraph Hill as the site and to put up a monument. It was never clear if the monument was for Lillie Coit or for the firefighters she adored. When the plans for the tower were unveiled many artists and architects were unfavourably shocked – they thought the 210-foot column looked like a firehose nozzle. The designers, architect Arthur Brown Jr and his associate Henry Howard, were offended by the idea and insisted the design had no precedent. It was designed, they insisted, to fit the landscape and the budget.

Coit Tower rose, according to the original plan, during the darkest days of the Depression, providing much needed work for San Franciscans. Constructed of reinforced concrete, the tower was fluted and tapered at the top.

It took most of 1933 to build. By a happy coincidence, the federal government was at this very time setting up agencies to create jobs for unemployed workers in every field. San Francisco artists proposed that local artists be hired to create decorations for the interior of the tower. The timing was inspired, coming at just the moment when a federal project for artists was at the top of the Works Progress Administration agenda. The Coit Tower murals became the first work commissioned by the Public Works of Art Project.

Twenty-six professional artists, including four women, Maxine Albro, Jane Berlandina, Edith Hamlin and Suzanne Scheuer, were hired to execute fresco murals inside the tower's ground and second floors. Nineteen assistants were hired, many of them art students. About a third of the assistants were women. Inspired by the turmoil of the times, Mexican mural master Diego Rivera, social realism and a touching optimism about the human spirit, the artists and their assistants (all working for $38 a week) designed and painted a set of remarkable murals depicting California history, politics, workers, farming, industry, landscape and cultural life.

In another accident of timing, the murals were approaching completion just as the seminal 1934 San Francisco Waterfront Strike was coming to a head. Word went around town that the murals were 'communistic', prompting a showdown between city officials and the artists. Eventually, the tower opened involving the alteration of only one mural; a hammer and sickle and revolutionary slogan were removed. The mural's design counterpoint, a banner reading 'In God We Trust' was also obliterated. No one ever admitted to reworking the mural ('Surveyor and Steelworker,' Clifford Wight), but this dead-of-night compromise defused the crisis and allowed the other 'subversive' artwork to be grudgingly accepted.

The murals underwent a full-scale, first-rate restoration in 1989.

The Visit   The park at the base of the tower makes for quite a nice walkabout. The complete views of the bay are marvellous. If you happen to hit Coit Tower on a monster tourist day you might spend your time studying the views from the ground and forgo the wait for the elevator to the top of the tower.

The murals, however, ought not to be missed. Located on the ground floor and the small second floor of the tower, they are some of the richest, most beautiful public art in America. The Coit Tower murals are frequently cited as a near-perfect expression of public art, created by talented, mature artists, expressing a point of view and deeply rooted in place and time.

There was overall co-ordination of the work, but each artist designed his or her mural. The leftist bias that caused such consternation in the 1930s permeates the murals, though the overall message today reads not revolution but extreme anxiety. In 'City Life' (Victor Arnautoff), found on the first (ground) floor, for instance, downtown San Francisco bustles with activity but there is a dark undertow of turbulence: a car crash in front of the Stock Exchange, a well-dressed man being robbed at gunpoint and a newsstand stocked with leftist papers like the *Daily Worker* and the *New Masses*.

The only non-mural artworks, oil on canvas landscapes of the Bay Area, hang in the central elevator lobby. Even in these, which were painted in artists' studios away from the collective work at the tower, the tone is foreboding and grey, the light seeming to disappear rather than be about to break through the gloomy skies.

Throughout the murals, women are well represented, probably thanks to the leftist point of view. In Suzanne Scheuer's 'Newsgathering', based on the *San Francisco Chronicle* building, two women are prominently shown at work in the newsroom. Women workers are also central in 'Meat Industry' (Ray Bertrand), 'Industries of California' (Ralph Stackpole) while women are shown at vigorous play in 'Collegiate Sports' (Parker Hall).

Jane Berlandina's 'Homelife', on the second floor, is almost out of place among the murals with its mono-chromatic colour scheme and outline drawings. Her scenes of upper middle-class home life with grand pianos, card games and luxurious settings are stylistically and philosophically at odds with the other murals, yet they seem to round out the discourse, with its depiction of a serene American middle class, confidently riding out the bumpy patches.

Leaving the murals behind, take the elevator (the only way) to the tower crown. From the elevator you will walk up a half flight of stairs to a loggia-like open space. In a town saturated with great views, Coit Tower offers the best. The immediacy of the Bay, no windows and 360 degree accessibility make the tower experience one of the best in San Francisco.

There are numerous stairways around Telegraph Hill, legacies from the days when you could only get from here to there on foot. If you're the wanderlust type, you may enjoy just following your nose around the hill. It is a safe, calm neighbourhood and you will stumble across all manner of charming wooden stairs, little cottages and gardens on your own.

Two stairways run downhill from Coit Tower. The Greenwich Steps are to the north of the tower and will take you all the way downhill, through several lovely streets. The Filbert Steps, a bit to the south, are more famous and probably the most beloved stairway in San Francisco, thanks to a remarkable woman named Grace Marchant (see below).

To get to the Filbert Steps, walk downhill from the tower alongside Telegraph Hill Boulevard; when the road bends downhill to the west, take the stairway in the opposite direction. You will descend to Montgomery Street.

Notice the striking Moderne apartment building at 1360 Montgomery. It was built in 1936, one of the first new structures on Telegraph Hill. Architectural historian Gray Brechin has aptly described it as a 'streamlined ark beached on a Telegraph Hill cliffside'. The marvellous exterior embellishments of Commerce, Discovery and California (the female figure over the entrance) were almost an afterthought, added by architect Irvin Goldstine's friend Alfred du Pont after a trip to Bali.

The building was immortalised in the 1947 Lauren Bacall-Humphrey Bogart film, *Dark Passage*. Bacall takes in San Quentin escapee Bogart in one of the great noir tales. The interiors were filmed in Hollywood but were exact replications, down to the illuminated elevator cage.

Continue down the Filbert Steps, crossing Darrell Place and Napier Lane, which are little more than paths. The verdant, well-tended gardens here are a memorial to one woman's contagious generosity. Grace Marchant moved to Telegraph Hill in 1949 when she was 63 and newly retired. She immediately set about cleaning up her new home. At that time, the Filbert Steps were a rickety wooden passageway and the ugly, excavated hillside was used as a dump by residents and construction people. Marchant began rooting out all the junk by dragging it to the side of the cliff and dropping it off. Later she got permission from the city to burn it in a little backyard fire that took three days to demolish all the stuff.

Once she had cleaned up the area, Marchant launched into her real purpose, gardening. She planted simple groundcover at first, then began bringing in grasses, flowers, shrubs and even trees. Her neighbours responded by doing a bit of sprucing up around their own homes, then gradually began to aid Marchant in her unannounced, unheralded one-woman crusade to heal Telegraph Hill. Marchant died in 1982 at the age of 92, busy on her hillside until the end. Neighbours, led by her protégé, Gary Kray, have continued the garden ever since.

In her busy, always cheerful life, Marchant was a Hollywood stuntwoman, a wardrobe mistress for RKO studios and a dockyard worker. A plaque on the Filbert stairs quietly calls attention to her life's greatest work: 'In appreciation of Grace Marchant for unselfish, devoted energy in the beautification of Filbert Gardens'.

A number of the houses on this side of the hill are pre-earthquake. The story goes that many of the Italian families were able to save their hillside homes from the 1906 fires because the area was too inaccessible for the army to send in troops for forced evacuation, as they did in other areas; and families hauled out the household wine vats, using their homemade wine to wet down roofs and soak their rudimentary fire fighting tools like blankets and brooms.

At the bottom of the hill you will see other buildings that escaped the flames, primarily warehouses. Blending in beautifully is Levi's Plaza, a 1982 addition to the landscape and the headquarters for Levi Strauss Corporation. Cross Sansome Street and enter this carefully designed plaza bordered by Union, Greenwich and the Embarcadero.

Levi Strauss is one of the great San Francisco companies. Its basic product, denim jeans, was born during the Gold Rush. Miners complained to Levi Strauss, a German-born pedlar, that their trousers were being shredded by their rough work. Particularly vexing were the way that seams were always ripping. After some experimentation, Strauss began producing overalls made of tough denim and put together with metal rivets originally designed for saddles. 'Levi's' became the Western uniform. Happily, this company that makes such a quintessential American product is a model corporation, regularly topping polls as one of the best workplaces for women, minorities and gays. Levi's is often held up as an example for American business by conservatives and liberals who point out (with different emphasis) that a large, profit-making corporation can make a healthy profit and be socially responsible.

Today, the very social and respected Haas family, Strauss's descendants, run the company. The Haases are deeply involved in community affairs and also own the Oakland A's baseball team.

The Levi's factory and design shop is across town in the Mission. Limited tours are available by calling ahead (tel. 565 9159). Headquarters is not for touring, but to enjoy. The relaxed plaza setting is a public place, available to all. Especially impressive is the landscaping by Lawrence Halprin. The fountain at the centre of the campus, as Levi's calls its offices, is a bubbling, cascading wonder which Halprin designed to invoke a Sierra mountain stream.

RUSSIAN HILL

Nob Hill has always been read as wealth and Telegraph Hill has translated as bohemian. Russian Hill combines both into a reputation as a well-heeled bohemian enclave – home to artists and writers as well as prosperous lawyers, stockbrokers and the merely independently wealthy.

Russian Hill is a name that pre-dates the Gold Rush. Among the sharp series of hillsides north of Nob Hill and west of Columbus Avenue, was the resting place of Russian seal hunters who had the misfortune to die during winter layovers in Yerba Buena.

Russian Hill is a bit of a mystery, even to locals. Unlike Telegraph Hill and Nob Hill, it has no central public place nor shopping areas like exclusive Pacific Heights. In addition, Russian Hill is geographically secluded which means it is not a corridor to anywhere else. To get to Russian Hill, you must intend to go there; there are a number of good reasons to brave the uphill walks and spend time in the neighbourhood where you can visit some interesting literary landmarks, look over the classic architecture and experience Lombard Street, 'the crookedest street in the world', Russian Hill's one bona fide tourist spot.

Russian Hill began to develop when the cable cars came in, making it, like Nob Hill, truly accessible. Russian Hill is still benefiting from the cable cars, having more service than any other city neighbourhood. The Powell-Hyde and Powell-Mason lines run over Russian Hill – a great bonus for visitors, saving walking and parking (which is non-existent, anyway).

Prepare for some serious walking on Russian Hill. The streets are steep but manageable, even if you're not in great shape. Just follow the example of residents who walk steadily but slowly, often taking little breathers on the sharpest climbs. Cafés, shops and public conveniences are thin on the ground here. What there is may be found along the cable route on Hyde Street.

Lombard Street

Between Hyde and Leavenworth streets.

The pleasantest route is to take the Powell-Hyde Street cable car, which you can catch at the Powell Street turnaround or at Aquatic Park, across from the Cannery. Get off at Filbert or Greenwich, two streets south of Lombard. The Hyde-Lombard corner, as you will see, is usually a madhouse. This one block, a one-way zigzag street, was just another San Francisco topographical adaptation in the

1920s when the steep grade was reworked. It was a natural response by a San Francisco mind, where cars and carriages negotiated the straight-up hills the same way, driving from side-to-side in an 'S' pattern to avoid the strain of a straight-ahead assault.

The terrace gardens evolved in the 1940s and are still a communal project for people on the block. Gradually the street itself became an object of curiosity and it is now one of the city's top ten attractions. Tour buses are banned from the squiggle (and most of Russian Hill's steep streets) which adds to the huge number of cars. In fact, visitors have been known to rent cars just so they can drive down Lombard Street. A walk is better because you can actually look at the street, houses and gardens, and pause at the top and bottom to take in the views and the delightful symmetry of it all. Being car-bound is to be on a non-stop conveyor belt. Even when you leave Lombard Street, there's no easy place to park for you and your passengers to get out and walk back to take photos or get another look.

At the top of the hill take notice of the sprawling house at 1100 Lombard St, the last home of Fanny Osbourne Stevenson, the widow and great love of Robert Louis Stevenson (see p. 104). After Stevenson's death in Samoa in 1894, she returned to the Bay Area and commissioned architect Willis Polk to design a house for her, which was built in 1900. During the 1906 fires a group of newspapermen, writers and artists impulsively decided to try and save Mrs Stevenson's house as the fires climbed Russian Hill. Armed with brooms, buckets and burlap bags soaked in water they actually fought off the encroaching fire.

AROUND RUSSIAN HILL

After leaving the Lombard Street squiggle, look for two of Russian Hill's little hidden streets that are the sites of unmarked literary points of interest. Neal and Carolyn Cassady, Jack Kerouac's intimate friends and literary fodder, lived at 29 Russell St (a dead-end street off Hyde, between Union and Green) in the early 1950s. Kerouac lived in the attic room for several months in 1952 working on *Doctor Sax, Visions of Cody* and *On the Road*. Cassady encouraged his wife and best friend to become lovers, creating a lifelong triangle among them. Carolyn Cassady's memoir, *Heartbeat*, is an insightful and thorough examination of the Cassady-Kerouac-Cassady story as well as that rarest of species, a woman's view of the Beat experience.

Macondray Lane is a block away across Hyde Street, off Leavenworth between Union and Green. This magical little pathway is a near-perfect blend of gardens and houses. It is often identified as the model for Barbary Lane, the setting for Armistead Maupin's *Tales of the City*. Though it looks private, it's a public throughway, covering two blocks, ending with the wooden stairway down to Taylor.

800 Chesnut St, tel. 771 7020. Diego Rivera Gallery, open daily 10 a.m.–5 p.m.; Walter/McBean Gallery open Tues–Sat, 10 a.m.–5 p.m. and Thurs, 10 a.m.–8 p.m.; Art Institute Café, open Mon–Thurs 8 a.m.–9 p.m., Fri 8 a.m.–4 p.m., Sat 9 a.m.–2 p.m., shorter hours between terms in May and September.

SFAI is one of the country's leading independent art schools, which had its beginnings as an art association in 1871. Later the club's classes were moved to the Mark Hopkins mansion on Nob Hill as the Mark Hopkins Institute of Art. After the 1906 fires destroyed the mansion, the school sold the lot and commissioned a new building on Russian Hill.

The school was renamed the California School of Fine Arts, then San Francisco Art Institute in the 1950s. The institute was a popular outpost for New York artists who enjoyed 'coming out to the coast' for a term or two of teaching. Mark Rothko and Clyfford Still were very influential teachers in the 1940s. It was around the Art Institute that one of the new significant challenges to the hegemony of Abstract Expressionism developed in the 1950s. A return to figurative work was championed by a loose regional school known as Bay Area Figurative Art. The artists, which included Richard Diebenkorn, Manuel Neri, David Park, Nathan Oliveira and Joan Brown, were almost totally ignored by the make-or-break New York critics. In the late 1980s, the Bay Area Figuratives were rediscovered and major retrospectives mounted on the East and West coasts.

The Art Institute's other well-known students and faculty have included performance artist Karen Finley, photographer Annie Liebovitz, water-colourist Beth Van Hoesen, sculptor David Ireland, painters Maynard Dixon, Ad Reinhardt and Maurice Sterne.

Non-students are welcome at the Art Institute where the two galleries and excellent (and inexpensive) café are popular with artists and local residents. A 1931 Diego Rivera mural dominates the hall used for the student gallery. This homage to American workers was produced during the same visit for Rivera's Pacific Stock Exchange commission (see p. 73).

The Walter/McBean Gallery is an important venue for new artwork, frequently devoted to avant garde conceptual artists.

Ina Coolbrith and Russian Hill Summit

Jones and Vallejo streets.

'You know I have never cared for cities,' Laura Ingalls Wilder wrote to her husband back home on the family farm in Missouri during her 1915 visit to the city, 'but San Francisco is simply the most beautiful thing. Set on the hills as it is with glimpses of the bay here and there and at night with the lights shining up and down the hills and the lights of ships on the water, it is like fairyland.'

Wilder, whose classic *Little House on the Prairie* books would endear her to generations of children, came to California to the world's fair, the Panama Pacific International Exposition, and to visit her only child, newspaper reporter Rose Wilder Lane. Her enchantment with San Francisco was reinforced by living on Russian Hill where Rose and her husband had an apartment in a rambling brown shingle house that had some resemblance to the enchanted cottages of fairytales. Their flat, 1019 Vallejo, is part of a six-level house beginning at No. 1013 and built by architect Willis Polk in 1894 for Doris Williams, an artist and the widow of the founder of the school that became the San Francisco Art Institute.

LITTLE HOUSE ON RUSSIAN HILL

The writer Rose Wilder Lane only lived in San Francisco for nine years (1909–18), but she was the archetype of the adventurous turn-of-the-century young woman who wanted to participate in life outside the domestic sphere, many of whom seem drawn to San Francisco and often ended up as writers. As with Wilder Lane, many of the writers weren't actually very talented, but possessed of tremendous drive and ambition; reporting or fiction writing was often the only possible outlet that could provide income and some patina of respectability.

Wilder Lane, who referred to her brief wifehood as being a 'parasite' and seemed not to miss having children, continued to use her unlamented husband's name all of her life. It was a common custom among divorced, widowed, even never married reporters and writers, who found it useful to be perceived as matrons rather than available women. One of the sneering epithets for early women journalists by their male colleagues was 'the three-name ladies'.

Fremont Older, a classic cigar-smoking, hard driving newspaper editor, was impressed with Wilder Lane's unquenchable curiosity and boundless energy. Older made her a star writer on the *Bulletin* (later merged with the *Call* and both folded into the *Examiner* in the 1950s), setting her to writing multi-part series about Charlie Chaplin, Henry Ford and barnstorming pilots.

In San Francisco Wilder Lane was an enthusiastic participant in the gently bohemian life that swirled around her on Russian Hill. Unlike Ina Coolbrith (see p. 130) (whom she doesn't seem to have ever met), Rose Wilder Lane was able to leave San Francisco for the bigger world, travelling widely in Europe and even living in Albania for a year. Her books about faraway places and novels of independent young women were big sellers in the twenties and thirties. Her mother, Laura Ingalls Wilder, didn't begin to write until she was sixty, setting down the lovely stories of her pioneer childhood.

Wilder Lane produced little after she was sixty, despite a vigorous old age, slipping deeper into the Ayn Rand philosophy of rugged individualism. A woman who had broken barriers through sheer force of will, she saw no reason others couldn't take charge of their lives as well. During World War II, living at her country house in Connecticut and raising her own food, Wilder Lane refused to accept a food ration card. At age 79 she was offered an assignment to Vietnam by a woman's magazine. Wilder Lane was undecided about taking it until the State Department tried to block her credentials because of her age. Like an old fire horse responding to the bell, she stubbornly demanded, and got, press credentials for Vietnam, flew to Indochina and filed a long report.

Towards the end of her life she adopted a Virginia attorney, Roger McBride as her 'grandson'. He was made executor of her work and that of her mother. In the 1970s McBride, also an exponent of rugged individualism, ran for the US presidency under the aegis of the tiny Libertarian Party.

The Polk-Williams house (Polk and his family lived in one of the apartments) is a marvellous example of the indigenous architecture that evolved in the Bay Area in the 1890s – a melding of Arts and Crafts Movement ideas with native materials and sensitivity to the local landscape. Polk was a master of what came to be called the Bay Region Tradition, which architectural historian Sally Woodbridge has defined as, 'woodsy, informal, anti-urban'.

The Polk-Williams house is at the centre of what is now called the Vallejo Street Crest District, a preservation area on the National Register of Historic Places. Enter through an archway at the top of Jones Street. Vallejo Street turns into stairways at this point to cope with the steep grade. It becomes a street again a block and half downhill at Mason. On top of the hill the centre lot was originally kept as an open space for a carriage turnaround, but is now a garden, maintained by people on the crest.

Take the stairs down to Taylor Street noticing the Mediterranean villa at 1001 Vallejo. This was the home of Paul Verdier, scion of the French family that ran the fabled City of Paris department store, until the 1930s when he leased it to Sally Stanford, perhaps San Francisco's most famous madam. Reproached by friends for allowing that woman to move into the family home, Verdier was unmoved. 'I do not care what she does there,' he sniffed, 'only that she pays the rent, which is considerable'.

At Taylor and Vallejo in lieu of the street is a small park, mostly vertical but adequate for contemplation, a brown bag lunch or tai chi. Ina Coolbrith Park is dedicated to California's first poet laureate, a beautiful, mysterious woman who came to San Francisco in 1862. Coolbrith (1841–1928) lived in Russian Hill at 1604 Taylor St, which burned in the 1906 fires, destroying a lifetime of letters, journals, manuscripts and Californiana.

Coolbrith's poetry faded quickly ('Lo! I have waited long!/How longer yet must my strung harp be dumb,/Ere its great master come/'), but her life is still well known. Coolbrith, darkly beautiful, clever and seemingly light-hearted, worked with Bret Harte, Mark Twain and Charles Stoddard on *The Overland Monthly*, a seminal

Western literary magazine. Surrounded by attractive men, Coolbrith was never actually romantically linked with any of them, although rumours were rife, including one that had Twain and Harte coming to blows over her, although Harte was married with children.

With Harte and Stoddard, Coolbrith was called 'the Golden Gate Trinity' and part of a boisterous crowd who enjoyed teasing each other with mild limericks and long evenings of banter. Gradually this first San Francisco literary set unravelled, with almost everyone departing for Europe except Coolbrith. She dreamed of going to Europe, but found herself with three children to raise: her widowed sister's two children, plus poet Joaquin Miller's half-Indian daughter, Cali-Shasta (simply deposited on Coolbrith's doorstep when Miller took off for England). In addition, Coolbrith's now widowed mother, in failing health, came to live with her.

By all accounts the disappointed poet simply buried her aspirations for a bigger world, put on a cheerful face and carried her load. To support her instant family, she continued to write for publication and acquired a demanding job as librarian for the public library in Oakland where she was popular and respected. At the height of their careers, both Jack London and Isadora Duncan paid emotional tribute to Coolbrith for encouraging and sustaining them as children hungry for knowledge and ideas.

Coolbrith was unceremoniously fired from the library in 1892 after she confirmed to an *Oakland Tribune* reporter that yes, the neglected old library building was unsafe. The loss of the job was a financial disaster for Coolbrith but allowed her to move home to San Francisco and Russian Hill, which she celebrated in poetry as her 'Hill of desire and dream'.

Coolbrith's old friends came to her rescue appointing her librarian of the all-male Bohemian Club. Originally a genuine gathering of bohemians, the club has become the preserve of the rich and established, the authentic writers, artists and poets retained for their entertainment value. Coolbrith was one of the handful of women to be made an honorary member, a tradition that ended early this century.

Friends and admirers orchestrated another 'job' for Coolbrith, poet laureate of California, which carried a small yearly stipend and enormous prestige. Crippled with arthritis, she built a new house after the fire, using funds that were raised for her all over the state. She continued to write, encourage young artists and hold a veil over her emotional life.

Coolbrith's tangled life story only surfaced after her death in 1928. She had been born in the Midwest to a younger brother of Joseph Smith, the mystic founder of the Mormon Church, where she was Josephine Donna Smith. Her father died when she was a child and her mother, alarmed at the growing cult of polygamy within the Church, remarried, renouncing Mormonism and swore her daughter to secrecy over their Smith heritage.

The new family moved west, eventually crossing the Sierra Nevada mountains into California. Young Ina, as she was called, and her family, were in danger of dying in the mountains when legendary mountain guide Jim Beckwourth came across their exhausted wagon train. A free black man, Beckwourth took pity on the confused settlers and led them through what is now known as Beckwourth Pass. Ten-year-old Ina, riding with the scout, was said to be the first white child to cross into California through the Sierra Nevada. Although she was often enigmatic about the specifics of her childhood, Coolbrith liked to tell this story, adding that at the summit Beckwourth paused and gestured ahead.

'There little girl,' he said to her, 'there is California. There is your kingdom.'

Ina's new family eventually settled in the small town of Los Angeles where she became one of the town's most popular belles. At seventeen Ina married a dashing young business-actor named Robert Carsley, who turned out to be psychotically jealous. Their one son died in childhood and by age twenty Ina was childless, divorced and locally famous because her sensational divorce case had been avidly followed by the public. Ina's stepfather had at one point been forced to defend her against Carsley's rages by shooting him in the hand, which was amputated.

The next year Ina moved to San Francisco with her younger sister's new family and constructed a new persona named Miss Ina Donna Coolbrith, using her nickname, birth name and her mother's maiden name. Here, as Beckwourth had prophesied, she found a kingdom.

FISHERMAN'S WHARF

Fisherman's Wharf ranks only behind Disneyland as the biggest tourist attraction in California, drawing 10.5 million visitors to Disneyland's 13 million. And both are Nos. 2 and 3 in the world (not just the US), outdistanced only by Florida's Walt Disney World and its 25.1 million annual attendance.

San Franciscans, however, turn up their nose at the ever-popular Fisherman's Wharf with a dismissive snort. 'Only tourists go there,' they say.

Tourists and their own children, that is. Fisherman's Wharf was named by Bay Area kids as their No. 1 favourite place in the city, far out-polling Golden Gate Park, shopping malls and even home. Like these junior San Franciscans, if you know what you want, you will be a very pleased visitor to Fisherman's Wharf and its honky-tonky offerings. If, on the other hand, you have looked at flashy brochures that promise an old world harbourside and romantic sunsets starring the Golden Gate you are in for a bit of a jolt.

Fisherman's Wharf is a highly developed tourist ghetto, groaning with T-shirt shops, candy stores, bad restaurants with fabulous waterfront views, souvenir shops, garish entertainments, street performers and even a few surprises. This is the fast-buck strip found in every city with a significant tourist population.

Whatever you may think of Fisherman's Wharf for yourself, it never fails to delight and thrill children and teenagers. If your children are on museum-historic site-California cuisine overload, they can be easily restored to happy campers with a half day at Pier 39, the Wax Museum and watching the street performers.

Fisherman's Wharf has always drawn an audience. Even in the days when it was a serious, working fish wharf, San Franciscans enjoyed coming down to the waterfront on weekends to promenade and chat with the Italian fishermen mending nets and swapping stories. On weekdays housewives came to the wharf by auto and cable car to buy their fish fresh off the boats. The little waterfront cafés that served the boat crews and dockworkers began to expand and draw customers who came for the fresh seafood.

The fishing business declined after World War II, as the effects of pollution and unrestricted fishing cut into the profit margin. Fisherman's Wharf remained home to many of the Italian families who shifted their focus from fishing to food brokerages and waterfront restaurants.

One of the most famous restaurants was DiMaggio's (closed in the 1970s), a venture of the great baseball star, Joe DiMaggio, and his brothers.

Joe DiMaggio was not at all fond of the fisherman's life, finding it gruelling, dirty and endlessly repetitive. In his autobiography he recalled, not entirely happily, that, 'my earliest recollection was of the smell of fish at Fisherman's Wharf'. Two of the other DiMaggio boys, Vince and Dominic, also played professional baseball but neither achieved the godlike status of Joe, 'the Yankee Clipper'.

In 1954 Joe DiMaggio married Marilyn Monroe in the San Francisco City Hall, a match made in god and goddess heaven. Their official home was San Francisco where Joe bought a house in the Marina, near the Wharf. He was retired from baseball and Marilyn was often seen around the neighbourhood, shopping like the other wives. The DiMaggios separated after nine months of marriage. Some wags say the split happened the day that Marilyn returned from Korea, where she had entertained the peacekeeping troops as part of a USO tour.

'Oooooh Joe, you never heard anything like it!' she reportedly cooed to her husband, 'Ten thousand men, all screaming for ME!'

'Oh yes I have,' he told her with a sigh.

Joe, then in his late thirties, wanted peace, quiet and a nice Marina wife and lots of babies. Marilyn, in her twenties and just hitting her stride, wanted 10,000 men screaming for her. Despite their divorce, the courtly DiMaggio continued to look out for Monroe the rest of her life, even making the funeral arrangements after her death in 1962. DiMaggio still has a house in the Marina and is sometimes seen around town.

If you are here for the kids, the best place to start is Pier 39. If you are here to shop, take yourself to the Cannery and/or Ghiradelli (pronounced GEAR-ah-delly) Square. If you are here to eat the best deal is the take-away seafood cups that you buy from sidewalk vendors. The fish, shrimp and crab are freshly cooked and reasonably priced. At any of the waterfront eateries you will get indifferent seafood, hit-or-miss service and a big bill. The city's best seafood restaurants are nowhere near the Wharf.

If you absolutely, positively have to have a meal with linen napkins seated beside a window with a sweeping view of the bay, try McCormick & Kuleto's in Ghiradelli Square which is not cheap, but does have good service and fairly reliable food.

Pier 39

The Embarcadero (foot of Powell Street). Open daily, 10.30 a.m.–8.30 p.m., usually later in the summer; restaurants are open until 11 p.m.

Built in 1977, Pier 39 is an attempt to provide something for everyone, even snobs. The restrained grey nautical design for the two-level, hundred-shop complex is meant to be a non-verbal assurance that this is a nice place, not part of the tacky Fisherman's Wharf hucksterism.

Though predictable and totally commercial, it is quite pleasant. The T-shirt shops, for instance, have not been allowed to run amuck. Food, however, is everywhere, from fudge to pasta to sausages to a fresh fruit market. The Eagle Café on the second level is well worth stopping by. This was a genuine waterfront hangout, first opened in 1928 and originally located across the street. The café was on the wipe-out list for the Pier 39 construction site, but a local outcry not only saved it, the preservationists came up with the bright idea of integrating the Eagle into the new complex. Accordingly, a crane hoisted the old café aloft to its present site. Some of the old waterfront folk still come here and its colourfulness quotient is increased by the street performers who hang out here between shows.

Among the Pier 39 shops there is a decided slant towards kids and teens with stores devoted to kites, puppets, teddy bears, posters, sweatshirts and the sort of over-done jewellery so dear to the hearts of teenage girls.

A colourful carousel is the centrepiece downstairs and older children will love the Namco Cyber Station with its dozens of video games.

'The San Francisco Experience' on the upper level is a multimedia tour of the city, using video, props, music and even a special shaking effect that allows the audience to 'feel' an earthquake. The half-hour show is a painless introduction to the city which employs historical clichés as entertainment.

Street performers, who can be found all around the wharf area, have their own stage at Pier 39. Jugglers, clowns, acrobats and jokesters perform almost every day on a very flexible, unplanned schedule. The performers' pay comes in the form of passing the hat after their act.

Pier 39 is a useful spot for taking care of business. The complex is well-stocked with clean restrooms, benches, telephones and has a Thomas Cook exchange office on site.

Sealions   California sealions are big, slick looking mammals that many people mistakenly call seals. They can be glimpsed here and there on the coast or seen close up on the K-Dock adjacent to Pier 39. The sealions, who suddenly began gathering at Fisherman's Wharf for no known reason in 1990, have become the waterfront's favourite show.

'They stink, they snore, they slobber. And they're adorable,' said *Newsweek* magazine trying to explain how San Francisco had gone ga-ga over the big guys. Weighing up to a thousand pounds, clownish on land and balletic in the water, the sealions are simply great fun to watch. They lumber up on the floating docks with loud honks, push their smaller brothers out of the way, engage in farcical battles and generally provide an ongoing comedy worthy of Laurel and Hardy.

To the consternation of some Fisherman's Wharf businesspeople, there doesn't seem to be any way to actually make money from this wacky show. The Marine Mammal Center has wisely provided guides who talk to anyone interested about the sealions while unobtrusively slipping in messages about the centre's worthy volunteer efforts to rescue and protect sea animals.

The sealions migrate up and down the Pacific Coast so it's not a sure thing when they're at Fisherman's Wharf and when they move on. To find out if they are in residence or where to see other sealions, call the Marine Mammal Center, 289 7325.

Walking west from Pier 39, you enter the heavy metal entertainment zone. Note, however, Piers 41 and 43 1/2 where you catch sightseeing ferries and boats to Sausalito (see p. 236), Angel Island and Alcatraz.

Berthed alongside Pier 43 is a World War II vintage submarine, the USS *Pampanito*, restored and maintained by the National Maritime Museum at Aquatic Park. It's an interesting time capsule (and it is a capsule) to tour, but you might have second thoughts if you are prone to claustrophobia. The *Pampanito* is open daily, 9 a.m. to 9 p.m., admission $1–$5.

The so-called museums that are clustered on Jefferson Street are cheerful frauds that showcase the freakish and grotesque. The Guinness Museum of World Records, 235 Jefferson, is probably the least offensive, with its models of the world's tallest man and so on. Ripley's Believe Or Not Museum, 175 Jefferson, is incredibly patronising to the people of the world in these sensitive times. The Wax Museum, 145 Jefferson, is a daffy mix of the nearly forgotten (Boy George), religious tableaux ('The Last Supper') and a predictable sampling of world leaders and celebrities. Under the same roof is the Haunted Gold Mine, a maze with holograms and the futuristic Lazermaze. (See under children's listings for details.) A word of warning about another putative museum at 145 Jefferson, the Medieval Dungeon which shows more than forty ancient torture techniques being performed in graphic detail on life-size wax models (discards from the wax museum, one supposes). It is difficult to imagine who could find this gruesome display interesting aside from mass murderers and drooling sadists. This repulsive showcase is guaranteed to provide children with nightmares.

The Boudin Sourdough French Bread Bakery, 156 Jefferson St, offers a window on one of San Francisco's culinary traditions, sourdough bread. The bread is baked at the shop and you can watch the baker at work through an outside window from 4 a.m. to about 1.30 p.m. There's a take-out café here with pleasant outside tables and chairs.

The Boudin Bakery has been around since 1853, capitalising on the SF mania for good bread. Sourdough is a crusty white bread that is made from a starter that is fermented without yeast. It has its murky origins in the Gold Rush when the mining camps learned about 'French bread' from the Mexican miners who showed their brethren how to make a sourdough leaven from flour and water, or milk or wine, letting it sour, then using it in breadmaking. Miners always kept a little bit of the sourdough with them, calling it 'mother'. The miners and their 'mothers' who headed to Alaska for the Klondike gold strike of the 1890s were called sourdoughs.

San Franciscans take it as an article of faith that the sourdough
bread made here is superior to any made anywhere else, owing to
the particular composition of the Bay Area's fog-dense air which
gives the dough a special chemical zap. Scientists say this is all non-
sense, but the city remains convinced. Try the sourdough and decide
for yourself.

FISHERMAN'S WHARF SHOPPING CENTRES

San Francisco pioneered the outdoor festival market-place trend
with Ghiradelli Square, the red brick complex at Beach and Larkin
streets. The old chocolate factory was abandoned by the Ghiradelli
company in 1962 and its future was bleak until the civic-minded
Lurline Matson Roth and her son, William, heirs to the Matson
shipping fortune, bought it. After a $10 million renovation,
Ghiradelli Square opened as an innovative shopping and restaurant
complex in 1964.

The reclaimed factory has not only been a success in itself, but
blazed a new path for American preservation, showing a lively alternative to the 'Williamsburg-sation' of old buildings. Instead of placing outmoded structures in historic deep freeze, Ghiradelli Square
demonstrated how they could be retooled for contemporary use
without sacrificing the building's integrity and historic interest.

The core of Ghiradelli Square dates back to the early 1860s
when it was built as a woollen factory to supply uniforms to Union
troops during the Civil War. In 1893 the Ghiradelli family bought
the factory and began expanding it for their chocolate manufacturing business. The last building added was the landmark Gothic
clocktower in 1916, inspired by the Chateau Blois in France.

Ghiradelli chocolate was another Gold Rush business. Italian-
born Domingo Ghiradelli came to California from his adopted
home in Peru to make his fortune in the gold fields, but soon
returned to his chocolate-making trade. The business flourished and
is still controlled by the Ghiradelli heirs. In the early 1960s the
Ghiradellis moved their operations to the East Bay, where
Ghiradelli chocolate is now produced. The company isn't involved
with the square's management, but the Ghiradelli Chocolate
Manufactory, an old-fashioned candy shop and ice cream parlour
on the ground floor, is one of the complex's most popular stops.

The Roths and their architects retained the separate, distinctive
buildings of the old factory, as well as the distinctive Ghiradelli
neon sign. The central plaza where workers used to take their
breaks is now home to a pretty fountain of mermaids by Ruth
Asawa and a space for street performers.

Ghiradelli offers more than seventy shops, with a heavy list
towards clothing, jewellery and accessories.

Nearby at Jefferson and Leavenworth is the Cannery, another

successful factory makeover. Built in 1906 to can Del Monte peaches, the brick building was reopened in 1968 as the Cannery with the familiar mix of boutiques, shops, restaurants and free entertainment.

The Museum of the City of San Francisco is on the third level of the Cannery, an interesting little exhibition space staffed by volunteers who are well-versed in San Francisco lore. There are changing exhibitions, but artefacts and souvenirs from the 1906 earthquake and fire are a speciality here. The museum is free (tel. 928 0289), open Wed–Sun, 11 a.m.–4 p.m.

Next to the Cannery on Jefferson, between Jones and Leavenworth, is the Anchorage, yet another multi-level shopping centre. The Anchorage is of newer vintage, built to blend in with the tone set by the Cannery and Ghiradelli Square. Free entertainment in the courtyard is a staple here, too.

Another kind of shopping landmark is close at hand from Fisherman's Wharf. As Ghiradelli Square is the archetype of festival shopping centres, Cost Plus is the mother ship of the now familiar kind of store that sells colourful, budget import items from a no-frills warehouse showroom. Cost Plus has become a small chain, but the first store (see p. 357) is a short walk from the wharf at 2552 Taylor St, at North Point Street. Cost Plus is where every person in the Bay Area buys dishes, glasses, flatware, table-cloths, folding chairs and area rugs for that first apartment or dormitory room. The stores stock housewares, linens, furniture, clothes, baskets, tea, coffee, candy and tons of other items from all over the world.

The prices are good but hardly the breathtaking bargains that are promised. You can find a good selection of items stamped with 'San Francisco' for souvenirs, ranging from T-shirts to teas.

San Francisco National Maritime Museum and Hyde Street Pier Aquatic Park

Museum (Polk and Beach streets), tel. 556 3002. Open daily, 10 a.m.–5 p.m. Free. Hyde Street Pier is at the foot of Hyde Street. Open daily, 9.30 a.m.–5 p.m., $1–$3, admission is free the first Tuesday of every month. Both are located in Aquatic Park, along the waterfront, Hyde Street to Van Ness Avenue.

The Maritime Museum's wonderful Streamline Moderne building (1939) was an ill-fated Works Progress Administration project to turn Aquatic Park into a beach. The casino, dreamed up as 'a palace for the public', was conceived with every amenity possible. Oddly, none of the planners appeared to have considered the San Francisco setting, with the icy water of the bay, the damp sand and the daily visitation of fog, particularly in summer. The beach casino idea was an expensive flop, but happily the building was ideal for a maritime museum.

Karl Kortum, a man in love with the idea of the sea and its heritage, led several campaigns that resulted in the opening of the museum in the old casino in 1951, and the restoration of historic ships, all tied together in a waterfront park. The museum and park, now part of the US National Park Service, is a fitting and engaging homage to San Francisco's waterfront.

Some of the museum exhibitions are perhaps over-detailed for the non-expert, but they give proper weight to the importance of their subjects. Using photographs, maps, models and even parts of ships and boats, the museum's two floors trace the history and culture of maritime life in San Francisco, examining the Gold Rush frenzy, the whaling industry, the military's long history with San Francisco Bay, fishing, pleasure boats, waterfront unions and maritime technology.

San Francisco's personality and fortunes have been inextricably tied up with its port. Even today, when Oakland has replaced San Francisco as the primary shipping point on San Francisco Bay, the city's No. 1 industry, tourism, is heavily tied to the water which gives San Francisco the physical beauty that visitors fall in love with.

During March the museum presents a lively series of programmes about sea-going women to mark Women's History Month. Wives of captains often sailed aboard whaling ships; a surprising number of women also went to sea as cooks on coastal ships. The Maritime Museum has been diligent in uncovering the forgotten history of women and the sea.

The ideas and history outlined in the museum can be fully understood through visiting the fleet of historic ships anchored on the Hyde Street Pier. The six boats paint a clear picture of the commerce and life on the bay. Newly restored is the *Alma*, an 1891 scow schooner. It is the last known survivor of what was once hundreds of these little flat-bottomed ships, busily moving loads of hay, lumber, bricks and grain between the small towns around the bay and San Francisco.

The star of the pier is the gorgeous *Balclutha*, one of the last square-rigged sailing ships that came around Cape Horn. Launched from Scotland in 1886, it is typical of the graceful sailing ships that once filled San Francisco's wharves. The *C.A. Thayer* (1895) is representative of the coastal ships that carried lumber and fish between Alaska and the Northwest coast and California. The *Eppleton Hall* (1914) is one of the paddle tugs that towed ocean-going ships in and out of San Francisco Bay. The *Eureka* (1890) was one of the bay's once huge fleet of commuter ferries. During its heyday, from

1922 to 1941, the *Eureka* could carry as many as 2300 passengers and 120 automobiles at one time. The *Hercules* (1907) is an ocean-going tug boat that came to San Francisco from the East Coast, braving Cape Horn. During the first part of this century the *Hercules* herded logs down the Pacific coast to factories and towed ships out of the bay to the ocean.

The ships are marvellous floating museums. Children love them, being allowed to roam the decks, go below and touch almost everything, a vast improvement in most kids' minds to the average museum environment.

Aquatic Park is a fairly well-maintained green space. It has developed into a weekend jam spot for musicians who show up with an amazing variety of drums for spontaneous sessions. The high-energy rhythm makes for a good soundtrack to the waterfront visit.

On the Water

It is an easy matter to get off land and on to the bay. Sightseeing boats are available almost hourly from the Blue & Gold Fleet, tel. 705 5444, or the Red & White, tel. 546 2628, both headquartered right outside Pier 39.

Dinner cruises on the bay are a popular entertainment, favoured by couples for anniversaries and birthdays or booked by groups of friends for other special events. The ferry lines run dinner cruises during the summer months. But Hornblower Yachts is the biggest company in the field, scheduling moonlight trips all year long. Hornblower's cruises include evening dinner-dances, Sunday brunches (good for children), luncheon tours and a steady schedule of theme parties, such as a solve-it-yourself murder mystery onboard, $30–$65. Call 394 8900.

A dozen boats berthed at Fisherman's Wharf are available for fishing charters, taking out 15 to 25 passengers to fish for salmon, sturgeon, shark, bass or halibut. Passage is about $45; boats may also be rented for solo trips, which is rather expensive. Jacky Douglas, one of the very few women captains, is the fleet coordinator for fishing, tel. 586 9800.

For something a little more adventurous the Oceanic Society takes out day trips to the Farallon Islands, thirty miles out in the Pacific. Passengers (who must be at least ten years old) get close-up looks at whales, dolphins, porpoises, sea turtles and birds. Tickets are $50–$60 each, tel. 474 3385.

If you are visiting during the winter, ask the Oceanic Society about whale watching trips, which take observers out to ride along with migrating whales. Dates vary, but the whales are on the move to Mexico between November and February.

Accessible only by Red & White ferry, tel. 546 2700. Open daily; frequent departures from Pier 41, $4.25–$8.75, children under 5 free.

Windswept, grey and melancholy, Alcatraz Island sits in the middle of sparkling San Francisco Bay like a dour relative at a festive family wedding. Small (22 acres), arid and rocky, Alcatraz is geologically different from the other bay islands, Angel and Yerba Buena, which are lush with plant and animal life. It would seem that nature, rather than the US government, had pre-ordained Alcatraz to be a place of misery.

The island is most famous for its years as the federal government's toughest prison (1934–63) populated by the likes of George 'Machine Gun' Kelly, Al Capone and Robert Stroud, the 'Birdman of Alcatraz', but it was a prison long before that. The army began keeping prisoners on Alcatraz in 1861. A lighthouse had been built in 1853, the first on the West Coast, and the military put a garrison there about the same time.

For all of those men, soldiers, guards, lighthouse keepers and prisoners, life on the cold, damp, foggy island was rather similar – isolated and grim. There was no water supply, no plant life and no animal life, only the pelicans and cormorants that inspired its Spanish name, *Isla de los Alcatraces* (Island of the Pelicans) that was eventually corrupted into Alcatraz. Water and topsoil were both imported from the mainland and a bit of vegetation took root.

As a federal prison, Alcatraz was an end-of-the-line place, reserved not for the most dangerous criminals but for the most intractable. Troublemakers, men with discipline problems and incorrigibles were sent to Alcatraz where they were placed in single cells, forbidden to talk, fed rich, heavy food and allowed very little mail, reading matter or visiting privileges. The prison was heavily staffed and the inmate population kept small, ensuring a stifling regimented life. A small community of guards and their families also lived on the island, with the children commuting to school in San Francisco by boat.

Visiting the island is a powerful experience. Its caretakers, the National Park Service, have carefully avoided trivialising or sensationalising the island. Ranger-led tours emphasise the rigid, soul-killing nature of prison life without making heroes of the prisoners.

The island is something of a ruin, intentionally left that way. When the federal government closed Alcatraz prison in 1963 as too expensive, eager visitors swarmed over the island. From 1969 to 1971 a group of American Indians occupied it in a much publicised reclamation of native lands, but they were unable to patrol and/or control the behaviour of everyone who came ashore. This led to a serious amount of vandalism, including the burning of the warden's house. What you will see, oddly enough, is a somewhat restored Alcatraz courtesy of Clint Eastwood. His 1979 film, *Escape from Alcatraz*, was filmed on the island in a deal that involved the movie company paying its rent through restoring the prison complex to its 1963 pre-vandalism condition. Eastwood's documentary-style film detailed the one perhaps successful escape from Alcatraz by three inmates in 1962 (they were never found and presumed drowned).

In the last few years birds have begun returning to Alcatraz for nesting and the Park Service has recently added nature tours to the cellblock visits. Birdwatchers find the island a rich resource and often come in groups, equipped with binoculars and bird-spotting books.

Angel Island

A state park accessible by private boat or ferries, tel. 435 1915; Red & White ferry service from SF's Pier 43, tel. 546 2896; daily during the summer, weekends only during the winter, $4–$7, the state park ferry, tel. 435 2131, runs from Tiburon every day on the hour during the summer; winter service is on a more limited basis, $3–$5.

No one ever mistakes Angel Island for Alcatraz. Called 'the Rock', Alcatraz is literally a rock outcropping in the middle of the bay. Angel Island, in contrast, seems to float just off the Marin shore like a green Neverland, sometimes lost in a dreamy white mist. If Alcatraz is known all over the world, Angel Island is a Bay Area secret that the hikers, bikers, picnickers and sun worshippers who frequent the island aren't necessarily eager to share.

Angel Island is a state park, accessible only by boat and uninhabited by cars, except for a few official maintenance vehicles. Walking and biking paths criss-cross the island which also has a grassy picnic area with tables, benches, barbecue pits and clean restrooms. Private sailboats and motorboats anchor in the cove, while ferries put-put to and fro all day long. The island is only one square mile in all, and can be easily circumnavigated in an hour via the trail near the top.

Deep within the island there's another story besides the view. Once called the Ellis Island of the West, Angel Island was the immigration entry point for Asians from 1910 to 1940. The immigration station was actually the enforcement arm for the Chinese Exclusion Act, putting all Chinese travellers through a rigorous and usually insensitive examination. Even other Asians were processed fairly quickly and painlessly. Europeans and other non-native whites entered the country almost without question.

In 1970, a park ranger named Alexander Weiss noticed Chinese characters inscribed on the walls of one of the old immigration buildings slated for demolition. He contacted Dr George Araki of San Francisco State University who was immediately intrigued about the writings. Araki saw to it that they were documented and translated. The writings, most of them unsigned and undated, give voice to the anxieties and sense of persecution that the immigrants experienced in their Angel Island limbo.

America has a power, but not justice.
In prison, we were victimised as if we were guilty.
Given no opportunity to explain, it was really brutal.
I bow my head in reflection but there is nothing I can do.

More than 130 poems have survived and been recorded, each in classical Chinese style, of four to eight lines with a fixed number of characters per line. All of the known poems are by men, having been written in the men's barracks. The women's quarters were in the Angel Island administration building which burned in 1940. Women who were interned there recall seeing poems but unfortunately, none seem to have been copied down before the fire.

The writings can be seen in the men's barracks building in China Cove. The poems were collected into a book, *Island* (University of Washington Press, 1980) by Him Mark Lai, Genny Lim and Judy Yung, descendants of Angel Island immigrants.

Angel Island is for day trippers only. A very well-kept secret is the handful of overnight camping sites on the island, but they are available only through making a reservation – difficult to come by. Otherwise all visitors must be off the island before sundown.

THE MARINA

When you hear the term the Marina, it most likely doesn't mean actual waterfront berths of the yachts and private boats tied up near the St Francis Yacht Club along Marina Boulevard. To San Franciscans, the Marina means the luxuriant park that parallels the waterfront and the expensive neighbourhood behind that.

The Marina is a twentieth-century addition to San Francisco. Much of the area is landfill, a fact that became painfully clear during the 1989 earthquake when buildings simply crumbled during the big shake. That's all been rebuilt now, with houses and apartment buildings getting over and above the foundation reinforcements demanded by the tough California earthquake retrofitting laws. At the same time, the Marina has quickly regained its popularity as a desirable address and a favoured place for recreation.

The Marina Green is a flat, safe park popular with skaters, runners, walkers, kite flyers and sedentary types who like to sit in the sun and watch the bay.

Fort Mason, a former army base, shares the waterfront and

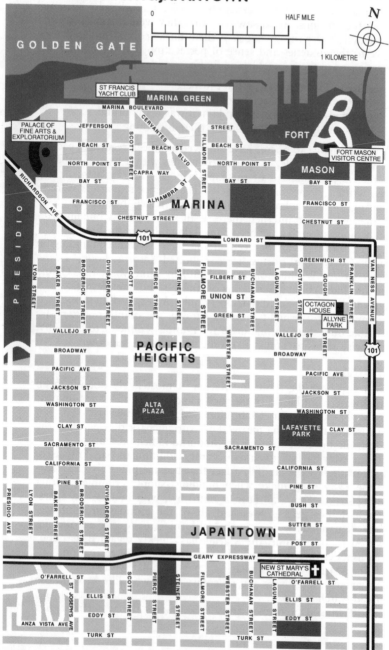

makes splendid use of it. Now an arts and culture complex, Fort Mason was in heavy use from 1910 to 1963 as an embarkation point for troops headed for the Pacific. The area was first called Black Point for the mass of dark green laurel trees that covered the bluff above the water. This promontory and natural landing have been used by the military for various purposes since the time of the Spanish.

Today you can visit museums, attend the theatre, take art and yoga classes, go to poetry readings and dine on world-class vegetarian fare at Fort Mason. It's a cultural nerve centre for the city owing to the diversity of groups and organisations that call the complex home. The one-time barracks and officers' quarters above the fort continue to house some military personnel, but is also headquarters for the park district, the Golden Gate National Recreation Area, which includes everything from Alcatraz and Aquatic Park to Point Reyes in Marin County.

Leaving the waterfront, the Marina is a safe and attractive neighbourhood to explore. Along Chesnut Street lies a café and shopping area, while Lombard is full of rather sweet old-fashioned motels. When the Golden Gate Bridge was completed, Lombard Street became the prime artery on and off the bridge.

Across Divisadero Street, the dividing line for western San Francisco, the Palace of Fine Arts sits in all its splendour, the lone remnant of the 1915 Panama Pacific International Exhibition. Staged to announce San Francisco's full return from the earthquake and fires, the PPIE is the mother of the Marina. The marshlands were filled in to give San Francisco a bayside arena for the fair. After it was over, a residential neighbourhood began to take shape on the landfill.

Fort Mason

You can walk to Fort Mason from Fisherman's Wharf and Aquatic Park, or you can arrive by bus (Muni buses 22, 28 or 30) or car as most people do at the gate on Marina Boulevard and Laguna Street.

Coming along the bayfront from Aquatic Park or along Bay Street a bit inland, consider turning into the residential section of Fort Mason, once the preserve of officers and their families. Black Point Battery, a Civil War era fortification, is still in place over the water and many of the pre-1906 houses are in use today. One of the first houses built here, but no longer standing, was put up by Col. John Frémont for his wife Jessie (see p. 79). The Brooks, Haskell and Palmer houses are from that same period. Across the road from these Greek revival houses is a wildly popular hostel, the San Francisco International Youth Hostel (see p. 286), fashioned from a Civil War era barracks compound.

Also at the 'upper fort', notice the community gardens that date from the time when military families lived here. The post wives first began to try to soften the windswept hill in the 1860s, with gardens which have survived to this day.

The Great Meadow, which begins the slope downwards to the waterfront fort, is greatly prized by Marina residents for running, walking and watching the bay. Every September, however, it becomes the home of blues fanatics who gather for the San Francisco Blues Festival, one of the last mellow, low-key outdoor music gatherings.

Fort Mason Center, entry at Marina and Laguna.

Greens Restaurant & Tassajara Bakery

Begun as a project of the San Francisco Zen Center, Greens has transcended genres (it is a completely vegetarian restaurant) to rank as one of San Francisco's top restaurants. The dining room has a lovely bay view to go with the elegant food. Tassajara, the Zen Center bakery, has a take-out counter in the lobby. Open Tues–Sat 11.30 a.m.–9.30 p.m., Sun 10 a.m.–2 p.m., Building A, tel. 771 6222.

Magic Theater

Established in the late sixties to showcase new plays and new playwrights, the Magic was the West Coast home of Sam Shepard for many years, but has been trying to redefine itself over the last few seasons. The work is erratic but sometimes stunningly good and, sometimes aimlessly avant-garde. Building D, tel. 441 8822.

Mexican Museum

Concentrates on Mexican and Mexican American artists, but shows artists from all over Latin America. The gift shop is one of the best places in San Francisco for finding Mexican toys, handicrafts and art books. Open Wed–Sun, 12 noon–5 p.m., admission Building D, tel. 441 0404.

Museo Italo Americano

Changing exhibits, history and art, concentrating on Italians and Italian-Americans. Open Wed–Sun, 12 noon–5 p.m.; free, Building C, tel. 673 2200.

San Francisco African American Historical & Cultural Society

The history of African Americans in California is the focus here, with changing art exhibits that include local black artists and African artists. Open Wed–Sun, 12 noon–5 p.m.; free, Building C, tel. 441 0640.

San Francisco Craft & Folk Art Museum

One of the city's best small museums, mounting its own shows of contemporary and historic arts and crafts and bringing in a wide variety of travelling exhibitions. Keeps a steady focus on the Bay Area's rich arts and crafts tradition. Open Tues–Sun, 11 a.m.–5 p.m.; admission, Building A, tel. 775 0990.

S.S. Jeremiah O'Brien

This World War II Liberty Ship is tied up at Pier 3, but is occasionally fired up and taken out on the bay for a spin. Considered part of the historic fleet at Hyde Street, rangers give tours of the ships, discussing how they were built with a good thumbnail history of 'Rosie the Riveter', the mass mobilisation of women during the war. 'Rosie the Riveter' was the nickname given to the corps of female defence workers who stepped from their kitchens into factories and shipyards, handling power tools as easily as their mixers and vacuum cleaners.

Open daily, Mon–Fri, 9 a.m.– 3 p.m., Sat–Sun 9 a.m.–4 p.m.; admission tel. 441 3101.

AROUND THE MARINA

Leaving Fort Mason and walking towards the Marina Green, you can continue walking all the way to the Golden Gate Bridge – and across the bridge to Marin – if that suits your fancy. The interconnected pathways and pavements from Aquatic Park to Fort Point underneath the Golden Gate Bridge form the Golden Gate Promenade, a three-and-a-half-mile stretch that's one of the most beautiful walks in the world.

The Marina Green is a pleasant spot to watch San Francisco go by. Even on sunny days, though, it can be windy so it is a good idea to keep a jacket or pullover handy.

Unless you walk up to Chesnut Street you are not going to see much in the way of business or commerce, a plus from most people's point of view, but annoying when you need a toilet or a snack. Make use of the restrooms at Fort Mason. If you can't get in at Greens restaurant (or don't want to pay top dollar) the huge Marina Safeway across Marina Boulevard from Fort Mason is a great spot to buy fruit or an entire meal from the take-out counter. It is also a great improvement over the only other eatery in Fort Mason, a counter sandwich-espresso shop in Building B called Cooks & Co which is renowned for its rude service.

The supermarket is famous too, but beyond San Francisco through Armistead Maupin's *Tales of the City*. This is the 'singles Safeway' where work-obsessed San Francisco singles, gay and straight, come to meet other singles under the cover of grocery shopping.

The Marina Green is equipped with a parcourse, a do-it-your-self fitness test that combines exercise and running – just follow the signs. The St Francis Yacht Club at the end of the Green is private, but their boat races are for everyone to enjoy.

Not terribly well advertised but also there to enjoy is the wave organ, a marvellous installation that magnifies the sounds of the ocean. Dreamed up at the Exploratorium, in the Palace of Fine Arts, the wave organ is located at the end of the outer seawall beyond the yacht club. Follow the roadway past the red-tile roofed St Francis (a 1928 Willis Polk building). The wave organ is constructed of stone chambers beneath the water; pipes send out the soothing sounds of the water.

Palace of Fine Arts and Exploratorium Museum

3601 Lyon St (at Marina Blvd) Exploratorium, tel. 561 0360, open Tues–Sun, 10 a.m.–5 p.m. and until 9.30 p.m. Wed; $4–$8, free under 6; free admission for all on first Wed of each month. The park is open all the time, free.

The Exploratorium is a hands-on science museum within a complex called the Palace of Fine Arts that includes a theatre and a park. The actual palace is a romantic, recontexturalised temple and colonnade created for the 1915 Panama Pacific Exposition and now surrounded by a slippery lagoon and walking paths.

PANAMA PACIFIC INTERNATIONAL EXPOSITION OF 1915

'We saw shining, almost imaginary buildings full of unbelievable works of sculpture, painting, weaving, basketmaking, products of agriculture, and all kinds of mechanical inventions,' author William Saroyan recalled of his boyhood visit to the Panama Pacific International Exposition.

All in all, Saroyan remembered it as 'a place that couldn't possibly be real'.

Looking at sepia-toned old photographs of the 'PPIE,' today, one is inclined to agree. The fair was a mammoth undertaking that eventually cost something like twenty million dollars and covered 635 acres, much of it marshes that had to be filled in by the Army Corps of Engineers. It could have been a huge garish carnival, but instead was an elegant, mindbending display of architecture, art, landscaping, colour and technology. Architectural historian Gary Brechin has described it as 'a miniature Constantinople'.

Ostensibly held to celebrate the opening of the Panama Canal in 1914, the PPIE was more correctly San Francisco's re-entry into the mainstream. More than seventeen million people streamed through the fair during its ten months and all were constantly reminded that San Francisco had not only survived the devastating 1906 earthquake and fire, but had rebuilt on an even grander scale.

In San Francisco lore, the PPIE is a high mark of American optimism and success, the huge fair grounds lit up by the magic of electric lights (indirect lighting at that, giving San Francisco an early jump on tasteful entertaining). The fair, San Franciscans felt, showed that they deserved the accolade awarded to them by President William Howard Taft when he designated the city to host the exposition.

'San Francisco,' said Taft, 'the city that knows how'.

The war in Europe hung over the happy throng even as the French and German pavilions opened as planned.

When the Exposition closed in December, much of the magic was unceremoniously torn down, ripped apart and in some cases, floated to other towns around the bay on barges. Holding on to the Palace of Fine Arts was the city's way of remembering that its magical kingdom – the place that couldn't possibly be real – had actually existed.

The Rotunda and Colonnade

The palace was designed by Bernard Maybeck, a free-spirited Berkeley architect whose work consisted primarily of residential structures in the Arts and Crafts tradition. The rotunda and colonnade fully express Maybeck's idea to create 'an old Roman ruin, away from civilisation, which 2000 years before was the center of action and full of life, and now is partly overgrown with bushes and trees – such ruins giving the mind a sense of sadness'.

Maybeck was vague about why the building dedicated to the fine arts should be permeated with sadness, but there it is. The architect used female figures to adorn the top of the colonnade – sad, classically Greek forms whose backs are turned as they peer downwards through the boxy planters atop the columns. (Maybeck's design called for the boxes to be planted with native California trees and vines, but he was overruled by head landscape architect John McLaren, of Golden Gate Park fame, who pointed out there was no way to water or maintain the plants).

The Palace of Fine Arts was so popular with the public that San Francisco decided to keep it as a kind of souvenir of the Exposition (see above), which had been a huge success. Built of stucco, the structure was a genuine ruin by the 1950s, when a campaign was launched to preserve it. Maybeck, always the puckish dreamer, wasn't particularly enthusiastic about the preservation plans, seeing his faux ruin turning into a genuine ruin. But the palace lovers forged ahead. A couple of million dollars later, the buildings were recreated in concrete and continue to be a favourite San Francisco backdrop for wedding photos, meeting friends and contemplative walks. Ducks and geese populate the lagoon, adding another romantic touch to the little park.

The Exploratorium

While the focus here is kids, the Exploratorium is a favourite with just about everyone who walks through the door. There are 700 exhibits, all of them for you to touch, manipulate or play with. A human-size bubble wand creates huge, wavy bubbles, a working internal combustion engine shows how the modern world runs and strobe lights, interactive videos and a zillion other delights fill the enormous, warehouse-like museum.

The Exploratorium is very big on programmes and how-tos, so call ahead and find out what is going on during your visit. You may have to go back more than once if you have science-attuned children.

This new kind of museum was established in 1969 by Dr Frank Oppenheimer, the infamous brother of Dr Robert Oppenheimer, head of the team that developed the atomic bomb in Los Alamos, New Mexico. Robert Oppenheimer had his security clearance yanked in the neurotic postwar years. He was accused of having too-liberal views and a commie brother. All true. Frank Oppenheimer, also a respected scientist, had been a serious Marxist as a young man and was hounded by the McCarthyites in the fifties but his radical past wasn't a handicap in San Francisco.

After you have experimented with as many things as possible, visit the gift shop. It is excellent, with a good array of educational toys and games. You can do all your Christmas shopping in one stop.

PACIFIC HEIGHTS

The boundaries of Pacific Heights are open to debate. One sharp-tongued observer has suggested that Pacific Heights is primarily a state of mind, bounded by Ambition, *Vogue* magazine, Dun & Bradstreet and the Social Register.

ANN GETTY

In a city that seems to produce remarkable rich women the way that Kentucky produces thoroughbreds, Ann Getty stands out in a very crowded field. As the wife of Gordon Getty, one of the richest men in the world, Ann Getty would be notable no matter what. But this billionaire's wife is 5ft 10in, with flaming red hair and has demonstrated an interest in building her own empire.

While husband Gordon is content to compose operas and look after the multi-billion dollar family business left in his care by his father J. Paul Getty, Ann Getty, 54, spends big chunks of time in New York and London while sitting on the boards of heavyweight corporations such as Revlon and MGM/UC Communications. She is also a partner in Grove/Atlantic Press. The daughter of a prosperous Northern California farmer, Ann Gilbert met Gordon Getty when he was on his father's black list, which meant that his net worth was approximately the same as a successful downtown attorney. They married, settled in San Francisco and lived a low-key upper-class life, gradually becoming richer as the elder Getty went through one son after another (he had five), finally making peace with Gordon and leaving him in charge of the family fortune.

Ann Getty spent her twenties and thirties raising the couple's four sons. Like the heroine of a feminist novel, she seems to have come into her own in her forties and fifties, first accelerating her social career to become the most sought after hostess/guest patron in San Francisco, New York and London, then returning to college full time at the University of California at Berkeley, to study archaeology, before plunging into a varied business career. Her enterprises, if not always flourishing are nevertheless interesting. 'The worst thing you can say about Ann is that she is a dilettante,' commented her great friend and publishing partner, Lord George Weidenfeld, 'and you can't really say that'.

As San Francisco's most prestigious address, Pacific Heights is home to millionaire Gordon Getty and his wife, publisher Ann Getty, singer Linda Rondstadt, romance writer Danielle Steel, former California Governor Jerry Brown, SF Mayor Frank Jordan and tons of others who are merely rich but not necessarily famous.

Lafayette Park is the centre of Pacific Heights, occupying the highest point (378 feet), a twelve-acre hilltop with sweeping views of the bay and the city. The park is bounded by Laguna, Sacramento, Washington and Gough streets. The other commonly accepted boundaries of Pacific Heights are Van Ness Avenue to the east, Union Street to the north and California Street to the south. The area around Union Street, where the hills begin to flatten out, is called Cow Hollow, although no one now living can remember when dairy farms covered the area.

HOW TO SUCCEED IN SAN FRANCISCO SOCIETY

Delia Fleishhacker Ehrlich, whose family dates back to the Gold Rush, laid out the rules for *San Francisco Focus* magazine before a recent social season: 'Have a lot of money. Get seats to Series A at the Opera. Buy a home in Pacific Heights, Nob Hill, or Russian Hill. Buy tickets to all the top charitable events. Choose your friends carefully. Be well-dressed, but not so well-dressed that you intimidate. Be willing to work for the Opera, Ballet or Symphony, but don't expect a committee chairmanship until after the first year.'

For the non-resident, the pleasures of Pacific Heights are the visual delights of beautiful houses in a beautiful setting, a number of historic houses open to visitors and some first-rate shopping areas.

Pacific Heights developed rapidly after the 1906 earthquake and fire. Van Ness Avenue, which had been a boulevard of fashionable homes, was destroyed. The authorities made desperate use of dynamiting whole areas, trying to establish firebreaks as the inferno raced west and south from the bay. Van Ness, the city's widest thoroughfare and first physical break in the fire's path, was dynamited to create as big a firebreak as possible. The line was held at Van Ness and the fire began to wind down on its third day. Historians of the disaster credit a change in winds with the fire's demise rather than the dynamiting which actually spread the fire in some cases.

In rebuilding, Van Ness became a commercial thoroughfare. The displaced wealthy families joined their brethren on Pacific Heights.

GERTRUDE ATHERTON

California's first native-born novelist of note, Gertrude Atherton (1857–1948) was a formidable woman whose name is still heard in San Francisco though her books have completely passed from the stage. Restless, independent and very attractive, Gertrude Horn Atherton's talent was more for self-promotion and excitement than for first-rate writing. If she had been born a century later it is easy to imagine her as a corporate raider, movie studio president, senator or editor of *Vanity Fair*.

San Francisco-born Atherton turned to writing almost in desperation for an outlet from her suffocating marriage to an ineffectual upper-class twit. In what seems to be a bid for Freudian sweepstakes immortality, Gertrude at nineteen eloped with her divorced mother's much younger beau, George Atherton, whom she despised. He conveniently died at sea and she used her widow's income to travel to New York and London to establish herself as a writer. She had little interest in her two children. Her son died as a baby and her daughter was consigned to her doting grandmother.

Atherton talked the literary talk, but in truth she saw fiction as a means to support herself and propel her into interesting circles. She travelled widely, armed with the compelling need to research her next book. Atherton wrote very fast and resisted any efforts to revise or rework her stories, which badly needed editing. She was fiercely competitive with other women and deeply resented the attention given to her contemporaries, Edith Wharton and Willa Cather, whom she regarded if not as lesser talents then as barely her equals.

Despite her elevated opinion of her own work, it is doubtful if Atherton's modest talent would have outlasted her life, even with careful handling. Atherton's gift was to reflect the spirit or idea of the day which she delivered in florid, tangled stories. Her early novels were full of spirited Western girls making their way off their ranches into English drawing rooms. Her later novels pushed the idea of hormonal injections as a fountain of youth, a reworking of Atherton's own experimentation with various treatments to retain her impressive looks.

Although she was linked with several men after her husband's death (most notably satirist Ambrose Bierce), Atherton seems to have had little interest in men as sexual partners. She enjoyed being admired, but her true nature was puritanical and relentlessly anti-introspective. Atherton championed women's rights, but held herself away from the street fighters. A terrible snob, she managed to keep bohemians out of San Francisco PEN, the literary society, by decreeing that evening meetings required black tie for men, evening dress for women.

Atherton's warm friendship with Gertrude Stein and Alice B. Toklas (see p. 243) comes as something of a shock, given her competitiveness and lack of sympathy for non-conformist sexuality. The Gertrudes met in Paris, liked each other, and Gertrude Atherton made extensive arrangements for Stein and Toklas's 1935 visit to San Francisco.

The Gertrudes' friendship was based on mutual blindness. Atherton considered Stein a writer *poseur* of no talent and silly theories and, although she thought herself one of the most sophisticated people in the world, doesn't seem to have grasped the sexual nature of the Stein-Toklas partnership. Consequently Atherton did not feel threatened sexually or professionally and enjoyed Stein and Toklas as literary gossips and San Franciscans from the old days. Further, the imperious Atherton put herself to considerable trouble (quite unlike her) for Stein's visit, organising parties, lectures and handling the press.

Gertrude Stein, for her part, saw Atherton as a hack who existed on the sufferance of her social connections. Stein thought it was only natural that the pathetic Atherton would be grateful to do handmaiden duty for a real writer.

Later Gertrude Stein wrote of the triumphant visit to San Francisco, 'Gertrude Atherton was to do everything for us and she did'.

WESTERN ADDITION

The Western Addition is a once-smart neighbourhood that blends into Pacific Heights below California Street. In 1858 the city decreed that the street grid would be extended past the city limits at Van Ness Avenue, adding the area to the west to the city. The Western Addition was a popular, upper middle class neighbourhood in the late nineteenth century which accounts for its heavy population of Victorian houses.

San Francisco's Victorian signature is here in the Western Addition on 'Postcard Row'. The late nineteenth-century houses facing Alamo Square on Steiner Street (between Fulton and Hayes) compose one of the most famous San Francisco scenes of all. The houses, most restored to their glory in the 1960s, are backed by the San Francisco highrise skyline with big splashes of the bay beyond that.

Even with its pockets of gentrification, the Western Addition is a dangerous neighbourhood that many San Franciscans of all races give wide berth. But the compact nature of the city means that no area is completely written off – or completely safe. Within the Western Addition are two important neighbourhoods with rich ethnic traditions: Japantown, the centre of Japanese American life, and the Fillmore, once the main street of African American life in San Francisco. Both Japantown and the Fillmore were almost swallowed up by the slash and burn policies of 1950s' era urban renewal. The shabby Victorians, marginal businesses and ethnic populations were seen as problems to be solved rather than the self-sufficient working-class enclaves that they were.

Union Street

Muni buses 22 and 45.

One of San Francisco's premiere shopping and dining districts. Union Street has faded a bit in the last few years as if being No. 1 was just too much of a strain. Fillmore Street, also in Pacific Heights, is trendier for shopping while the hot South of Market scene has siphoned off most of the cool singles from the Union Street saloons.

Union Street remains a pleasure though, with its boutiques and cafés offering up a textbook example of why people want to live in cities. From Van Ness to Steiner, Union Street is home to clothing stores, jewellery shops (especially), stationery-gift stores, flowers, hairstylists and eateries.

Around Cow Hollow

Downhill from Union Street, where Pacific Heights and Cow Hollow blends into the Marina is the mildly infamous 'Bermuda Triangle' area at Greenwich and Fillmore streets.

The Bermuda Triangle in the Atlantic Ocean is famous for swallowing up aeroplanes and yachts.

The San Francisco 'Triangle' is famous for attracting little knots of twentysomething singles who make the rounds of bars. The name comes from the not very mysterious disappearances; friends wander off with attractive new acquaintances and are not seen again until Monday morning. Whether or not the instant dates are as exciting as advertised, the bars clustered at Fillmore and Greenwich do a roaring business on weekends and drinking holidays like St Patrick's Day and Super Bowl Sunday. The Balboa Café (see p. 300), 3199 Fillmore, is a quite good restaurant that anchors the triangle. The Golden Gate Grill, 3200 Fillmore, the Pierce Street Annexe, at No. 3138, and Baja Cantina, at No. 3154, are barely mediocre restaurants that are there just to accommodate the roving bands of singles.

The Octagon House

2645 Gough St (at Union), tel. 441 7512. Open second Sun, second and fourth Thurs of every month but Jan, 12 noon–3 p.m.; $2–$4 admission.

This is one of five octagon houses built in San Francisco, a local manifestation of a mid-nineteenth century fad sparked off by Orson S. Fowler's book, *A Home for All*. Fowler proclaimed the octagon the optimal healthy space for living. A prosperous businessman named William C. McElroy built an octagon house for his family in 1861 on Gough (pronounced goff) Street where they seemed to have been reasonably happy. In 1951 the deteriorating house (it had long passed out of the McElroy family) was acquired by the California chapter of the National Society of the Colonial Dames of America. The house was moved across the street from its original location and carefully restored by the Dames who did not shirk from reworking the floor plan. The museum is only open three days a month and is notable for its collection of Colonial (1600–1785) and Federal (1785–1810) era furniture, cutlery, ceramics, portraits, pewter, handiwork, rugs and lacquerware. The artefacts and antiques are family heirlooms that have been deeded to the Colonial Dames from its members. None are original to the house, which very likely had no authentic Colonial and Federal furnishings. The museum is a little odd, its contents being unconnected to the history of San Francisco or California, but it is popular with visitors interested in historic furniture, silver, dishes and the Early American era. Volunteers staff the house on open days giving cheerful walkthroughs. A Colonial garden has been added to the grounds, quite authentic in its flower and kitchen beds. It's a lovely place for a quiet break.

FAMILY TIES

The National Society of the Colonial Dames of America is one of a handful of ancestor-worshipping sororities that seem to be a peculiarly American phenomenon.

Established in the late nineteenth century as white, Christian, Anglo-Saxon America was becoming a more diverse society, the Colonial Dames and their sisters, the Daughters of the American Revolution and the United Daughters of the Confederacy, combined elitism and historic preservation for a sometimes combustible mix of genuine service and appalling snobbery.

The key element in all the groups is ancestry; the DAR is for descendants of those who fought against the British in the War of Independence (1775–83); the UDC is made up of women whose direct ancestors served the Confederate cause (1860–5), but the queen of them all is the Colonial Dames which demands that a direct male ancestor must have arrived in one of the original thirteen colonies well before 1700; further, said ancestor must have been a person of wealth or position (indentured servants or exiled convicts most emphatically do not count). The Mayflower Society has a certain cachet, with a membership restricted to those whose family came over in 1620 with the settlers of Massachusetts, but the Dames are said to sniff at the Mayflowers in private, pointing out that any nobody could have got on board the *Mayflower*.

The Society of California Pioneers, founded in 1850, is the Golden State counterpart to these Eastern societies. It is open only to men descended from men who were in California before 1850. That would seem to indicate a Californios heritage, but the focus is relentlessly geared to non-Hispanics who settled in California before the Bear Flag Revolt and Forty-niners who came at the beginning of the Gold Rush. The Society is unusual in the genealogical clubhouse for being a male-only group with no equivalent for women. The DAR and UDC were both founded to give women their own place and quit bothering the men who had their veterans' organisations and groups such as the Sons of the American Revolution.

Allyne Park

Gough and Green streets.
As with Octagon House next door, this fairyland of a park owes its existence to two sprightly maiden ladies, the Allyne sisters. Lucy and Edith Allyne, the daughters of a sea captain, grew up on a small estate that was once here. There were cows, horses and outbuildings but the Allynes' domain urbanised with the neighbourhood. The sisters donated part of their lawns to the Colonial Dames (they were

avid members of the organisation) in 1951 for Octagon House. The Allynes' other property was left to the city. Their house was torn down and the glade of redwoods, pathways and lawn opened to the public in 1966. The homeless have also discovered this park, but the setting seems to work on them as well; the homeless people who come to Allyne Park are quiet and well mannered.

The park is surrounded by a rustic picket fence. Just open the gate and let yourself in.

Historic Houses

Pacific Heights' houses are old, beautifully maintained and fiercely private. There are three well-known historic houses that merit a look-see, but only two are open to the public.

The Spreckels Mansion, 2080 Washington St (at Octavia Street) is a San Francisco landmark. Built in 1913 for Alma deBretteville Spreckels, the upstart bride of ageing sugar heir Adolph Spreckels in 1913, this enormous palace of white limestone was based on the Grand Trianon.

Alma Spreckels, who stood six feet tall and was the model for the Victory atop the Dewey monument in Union Square, lived life on a very large scale, as a domineering patron of the arts who bankrolled the Maritime Museum on Fisherman's Wharf and more grandly, the Palace of the Legion of Honor in Lincoln Park. Her house was the scene of hundreds of soirées, balls and gatherings. A coming out party for her daughter Dorothy in 1930 was reported in *Time* magazine, it was so incredibly lavish. There were orchestras, tented grounds and 'Big Alma' touches such as mounds of caviare in ice sculpture bowls and page boys in Nubian slave costumes of loin cloths and rhinestone collars that were exact copies of the statues in her Italian Room.

The 55-room house, which includes a Louis XVI ballroom and panoramic views of the bay, was bought by romance novelist Danielle Steel in 1990 for a reported thirteen million dollars. Steel commissioned an intensive thirteen-month renovation and re-decorating before moving in with her fourth husband, shipping heir John Traina, and their his-and-her brood of nine children. The house is not open to the public in any way except to stroll by and hope for a peak of the sixty-million dollar woman who lives and writes there.

The Haas-Lilienthal House, 2007 Franklin St, is open to the public. Embellished with a turret, gables, porches and gingerbread woodwork on the outside and boasting a well-preserved nineteenth-century interior, this 1886 villa is a Victorian theme park. Built by one of the Jewish merchant families, the house was lived in continu-ously by the descendants of William Haas until 1972. The house was then turned into a museum, complete with decades of family pieces. The house is open for tours on Wed and Sun, $2–$4, tel. 441 3000.

DANIELLE STEEL

Danielle Steel is easily one of San Francisco's most productive industries. Since 1972 she has written thirty novels which have sold upwards of two hundred million copies. In 1992 she signed a sixty-million dollar, five-book contract with Dell/Delacorte publishers. Considering Steel's awesome sales, some observers think the publishers have got her cheap.

No matter how many nasty, snickering, condescending reviews Steel's novels rack up, readers just can't resist the plucky heroines who go from rags to riches, or riches to rags as they find and lose love while wearing gorgeous clothes, working in glamorous professions or when it all gets too much, giving up the fast lane for a sensitive cowboy on a fabulously beautiful ranch or a hunky doctor on a rustic winery.

Steel's life provides the grist for her pulp mill. The daughter of a German businessman and a Portuguese socialite, she was raised in New York and married at eighteen to a French-American banker ten years her senior. Driven to write, she divorced the banker and took her young daughter to live in San Francisco. Working on a magazine story about prisoners, she met a charming car thief and married him in the prison recreation room. She divorced him when he was re-arrested and married a charming recovering heroin addict in 1978 with whom she had one son. Steel's novels began hitting the big time in the late 1970s and when the ex-addict reverted to old patterns, she dropped him. Soon after she married John Traina in 1981, the scion of an old Italian American shipping family, who had just gone through a very public, nasty divorce in San Francisco.

Steel's writing accelerated even as she went on to have five children with Traina. She reluctantly called it quits after a daughter was born in 1987 telling friends, 'Further children would be dangerous to my health – my husband would kill me!'

Steel lives a high profile society life while adroitly sidestepping interviews and suing to halt publication of an unauthorised biography. The Queen of Romance wants final say on all plot lines, fiction and real life.

The Whittier Mansion, 2090 Jackson St (at Laguna), is a stolid 1896 house that is now home to the California Historical Society. Built for William Frank Whittier, who headed the utility conglomerate that has become Pacific, Gas & Electric, the red sandstone structure withstood the earthquakes of 1906 and 1989 thanks to its steel-reinforced walls. Tours of the house are given Tues–Sun, interesting for the exhibitions of California art and the richly panelled interiors. A donation is asked, tel. 567 1848.

JAPANTOWN

Japantown is smaller and less textured than Chinatown, being primarily a commercial area. This is unfortunately easily explained by the uprooting of the Japanese American community in 1942 in the hysterical aftermath of Pearl Harbor and the declaration of war with Japan.

THE LONG SAYONARA

The overnight emptying of San Francisco's 'Little Osaka' was the Japanese American war experience writ large. The anti-Japanese frenzy unleashed by the bombing of Pearl Harbor was ultimately channelled into Executive Order 9066, President Franklin Roosevelt's empowering of the military to detain Japanese Americans in the cause of national security.

Despite absolutely no evidence of treason, disloyalty or even wavering allegiances, Washington was swayed by a nasty public atmosphere. Intelligence experts argued against taking any stops at all against Japanese Americans, pointing out in confidential reports that their spying had shown that the Japanese were contemptuous of their American cousins as traitors to the race and unreliable on loyalty to the homeland.

A clumsily drawn-up plan was put into action in early 1942. Japanese Americans in California, Arizona, Oregon and Washington were ordered to leave their homes and businesses, allowed to take only what they could carry. Most San Franciscans were sent to the Topaz Relocation Camp in Utah. No distinction was made between American citizens and foreign nationals. While a few Italian and German citizens were interned for part or all of the War, there was nothing like the mass action against Japanese Americans.

Leaders in the community counselled compliance, determined to demonstrate their patriotism beyond all doubt. Sent to crude encampments in remote parts of California, Utah, Wyoming, Idaho and even Arkansas, the Japanese Americans made valiant efforts to carry on with their lives. They took classes, tried to make their arid deserts and mountain camps bloom and proudly supported the war effort.

Japanese American soldiers fought heroically in Europe. The famous 'Go For Broke' company, the 442nd Regimental Combat Team, was the most decorated American military unit in the War. Nisei (second generation) women joined the military, too. An all-Nisei woman's unit was trained in the Army language school to work in postwar Japan. When the American military suddenly realised the urgent need for Japanese translators, it hurriedly turned to the internment camps. The recruiters were puzzled to find that many of the so-called Japanese spoke only unaccented American English with a passing understanding of spoken Japanese. These American translators had to be trained in the language just like the farm boys from Iowa.

In retrospect, the internment of Japanese Americans was not only patently racist but quickly shown to be useless. For instance, Japanese Americans made up almost a third of the population of the Hawaiian Islands, the most vulnerable American territory (it didn't become a state until 1959), yet there was no internment nor evacuation from Hawaii. Nor was there ever any incidence of spying, sabotage or fifth column activity among Japanese Americans anywhere in the continental US or its territories.

President Gerald Ford officially rescinded 9066 in 1976 and issued a presidential apology to Japanese Americans for their treatment during World War II.

Kristi Yamaguchi, the perky East Bay teenager who won the Olympic gold medal for figure skating in 1992, is the daughter of a Nisei couple who met growing up in Manzanar, a camp in the California desert. As the medal was put around Kristi's neck the TV cameras zoomed in on her father in the stands, his hand on his heart, pledge of allegiance style, singing along with 'The Star Spangled Banner' as tears streamed down his face. Now an affluent dentist, he was asked how he felt, looking back to the dark days of internment and seeing his daughter become an American heroine. 'Oh, that was a long time ago,' he said. 'We're all proud to be Americans.'

In a kind of tacit apology, the urban redevelopment plan of the early 1960s insisted on giving Japantown a pedestrian mall and plaza. Razing Victorians and displacing occupants, the five-acre Japan Center complex was created on three blocks between Post and Geary streets while the Nihonmachi Mall (Japanese village) was formed by closing off a block of Buchanan Street. The buildings are big, brutish and uninviting. Small boutiques, cafés and businesses do their best to reverse the impersonality of the place.

Built over an 800-space parking garage, Japan Center has more than twenty restaurants and a movie complex (the Kabuki 8) that is a local favourite for its clean theatres and good mix of blockbusters and 'little' films.

Kabuki Hot Spring

1750 Geary Boulevard (lower level of Japan Center), tel. 922 6000. Open daily 10 a.m.–10 p.m.; reservations needed for massage.

If you know and love saunas, steambaths and massages, you will find the Kabuki a dream come true. If, on the other hand, you haven't tried these delightful body treats, the Kabuki is an ideal introduction. Deep within the Japan Center the place recreates the ideal Japanese bath house with clean pools, quiet atmosphere and dim lights.

MASSAGE & ALL THAT

Massage, bodywork, saunas and hot tubs are not luxuries but necessities to many San Franciscans. The Bay Area's welcoming attitude towards New Age ideas and Eastern spiritualism has created a mass market locally for some of the offshoots such as acupuncture and massage. Kabuki Hot Spring is one of the best places for a good soak and massage. Here are some other clean, well-run, easy-to-like massage and bodywork places:

Family Sauna Shop, 2308 Clement St, tel. 221 2208. A staff of wonderful massage therapists and attendants offer treatments such as herbal facials, Finnish sauna and whirlpool. Open daily, 12 noon–10 p.m.; prices from $7 for sauna to $42 for an hour-long massage.

Osento, 955 Valencia St, tel. 282 6333. A woman-only bath house in a funky Victorian building. Communal in nature, you can get a sauna, hot tub or massage here. In the Mission (near Old Wives' Tale bookstore). Call for hours and charges.

Piedmont Springs, 3939 Piedmont Ave, Oakland, tel. (510) 652 9191. A favourite East Bay hot tub and massage shop with a variety of massage styles (Japanese shiatsu, Swedish, combinations). Redwood hot tubs are outside but very private. Facials are done, too. Open daily, 11 a.m.–10 p.m., $8 hot tub to $50 for an 80-minute massage.

The communal pools are reserved for women three days a week (Wednesday, Friday, Sunday) and for men the other four. Visitors may come for the baths, hot and cold pools only, or sign up for a massage. The staff is uniformly polite, instructive and low-key. Be aware, however, that massages are given in a room of six or more unless the visitor asks for a private room. Massages are given by men and women, so ask for a woman masseuse if you don't feel comfortable with a man.

Cost depends upon the service: $10 for the basic use of the baths; $65 for baths and a private 90-minute massage.

Around Japantown The Ikebana Society of America on the first floor of the Japan Center, has ongoing exhibits of its delicate flower arranging art. Demonstrations of *ikebana* are usually scheduled for Saturday morning. Call 567 1011 for information. The Nichi Bei Kai Cultural Center, 1759 Sutter St, performs the traditional tea ceremony for visitors by arrangement. Call 751 9676.

Japanese religious groups are based in the neighbourhood. The Buddhist Church of San Francisco, 1881 Pine St, is deceptively plain from the outside, with an impressive, detailed interior. The Konko Church of San Francisco, 1909 Bush St, is a fairly recent building (1973) for the religion that blends Shintoism with revelation. The altar area is very handsome.

The Cherry Blossom Festival, held in April, is worth putting on your agenda. The festival is programmed for the whole month with *ikebana* demonstrations, bonsai exhibits, folk dance performances, taiko drumming and a variety of other events, culminating in a marvellous parade through Japantown, usually on the final Sunday. The festival is in the spirit of the celebrations in Japan, but can't completely emulate them as cherry trees are scarce and on a slightly different schedule in San Francisco. The festival is a thoroughly Japanese American event with Boy Scout troops carrying their very own handmade Japanese icons, housewives dressed in kimonos performing ceremonial fan dances and other cultural representatives, such as a group of black baton twirlers. Write to Cherry Blossom Festival, P.O. Box 15147, San Francisco, California 94115 for dates and programme plans.

St Mary's Cathedral

1111 Gough St (at Geary). Open daily, 6.30 a.m.–5 p.m. Free.

'What is that?' visitors ask from a variety of viewpoints of the city. Whether at the top of a highrise or on Twin Peaks, they are pointing at a dramatic white structure that resembles a giant spaceship.

It is St Mary's Cathedral, a bold, uncompromising church that presents the sign of the cross in its soaring, parabolic dome.

Construction The new St Mary's was commissioned to replace
the redbrick, Germanic cathedral on Van Ness that burned in 1962
after surviving the 1906 earthquake and fire. Designed by a team of
American and Italian architects, led by Pietro Bellusch and Pier
Luigi Nervi, the new cathedral was finished in 1971 and covers two
blocks.

The structure's concrete form is covered by Italian travertine
marble, giving it the dazzling white shimmer that can be seen from
all over the city. The redbrick used in the outdoor plazas that lead
up to the cathedral doors are meant to echo California's mission
past.

The visit New St Mary's is beautiful in the way that a sheer, rock
cliffside is beautiful: it is big, powerful and a little intimidating. The
interior of the church has a cavelike feeling with the 190-foot ceiling
drawing the eye upwards to the light that filters through the narrow
stained glass windows that form a cross.

More light comes through the floor-to-ceiling windows at each
corner of the sanctuary. The windows provide beautifully framed
postcards of the San Francisco skyline, suggesting the possibilities of
melding the spiritual life and the secular life outside of the church.

The centrepiece of the 2500-seat interior is a Richard Lippold
mobile sculpture of thin, aluminium rods that give the appearance
of a perpetual silver rain caught in midair over the altar.

Representations of Mary are diverse and splendid. Enrico
Manfrini's larger than life carvings in rich woods hang in niches
throughout the interior. They depict the assumption, the visitation
and flight into Egypt. Another view of Mary as Our Lady of
Guadeloupe is presented in a contemporary mosaic from Mexico.
This Latina Mary is tied to the Italian Marys with Manfrini's
carving of the burning bush which completely frames the mosaic
portrait.

THE FILLMORE

Jack Kerouac rhapsodised about the bars and jazz clubs in the
Fillmore. Among blacks in the Bay Area, 'goin' to the 'Mo' was
going home where they could get a haircut, talk to a lawyer, run
into friends and dine in restaurants that wouldn't put them in isolated tables.

The Fillmore is more of a state of mind than a precise geographical designation. Clustered around lower Fillmore Street,
downhill from the grandness of Pacific Heights, the Fillmore was
once the heart of the city's black community. As Japanese
Americans were being shipped out of the Western Addition during
the Second World War, African Americans from Louisiana and
Texas were streaming in. Brought to San Francisco to work in the

war industries, these eager new residents found housing in the suddenly vacated Western Addition. Black businesses soon sprang up on Fillmore. After the war, many of the black workers decided to stay on in San Francisco, settling permanently in the Western Addition which was beginning to be called the Fillmore.

Once known as the Harlem of the West, the Fillmore suffered the same fate of downward mobility. The combined effects of redevelopment and upward mobility depleted the community.

Some interesting cultural landmarks remain. Look out though; the area is gentrifying, but can be unpredictable. Be alert and don't advertise yourself as a tourist.

Marcus Books

1712 Fillmore St (across from the Japan Center, tel. 346 4222). Open Mon–Sat, 10 a.m.–7 p.m., Sun, noon–6 p.m.

More than a bookstore, Marcus Books is a community resource and meeting place. Opened in 1960 and named for the African nationalist, Marcus Garvey, the shop and its Oakland branch have the most comprehensive selection of black literature in Northern California. Family owned, Marcus Books hosts a steady schedule of author readings, book signings, community forums and children's events.

Fillmore Auditorium

1807 Geary Blvd (at Fillmore).

There's not really much to say about this 1912 building unless you have a weakness for rock'n'roll holy ground. The late impresario, Bill Graham, first rented the hall in June 1967 for a concert with Jimi Hendrix, the Jefferson Airplane and some forgotten names. The rock concert was created here, with deafening sound, spontaneous dancing and light shows.

The hall has been undergoing a seismic upgrading and is scheduled to open for a new era of rock shows in 1994.

MARY ELLEN PLEASANT

For generations San Franciscans enjoyed scaring themselves with stories about the 'House of Mystery' at the corner of Bush and Octavia streets in the Western Addition. It was famous beyond the city; visiting cousins asked their hosts to take them to see this strange place of intrigue.

The 1879 Second Empire mansion with its mansard roof, thirty rooms, coach house and gardens is gone now, but some eucalyptus trees planted by the house's builder, Mary Ellen Pleasant, and a small memorial tablet to her memory mark the spot. Pleasant (1814–1904) was one of San Francisco's most remarkable pioneers, male or female. Called Mammy Pleasant in some accounts, but always Mrs Pleasant or Madame to her face, she was a black woman who came to San Francisco in 1849 with the first flood of gold seekers. Presenting herself as a cook and housekeeper, she progressed to owning boarding houses, acquiring stocks, real estate and substantial wealth.

Pleasant had been born a slave in Georgia. Part white and Indian, she made her way to Boston either as a freed slave or a runaway, where she came into contact with the abolitionists. In San Francisco, Pleasant was the Western terminus of the Underground Railroad, welcoming runaway slaves. She schooled the new arrivals in how to survive in the free world and quickly placed them in jobs as cooks, housekeepers, grooms, waiters, porters or whatever else she could get. Every white person in San Francisco was convinced that Pleasant operated a huge intelligence network through this corps of domestics and, furthermore, converted her inside information into a blackmail machine. This was in the same way that every white San Franciscan knew 'for a fact', that all of Chinatown was linked by a vast system of sophisticated underground tunnels and stairways.

Pleasant helped bankroll the activities of John Brown, the anti-slavery crusader who attempted to spark a slave rebellion in 1859 by seizing a federal arsenal in Harper's Ferry, West Virginia. In San Francisco, although she had her own coach and driver by this time, she sued the streetcar companies more than once for rude treatment or nonservice to blacks.

Pleasant's personal civil rights and anti-slavery campaigns have been mostly brushed aside in favour of lurid retellings of her story which trade on skulduggery, murder and voodoo. She has been villified from her lifetime onwards as a procurer of beautiful young women for rich old men. Pleasant did become deeply involved in several famous courtships, divorces and affairs, most notably Sarah Althea Hill's lawsuit against the rich, rich, rich Senator William Sharon. Hill, Sharon's mistress, sued for a divorce, claiming that she and the widowed senator had been secretly married. She produced a marriage contract, widely said to be a forgery concocted by her friend Pleasant. The case ended in chaos; Hill won, Sharon died, whereupon she married one of her supporters, Judge David Terry. The case was reversed on appeal, Terry threatened one of the judges on the case, the judge's bodyguard shot and killed Terry and Hill went mad.

Pleasant's ostensible employer, banker Thomas Bell, fell to his death in the Octavia Street house in 1892, sealing her reputation as a voodoo queen manipulator. Pleasant was never accused of his death but, as always, San Francisco 'knew it for a fact'.

Revisionist historians are in the process of making over Madame into a freedom fighting, free enterprise role model without adequately studying the dark side of her life. Actually, without the taints of sexism and racism, Mary Ellen Pleasant emerges as typical of San Francisco's great swashbuckling personalities. She believed in herself and her causes passionately, she was fiercely loyal to her friends, she amassed and lost great wealth and, when she felt it was necessary, indulged in activities that were variously illegal, unethical, immoral or deceitful – in a word, a great San Franciscan.

CIVIC CENTER

San Francisco's Civic Center was initially visualised as a twentieth-century *Place de la Concorde*. The seat of city offices, surrounded by palaces of arts and music would be approached through wide avenues and parks.

'Make no little plans,' advised Daniel Burnham, the Chicago

architect brought in to work on a civic master plan in 1904. 'They have no magic to stir men's blood, and probably of themselves will not be realized. Make big plans.'

Burnham, who had created spectacular Chicago's Columbian Exposition Fair in 1893, made huge plans for San Francisco and when the 1906 earthquake and fires presented the city with a *tabula rasa* it looked as if the visionary Burnham Plan would be realised. Instead, a nasty, drawn-out investigation of municipal corruption and the frenzy to rebuild as fast as possible sidetracked many of Burnham's grandiose ideas. But the Big Plan mentality took hold and the spirit of Burnham is certainly visible today in the plazas that approach City Hall and the building itself, an imposing palace of the government.

When Civic Center took shape, San Francisco was still the unofficial capital of California, indeed the entire Pacific Coast. Today the city is barely the capital of the Bay Area. San José, to the south, is bigger in population and size, and with the importance of adjacent Silicon Valley, the city would seem headed towards a powerful role in California and even the nation. However, San Francisco continues to have an impact far in excess of its size. With a population of 725,000 a few thousand votes can swing a local election, but the city doesn't really matter for winning or losing a statewide or national election. Yet San Francisco produces statewide politicians while San José and the ever-growing Los Angeles suburbs stay mired in provincialism. Dianne Feinstein (see p. 38), supervisor-mayor-gubernatorial candidate-senator, is the most compelling example of how San Franciscans take themselves seriously, invest their small political stage with importance and in turn convince everyone else: so goes San Francisco, so goes everything else.

San Francisco's municipal seat, which is ringed by representatives of the arts, is often cited as the most complete expression of the City Beautiful movement with its classical architecture and unifying vision. In the last few years visitors have often been shocked to compare the travel brochure image of Civic Center's beautiful buildings and the reality of a rather grimy district populated with even grimier street people. The more sophisticated homeless have been camping out around Civic Center while a battle rages in the halls of government over quality of life (some of us want a nice, clean city) versus individual freedom (some of us believe arresting people for sleeping on public property is undemocratic). Wearing tattered layers of clothes, pushing all their belongings in a shopping cart (or two) and sometimes accompanied by a dog on a leash, the Civic Center homeless population is a dispiriting sight. Most of these people are harmless, but occasional screaming fights and pushy panhandling make workers and visitors uneasy.

In addition to the homeless, Civic Center is unlovely at present because of massive construction and changes that are being put into place. A new main library is under construction at Larkin and Fulton, across from the current library and several buildings are surrounded by fences awaiting seismic upgrading work. City Hall will close in 1996 for two years to undergo renovations and earthquake reinforcements, by which time the San Francisco Museum of Modern Art will have moved from the upper floors of the Veterans Building at Van Ness and McAllister to a dramatic new building South of Market, and the mayor, board of supervisors and city employees will move in. Work is also planned for federal and state buildings on the perimeter of Civic Center which should make for a construction trades' Disneyland.

For the visitor, the best plan is to ignore the distractions, make a determined effort to look past the noisy construction work and late twentieth-century social disharmony and see the city that lies beneath it all.

Despite all this confusion, Civic Center will continue to be busy and full of people. San Francisco's cultural life is played out here, not only the ballet, opera and symphony, but the Civic Auditorium which hosts major rock shows. Across Franklin Street, behind Davies Symphony Hall, the Opera House and the Museum of Modern Art-Veterans Building, Hayes Valley is a rapidly gentrifying neighbourhood of cafés, art galleries and shops. If you are in town for a trade show and trying to find Brooks Hall in Civic Center, it is underground, adjacent to the subterranean parking lot under Civic Center Plaza. Take the elevator down.

Also within the Civic Center boundaries is the Tenderloin, San Francisco's high profile druggie-porno-sleazy district. It is not a pretty sight but it is almost an anachronistic kind of evil place, its little 'Naked City' dramas played out on crowded city streets instead of burned out ghetto neighbourhoods. The Tenderloin is too small and too visible for drive-by shootings and gang wars. It is actually quite a stable area, with the pimps, hookers, addicts, petty criminals and hangers-on involved in their own subculture of sleaze rather than lying in wait for clueless passersby.

Southeast Asian immigrants have moved into the crumbling residential hotels, opened little cafés and given the Tenderloin a few soft edges. San Franciscans often pass through the area going to and from their jobs and venture into the Tenderloin to attend touring Broadway shows at the grand Golden Gate Theater and dine at some of the good restaurants which are scattered around the area.

City Hall

Civic Center Plaza (Grove, Polk, Van Ness and McAllister streets). Open Mon–Fri.

Finished in 1915, City Hall is a reconceptualisation of the US Capitol Building as a French Renaissance palace. Based on Burnham's ideas and designed by Arthur Brown Jr and John Bakewell Jr, the huge building is often cited as a high point in the City Beautiful movement of the early 1900s. (Hollywood often uses the building as a stand-in for Washington.) The soaring dimensions, rich detailing and sense of grandeur give the visitor a clear reading of San Francisco's sense of itself as an imperial city-state.

The interior rotunda is dazzling. During a 1980s' Black & White Ball fireworks were staged here. Political junkies might enjoy dropping in on a Board of Supervisors' meeting where politics is carried out on the level of a no-holds-barred family vendetta. The Supervisors meet every Monday at 10 a.m.; on other weekdays the various board subcommittees hold public hearings at 10 a.m. and 2 p.m.

Louise B. Davies Symphony Hall

210 Van Ness Ave (at Grove Street), tel. 431 5400. Open for performances; box office.

Louise B. Davies, one of the great San Francisco philanthropists, underwrote the $31 million it took to build this symphony hall. Home to the world-class San Francisco Symphony, it also hosts touring orchestras, recitals and other classical music programmes. There has been a struggle with the hall's acoustics, but the music will sound grand to the garden variety concert-goer.

Architecturally the 1981 building is rather a mess. Designed by the high priests of Modernism, Skidmore Owings & Merrill, the softened contours and light detailing were meant to be a nod to the classicism of the other Civic Center buildings. Instead of being a transition, Davies is a Modernist oddity as the new buildings and renovations planned for Civic Center will all be neo-classical.

War Memorial Opera House

301 Van Ness Ave (at Grove Street), tel. 621 6600. Open for performances; box office.

Built in 1931, the Opera House echoes the old world richness of City Hall with marble floors, marvellous detailing and comfortable, old-fashioned seats. The San Francisco Opera, one of America's top opera companies, is at home here in the autumn while the San Francisco Ballet take up residency in the winter.

In early September the Opera House is the scene of one of the last great public displays of American society. The San Francisco Opera season's opening night brings out the city's elite, as well as politicians, celebrities and good-natured gawkers. Socialites engage in an updated street duel, establishing who is queen of the hill with 167 fabulous couture dresses that they spend the rest of the year searching for. Designers, such as Bill Blass, Herbert Givenchy and Carolina Herrera, sometimes show up to see how their representatives are faring.

San Francisco Museum of Modern Art/Veterans Building and Herbst Theater

401 Van Ness Ave (at McAllister Street), tel. 252 4000. SFMOMA is on the third and fourth floors, open Tues–Fri 10 a.m.–5 p.m. (and to 9 p.m. Thurs), Sat–Sun 11 a.m.–5 p.m.; $2–$4, free for children under 13; free admission to all the first Tuesday of every month. Herbst is open for performances.

The San Francisco Museum of Modern Art shares this graceful old building (Bakewell & Brown, 1932) with the Herbst theatre, a much-used lecture hall and various other organisations. By 1995 the museum is supposed to be established in its high-impact new building by Swiss architect Mario Botta in the Yerba Buena area, South of Market. Until then the museum continues to make do with a building that it has long outgrown.

Founded in 1935, this was California's first museum devoted to twentieth-century art. It was also San Francisco's first art museum that grew out of the art community rather than a *noblesse oblige* urge from the rich. Grace McCann Morley was the museum's founding curator and highly regarded director until her retirement in 1958. She was unusual among American museum directors for her heavy emphasis on community education.

The museum's permanent collection is a respectable mixture of American and European artists, anchored by the patronage of several San Francisco families, particularly the Haas-Levi Strauss dynasty. Highlights among the painting collection include Matisse's 'The Girl With Green Eyes' (1908) and his portraits of Michael Stein and Sarah Stein, Gertrude Stein's brother and wife (1916). Harriet Lane Levy, who grew up next door to Alice B. Toklas on O'Farrell Street and later became a part of the Stein-Toklas (see p. 243) circle in Paris, donated her collection of Matisse paintings and sculpture to the museum – part of the significant French core of the collection.

The Museum of Modern Art also has a respectable sampling of Picasso, Rivera, O'Keeffe, Kandinsky, Mondrian and the New York School of Abstract Expressionism. While the museum tries to avoid a regionalist outlook, it has quite rightly been attentive to California artists such as Viola Frey, Robert Arneson, Richard Diebenkorn, Manuel Neri, David Park and Sergeant Johnson.

MUSEUM OF MODERN ART

Video and architecture have full departmental status within the museum, both rarities. The photography department, which dates to its beginnings, is arguably the museum's strongest area.

Currently under the leadership of director John Lane, SFMOMA has been relying on travelling shows for the majority of its big events in the limbo of preparing for the new museum.

The museum café and bookstore are both outstanding. The bookstore is small, but takes its role as a key art book marketplace seriously. It's also big on sales and mark-downs to keep commerce flowing.

San Francisco Performing Arts Library and Museum

399 Grove St (at Gough), tel. 255 4800. Open Tues–Fri 10 a.m.–5 p.m., Sat 12 noon– 4 p.m.; donation requested.

Depending on what is being showcased in the exhibition space, you might see a jar of Lola Montez's specially-formulated face cream, soprano Kirsten Flagstad's dressing room china, diva Luisa Tetrazzini's costumes or programmes from Isadora Duncan's performances (see p. 86). The Performing Arts Library & Museum has an unmatched collection of theatrical, musical and dance memora-

LOLA MONTEZ

Lola Montez's association with San Francisco was fairly brief, but the actress-adventurer-dancer bonded instantly with the brash, thrill-seeking city.

Still notorious for her liaison with Ludwig I of Bavaria and championing of the peasants in the revolutions of 1848, Montez swept into San Francisco in 1853, dazzling the mostly male audiences with her 'spider dance'. Theatre historian Misha Berson has observed that Montez's pièce de résistance sounds uncannily like avant garde performance art. After a programme of recitations and songs, Montez appeared in a diaphanous dress, dancing to a rhythmic beat. She acted out a woman being attacked by spiders, ending in an orgasmic frenzy as she tried to rip away her flimsy costume to get at the spiders next to her skin. The New York critics trashed Montez, but rough and tumble San Francisco loved her.

Montez, born Eliza Gilbert in Ireland in 1824, became the Madonna of her day, widely denounced as a talentless charlatan who beguiled and abandoned men. Montez was equally adored by quite a few of her many husbands, as well as audiences and benefactors who enjoyed a kind of voyeuristic freedom through the performer's hedonism.

Montez liked San Francisco so much that she married a local journalist before moving on. She lived for a while in the Gold Country where she encouraged the young Lotta Crabtree (see p. 75). Montez left for Australia, returning to San Francisco for her final stage engagement in 1858. The magic was gone and she was booed. Montez, who had horsewhipped critics for unfavourable notices in other years, didn't seem terribly bothered. She wasn't interested in the stage any more. She left for New York and spent the final three years of her life lecturing and writing on spiritual subjects – New Age before her time.

Adah Menken

In the 1860s, Adah Issaacs Menken assumed the Montez mantle of putting sensuality on-stage. A onetime New Orleans prostitute, Menken launched a stage career by appearing in flesh-coloured tights onstage in male roles. In her signature role, Mazeppa, she rode a cantering horse across the stage and up a prop mountain. It was a sensation.

Menken lived a free life offstage, too, dressing in men's clothes to amble around the Barbary Coast with her men friends, who included Bret Harte, Joaquin Miller and Mark Twain. Her third husband left Menken during her San Francisco stay, saying that the city encouraged her wildness.

San Francisco had shorter infatuations with Lillie Langtry, Lillian Russell and Sarah Bernhardt, all of whom were warmly received. But Montez and 'the Menken' were embraced as home girls, whose passion for drama and genius for finding it, paralleled the city's own personality.

As with Montez, Menken's contact was brief (a year) but ecstatic. She died penniless in Paris, aged 33.

bilia and scholarly materials dating from the Gold Rush.

PALM's work is an apt reflection of San Francisco's infatuation with the stage. The organisation has one of the most comprehensive collections of Isadora Duncan materials in the world. Also part of the archive is the Lew Christensen Collection, the personal papers and souvenirs of one of the founders of the San Francisco Ballet. The Utah-born Christensen (1909–84), worked in vaudeville and later with George Balanchine, trying to find a way to be a male ballet dancer without having to go to Europe.

While the museum's exhibition space is very small, accommodating only one show at a time, the exhibitions are consistently interesting.

AROUND CIVIC CENTER

At the imposing Main Library (Larkin and Fulton) the San Francisco History Room and special collections on the third floor make an interesting stop. The History Room staff can answer most queries about city history off the top of their heads; if you want to get serious and look it up, the resources are here. Intriguing memorabilia, such as old photographs, programmes, announcements, awards and maps, is also on display. The Museum of the Book, next door, has displays of early children's books, California writers and rare books. The exhibitions are in no way interactive, some might even call them boring. Bibliophiles, however, will be riveted.

The new library, again scheduled for completion in late 1995, is a visionary project that will be heavily invested in electronic access, while making enormous expansions in the institution's range. A million-dollar Chinese Center will house an in-depth collection of

Chinese language books and rare materials, but the most unusual aspect of the new institution will be the $1.6 million Gay and Lesbian Center, which will be an archive, resource centre and ongoing historical documentation project.

The San Francisco Art Commission Gallery, 155 Grove St, is a municipal gallery that rides the cutting edge of local work with videos, conceptual art, interactive events and a wide range of artist talks and demonstrations. Open Thursday 12 noon–8 p.m., Fri–Sat, 12 noon–5.30 p.m.

If you are in town around Labor Day (the first Monday of September) check out the annual San Francisco Fair, held in Civic Center Plaza. The fair is a citywide celebration, taking the concept of an old-fashioned county fair and reapplying it to an urban setting. Popular events have included the Fog Calling Contest, with entrants imitating fog horns, and the Impossible Parking Space Race, which gives racers a list of tough streets to find a legal parking space, assigns a referee with a stopwatch to each car and sends the field hurtling towards Chinatown, Russian Hill and other parking impossibilities (the city's traffic commissioner was placed fifth last year). There are also food booths, music, crafts and the more familiar trappings of a street fair.

United Nations Plaza is a wide, bricked pedestrian mall that links Civic Center with Market Street. The Plaza, presided over by a magnificent statue of Simon Bolivar, comes alive every Wednesday and Sunday when the Heart of the City Farmers' Market fills the pavements with vegetables, fruit, flowers and even fish. The shoppers run the gamut from Vietnamese grandmothers in their native pyjama uniforms to devoted foodies looking for that one perfect artichoke. The market is open all day, 10 a.m. to 6 p.m., but come in the morning for the full benefit of the gorgeous produce and happy shoppers. If you are inclined, it's usually an easy matter to make a picnic of fruit, bread and other bounty on sale.

AROUND HAYES VALLEY

The name Hayes Valley has been on city maps since the nineteenth century, but the neighbourhood was dormant for decades, crisscrossed by freeways and stamped uncool. Some of the freeways are coming down – part of the rethinking of elevated highways after the Loma Prieta earthquake – and the idea of living near an arts neighbourhood has taken on a distinctly hip tint.

Hayes Valley wraps around the south and west edges of Civic Center, extending, in theory, far into the Western Addition. In current terms, Hayes Valley mostly refers to the rapidly gentrifying area along Hayes Street, between Laguna and Franklin. New ventures are popping up almost daily, as every kid who ever worked an espresso machine or helped friends hang paintings is opening a café or gallery. As one of the shock troops told a newspaper reporter, 'We're the frontline for gentrification. Artists are expected to go in and clean things up so the middle class can move in.'

Whatever the case, Hayes Valley is a major fun spot at the moment. A couple of women-owned cafés, Momi Toby's Revolution Café, 528 Laguna St, and Mad Magda's Russian Tea Room & Café, 579 Hayes St, set the funky tone. Art shops are thick on the ground here, with jewellery, sculpture and various types of artwork. De Vera, 384 Hayes St, has marvellous glass work; F. Dorian, at No. 388, stocks fey little one-of-a-kind items such as handmade birdhouses and a variety of delicate jewellery; and Velvet da Vinci, No. 508, is known for its off-the-wall artists' pieces, like a robot made of old teapots.

THE TENDERLOIN

Supposedly the name was imported from New York; the police beat officers wanted the district because it was a 'prime' area for kick-backs and pay-offs.

What is now San Francisco's Tenderloin was one of the first areas rebuilt about 1906. There was a tremendous demand for residential hotels after the fires. With the tourist bonanza of the 1915 Panama Pacific International Exposition on the horizon, hotels were considered an excellent idea and the area was seriously overbuilt. Inevitably, the hotels became prostitution nests and home to society's marginal members.

The area already houses many 'respectable' parlour houses, those well-organised brothels where prostitutes resided under the iron rule of a madam. The parlour house girls lived quite a regulated life with strict house rules, such as fixed hours for meals, dress and room checks by the madam and little time off. According to evidence pieced together by San Francisco folklorist Jim Riggs, one of the women's favourite time off spots was Aunt Josie's Place in the 100 block of Mason Street. It is a parking lot now (next to the Powell West Hotel), but in 1906 the two-storey building which stood on the spot was a club for women only.

'Twelve handsome stalwart men for your amusement,' said the discreet cards for Aunt Josie's. The clients – prostitutes having a bus person's holiday – could select their stalwart man from photos in the reception room, pay their $10, and be shown to a private room. Aunt Josie's was reportedly a huge success, but the city's pimps were so incensed by this display of unfettered female sexuality that they forced Aunt Josie to close down. At this point in time, it is difficult to discover exactly what was going on almost a century ago in the shadow world of prostitution, but Riggs says that the pimps were furious that the working girls were 'wasting their money'. If the women were going to have sex anyway, then the pimp establishment felt it should be making money from it. The Aunt Josie's situation must qualify as the all-time champ for insidious male double standardism.

'I SHOT HIM 'CAUSE I LOVE HIM, GODDAM HIM!'

Tessie Wall shocked and delighted San Francisco when she shot her ex-husband down on Anna Lane (now Cyril Magnin Street) on a rainy December day in 1917. She was a flamboyant madam who had bitterly contested the divorce suit of Frank Daroux, a gambler and Republican political boss.

Standing over his body, both triumphant and distraught, Tessie told everyone around that she had shot Frank because she loved him so. To San Francisco this was a fitting dénouement to the Frankie and Johnnie-esque melodrama to Tessie and Frank.

Tessie was widely admired in San Francisco as a working-class girl from the Mission who had enough gumption to leave her alcoholic fireman husband and take care of herself. She drifted into prostitution from housework and set up a famous parlour house on O'Farrell Street in the Upper Tenderloin. Tessie's fame rested on her warm, Irish personality and her reputation for hard-headed business. As John Steinbeck once said, 'There is something very attractive to men about a madam. She combines the brains of a businessman, the toughness of a prize fighter, the warmth of a companion, the humor of a tragedian.' Tessie typified this male dream logic for a sexually voracious woman who was outwardly independent and self-sufficient, yet utterly dependent on men's patronage and largess.

Tessie was obsessed with Frank Daroux, who was seen as hen-pecked for having agreed to Tessie's determination to have a church wedding. Daroux survived his wounds, married another woman and moved east. Tessie eventually got out of 'the life' with quite a tidy sum. She retired to her apartment buildings in the Mission which were furnished with her eclectic collection of antiques, another foible San Francisco enjoyed laughing about. In one matchup, though, Tessie had the last laugh. She was as avid to be a part of society as to marry Frank. Finally she somehow contrived to get an invitation to a society ball. The ball-goers were shocked but distantly polite. Tessie, who knew that press reports routinely omitted the names of the scandalous, was not about to let the society columnists cheat her out of her victory. A perfectly straight-faced story that never mentioned the ball appeared in the next day's *Examiner*.

REPORTED LOST

Tessie Wall reported to police early this morning the loss of one diamond brooch, of great monetary and sentimental value, the gift of Frank Daroux. The loss is said to have occurred somewhere between O'Farrell Street and the Hotel St Francis last night sometime between the hours of ten and midnight.

Translation: Tessie Wall, accompanied by her lover, had been at the Mardi Gras Ball at the St Francis hobnobbing with all the swells.

Prostitutes still roam the Tenderloin. It is also home to the creepy porno movie theatres, peep shows and adult bookstores. It is more than a little wrenching to see groups of Vietnamese, Thai and Cambodian children darting through the mean streets on their way home from school or running errands for their families. O'Farrell Street is the spine of the Tenderloin with its changeable borders extending to Mason Street towards downtown, Market, Polk and Post with a *baja* Tenderloin crossing Market along 6th Street, San Francisco's historic Skid Row.

In the midst of the Tenderloin are a number of surprises. The Phoenix Inn (see p. 284), 601 Eddy St, is a fifties' motel retooled as a very cool kinda rock'n'roll hotel with a guest list that includes John F. Kennedy Jr, the Red Hot Chili Peppers, kd lang, Bonnie Raitt, the Sex Pistols and Sinead O'Connor. The motel restaurant is a Caribbean hot spot, Miss Pearl's Jam House (see p. 302).

Glide Memorial Methodist Church, at 330 Ellis St, is a free-form congregation that is exactly what all the high church elders of every denomination feared would happen when the old ways were loosened the teensiest bit. Headed by the extremely influential Reverend Cecil Williams, a hard-driving black minister who takes his text from the social gospel, Glide is home to an eclectic, multi-racial congregation. Services, or in Glide-speak, celebrations, are a popular entertainment form for San Franciscans of all religious backgrounds. Call 771 6300 for times.

SOUTH OF MARKET

THE MISSION, CASTRO AND NOE VALLEY

For most of its history, South of Market has been San Francisco's gritty industrial working-class backyard.

'Whether you know your location or not, the heart of the city is South o' the Slot!' went one popular ditty of long ago, when Irish, Greek, Jewish and German immigrants lived in the plain workingmen's Victorians and walked to their jobs in warehouses, on the waterfront, with the railroad and at factories and foundries.

There was a tremendous sense of pride that bordered on tribal for the South of the Slot residents (the slot referred to the cable car groove cut down Market Street) who saw themselves as independent, hard-working and beholden to nobody.

Today South of Market has a different image, the name calling up a hip mélange of pulsating dance clubs, artists' lofts, trendy restaurants, hordes of youthful fun-seekers, slick condo buildings and the new arts district, Yerba Buena Center. The old warehouses and railroad tracks are still there, but most are unused or for sale. As the last undeveloped region of San Francisco, South of Market is headed towards massive redefinition.

Artists and young people were the first to begin moving into the area which they discovered in the 1970s. A lively subculture of restaurants, music clubs and semi-legal warehouse apartments grew up along Folsom, Bryant and Brannan streets parallel to Market.

South of Market has remained separate from land-hungry San Francisco for several reasons, but chief among them is the physical barrier. The street grid above Market is completely different from the streets South of Market, with few direct intersections. It is more than a psychological barrier to travel across Market Street; if you are driving it requires a major strategic plan to go north to south or vice versa.

This odd state of affairs came about in 1847 when the new American administrators hired surveyor Jasper O'Farrell to expand and formalise the Mexican street plan. O'Farrell thought the Mexican blocks were too small and the streets too narrow, so he

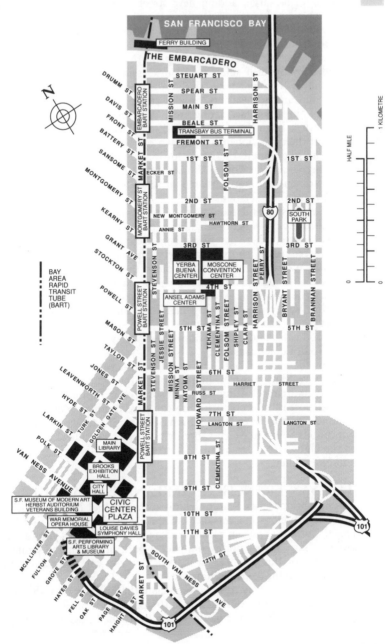

attempted to correct that by making the blocks South of Market four times as large, adding new street patterns to accommodate them. Instead of spurring development, the O'Farrell plan created a barricade that has lasted for almost a century and a half.

South of Market runs from the bay to South Van Ness Avenue where it becomes the largely Hispanic Mission. Mission Dolores, founded by Spanish soldiers and priests in 1776, is anchor of the city's most vibrant neighbourhood. Unlike Chinatown, tourists don't outnumber residents on the streets. The Mission warrants caution, but it is a fascinating area. While most known as a Latino area with a huge Spanish-speaking population, it is also home to many of the city's bohemians, drawn by the (relatively) cheap rents, good cafés and interesting street life. San Francisco's women's quarter is here – a collection of shops, bookstores, clubs and the venerable Women's Center gathered around Valencia Street which is sometimes called "Feminist Ave."

The Mission is flanked by the Castro and Noe Valley, two residential-shopping-hangout neighbourhoods. The Castro, of course, is the gay centre, where gay men's bars are interspersed with clothing stores, ice cream shops, stationery shops, all gay-owned, gay-staffed, gay-oriented. There are women on the streets and at work on Castro, though it's a predominantly male scene. It is not, however, a male place where women feel the least bit out of place.

Noe Valley, on the other hand, is almost completely off the tourist track, but a pleasant place of bookstores, boutiques, neighbourhood cafés and quirky shops. Noe Valley is a window on how typical San Franciscans live.

For the visitor, South of Market isn't as easy to traverse as the area above Market Street. In addition to the wide open spaces that make walking more arduous and in some cases, not at all safe, public transport isn't as colourful (no cable cars) nor as plentiful. Keep in mind you may have to do a bit more planning to get to the neighbourhoods South of Market, but by all means go; take taxis at night to the clubs, use buses and BART to go to the Mission, the Castro and Noe Valley.

THE SAN FRANCISCO-OAKLAND BAY BRIDGE

The Bay Bridge casts a large shadow over South of Market which is riddled with exits and entrances to the elevated roadways that feed into the bridge. You can't walk across the Bay Bridge as you can the Golden Gate; there's not even a pocket park or designated sightseeing point for this engineering marvel. But you can walk along the Embarcadero for some dazzling views.

An excellent way to fully appreciate the bridge's overwhelming scale and masterful construction is to approach it on foot from the Ferry Building. From the bay-front walkway the bridge looms larger and larger. You will begin to hear what Jack Kerouac called 'the boomcrash of truck traffic' hurtling across the 'glorious girders of the Oakland Bay Bridge'.

The Bay Bridge is the ugly duckling to the Golden Gate's beautiful swan; it gets overlooked by the other bridge's perfect aesthetics and perfect placement. The Bay Bridge, though, is the backbone of Bay Area transport. In the 1989 earthquake a section of the bridge gave way, creating a gap which caused one car to crash. No cars went off the bridge or into the water. Authorities shut down the bridge for a month which was one of the most disastrous repercussions of the earthquake, since thousands upon thousands of people couldn't get to work, get home, visit their families, in short, carry on with their daily lives.

EMPEROR NORTON

Joshua Abraham Norton (1819–80) set a standard for eccentricity that San Francisco has been hard-pressed to match. Dressed in a blue uniform and plumed hat, the once wealthy speculator gravely carried out daily inspections of the city from 1857 to his death in 1880.

An Englishman who arrived in San Francisco in 1849, Norton was known as a keen businessman well on his way to his first million. In 1853 he was wiped out in an attempt to corner the rice market and lost his senses. When he reappeared in the city in 1857 he had declared himself the Emperor of America. Possessed of a touching dignity, Norton I issued edicts, attended public functions and observed his subjects. He even travelled to Sacramento to sit in on the Legislature. Printing shops printed his proclamations (for free), which included the far-sighted idea of a Bay Bridge, although His Majesty inexplicably included the uninhabitable Farallones. Tailors presented him with a new uniform every decade or so and restaurants honoured his royal currency, another gift of the city's printers to His Majesty.

Part of Norton's success was his infallible sense of decorum and propriety. He never asked for much nor pushed too hard. A good Londoner even in his madness, he carried an umbrella about during the rainy season. He was listed in the city directory as 'Norton, Joshua (Emperor, Protector of Mexico)'. He added Mexico to his domain when one of his subjects suggested their citizens needed his help, too. Norton I died of a heart attack at the corner of California and Grant. More than 10,000 people attended his funeral.

A bridge connecting Oakland and San Francisco had been proposed as early as 1851. Emperor Norton, San Francisco's favourite eccentric, issued proclamations ordering the building of a bridge in the 1860s. The talk turned serious during World War I and plans began to take form in the late 1920s. President Herbert Hoover, an engineer and Stanford graduate, used his power to nudge the plans along and construction began in 1933, to finish three years later. It was the world's most expensive project at that point, costing $78 million and involving more concrete than was used for New York's Empire State Building, eighteen per cent of all American steel produced in 1933 and a mind-boggling amount of cable, timber and manpower.

GIVE ME A BRIDGE OR GIVE YOU DEATH
Whereas, it is our pleasure to acquiesce in all means of civilization and population:

We, Norton I, Emperor of the United States and Protector of Mexico, do order and direct first, that Oakland shall be the coast termination of the Central Pacific Railroad; secondly, that a suspension bridge be constructed from the improvements lately ordered by our royal decree at Oakland Point to Yerba Buena (Island), from thence to the mountain range of Sausalito, and from thence to the Farallones, to be of sufficient strength and size for a railroad; and thirdly, the Central Pacific Railroad Company are charged with the carrying out of this work, for purposes that will hereafter appear. Whereof fall not under pain of death.
  Given under our hand this 18th day of August, A.D. 1869. Norton I

The Bay Bridge was – and is – beloved among San Franciscans not only for its usefulness but its saviour-like role in the Depression. Begun and finished before Golden Gate, the Bay Bridge put hundreds of men to work on its construction while creating a powerful economic ripple effect throughout the Bay Area. For many San Francisco families the bridge symbolised not just the Bay Area's emergence from the Depression but their own ability to survive as a family.

The bridge consists of two levels and two bridges: San Francisco to Yerba Buena Island is a suspension bridge; Yerba Buena to Oakland is a cantilever bridge. The two are seamlessly connected by a tunnel that was blasted through hilly Yerba Buena Island. Originally cars used the upper deck while trains and trucks travelled the lower level. With the dominance of the automobile, both levels were given over to cars in the late 1950s – westbound on the upper deck, eastbound on the lower.

Few sights are as exhilarating as coming into San Francisco from the top deck of the Bay Bridge on a sparkling day, bursting into the light from the tunnel, gaining the top of the slight arch and seeing San Francisco spread out like a dream world in front of you. If you don't have a friend to drive you, take a bus or BART (which has its own underground tunnel) to the East Bay just so you can ride a bus back across the Bay Bridge.

South Park

Bounded by Bryant, Second, Brannan and Third streets.

Increasingly, people are discovering South Park but it is still a more secret place than not. You can only find this hidden oval park by looking for it. A fashionable neighbourhood that peaked early, South Park isn't visible from the surrounding busy main streets and is accessible only by narrow valleys: South Park Avenue from Second and Third; Jack London Street from Bryant and Brannan.

Reclaimed by new residents in the early eighties, South Park evolved from a scuzzy drug dealer haven to a neighbourhood gathering place. There's a sturdy little playground with slides and sandpit for the kids and benches for grown-ups. South Park is also home to three very good cafés. Caffe Centro, 102 South Park, is a coffee house with seating that spills out onto the pavement. A few doors down, at No. 108, is the South Park Café which feels for all the world like a Parisian bistro set down in San Francisco. Across the park is Ecco, a terminally chic Italian restaurant with attitude and first-rate food to match (see p. 305).

An Englishman, Gold Rush financier George Gordon, developed South Park in 1856, inspired by Berkeley Square. He envisioned elegant Georgian townhouses centred around a private park. At the time, South Park was almost next door to the city's most prized neighbourhood, Rincon Hill (now totally obliterated by the Bay Bridge anchorage), and for a while was a rising area. By the early 1870s, however, Rincon Hill was slipping, soon to be completely overshadowed by Nob Hill. South Park never achieved Gordon's dreams. Later he suffered the financial reverses familiar to the time and died penniless, further shamed by his alcoholic wife and their wanton daughter, Nelly, said to be one of San Francisco's earliest examples of a rich girl gone bad (she drank and married badly). Gertrude Atherton (see p. 152) used the Gordons' tragic story as fodder for her first novel, *Daughter of the Vine*.

After more than a century of neglect, San Francisco is once again coming to South Park. The park is almost at the heart of the city's new discount shopping circuit which makes it a convenient lunch and dinner stop for all those tired, hard-working shoppers. Third Street is lined with discount places, from the Jeanne-Marc outlet to the mall-like Six Sixty Center.

The Jewish Museum San Francisco

121 Steuart Street (at Mission, off the Embarcadero), tel. 543 8880. Closed Mon and Sat, open other days, 10 a.m.–4 p.m.; $1.50–$3, children under 12 free.

This is one of San Francisco's lively little museums with changing exhibits, knowledgeable guides, lectures and multi-media presentations. Devoted to Jewish culture and art, the exhibits range from the whimsical, such as Jewish greeting cards and Outsider art, to the serious issues of history and society. Important shows have included exhibitions of political artwork from Israel and the work of San Francisco cartoonist Art Spiegelman, whose controversial retelling of the Holocaust (*Maus*) using animals in cartoon drawings, won the Pulitzer Prize.

Yerba Buena Center

Bounded by Fourth, Mission, Third and Folsom streets.

Opened in late 1993, Yerba Buena Center is an ambitious arts and business complex that could become San Francisco's most exciting arts centre.

Yerba Buena is across Howard Street from the Moscone Convention Center. The new San Francisco Museum of Modern Art is rising across Third Street, while the Mexican Museum and the Jewish Museum plan to move to the area in the next two to five years. The Ansel Adams photography gallery is already in place on Fourth Street. A new theatre (designed by James Stewart Polshek) and art gallery (by Japanese architect Fumihiko Maki) are carefully integrated into an elaborate park that can also double as a performance site.

The quality of art and culture is an unknown. The theatre will programme dance, music and plays, but will have no resident company. The galleries, likewise, will not have a permanent collection but will exhibit travelling shows and exhibitions organised by its staff.

While San Francisco makes up its mind about the art and culture inside the buildings, the park and gardens were pronounced an instant hit. A monument to Dr Martin Luther King Jr, a perpetual waterfall, is an especially outstanding feature. There is also a butterfly garden and twenty species of trees.

The Center, which includes the Moscone Convention Center, plans to have a children's centre, cinema, shops and restaurants before the complex is complete. Three cafés launched themselves in Yerba Buena as soon as the doors opened to the public.

Yerba Buena represents a major gravitational shift in the San Francisco landscape. Civic Center has been the arts focus of the city for the last seventy years; it is unclear exactly how the new arts neighbourhood will affect that.

For information about programmes at both the theatre and the gallery, call 978 2787.

Ansel Adams Center

250 Fourth St, tel. 495 7000. Open Tues–Sun, 11 a.m.–6 p.m., $2–$4, under 12 free.

The Ansel Adams moved from Carmel to San Francisco in 1989,

settling into this spacious, well-designed building that houses five galleries, an outstanding photography bookstore and administrative offices that co-ordinate the seminars, photography classes and publications run by the Center's parent organisation, the Friends of Photography.

The gallery shows are varied. One exhibition room is devoted to the work of Adams, the great camera poet of nature. The Adams work is curated with verve and imagination rather than presented as a shrine to the photographer, who died in 1984. One of the centre's biggest popular and critical successes was a retrospective of Adams' most famous photograph, 'Moonrise Over Hernandez, New Mexico'. The gallery mounted a roomful of 'Moonrises', showing how Adams had subtly worked with the image over the years in cropping and printing it.

The Center develops its own shows and exhibits important travelling photography. As with the handling of Adams's work, the philosophy of curating is adventurous while keeping an eye on the past. Photographs of the Ansel Adams vintage and earlier share the galleries with emerging photographers whose pictures are often wildly experimental. The Center has a relaxed attitude towards the past and the present, mixing the best photographers of both.

SOUTH BEACH

This is an old name, originally used to refer to the bay front area running south from Rincon Hill, where the anchorage of the Bay Bridge now sits, to Steamboat Boat Point around Piers 40–44. Younger San Franciscans often think South Beach is a contemporary developer's brainstorm, a slightly ironic borrowing from Miami Beach's neon-glitz-bikini district, also called South Beach.

There's no comparable scene happening in San Francisco's South Beach, once the province of longshoremen, ships, waterfront dives and cheap boarding houses. The development engine is beginning to turn over, however, and the signs of a different agenda for South Beach are unmistakable. You will find some upscale restaurants, new condo buildings and even a golf driving range that has become one of the town's big singles spots.

At Brannan Street and Embarcadero, look for a handsome neo-Mission style complex that looks to be a condo building, or perhaps a quiet institution of some sort. This is the Delancey Street Foundation, one of America's most successful drug and alcohol rehabilitation centres. Founded in 1972 by a charismatic alcoholic and felon named John Maher and Dr Mimi Silbert, a criminologist, Delancey Street takes its name from the New York street where many immigrants settled. The idea is that the residents are beginning a new life in a new world.

MIMI SILBERT

Mimi Silbert is the driving force behind Delancey Street. A frustrated prison criminologist, Silbert met ex-con John Maher in 1971. He was a recovering alcoholic, equally frustrated with the prison system.

They put their expertise and anger together and worked out a rehabilitation plan for criminals and addicts that they felt would really work. This plan called for a residential, self-governing group which was completely self-supporting. The people they wanted to reach had failed at every level of living their lives; Silbert and Maher wanted an environment that would force the residents of their programme to become responsible and fully conscious of their decisions.

Delancey Street has supported itself from day one. Maher and Silbert felt that government subsidies or foundation grant money would create a sense of 'them' being in charge, freeing the residents of the responsibility of paying their way. They began in a run-down San Francisco apartment with four ex-prisoners. Soon they had a hundred enrollees. By living frugally and pooling resources, they were able to buy a big house in Pacific Heights, once the former Soviet Embassy.

The Pacific Heights neighbours were shocked and tried very hard to keep Delancey Street out. Silbert and Maher were able to overcome the barriers and even win over the people in the big houses. The Delancey residents proved to be perfect neighbours and sealed their acceptance by performing chores, for free, around the neighbourhood. This good will continues today in Delancey Street's widespread support network among SF socialites.

Silbert and Maher fell in love and although they never married, became a personal and professional partnership, with Maher becoming father to Silbert's twin sons from a brief early marriage.

Silbert's common sense more than her Berkeley PhD has made the difference at Delancey Street. Early on she saw the opportunities for the organisation in unskilled labour, establishing the moving company and other services by trial and error. Today, the residents are required to learn three skills, one involving physical labour, one involving clerical or computer skills and one concerning interaction with other people.

Non-sexist by its very nature, Delancey Street holds all doors open to women. Job skills and domestic chores are assigned by a resident's rank and later, inclination. Women aren't frog-marched into secretarial jobs and men aren't pointed at heavy lifting. Silbert's current No. I career choice for all residents is truck driving which is fairly easy to get into and pays well. She often brags about the success of women residents in this once all-male field.

Silbert's sons are grown up now and on their own. Maher left Delancey Street in 1984 when his drinking began to plague him again. He died of a heart attack in New York City four years later. Silbert, who lives at Delancey Street and says she has no wish to marry again, continues to preach her gospel of hard work, self-discipline and self-reliance.

Delancey Street's requirements are simple but stringent. A candidate must ask to join the community. If accepted, he or she pledges to stay a minimum of two years. Usually this is the last desperate chance for veteran criminals who are pushed to go by the courts or their exhausted families.

Five hundred people live and work at Delancey Street. The

foundation is completely self-supporting from no-strings gifts and its businesses, which include a moving service, car repair, janitorial service, a picture-framing shop and a printing business. The newest foundation venture is the Delancey Street Restaurant (see p. 304).

Located on the ground floor with indoor and outdoor seating, the restaurant is indistinguishable from a commercial café with the exception of the staff's overwhelmingly enthusiastic service. The staff is trained by chefs, waiters and bartenders from some of the city's best restaurants such as Postrio, Perry's, Roti, Square One and the Washington Square Bar and Grill. There's a full bar on the premises, the idea being that recovering addicts are going to be around alcohol in the real world so a training ground is necessary.

If you're interested in how Delancey Street works, go to the main gate and ask to be taken to the office. The reception staff will cheerfully give out materials and even take you on a tour of this remarkable building. Delancey Street residents built the structure under the guidance of a few volunteer experts. It consists of several storeys built around a courtyard with 177 apartments, meeting rooms, a movie theatre, work spaces, shops, kitchens and even a swimming pool.

SoMa

Unlike South Beach, SoMa is a recent wrinkle on the San Francisco map, first introduced as a joke. Nobody remembers exactly when or who introduced this smirky contraction of South of Market, but it has taken hold and seems here to stay.

It is a borrowing from New York's SoHo (South of Houston) district, another warehouse-to-wonderful Cinderella story. SoMa's boundaries are a bit difficult to pin down, but it is clear that Folsom Street is the main drag and the heart of SoMa is at the club-encrusted corner of 11th Street and Folsom. The trendmeisters have pronounced that 11th Street is 'over but not dead', saying that the club epicentre has shifted to the Mission. For the untutored, it would be difficult to tell that this two-block club loop isn't the centre of the universe on Friday and Saturday nights, when lines of would-be patrons snake down the street, limousines circle the block and groups of friends walk from club to club.

The crowds are usually under thirty, but a good band will bring out the baby boomers, especially to Slim's, rocker Boz Scaggs' celebrated club (see p. 325).

The 11th Street Club Crawl
Slim's, 333 11th St, adroitly mixes blues, hiphop, funk, tex-mex and almost every pop music genre. The club's sound system is the city's best, the bar is good and there are even good seats scattered around the room. The club has become such a success on its own

that many patrons don't know, or don't care, that it is owned by a rock star.

Paradise Lounge, 1501 Folsom St, is a warren of different spaces: five bars, three stages and a pool room. Sounds like a mess? It is and the regulars love it. On a good night you might hit one of the unannounced stars such as Chris Isaak fine-tuning his new concert show.

DNA Lounge, 375 11th St, two bars, big dance floor, loud, loud music. Prince likes to pop in and try out his new stuff when he's in town.

Twenty Tank Brewery, 316 11th St, a good spot to sit down and have one of the beers brewed on the premises. Some food, but mostly acts as a relay station between club stops.

Hamburger Mary's, 1582 Folsom St, San Francisco's best hamburgers. The club kids come in before shows for sustenance and afterwards to hash over the evening.

Club 0, 278 11th St, disco fever in the '90s, a huge dance floor, multi-racial crowd who do a double-take when anyone over 25 walks in – mostly DJ music, some bands.

(See 'clubs' under listings, p. 321, for more details.)

Shopping South of Market

South of Market's discount shopping is a mixed blessing for the visitor. The variety and quality of the merchandise makes every shopper's heart beat a little faster, but studying a map of the widely spaced warehouses and stores causes consternation. If you are on vacation to shop, this will be no problem. If you want to merely dip into the shopping it gets a bit tricky because it can be confusing and extremely time consuming to criss-cross South of Market getting to the stores.

The serious shopper ought to consider getting a copy of Sally Socolich's *Bargain Hunting in the Bay Area* (Wingbow Press, 1993) the shopper's bible. Socolich, who often appears on local TV with her shopping tips, has mapped out all of Northern California, but grades the shopping outlets as shrewdly as a sommelier rates wines.

Another shopping aid that locals use is the shopping tour bus. Guided by board certified shopoholics, the buses cruise from outlet to outlet, the happy shoppers unconcerned about directions, addresses, parking or finding a cab. Shopping Safari, a San José company that specialises in bringing in suburbanities, will happily pick up shoppers in San Francisco for one of its all-day tours. Reservations are needed, tel. (408) 292 7467, $25.

Ten Fave Outlets

Jeanne-Marc Factory Outlet, 508 Third St, tel. 243 4396; the best designer outlet in town, elegant women's clothes, dresses, vests, skirts, jackets and more.

660 Center, 660 Third St, tel. 227 0464; two levels, a dozen shops, good bargains.

Toy Liquidators, 899 Howard St, tel. 243 8518; perhaps it is best to leave the children behind and do all your birthday and Christmas shopping alone.

Gunne Sax, Ltd, 35 Stanford St, tel. 495 3326; Jessica McClintock's romantic party dresses are a teenage girl's fantasies brought to life; McClintock's more grown-up clothes are here, too.

Bed & Bath Superstore, 555 9th St, tel. 252 0490; one of the biggest single stores in San Francisco, stuffed with towels, sheets, storage bins, kitchen implements and more.

Christina Foley, 430 9th St, tel. 621 8126; beautiful sweaters for children and adults, gorgeous markdowns.

Harper Greer, 580 Fourth St, tel. 543 4066; sophisticated women's clothes for the office and leisure in large sizes.

Esprit, 499 Illinois St (Potrero Hill), tel. 957 2550; the only place Chelsea Clinton specifically asked to see on her San Francisco vacation; teenagers love this place and the jazzy clothes – mothers are less impressed with the skimpy discounts.

Rainbeau Factory Store, 300 Fourth St, tel. 777 9786; exercise wear, much of it in cotton, leotards, tights, unitards for men, women and children.

Golden Rainbow Factory Outlet, 435-A Brannan St, tel. 543 5191; kids' clothes, kids' clothes and more kids' clothes.

THE MISSION

The Mission throbs with life. Low-riders cruise the slow-moving, crowded streets with Mexican pop music cranked up to ear-splitting decibels while families fill the sidewalks on Mission Street and 24th Street, shopping in the little markets.

Undeniably shabby, the Mission is full of pleasant contradictions. Street murals that echo the work of the great Mexican muralist Diego Rivera and José Clemente Orozco pop up at unexpected places. In the middle of this machismo-flavoured neighbourhood a women's district has come alive. Cafés that could just as easily be found in Managua, Guadalajara or Guatemala City sit cheek-by-jowl beside non-smoking vegetarian, politically correct coffee houses.

San Francisco's oldest district and more often than not a working-class neighbourhood, the Mission is now a predominantly Latino district, the Germans and Irish having moved up and out. It comes as a shock to some newcomers that the Mission hasn't always been a Hispanic district. Mission Dolores, site of San Francisco's founding and the oldest building in the city, exudes a heavy air of Spanish colonialism while the streets of the Mission have the stamp of the Spanish past upon them: Valencia, Sanchez,

Dolores, Mission, Guerrero, Noe, Ramona, Hidalgo. In one of those amusing twists of history, the streets were named after some of the early Spanish and Mexican settlers and to give the district a nostalgic air for the days of the Californios. Now the re-Latinisation of California brings the Spanish influence full circle.

There are two BART stops in the Mission, 16th Street and 24th Street. Both are full of street life and should be approached with caution, especially if you're alone. Avoid them altogether at night. Because they are gathering spots, the street corners around the BART stops (the stations are underground; you take an escalator to street level) can attract a marginal element. But these areas are heavily patrolled by police and used every day by thousands of women who live and work in the Mission. Switch your urban alertness to 'on' – watch what is going on around you, move with a sense of confidence and leave if you feel the tiniest bit uncomfortable.

Mission Street and 24th Street are the district's main thoroughfares. Spanish is the first language spoken everywhere, even in Asian grocery stores where the owners have cheerfully learned their customers' language. If you have an ear for Spanish you will notice a variety of accents. Unlike most *barrios* in the American West, the Mission is not an exclusively Mexican neighbourhood. Immigrants are just as likely to be from Central America, particularly the war-ravaged countries of Nicaragua, El Salvador and Guatemala. South Americans, too, have come to the Mission in significant numbers in the last decade.

Food is a big entertainment item in the Mission; everyone in San Francisco seems to have his or her favourite *tacqueria*. There are also art galleries, tiny performance spaces and Valencia Street, San Francisco's only visible women's area.

Mission Dolores

320 Dolores St (at 16th Street), tel. 621 8203. Open daily 9 a.m.–4 p.m., some restrictions during services. Donation requested.

History Properly the Mission San Francisco de Asis, this adobe church is the oldest building in San Francisco. Built between 1785 and 1791, the Mission has survived three major earthquakes and years of desecration. The unshakeability of Mission Dolores is an article of faith among San Franciscans, whatever their spiritual persuasion.

The church was established as part of a 1775–6 mission by the colonial government to strengthen its claim on Alta California. Led by Captain Juan Bautista de Anza, the party of thirty soldiers and four male civilian settlers, all with their families, arrived from Mexico in Monterey in March 1776. De Anza and a group of

soldiers continued on to San Francisco Bay which the Spanish had only discovered in 1769. They chose a spot high above the bay for the *presidio* (fort) and a sunny spot three miles inland for the Mission. The Mission would be called San Francis in honour of the founder of the Franciscans, the priests in charge of California missions. De Anza picked the spot because it was sunny and near fresh water in the form of a small lagoon he called *Laguna de Nuestra Señora de los Dolores*, as it was the Friday of Sorrows on the religious calendar, referring to Our Lady of Sorrows, the Virgin Mary. The pool is long gone, but the name became more identified with the church than Saint Francis. Even the church puts 'Mission Dolores' on its publications.

In June, the 193 colonists made their way up the coast and set up camp around the mission site. Father Francisco Palou said mass on 29 June, five days before the Declaration of Independence was proclaimed in Philadelphia.

Palou organised the mission under the principles set forth by Father Junipero Serra, the Franciscan priest in charge of the California missions. Although they served the Spanish and Mexican settlers, the main purpose of the missions was to convert the Native Americans who were herded into them by the soldiers and punished for resisting or leaving. The Native Americans were taught European farming, husbandry and carpentry methods and expected to adapt their behaviour to the priests' demands. The results were ruinous. Diseases such as measles killed people by the thousands while the agricultural schemes never fully took hold.

Interdependent *presidios* and missions were the standard method of Spanish settlement, but there were enormous tensions between the two institutions. The soldiers were generally ill-trained, badly paid and harshly treated. Bored and lonely, they vented their frustrations on the Native Americans. The women were particularly vulnerable to rape by the soldiers. In a particularly horrific case, three San Diego garrison soldiers kidnapped two girls, raped them and killed one. The soldiers were sent to Mexico for trial and found guilty, whereupon their punishment was to live out the rest of their lives in California, at that point the Devil's Island of colonial Spain.

While the priests did try to protect the Native Americans from the soldiers, the latter were in place to protect the missions from the Native Americans. All of this created a complicated and deeply unsatisfying web of alliances and dependencies for everyone concerned.

In 1834 the Mexican government washed its hands of the hugely expensive missions.

Secularisation destroyed the already fragmented mission system and left the remaining peoples adrift. Although Mexico City ordered the missions to be given to the Native Americans, or if they did not want them, sold on their behalf, the mission farmlands, vineyards, buildings and supplies were simply gobbled up by greedy landowners. Mission Dolores went through a variety of uses, including a saloon. In 1846 the new American government returned the missions to the Catholic Church. Mission Dolores was mired in deed squabbles and wasn't fully regained by the church until 1858. It became a parish church and has remained one ever since.

Construction   Work on a permanent church began in 1785 under Father Palou. Four makeshift chapels had been built and torn down around the original camp site, about a block away from the present church. The San Francisco mission church was neither the most elaborate nor the plainest building among the 21 missions.

Rectangular with a central aisle, the building has adobe walls that are four feet thick. All work was done by Mission's native peoples who were getting on-the-job training in Spanish-Mexican building crafts. No nails were used by the carpenters who employed other adaptive techniques such as the use of pegs, securing the wooden beams with leather thongs. The roof tiles and adobe bricks were all made on site.

During the building Father Palou departed for Mexico and two new priests, Marin Landaeta and Antonio Dante took over. Enthusiastic builders, they completed the church in 1791 and the entire quadrangle compound in 1798. Their draconian methods, however, caused so many people to run away that the Presidio *commandante* was forced to intervene. He insisted that the priests at least provide one hot meal a day instead of the cold grain (most missions prepared three hot meals a day for the neophytes) they were given.

Many of the church's embellishments were brought overland from Mexico, some originating in Spain. While the building's design and workmanship are modest in terms of great world architecture, the achievement of the workers, labouring under miserable conditions to construct something they had never heard of, much less ever seen, is remarkable.

The Visit   Mission Dolores sits side-by-side with a much larger church, the 1913 Basilica of San Francisco where most masses and parish events are held. The Basilica is done in the ornate Spanish Colonial style, suggesting the sort of church that might have been built in San Francisco if it had been a successful colony. In contrast Mission Dolores is a humble church with its squat dimensions and recessed stumpy columns. Yet it projects a quiet, age-old dignity that blends nicely with its fancier neighbouring basilica.

The Mission's facade is a campanario, a design that incorporates bells. These three bells are worth noting as they are original, cast in Mexico in 1792 and 1797 specifically for the Mission and brought overland to California.

Enter the church through a side door, clearly marked, where you are given a brochure and asked for a donation ($1). The church is cool, dim and pregnant with history. The interior's most remarkable features are the Native American designs painted on the ceiling and arches. Adapted from Costanoan basketry designs and originally executed in vegetable dyes, these chevron patterns are the only tangible legacy of the tribe. The designs, repainted in 1890, are vivid and powerful.

The baptistry, midway down the left side of the nave, is still used for all baptisms in the parish. The handcarved altars came from Mexico in the early 1800s. The statues and the reredos behind the altar may also have come from there, but new scholarship indicates that the statues may be made of redwood which would mean they originate from San Francisco or nearby.

Some of the early parish stalwarts are buried within the church. You can see the stones at the rear of the building, embedded in the floor. They include members of the Noe family and William Leidesdorff, one of San Francisco's first black businessmen. He came to the city in 1841, already rich, a native of the Virgin Islands where his father was a Danish planter and his mother a slave woman.

Leaving the church you can enter the basilica next door. Built to replace an 1860 church that was so damaged in the 1906 earthquake that it had to be torn down, the 1913 replacement church's interior is unexceptional. The most interesting features are its Madonna shrines and stained glass windows depicting all 21 California missions.

A small but instructive **museum** lies behind the mission church. Though in need of maintenance itself, the museum shows how the Mission was built and displays fascinating artefacts.

From the museum follow the signs through a small patio area to the walled garden **cemetery**. Quiet and green, this burial ground is only a sliver of the original.

You'll notice a statue of Father Serra (1713–84), architect of the mission system. He is buried in Carmel, but was a careful overseer of Mission Dolores. Serra has been proposed for sainthood and is only one step from canonisation. However, his case has stirred a protest among Native Americans and their supporters – both in and out of the Church – who angrily point out Serra's implicit racism in his dealings with non-whites. The protests seem to have slowed Serra's case, but the outcome remains far from clear.

The focal point of the garden is the **Grotto of Our Lady of Lourdes**, a contrived ruin that pays homage to the estimated 5000

Native Americans who were buried around Mission Dolores.

Another memorial is a statue of the Mohawk convert, Kateri Tekawitha. A small statue of Tekawitha, her eyes turned heavenward, tops a column which reads, 'In prayerful memory of our faithful Indians'. Tekawitha is the first Native American candidate for sainthood. She has been declared 'venerable', one of the three steps to sainthood. Like Father Serra, Tekawitha's case is moving slowly through the Vatican satin bureaucracy.

The cemetery is interesting for the fact that it is one of only two remaining in the city. Realising that burials were far too land-intensive for the unexpandable city, the municipal government banned burials within San Francisco in 1902 and in 1914 evicted all cemeteries except Mission Dolores and the Presidio's National Cemetery.

Many of the headstones are of late nineteenth-century vintage, touching in their elaborate sentiments and decorations. Predictably, there are many children and women buried here, struck down by disease, accidents or childbirth. This being a frontier cemetery there are also headstones that are more about settling old scores than offering prayers to heaven. Several of the victims of the Committee of Vigilance (VC) are buried here. Formed in 1851, when the more settled San Franciscans felt crime had got out of hand, the VC was an amazingly well organised and bureaucratic lynch mob with officers, companies, insignia and its own court system. Of course, these were generally the same aspiring millionaires who refused to pay taxes for a full-time police force and themselves made use of the rough-and-ready ethics of the day.

The Committee reformed in 1856 when a number of events convinced the community leaders that lawlessness was rampant. Among those hung were James P. Casey, who shot his sworn enemy, a newspaper editor, in the street. 'May God Forgive My Persecutors', reads his memorial. James Sullivan's tablet is more direct: 'Sacred to the memory of the late deceased James Sullivan who died by the hands of the V.C. May 31, 1856, age 45 years'.

Charles and Belle Cora are buried together under a sweet marble headstone. Charles, a gambler, was hung by the Vigilantes in 1856 and Belle, a madam, spent the rest of her life (six years) extracting revenge. Charles Cora was originally buried in another city cemetery. In 1916 newspaper reporter Pauline Jacobson became fascinated with Belle's story and tracked down the forgotten graves. She campaigned to have them moved to Mission Dolores when the other cemeteries were being dug up.

BELLE CORA

Belle Cora was perhaps San Francisco's leading madam when her lover and partner, gambler Charlie Cora, was executed by the Vigilantes.

They had arrived in San Francisco in December of 1849, Charlie, 33, a shrewd riverboat gambler, and Belle, 22, already a prostitute, beautiful and proud. Their history is shadowy, Charlie was born in Italy and came to America as a child, but to where? Belle was born in Baltimore and told a number of different stories about how she came to prostitution, her most repeated tale being that she was a sheltered minister's daughter, seduced and abandoned. Belle's short history in San Francisco suggests a wilful woman who positively revelled in her freedom and power.

While later accounts reviled them as 'Oh, so foul!' the Coras were well-liked and respected in early San Francisco. Belle's clientele included judges, senators, millionaires and city officials, while Charlie was known as a stand-up guy whose word was always good.

Not married but completely committed to one another, Belle and Charlie made a formidable team. Their downfall was perhaps fated as San Francisco began attracting families and women who were bent on establishing an approximation of respectability. Belle and Charlie's ruin began at the theatre. One evening in 1855, US Marshal William H. Richardson and his wife were seated in front of the Coras. When Mrs Richardson realised she was next to San Francisco's leading scarlet woman, she told her husband to do something. The Marshal asked the Coras to leave. Belle and Charlie refused, with Belle taking particular delight in Mrs Richardson's discomfort, and the manager was called. In the end, the Richardsons left, much to the amusement of the audience, mostly male and many of Belle's customers.

Richardson, a shady character who was known as a bad drinker, swore revenge. Sober, he was talked out of gunning down Charlie, drunk he stalked the bars. Charlie, a prudent man, evaded him. Finally a heavily intoxicated Richardson cornered the gambler who drew his own gun and shot Richardson dead. After a sensational trial with the state's best lawyers defending Charlie, arranged for and paid for by Belle, he was acquitted.

Charlie's self defence was decried as a mockery of justice and the self-righteous began to talk about reforming the Committee of Vigilance of 1851. When Charlie's friend Charles Casey shot an enemy in the street the Vigilantes began tolling their dreadful bell. The Vigilante men met at their headquarters, 'Fort Gunnybags', a fortified warehouse on Sacramento Street. Charlie and Casey were taken into custody by the Vigilantes and shortly thereafter given a pro forma trial. Told of his death sentence, Charlie's only concern was to see Belle. A priest married them in his cell the night before he was hung.

Belle arranged a lavish funeral for Charlie, donned widow's weeds and ignored an open letter to her from 'Many Women of San Francisco' who said the Vigilance Committee's work wasn't done until Belle Cora left town. Eventually Belle reopened her houses and was as successful as ever. She secretly funnelled her great wealth into a couple of scandal-mongering newspapers, the tabloids of the day. Belle's name was never associated with the papers, but a careful reading shows that the men who were revealed to have second wives back East, involved in crooked finance schemes, suffering from venereal disease and having affairs were always Vigilantes.

Belle Cora died at 36, not an unusual occurrence on the frontier. She left little behind and was buried with her Charlie. There is little reason to think that she did not accomplish everything she set out to do.

Here in the mission garden one begins to understand the romantic mission cult that grew up in the late nineteenth century. By then Father Serra's old missions of cheerless drudgery had metamorphosed into sweet ruins. The courtyards, which had been devoted to vegetables, chickens or workshops in the missions' heyday were planted with colourful flowers and vines. What curious visitors, usually Eastern tourists, saw in the 1880s bore little resemblance to the ruthless collective farms that were the reality of pre-secularisation missions.

This curiosity was fanned by writer Helen Hunt Jackson, a passionate campaigner for the rights of Native Americans. After her factual study of their exploitation aroused little interest, she turned to fiction, hoping to create her own equivalent to *Uncle Tom's Cabin*. Her book, *Ramona*, came out in 1884 and created a sensation. To Jackson's dismay, however, the book was taken up for its love story and the romance of Old California rather than being a brief against an exploited people. Jackson, a Massachusetts-born writer who came to the West with her second husband, took on their cause well into middle age. She settled in San Francisco after the publication of *Ramona* and died in her Russian Hill home in 1885.

Leaving the Mission Dolores garden you will exit through a gift shop which has little to offer.

Dolores Street

When you are back on Dolores Street notice the long building across the street with the mansard roof. Until 1981 it was Notre Dame High School, the first school for girls in San Francisco. Founded in 1868 by the Sisters of Notre Dame de Namur, the original school was dynamited in 1906 as a fire break and, in fact, the fireline held at Dolores (the fire's deepest penetration was 20th Street, across from Mission Dolores Park). The school was replaced in 1907 with this building, which is now used for performances and offices for non-profit groups.

Mission Dolores Park (18th and Dolores) is a popular outdoor venue for summer entertainments such as Make-A-Circus and the San Francisco Mime Troupe (see p. 334). On warm weekends the upper rim is full of sun-starved San Franciscans trying to get a tan.

When two of the world's most famous feminists came to San Francisco, they stayed in the Mission. America's foremost suffragist, Susan B. Anthony was a guest at the luxurious Murphy house at 159 Liberty St, off Dolores, when she visited the city in 1896 to make speeches for the cause. Emma Goldman lived for about a year at 569 Dolores with her lover, Alexander Berkman, in 1916. Goldman had come to town to take part in the fractious Tom Mooney trial. Mooney, a radical socialist, was convicted of a bombing that killed ten people during a pro-military parade on Market Street in 1916. He spent 23 years in prison on bogus evidence before being pardoned. Goldman rallied support on his behalf and lectured to San Franciscans on feminism and birth control.

Valencia Street

This is called the women's street or "feminist ave." for the concentration of women-oriented shops and businesses that are sprinkled through the shabby storefronts and *tacquerias* that run from 16th to 24th streets.

The two centres of gravity are the Women's Building, right off Valencia at 3543 18th St, and the Old Wives' Tales Bookstore, 1009 Valencia. Like the women's area as a whole, the Women's Building and Old Wives' Tales are both uncompromisingly feminist, powered by a heavy infusion of lesbian energy and consciousness.

There's no clear line between straight women and lesbians in most women's organisations, which makes a comfortable mix for everyone. Straight women don't feel out of place on Valencia and gay women don't feel marginalised. Visit the Women's Building (or call 431 1180) to drop in on political meetings, read the bulletin board and catch up with the movement. In December the Women's Building hosts one of the Bay Area's biggest craft fairs which includes music, entertainments, childcare, food and networking. Spread over two weekends, it is possibly the biggest annual women's event in San Francisco.

Old Wives' Tales, which has been struggling financially, is more like a community centre than a business. The store is such a nerve centre for locals and visitors that the staff regularly prints up a list of women's businesses, cafés and happenings that it hands out free. Staff are also happy to chat about women's activities in the city. The shop itself is the only women's bookstore in San Francisco. As bigger bookstores, both independents and chains, have established women's and gay sections, Old Wives' Tales competes by stocking unusual and hard-to-find books, magazines and pamphlets on women's issues. Loyal customers often donate books back to the store for the used section, anxious to keep this landmark in business.

A block and a half away is another women's enterprise, Good Vibrations, 1210 Valencia St, a feminist sex store. It dates from 1977 and is owned and run by its women workers. The shop, which has recently doubled in size and has a thriving mail-order business, is not for the easily shocked. The Antique Vibrator Museum alone has been known to send clueless visitors rushing out the door.

Like Old Wives' Tales, Good Vibrations is as much a mission as a business. The women who run the shop are cheerful, attractive and dedicated to sexual openness. They will demonstrate vibrators, rate varieties of condoms, offer guidance on choosing an erotic video and discuss the fine points of safe sex with a straight-forward perkiness. Be sure and pick up a calendar of events. Good Vibrations schedules everything from serious discussions of female sexuality to a dress-like Madonna party to introduce the Material Girl's book, *Sex*.

Osento, a women's bathhouse, is at 955 Valencia, another stop on the circuit. It's a very casual place, where all fees are on a sliding scale. Massage, hot tubs and steam rooms are available in this funky old Victorian building, but the main attraction is Osento's reputation as a woman-centred kind of place.

WomanCrafts West, 1007 1/2 Valencia, offers the work of women artists and crafts workers from North America and Europe while Gifts of the Goddess, 973 Valencia, is a New Age mecca where someone will appear to wait on you if the karma is right.

The Bearded Lady Dyke Café is several blocks away from Valencia at 485 14th St, at Guerrero, but spiritually located between Old Wives' Tales and the Women's Building. Cosy and casual, the Bearded Lady serves standard SF café fare of espresso, fruit juices, sandwiches on freshly baked bread and hearty soups. Its real life, however, is a lesbian community centre where friends meet by plan or accident, news is disseminated through gossip and flyers, and housing and jobs are located through a crowded bulletin board. On Friday and Saturday nights the café hosts entertainments that range from rockabilly bands in drag to comedy and poetry. The Bearded Lady advertises itself as 'everybody welcome' and it is absolutely true. Straight women feel completely comfortable here.

Valencia Street is rich in restaurants and bookstores. Modern Times Books at No. 968 is the premier leftist bookstore in San Francisco. Run by a collective, the shop is sixties' idealism put into practice.

AROUND THE MISSION

In the early 1970s Chicano activists began organising mural projects around the Mission. It was an inspired idea, combining the Mexican mural heritage with a community-based expression of identity and pride. Today there are more than two hundred murals all over the Mission, some contained on a garage door, some covering three-storey buildings.

Twenty-fourth Street, which likes to call itself San Francisco's Avenue of the Americas, has a good concentration of murals (thirty) you can easily see from street level. Detour down Balmy Alley (between Harrison and Lucky) for a mural intensive. This was where the muralists began, working singly and in teams, in 1973.

The Precita Eyes Mural Center gives tours of the Mission

murals every Saturday. Call 285 2287 for information (sometimes special tours are given) and make reservations.

Galeria de la Raza, 2857 24th St, is a non-profit arts centre, founded by Latino arts activists in 1970. The gallery mounts eight major shows a year, concentrating on local artists. The gallery store, Studio 24, is a rich source of jewellery, artwork, T-shirts and books. It is particularly beloved by Frida Kahlo devotees who say that Studio 24 has the best single collection of Kahlo memorabilia, books and reproductions in San Francisco.

The Mission Cultural Center, 2868 Mission St, also has an art gallery. It is especially known for its 'Day of the Dead' installation in October and early November. As many as 24 artists create rooms in the upstairs gallery as interpretations of the Mexican celebration of All Saints and All Souls Days. Unlike the trick or treating Anglo Halloween, Mexican families recall the souls of loved ones by holding parties at the grave sites. Memorial masses with candlelight processions are another dramatic feature of *Dia de los Muertos*. San Francisco Latinos have reclaimed Day of the Dead and made it a major event in the Mission. A candlelight procession, usually from Mission Cultural Center, is a wonderful sight with hundreds of people dressed in costume parading through the streets.

Other Mission street parties include *Cinco de Mayo*, first weekend in May, and Carnival Festival, Memorial day weekend (last weekend in May). These events both include big parades, street fairs, music and dancing.

SUSIE BRIGHT

Susie Bright is a porn guru who has made the rejuvenation of eroticism her life's work. Not exactly the expected career for an ex-Marxist feminist lesbian mother.

Funny and savagely intelligent in her books, articles and popular film lectures, Bright is San Francisco's favourite contradiction. She breezily condemns anti-porn feminists such as Catharine Mackinnon and brushes off her own critics who are still aghast at her stint as X-rated movie critic for *Penthouse Forum*.

'No woman is going to get a better job or walk safely at night just because you burned your porno magazines,' Bright tells her audiences.

In her mid-30s and the mother of a five-year-old named Aretha, Bright has a huge following among straights, especially men who warm to her message of the need for more sexy men. Bright takes her changing film lectures on the road after fine-tuning them with appearances at the Roxie. She's a top attraction on American college campuses where the question of non-sexist sex is a No. 1 Topic.

Bright was one of the founders of the lesbian magazine *On Our Backs*, the first wildly sexy magazine for gay women (1984). 'I think women should be pissed that sex is a good old boys' club and they weren't allowed in,' she said of the magazine's *raison d'être*. 'We're letting them in.'

One of San Francisco's best repertory movie theatres is located in the Mission, the Roxie Cinema, 3117 16th St, at Valencia. The city's oldest continuously run movie house, the Roxie is a bit worn but comfortable and welcoming. It specialises in programme revivals of obscure movies that film buffs love, as well as showcasing new documentaries and art films. Special attention is paid to gay and women's films. The Roxie is also home to 'sex-pert' Susie Bright's periodic *Porn Reviews* – Bright takes to the stage to accompany a programme of film clips with a breezy commentary that is anything but politically correct.

THE CASTRO

The Castro district has been called the 'gayest place on earth' and it's an apt description in both the contemporary and old-fashioned meanings of gay.

Centred at Market and Castro streets, the area is roughly bordered by Church, 22nd, Duboce and Market streets and is home to thousands of gay men and lesbians. The gay influx began in the early 1970s when the retired Irish and Italian residents were selling off their run-down Victorians and moving to the suburbs. Gays loved the old houses and devoted themselves to rehabilitating them. Gay bars and businesses, encouraged by the gay liberation movement and a consumer base, soon followed.

THE GODMOTHERS

When Del Martin and Phyllis Lyon moved into the Castro in 1953 it was called Eureka Valley and home to blue collar Irish and Italian families. In fact, like many of San Francisco's residential neighbourhoods, it was even better known by its parish name, Most Holy Redeemer.

Martin and Lyon were more than roommates, they were lovers who had met in Seattle in 1949, working in the printing trades. Eager to make friends but weary of the bar culture, they founded a lesbian social club, Daughters of Bilitis, in 1955. Martin picked the name Bilitis out of a lesbian poem. They added the Daughters to give the group a solid sound, 'Like the Daughters of the American Revolution,' Martin recalled later.

Without quite realising it, the couple were making history. Daughters of Bilitis soon spread nationwide and in 1960 had its first national convention, in San Francisco, of course. Lyon and Martin publicised their meeting and complained about police harassment, setting a new example of lesbian activism.

In the 1970s the Daughters never quite got in step with gay liberation. Still fighting rearguard actions and protecting the identity of its cautious members, the Daughters were dismissed as too conservative by the defiant new breed of lesbians.

Martin and Lyon weren't discouraged. They continued to pour their enormous energies into issues that were important to them, such as healthcare and politics. The couple were among the founders of the Alice B. Tokias Lesbian and Gay Democratic Club, a serious power broker in SF politics. With a city-funded women's healthcare centre named after them, their names are stamped on the San Francisco fabric. Now in their early seventies, the couple are in the front lines in the fight against ageism.

We've been so busy over the years we got old without realising there are all these problems that older people face,' Lyon told a reporter after she and Martin were named 'Local Heroes' by the *Bay Guardian*. 'It's especially difficult for older lesbians and gays.'

In one of those amusing accidents of time and place, Phyllis Lyon and Del Martin have watched the world's most famous gay neighbourhood grow up around them and their unassuming crusade to live lives of dignity and meaning as gay women.

By the late seventies, the Castro was the hottest party going. Gay men owned the streets, strolling arm in arm, many of them brawny, muscled Adonises confounding the stereotype of the limp-wristed homosexual. AIDS surfaced in 1981 and by the mid-eighties had cut a deadly swathe through the male gay community. Yet the Castro continued to prosper and to solidify its position as a gay neighbourhood to San Franciscans and a gay mecca to homosexuals around the world. The Castro, in fact, has become a metaphor for the gay community's resolve to never go back into the closet. AIDS has been combated with incredible courage and resourcefulness in San Francisco's gay community, which has taught the world how to care for the sick and educate the healthy.

The Castro, pulsating with shops, cafés and streets full of happy people, demonstrates the ultimate in grace under pressure. The party continues, but these days it is usually an AIDS fundraiser.

Women are completely welcome in the Castro. Many women visitors say they prefer Castro bars, which they can enter confidently, knowing they are not going to be hassled in any way.

The street life, more than the restaurants, shops or bars, is the big attraction. The always colourful ebb and flow of locals and visitors cranks up to outrageous proportions on Halloween when everybody, even the hetero gawkers, come in costume. During Gay Pride Week (the week of June 27) the area is a perpetual Mardi Gras. The Castro Street Fair, usually held in early October, is another delightful open-air party.

The Names Project

2362 Market St (at 18th Street). Usually open Mon–Sat but hours vary; tel. 241 7933 or 882 5500 for current times.

The Names Quilt, which originated in the Names Project, is one of the most moving memorials to come out of the AIDS epidemic. In 1987 activist Clive Jones suggested that friends and lovers make quilt patches to honour the dead. The idea took off like a rocket, inspiring more than 25,000 handmade textile memorials. Not literally quilt, even in its early days, the memorial is displayed in football stadiums, convention halls and school buildings with the beautiful panels carefully arranged in blocks. Visitors tour it as if it were a garden, following footpaths through the acres of panels which range from crude lettering stencilled on inexpensive fabric to gorgeous needlework and intricate designs.

The Market Street storefront is now a visitor centre and volunteer workroom (the foundation's offices have been moved to larger quarters South of Market). You can see samples of the quilt and see volunteers at work on the endless maintenance tasks needed to keep it going. Guidelines on how to make a quilt panel are available here or the staff will help you make a panel during your visit.

Also on the premises is a gift shop called Under One Roof. Originally the shop was open only at Christmastime, offering crafts, ornaments, cards, photographs, books and sexual toys from local artists and writers. The profits went to the Names Project and other AIDS work. The shop was so popular that the sponsors, Visual AID, decided to go all year-round. The shop is open Mon–Fri 11 a.m.–7 p.m. and Sat 10 a.m.–8 p.m., tel. 252 9430.

AROUND THE CASTRO

The glorious Castro Theater, 429 Castro, is the neighbourhood's symbol, with its campy marquée and huge neon sign reading 'CASTRO'. Visitors love to have their photo taken with the sign as a backdrop. During busy tourist times you practically have to elbow your way into a good photo position on the street.

The theatre is more than a sign – it is one of the Bay Area's best repertory theatres. The 1924 Spanish Revival movie house hasn't been cut up into mini-theatres nor remodelled during the 1950s. The programming is as intelligent as the building with a gay-flavoured schedule that runs the gamut from Bette Davis retrospectives to new gay cinema. The annual San Francisco Lesbian and Gay Film Festival, held in June preceding Gay Pride Week, is headquartered at the Castro – one of the largest film and video events in Northern California.

Castro central is Café Flore, 2298 Market St, a pleasant café and coffee house that everyone passes through at some point or another. Men and women drop by looking for friends, assured that at least one acquaintance is probably to be found lounging at a table with an espresso, leafing through the daily paper and keeping an alert eye on the door.

Across the street at No. 2367, the Café (formerly Café San Marcos) (see p. 315), is the prime girl spot in the Castro. The upstairs deck is known as a girl watching spot and the pool tables are a popular hang-out focus for friends.

Among the bars that dot the Castro, one stands out as a historic site. The Twin Peaks Tavern, 401 Castro, was the first gay bar in America with clear glass windows. Gay bars, always vulnerable to police raids and outside harassment, were traditionally dark and secret places. The Twin Peaks marked the shift in history.

For a thorough, step-by-step visit to the Castro, Trevor Hailey's four-hour Cruisin' the Castro walking tour (see p. 60) is unbeatable. Hailey, a lesbian activist and former nurse, weaves history, culture and anecdotes into a seamless narrative as she takes visitors all over the Castro.

NOE VALLEY

One might call Noe Valley the straight Castro. It isn't as colourful or exciting, but it is a neighbourhood that has gone to great lengths to shape itself.

Noe Valley and Eureka Valley were settled about the same time, the 1880s, as home to the prosperous working class and lower middle class of San Francisco. Their snug little two-storey and single storey houses are much prized today by San Franciscans. These two areas, under the shadow of Twin Peaks, were without views of the water so never considered desirable by haute San Francisco.

Old residents are sometimes heard to grumble that Noe Valley is being ruined by 'all the yuppies'. The two-career couples who have moved into the area are different from the old blue-collar residents, but they are just as fiercely devoted to keeping Noe Valley small scale and residential as the old timers. The neighbourhood is a great favourite for professionals in their thirties and forties who want to stay in the city with their children, despite its problems. Generally these aren't rich people and they have to strain to meet rent and mortgage payments. They put a very high priority on quality of life which translates in a high ratio of coffee houses, good cafés, bookstores and children's shops.

Noe Valley is a neighbourhood where you can relax and follow your nose. Feel free to wander around looking at the Victorian houses, many of which have been meticulously restored. Twenty-fourth Street is the main street and good for a half-day's shopping, eating and poking around.

The San Francisco Mystery Bookstore, 746 Diamond St, at 24th, (see p. 354) is a little gem. Once a tiny storefront, this all-mystery shop is now two slightly larger than tiny rooms. Owner Bruce Taylor stocks new and used books and runs a fluid mystery salon on the days he's there. Taylor doesn't have enough room to have author readings, but it doesn't matter as many local mystery writers often drop by to see their friends and chat.

MYSTERIOUS SAN FRANCISCO

Mystery writers have always loved San Francisco. Whether they live in North Beach or the Bronx the authors of whodunnits are fond of setting scenes in enigmatic San Francisco alleys and on fog-bound piers. Dashiell Hammett's 1930 classic, *The Maltese Falcon*, claimed the city for all time as a place of mystery and intrigue.

In the last decade a new wave of San Francisco-based mystery writers have been part of a seachange in the genre, marked by the emergence of women-identified women in detective stories. Instead of Miss Marple getting her policeman nephew to do the dirty work the new heroine punches out the bad guys herself, then goes home to a fabulous lover whom she may or may not let stay all night. Sara Paretsky and Sue Grafton are the best known and most successful of the new breed of women authors, but both have acknowledged their debt to San Franciscan Marcia Muller who introduced the first feminist-attuned detective in 1977 with her Sharon McCone character of *Edwin of the Iron Shoes*.

The Bay Area has one of the biggest concentrations of published women mystery writers in America. Julie Smith, winner of the Edgar Award (the Academy Award of US mysterydom), is approaching cross-over status, while Janet LaPierra, Susan Dunlap, Marilyn Wallace, Gloria White, Janet Dawson, Linda Grant and Lia Matera have all established national reputations in the mystery field. There are also specialists within the speciality: Patricia Elmore writes mysteries for children and Mary Wings and Elizabeth Pincus have built their series around lesbian detectives.

The Bay Area writers, most of whom are involved in the Sisters in Crime authors' group, make frequent appearances in local bookstores reading from their work and participating in mystery roundtables. They also make unannounced appearances at Bruce Taylor's bookstore (above) which acts as a clubhouse for local mystery writers, male and female.

Small Press Traffic, 3599 24th St, does have author readings to promote its offbeat books, focus on poetry, drama, women's writing, Third World work and literary criticism.

Noe Valley Ministry, 1021 Sanchez St, is a Presbyterian church and community centre that offers a rich schedule of folk music, dance, poetry and children's events. This is a favourite spot for the babyboomers in the neighbourhood to hear music and bring their children along. Call 282 2317 for a listing of current events.

WEST OF DIVISADERO

The western side of San Francisco's peninsula is its open space. In contrast to the dense neighbourhoods and highrises of downtown and districts like North Beach, there is the Presidio, the huge military base poised to become a national park, and Golden Gate Park, one of the world's great public parks.

Aside from these two parklands, most of the real estate west and south of Divisadero (it ends just short of Market Street) is given over to residential neighbourhoods without any especially interesting history or architecture. Even beautiful cities like San Francisco have to have ordinary spots.

The main attractions outside of the Market Street core, however, are the big-ticket items: Golden Gate Park, the Pacific Ocean, the San Francisco Zoo, the Golden Gate Bridge and the Presidio. The one neighbourhood that is famous to outsiders is the fabled Haight-Ashbury, home of hippiedom.

Getting around is a little more complicated here. BART doesn't have any westward lines at all. You may have to change buses, but public transport is available and reliable to all the major sights. For Golden Gate Park and Ocean Beach, you might consider renting a bicycle to get around.

Golden Gate Bridge

Highway 101. Free to walk across, toll for westbound traffic.

It took engineer Joseph Strauss fifteen years to convince San Francisco to build the Golden Gate Bridge. It wasn't just the cost (eventually $35 million) or the Depression or the glacial pace of government projects. People all around the bay were horrified at the idea of marring the Golden Gate, one of the most beautiful natural land and water formations in the world.

Progress, of course, won the day but the result has been shocking to even the most unyielding environmentalist. Strauss' classic, clean-lined suspension bridge has actually enhanced the setting. Since its opening in 1937, 'the Golden Gate' has come to mean the mouth of San Francisco Bay and the heart-stoppingly beautiful bridge combined.

Construction Strauss, a Napoleon-sized engineer with a comparable ego, was passionate about bridges. 'I'll build a bridge to Hell if they'll give me enough money to do it,' Strauss said of his determination to span the Golden Gate.

The bridge is hung on two enormous towers that soar 746 feet above the water. The high passage underneath (260 feet) was necessary for Navy battleships to be able to enter the bay. Construction took four-and-a-half years. Unlike the Bay Bridge (see p. 176), Golden Gate is one level with six lanes. The lanes can be arranged to suit the flow of traffic, for instance more westbound in the mornings.

Golden Gate is one of the safest bridges in the world. It survived the 1989 quake without any significant damage and it can withstand winds of a hundred miles per hour.

The Visit Walking across the Golden Gate Bridge is a San Francisco must. The bridge has walkways on both sides which are open to walkers and bicyclists. The span is about one-and-three-quarter miles; most people make the roundtrip in about an hour and half, allowing for a slow pace and lots of looking around on the Marin side.

There is a small park below the Toll Plaza entrance to the bridge, reached by walking along the Golden Gate Promenade, the paved walkway that begins at Aquatic Park (four miles), or taking the Muni Bus 28 or 29. Note the Roundhouse, a gift shop, which also has restrooms for a last stop before tackling the bridge.

Even on a warm, sunny day bring along a jacket or sweater. The winds whipping through the riggings can be uncomfortably sharp. Visitors are surprised to find that the bridge is rust red in colour (officially 'International Orange'), expecting to find some shining, golden bridgeway. John C. Frémont named the bay opening Golden Gate in 1846, comparing it to the 'golden horn' of Byzantium. Frémont (see p. 79), ever the showoff, used the Greek name, Chrysopylae, and seemed annoyed that Californians anglicised it. The Spanish had called it simply *La Boca*, the mouth.

The bridge continues to attract people bent on suicide, although it has always puzzled San Franciscans why. The most popular theory is that the bridge represents the end of the continent which translates into a finality that people who want to kill themselves are seeking. Despite the 260 foot drop into icy, powerful currents, more than a few jumpers survive.

The bridge sidewalks have been blamed as a suicide aid, but

efforts to close the bridge to pedestrians and bike riders have thankfully come to nothing. Bridge authorities point out that many of the suicides actually drive on the bridge, stop, bolt from their cars and dive over the railing. The number of people who have jumped off the bridge (official toll) is approaching a thousand.

On the Marin side is a nice park. There's a small visitors' building with restrooms and water fountains.

Fort Point

Underneath the Golden Gate Bridge (accessible by paved walkways), tel. 556 1693. Open Wed – Sun, 10 a.m.–5 p.m. Free.

Fort Point, built between 1853 and 1861, was the new American government's gesture at securing San Francisco from sea attack or invasion. Built of granite from China and red brick, the fort was typical of the coast fortifications that the US built along the Atlantic and Gulf Coasts. Fort Point is the only fort of this type (they were phased out after the Civil War) built on the Pacific Coast.

Despite rumours of a Confederate invasion, Fort Point never saw any action, during or after the Civil War. The fort was lightly manned and sporadically used. San Franciscans have always taken a puckish pride in Fort Point, the fort that 'never fired a shot in anger'. In 1933 Joseph Strauss even altered his all-but-sacred bridge plans in order to spare demolishing the fort. Fort Point was last used by the military during World War II and in 1970 was made a national historic site.

Today's visitors will see a preserved, but not fully restored, nineteenth-century fort. Park rangers wear Civil War Uniforms (Union Army, of course) and give guided tours. The fort offers a number of activities on the weekends. Children love the daily cannon drills which they are allowed to participate in.

As with Golden Gate Bridge, this is a windy spot. Bring warm clothes even if you don't think you will need them.

The Presidio

Main gate at Lombard and Lyon streets.

A 1752-acre preserve with one of the most beautiful settings in the world, the Presidio has been in continuous use as a military base since 1776. This will come to an end 30 September 1994 when the Presidio is officially closed by the army and handed over to the National Park Service.

Plans for the Presidio's future are predictably turbulent as neighbourhoods, environmentalists, the Park Service, the city, the state and average citizens debate the correct course. Early signs

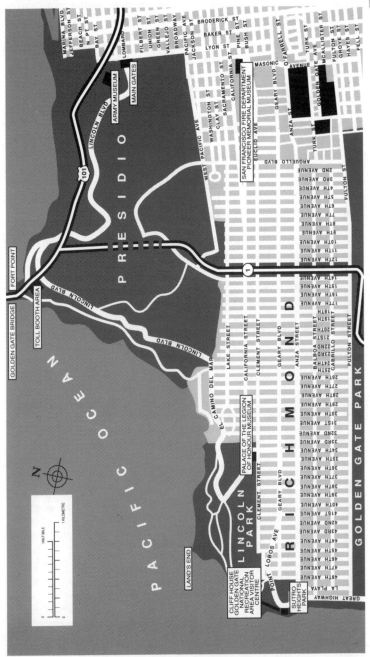

indicate that it will be a mixed use park with many of the architecturally significant army buildings converted to conference centres, non-profit organisation offices and given over to public use. The Sixth Army will continue to use the Presidio as its headquarters but it will be an administrative rather than a troop presence. Mikhail Gorbachev's new international foundation, which he says will work for world peace, is already a tenant, making the Presidio its American headquarters.

The Presidio has always been open to visitors and will continue to keep its gates open in its final days as an army post and during the transition to full-time park.

Construction Captain Juan Bautista de Anza selected the site for the Presidio in June of 1776, then set his small troop of soldiers to work building adobe barracks and offices.

Under the Spanish and Mexican governments, the Presidio was always a provincial backwater. During the Mexican years the handful of soldiers at the post could go for years without hearing anything from their superiors in Mexico. A British navy ship visiting San Francisco in 1825 found the Presidio in shambles.

CONCEPCIÓN ARGÜELLO

San Francisco's most famous love story began and ended at the Presidio. Concepción Argüello, the 15-year-old daughter of an early Spanish commandant, was swept off her feet by Nikolai Rezanov, a Russian aristocrat who arrived in 1806.

Rezanov, 43 and widowed, was trying to establish ties between the Russian colony in Alaska and California. An emissary of the Czar, he had almost starved to death in Alaska and realised that its fragile colony must have stronger Pacific coast ties to survive. The Spanish commandant, Don José Argüello, was polite but suspicious. The Russians did, in fact, have designs on California, but were never in a position to act on them. Rezanov, seeing he was getting nowhere with the commandant, decided a marriage of state would be the most reliable course.

Although his courtship was politically motivated, Rezanov was clearly smitten by lively Concepción whom he described matter-of-factly as 'beautiful' in his dispatches to St Petersburg. Further, she was 'active, venturesome' and had an 'overweening desire for ranks and honors'. Concepción, alone of her family, found California deadly boring and longed for an exciting life in Europe. When Rezanov proposed, she leapt at the chance. Her parents were beyond shock at this turn of events, but they could not shake her determination to marry the Russian. After much prayer and discussion with the mission priests, the Argüellos agreed to the marriage if Rezanov could secure the approval of the Pope and the Russian Orthodox Church. Disappointed that he couldn't seal the deal immediately, Rezanov agreed and Concepción promised to wait, realising it would be years before they could meet again.

He sailed away forever as it turned out; Rezanov died in Siberia during his arduous cross country trip to St Petersburg. His health had been destroyed by his Alaska mission.

Concepción waited faithfully in California. She joined a convent without taking vows. Thirty-five years after Rezanov left she heard of his death from a visiting English official.

Concepción took the vows of a Dominican, the first California-born nun at age sixty.

Gertrude Atherton wrote a florid romantic novel about Concepción and Rezanov and Bret Harte used the story for a long narrative poem. Concepción's story is still a powerful legend. Romantics continue to seek out her grave in the little East Bay town of Benicia and cover it with flowers. The Oakland Ballet commissioned a full-scale new ballet of the Concepción and Rezanov story a few seasons ago. It was not a successful dance, but audiences loved the idea.

'Little better than a heap of rubbish and bones, on which jackals, dogs and vultures were constantly preying,' wrote Captain Frederick William Beechey, who described the only symbol of authority as 'a tottering flagstaff upon which was occasionally displayed the tricolored flag of Mexico, three rusty field pieces and a half-accoutered sentinel parading the gateway ...'.

The Presidio you see today, forested and green, is not its natural state. When the Spanish first saw the area it was rocky, barren and windswept. An Army Corps of Engineers officer, Major W.A. Jones, proposed landscaping the Presidio in 1883, a plan that transformed the grim base to a beautiful haven.

The army continued to add to the Presidio after World War II. Building standards, however, changed dramatically and many of the ugly apartment buildings and the characterless Letterman Hospital are prime candidates for demolition in the new Presidio.

The Visit   You can enter the Presidio a number of ways. Walk up from the Golden Gate Promenade, drive in through the gate at Lombard and Lyon streets or take the Muni 28, 29, 43 or 45 bus. Inside, you are free to wander around but pay attention to signs that say 'Military Personnel Only' or 'Restricted'.

There aren't any tours on a regular basis, but that will probably change as the Park Service begins to take over more of the base. The trails that run through the grounds are open to everyone. Most are clearly marked.

Until the army leaves it will continue its flag-raising and flag-lowering ceremonies at 6 a.m. and 5 p.m., accompanied by a booming cannon.

Presidio Army Museum

Funston and Lincoln (near the Parade Ground), tel. 561 4115. Open Tues–Sun 10 a.m.–4 p.m.; donation requested.

Housed in the 1857 military hospital, the museum is a thoughtful and conciliatory survey of the Presidio's history and the army units and soldiers who have served there. Guns, swords and uniforms are on display, but the exhibits take pains to paint the lives of ordinary soldiers. Several artless dioramas using period costumes, furniture and memorabilia are attractive windows on the past.

Be sure to look for the photograph of Major Pauline Cushman Fryer, an actress turned Union spy who is buried in the Presidio cemetery.

'MISS MAJOR CUSHMAN'

Pauline Cushman was a minor actress of no known political leanings when she became a Union spy in 1863. Appearing in a play in Louisville, a Confederate prisoner of war offered her $500 to ad lib a toast to the South onstage. After secretly conferring with Union army officials, Cushman agreed to do it. Her passionate praise for Jefferson Davis in the middle of the play stunned the audience, but delighted the prisoners in the upper galleries.

Fired in disgrace, she retreated to the South which welcomed her as a daughter. Cushman cultivated key Confederate officers and was able to amass considerable information about troop movements, battle plans and supply lines. She made clandestine trips into the north to report to her superiors. Cushman often dressed as a man for her travels and several times eluded capture through bravura performances. Her luck ran out near the end of the war when she was found with detailed notes of military plans. Cushman was tried as a spy and sentenced to hang. Her luck returned when Union forces happened to capture the town where she was being held the day before her execution.

After the war Cushman was publicly hailed as a heroine. Given the rank of major, she enjoyed wearing specially made uniforms that showed off her 'well-curved' figure. Cushman insisted on being addressed by her rank. She married a musician and they settled in her childhood home of Michigan, where the couple had seven children and suffered unrelieved catastrophe. Terribly hard up financially, Cushman went back on stage to try to support them as well as writing her autobiography. The children all died in a diphtheria epidemic, four of them in one day. Cushman's husband died soon afterwards.

The 'Spy of the Cumberland' married at least two more times, neither happily. In the late 1880s she came to San Francisco where she had appeared in other days. Living in a rented room and scraping by on her army pension, life was difficult. She died in 1893, probably a suicide. The army suddenly remembered her and organised a splendid funeral at the Presidio with flags, an honour guard and a 21-gun salute.

Cushman is buried in the Presidio cemetery, one of the very few women who is not an army spouse. Interned under her last married name, Fryer, until a few years ago even that was misspelled as 'Tyer.' Her tombstone now reads: Pauline C. Fryer Union Spy.

Behind the building are two small 'earthquake cottages'. Only a handful of these sturdy little houses remain, but thousands were issued to earthquake survivors in 1906. The cottages replaced the tents that sheltered whole families after the city was levelled. The Presidio and Golden Gate Park became vast refugee camps after the earthquake. General Frederick Funston, the army's ranking officer in San Francisco, went into action immediately, mobilising all troops and opening up the Presidio to civilians.

Officers' Club

Moraga Avenue (at Pershing Square). Not open to the public.

This is often called the oldest building at the Presidio, dating back to the Spanish adobes. Actually, the original adobe garrison was rebuilt by both the Mexicans and the Americans. Some of the eighteenth-century adobe bricks are embedded in the wall.

Pet Cemetery

McDowell Road and Crissy Field Avenue (near the stables).

This is a must for animal lovers. Behind a little white picket fence, under the shade of evergreens, military families have buried their pets here for decades; cats, dogs, birds and hamsters lie underneath handmade markers.

PRESIDIO HEIGHTS AND THE RICHMOND

Presidio Heights, the neighbourhood that backs up to the Presidio has much in common with nearby Pacific Heights. It is residential, comfortable and upper-middle class. Sacramento Street is a smaller version of Union Street, with a heavy emphasis on upscale children's shops.

Further west, the Richmond extends to the Pacific Ocean, hills slowly unfurling to sea level at Ocean Beach. This is one of the few unpopular waterfront neighbourhoods in California. The fog clings to the Richmond even when the rest of the city is bathed in sunlight. Early maps simply labelled the area, 'Great Sand Waste'.

It actually follows that the city's great park, Golden Gate, and a smaller but still impressive one, Lincoln Park, are situated here. Development-crazy San Franciscans weren't about to give up extremely valuable land for parks. The public could have the 'sand wastes'. None of the early citizens dreamed that the windswept lands on the western side of the peninsula could be made to bloom like the great gardens of Europe.

Swedenborgian Church

2107 Lyon St (at Washington), tel. 346 6466. Parish office hours, Mon–Fri 9 a.m.–5 p.m.; free.

Built in 1895, this is San Francisco's favourite wedding chapel, no matter what the religious background of the bride and groom.

Officially the Church of the New Jerusalem, almost every important Arts and Crafts-inclined architect and designer in the Bay Area had a hand in this little jewel. A. Page Brown, Bruce Porter, Bernard Maybeck, Willis Polk, Ernest Coxhead and A.C. Schweinfurth all worked on the church in one way or another. A bell tower and walled courtyard give the chapel a Mediterranean feel from the outside, but the interior is classic Arts and Crafts with exposed redwood beams, handcrafted chairs rather than pews and paintings of California by nineteenth-century landscape artist William Keith.

The church, a branch of Swedish protestantism, welcomes visitors, but suggests a call ahead to check the schedule, especially on Saturdays, the prime wedding day.

Temple Emanu-El

Arguello Boulevard and Lake Street, tel. 751 2535. Open to visitors Mon–Fri 3–5 p.m.; free.

Emanu-El is San Francisco's oldest and largest Jewish congregation, dating from 1851. This splendid cream-coloured Roman-Byzantine temple is the synagogue's third building, put up in 1925 and designed by Bakewell & Brown, the architects of City Hall and Coit Tower. Bernard Maybeck was a consultant on the temple's design which fits in historically and stylistically with the Bay Tradition of reworking historical architectural schools to fit the Bay Area Arts & Crafts school. Incorporating courtyards and classroom wings, the temple complex is thoughtfully planned. The interior is rich in ornament and decoration of Jewish symbols and worship. Emanu-El's huge red tile dome, visible for blocks around, is a San Francisco landmark. Guided tours are available to visitors during the afternoon visiting hours.

San Francisco Fire Department Pioneer Memorial Museum

655 Presidio Ave (at Pine Street), tel. 861 8000. Open Fri–Sun 1–4 p.m., free.

Firefighters and the fire department are very dear to San Franciscans, dating from the Gold Rush when deadly fires regularly swept through the wooden town. This neat little museum displays memorabilia that dates back to 1849, as well as equipment, uniforms and photographs. The star artefact is the city's first fire engine, an 1810 hand-pumper that wasn't retired until the 1860s. The museum is next door to a working firehouse.

LINCOLN PARK

Clement Street and 34th Avenue.

A public golf course, windswept vistas and a very fine art museum are the attractions here. The California Palace of the Legion of Honor, a museum the city was railroaded into by socialite Alma deBretteville Spreckels, sits on a rise above the golf course, looking out over the Pacific towards the Golden Gate. The museum shut down in 1992 for extensive seismic upgrading and renovations and is not expected to reopen until early 1995.

Even without the museum the 270-acre park is a lovely place to visit. It blends with GGNRA parklands which run along the coastline. From the museum you can walk west on El Camino Del Mar, an old pathway that is paved, to the Coastal Trail that will take you to Land's End, a windy, wild cliffside that looks out to the Pacific. From here you can continue the Trail for ten miles if you want to, walking alongside the Pacific. Be very careful on these rocky paths and avoid the cliffs altogether where footing is very unstable.

California Palace of the Legion of Honor

(Within Lincoln Park.) To reopen in late 1994 or early 1995. Call 221 4811 for information.

History   This museum is the result of one woman's burning ambition. Alma deBretteville Spreckels (1881–1968) was a poor San Francisco girl who married one of California's richest men and devoted her adult life to leaving a mark on the city. A Francophile, she met the sculptor Auguste Rodin during her first trip to France in 1914 and began to formulate the idea of a museum devoted to French art.

Alma's husband, sugar magnate Adolph Spreckels, wasn't at all sympathetic to the museum idea – after all he had built her a French palace on Pacific Heights, the largest private home in San Francisco. But, just as she had managed to get the ageing bachelor to upgrade her status from mistress to wife, Alma brought him around. Spreckels spent more than a million dollars to build his wife's dream. World War I intervened, but Alma added patriotic lustre to her plans by announcing the museum would be a memorial for California boys killed in the war. The museum finally opened in 1924, bursting with paintings, sculpture and items of decorative art that Alma had bought all over Europe. The Spreckels' Rodin collection was the centrepiece for the new museum, including one of the five original castings of the sculptor's signature work, 'The Thinker'.

Alma was shrewd about enlisting museum supporters. She had been a prominent and effective fundraiser for war relief, a fact not lost on the French government which lent treasures from the Louvre to the museum's opening. The government also presented Alma with the Cross of the Legion of Honor to the consternation of her Pacific Heights critics who found Mrs Spreckels far too bossy and unpolished for full membership in San Francisco society.

Although the city accepted the gift of the museum, Alma ran it with an iron hand the rest of her life. Massively unhappy with the first director, she discovered that his passionate wish was to study Persian art in Persia and so presented him and his family with a lavish trip to that country. Of course, the tickets were one-way. Alma raised money, badgered art collectors to leave their art to the Legion of Honor, donated her own and worked ceaselessly for the museum. It was the blind devotion of mother to child with no clear understanding of what she was doing. Alma had been an art student at the Mark Hopkins Institute and an artist's model (most prominently for the full-figured Victory in Union Square) but her knowledge and understanding of art was sketchy at best. She seems to have been drawn to Rodin because of a friend's enthusiasm. Nor was her artistic outlook adventurous. She called Picasso 'communistic' and complained about 'screwy art' created to 'make the people miserable and dissatisfied'.

In the end, though, Alma had her way. She had a troubled relationship with her three children, she was never truly accepted by San Francisco society, but she left a permanent legacy that San Francisco could not ignore.

Construction   The Spreckels hired George Applegarth to design their museum, the same Ecole de Beaux Arts-trained architect who had designed their Pacific Heights mansion (see p. 156). Alma had picked out the design in 1915 when she saw the French Pavilion at the Pacific Panama Exposition, a scaled down reproduction of the Palace of the Legion of Honor in Paris. Alma's palace, of course, would not be scaled down.

Erected between 1921 and 1924, the building incorporated all the most advanced ideas about museum design and technology. Applegarth included specially-designed heating and cooling systems and provided massive reinforcements for the building which sailed through the Loma Prieta earthquake with minor problems. The $25 million work begun in 1992 is half seismic upgrading and half expansion of the underground galleries.

The Visit   Alma Spreckels' huge Rodin collection has been the museum's anchor since its inception. She donated more than seventy pieces, many of them shipped directly from Rodin's studio. 'The

Thinker' sits in front of the museum – one of San Francisco's most

The museum is more important than Alma's Rodin fixation. Thanks to long-time museum director Thomas Carr Howe who was able to forge a thirty-seven-year relationship with Alma despite her imperious ideas, the Legion of the Palace of Honor ultimately benefited from rather than drowned in Spreckels' largess. He gently but steadily took over the direction of the museum from Alma and was able to channel her untamed collecting and gift-mongering into productive avenues. Today the museum has the most comprehensive collection of French art in the world outside of France. The collection also includes many other European artists, though the focus is Gallic. When the museum reopens the galleries will retain the original plan which devotes rooms to Baroque, Rococo, the age of Louis XV, eighteenth-century decorative arts and nineteenth-century painting. The museum's permanent collection includes work by Claude Monet, Renoir, Edgar Degas, Georges de La Tour, Louis, David, Camille Corot, Gustave Courbet, Georges Seurat, El Greco, Rembrandt and many more.

The Achenbach Foundation for the Graphic Arts is an important collection of graphic arts with pieces dating back to the fifteenth century.

The Cliff House

109 Point Lobos Ave (at the Great Highway), tel. 386 3330. Restaurant open daily; take Muni bus 18, 38 or 38L.

Perched on a rocky cliff overlooking the Pacific Ocean, Cliff House is more of an institution rather than a restaurant. This unimpressive 1909 building is the fourth Cliff House. As early as the mid-1850s there was a road house-tavern on the spot, overlooking the Seal Rocks and off into the Pacific horizon.

Cliff House is at the centre of a little cluster of tourist shops and restaurants, an easy walk to the Sutro Baths ruins, Ocean Beach and the almost forgotten Sutro Heights gardens.

The first Cliff Houses were taverns and gambling saloons, but once a toll-road was built in 1868, making a trip from town less than a day, Ocean Beach became a popular destination for family outings. The earlier Cliff Houses burned and were replaced with a huge French Chateau-style Cliff House in 1896 by mining magnate Adolph Sutro. Sutro's Cliff House also burned in 1907 after surviving the previous year's earthquake. His daughter, Dr Emma Merritt, had the fourth Cliff House built, primarily to carry on her father's dreams.

Having made a fortune by building a tunnel to drain the dangerous Nevada mines, Sutro returned to San Francisco and invested heavily in real estate and his own brand of philanthropy. He spent most of his fortune bestowing upon San Franciscans 'health giving amusements' that he hoped would ease 'the struggles of life'.

Sutro's most impressive achievement was the Sutro Baths, a salt water sanatorium on the cliffs to the north of Cliff House. You can explore the ruins yourself or take a guided tour with a park ranger (Cliff House, Sutro Heights and Ocean Beach are all part of the GGNRA). The baths opened in 1896 with five indoor tanks (pools) in lavish surroundings that could accommodate up to 25,000 swimmers. The Baths declined after Sutro's death and burned in 1966.

You don't have to dine at Cliff House to enjoy it (the food is overpriced and undistinguished). Follow the outer walkway to the lower levels facing Seal Rocks and discover two of San Francisco's most amusing tourist attractions. You can also linger here to watch the sealions who congregate on the rocks, frolicking and yapping.

The Musée Mécanique

This is an informal museum of long ago penny arcades before the days of pinball and video games. The games will eat up your dimes and quarters, but you can have your fortune told by a mannequin, see a circus diorama constructed of toothpicks and play simple games of chance. Techno-addicted children might find this sort of silly but adults usually love this place. The Musée is open daily 10 a.m.– 8 p.m. in summer, 11 a.m.–7 p.m. in winter, tel. 386 1170.

Camera Obscura

Step inside and see the ocean a whole new way. This nineteenth-century magic show is still great fun. The Camera is open daily, unless there's rain or fog, from 11 a.m. to sundown, $1, tel. 750 0415.

GGNRA Visitor Center

Also located within the Cliff House, this is where to find out about ranger-led walking tours, pick up free maps or buy more detailed books and guides to the park areas. Open daily, 10 a.m.–4.30 p.m., tel. 556 8642.

Sutro Heights Park

Above Cliff House (enter at 48th Avenue and Point Lobos). Free.

Adolph Sutro built a large Victorian house here, but lavished most of his attention on his gardens which included a conservatory, statuary and exotic plants. He invited the public to stroll through his carefully landscaped twenty-acre grounds.

After Sutro's death the house and garden went to seed. The Sutro heirs gave the place to the city in 1920; eventually the ruined house was demolished while the gardens continued to fade into undergrowth.

In 1976, the GGNRA took over and turned the clifftop back into a garden. But not Sutro's garden. Now planted with less rarefied flowers and shrubs such as hydrangea, geranium and fleabane daisies, the garden is a treasure once again but a secret, quiet treasure this time. Often covered in fog and rarely having more than a few visitors, Sutro Heights is a romantic, haunting place. San Francisco photographer Anne Bement, who has produced an ongoing series about the garden, loves the place for its mysterious qualities. 'It didn't have the appearance of a ravaged park,' she has said of her stumbling upon the place. 'It only appeared that the hand of man had come and gone.'

Ocean Beach

Along the Great Highway, Muni buses 5, 18, 31.

For anyone expecting the silvery sands and warm blue waters of the movie California beach, Ocean Beach will be a keen disappointment. The sand is grey and damp, the water is cold and unfriendly. Yet this three-mile stretch of open coastline is where San Franciscans go when they plan a day at the beach. And they're not unhappy about it.

Ocean Beach is fine for walking, running, wading, sunning, kite flying and people watching. The Pacific Ocean makes a pleasant, lulling roar and in the distance you can see ships making their way to and from the Golden Gate.

You will see hardy surfers in wet suits out in the water trying to catch a wave, but don't even think about swimming here. Aside from the icy water, the undertow is vicious and drowning a very real danger, even for expert swimmers.

GOLDEN GATE PARK

Golden Gate Park (accessible by Muni buses 5, 7, 18, 21, 28, 29, 33, 44, 71 and the N Judah Muni Metro) is 1017 acres of woodlands, lakes, flower gardens, glades, dells, bridle paths, playing fields, museums, children's playgrounds and quiet little nooks. Visiting the park today it's difficult to realise that it is entirely artificial – a modern-day Garden of Babylon that took decades to shape and requires an army of gardeners to maintain.

In 1868 when San Francisco was making plans for a vast municipal park the three miles from Stanyan Street to the ocean was part of the undeveloped 'Outside Lands', the desolate sandy hills that covered most of the western part of the Peninsula.

Under the guidance of two remarkable men Golden Gate Park

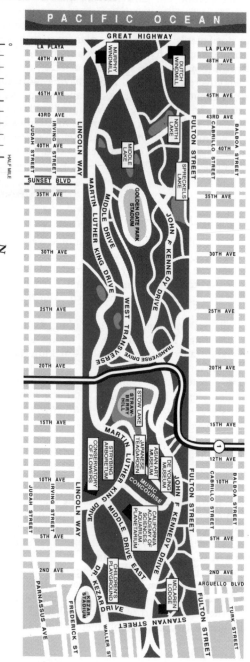

eventually took shape as a grand scale public park, heavily influenced by the English garden ideal of rusticity and the California impulse to make the outdoors another living space. Work began in 1870 under civil engineer, William Hammond Hall. He created the master plan for the park and began the seemingly hopeless campaign to convert the sandhills to a green land.

After several unremarkable park supervisors, a genius was appointed to the job. Scotsman John McLaren took over the park in 1887 and devoted his life to the park. Mandatory retirement age was waived for him and he died in office at age 93 (in 1943) after reigning as the park's loved and loathed despot for an amazing 56 years.

McLaren discouraged buildings, statuary and human intrusions. His vision of the park was a lovely natural world that offered respite and contemplation from the rigours of urban life. Inevitably, McLaren's pastoral idyll was at war with the needs of a burgeoning city population. To an amazing degree, however, he succeeded in keeping Golden Gate as a world unto itself. In 1906 the park became home to thousands of San Franciscans who were burned out of their homes and McLaren, the fierce guardian of every blade of grass in his domain, turned his energies to making it an efficient refugee camp. San Franciscans were fond of Golden Gate Park before 1906, but after the earthquake they regarded the park as a family shrine, the place that had taken them in, sheltered their families and then sent them back into a new world.

Unlike most great urban parks, Golden Gate is not near the heart of the city. The city grew up around it as San Francisco developed. The park's success in making the 'great sand wastes' attractive was part of the impetus in the development of the Richmond and the Sunset.

THE 1906 EARTHQUAKE AND FIRE

Most San Franciscans were shaken out of bed on Sunday morning, 18 April 1906. After the invention of the Richter Scale, the earthquake was rated as 8.3, one of the severest ever recorded. The shake lasted for 48 seconds, another factor in its destructiveness (the 7.1 Loma Prieta in 1989 lasted 15 seconds).

At 5.13 a.m., buildings tottered, leaned and fell. Some just leaned. After hurriedly dressing and grabbing up the children, San Franciscans ran into the street to see what had happened. Anxiety soon turned to relief. Most of the city had remained standing and rescue efforts were launched to find people buried in the buildings that did collapse. It was not until midday that the real danger became clear as fires began to burn all over town. Overturned wood stoves, damaged electrical wires and broken gas pipes started fires in every part of San Francisco. The fire department sprang into action (even though fire chief David Scannell had been killed in a collapsing stationhouse), but the firefighters quickly hit a dead end. Almost all of the city's water systems had been wrecked by the quake, leaving no water to fight the fires. Despite heroic efforts by firefighters and citizens and a few lucky breaks such as navy fireboats, the fires burned out of control for 72 hours, finally exhausting themselves.

The aftermath was bleak: more than 3000 deaths (although the number was drastically under-reported at the time as 300–600), thousands of injuries, 28,000 buildings destroyed, four square miles reduced to smoking rubble and losses totalling $500 million. San Franciscans who could retreated to Marin or the East Bay or down the Peninsula. Others moved in with family or friends who still had a house, but the great majority of homeless citizens found shelter in the vast refugee camp in Golden Gate Park (see p. 217) or smaller encampments at the Presidio and in other parks and vacant areas. First using army tents, later upgraded to boxy cabins and barracks-like buildings, the earthquake survivors quickly re-established their lives.

Cooking in the streets was one of the most vivid memories of 1906. For six weeks after the earthquake no fires of any kind were allowed indoors while every chimney in the city was inspected for safety. Families hauled their wood stoves out on the sidewalk and set up al fresco kitchens. The optimistic can-do attitude of the city was reflected in these outdoor rooms which were often decorated and sometimes festooned with signs identifying them as the city's finest restaurants, Delmonico's, the Poodle Dog, the Palace. One famous photo of the time showed an outdoor kitchen with the inspirational message, 'Eat, Drink and Be Merry, for Tomorrow We May Have to Go to Oakland'.

San Francisco women demonstrated their mettle in their quick adaptation to frontier living in the parks and in their own homes. There was some measure of tension over the indoor fire ban which hard-pressed housewives saw as overreaction. Their concern was treated as typical female inability to deal with the big picture by shell-shocked authorities.

Perhaps the city fathers saw a connection to the so-called 'ham and eggs fire', which assumed a wildly unbalanced importance in the fire's history. Supposedly it began from a Hayes Valley housewife starting breakfast on that fateful Sunday without checking for damage to the chimney. A fire ensued and unchecked, began slashing a path towards the downtown fires. This one lapse started a fire that increased the damage tenfold, according to stories told afterwards. In retrospect this analysis is lunacy. With no water to fight any of these fires and fire conditions at 100 per cent everywhere in the city, disaster was ordained. To single out one fire among at least fifty burning early Sunday morning is wishful thinking that there was some possibility of human control over nature. Still, accounts of 1906 often refer to the 'ham and eggs fire', pointing a long finger at the hapless Hayes Valley housewife.

San Francisco made an astoundingly fast recovery from the earthquake and fire. The city's affection for itself proved to be a valuable tool. As one of the many jovial poetic tributes to the city put it: 'From the Ferries to Van Ness you're a Godforsaken mess/But the damndest finest ruins – nothin' more or nothin' less.'

How to Visit the Park The great shame of Golden Gate Park is its lack of an inner-transport system. Public buses run there, but don't ferry passengers among the sights. While walking and biking are always pleasant options, it is a problem for anyone with children to get from one place to another without exhausting the kids and using most of the day to traverse the park.

You can take public transport directly to the museums. Buses (the 44 O'Shaughnessy) run through the museum loop with stops on the doorstep of the California Academy of Sciences and the de Young Museum. Driving in the park is also an option, although parking can be difficult on weekends. John F. Kennedy Drive is closed to traffic on weekends and becomes a thoroughfare of rollerbladers and cyclists. For bicycle rentals, there are several places near the eastern edge of the park in the Haight.

The upper park with the museum loop, Strybing Arboretum, the Japanese Tea Garden and the Conservatory of Flowers is the most heavily visited section, but it is only a fraction of Golden Gate's attractions. If you are particularly fond of the outdoors it will be rewarding to make several forays into the park.

Admission is charged to all the major attractions – all the museums, the Japanese Tea Garden and the Conservatory of Flowers. To avoid feeling that you are being nickeled and dimed to death, consider the $10 Culture Pass which is a good buy if you are planning to do the big venues all in one day.

McLaren Lodge, at the Stanyan Street entrance to the park, is Golden Gate Park headquarters. It's only open weekdays (8 a.m.–5 p.m.) and is a good central source for finding out about all park activities. You can also pick up park brochures and maps here, tel. 666 7200.

Asian Art Museum

Open Wed–Sun, 10 a.m.–5 p.m.; $2–$5, children under 12 free, tel. 668 7855.

This is the largest museum outside of Asia devoted exclusively to Asian art. The thousands of treasures, including sculpture, painting, tapestry, architectural elements, bronzes, ceramics, jades and decorative objects represent forty Asian nations. More than 80 per cent is taken up by the Avery Brundage Collection, the awesome lifetime work of the crusty Chicago millionaire who was perhaps better known for his role as chairman of the International Olympic Committee.

Brundage donated his collection to the city of San Francisco on the condition a special building was constructed to house it. The city accepted and put up a wing to the de Young Museum in 1966. The museums share an entrance court and storage facilities, but are otherwise completely separate. One admission, however, admits you to both museums.

The Visit The vast majority of the collection is devoted to Chinese art. In recent years the museum has been aggressive in adding to the various sections and building a strong educational component to introduce visitors to the subtleties of Asian art. Owing to space limitations only 15 per cent of the museum holdings can be displayed at one time. The museum is less reliant on travelling shows than other local museums as it tries to bring out its artwork from storage in revolving exhibitions.

The first floor is devoted to China and Korea, the second floor holds work from India, Tibet and the Himalayas, Japan and Southeast Asia. Highlights to look for include the world's oldest dated Chinese Buddha (338 A.D.). The Jade Room houses an exquisite collection of work, ranging from jewellery to sculptures. The museum also has an impressive collection of seventeenth-century Chinese blue and white porcelain and the largest collection of Indian statuary outside of India. Although Brundage only became interested in Japan late in his life and the Japanese element is small, there is a good collection of netsuke and inro – the largest in the US.

Daily guided tours (free) are a good way to see the museum. It hopes to move to Civic Center in the next four or five years after renovating the old Main Library building. If the money is found to do this, the Asian will turn over its space to the de Young.

M. H. De Young Memorial Museum

Open Wed–Sun, 10 a.m.–5 p.m.; admission $2–$5, child under 12 free, tel. 863 3330.

History Alma Spreckels liked to make fun of the de Young as a collection of art castoffs from Burlingame matrons. Spreckels' mean-spirited sniping had a quality of truth about it. Founded as a city museum after the 1894 California Midwinter International Exposition (see p. 148), San Francisco's first big fair, the Fine Arts Museum became more a receptacle for odds and ends than a genuine museum. In addition to the sculpture and decorative pieces left over from the fair, the early displays included stuffed birds, miners' equipment from the Gold Rush and (to Alma Spreckels' never-ending barbs) portraits of obscure ancestors donated by San Francisco socialites.

The museum was the idea of Michael de Young, editor of the *Chronicle*. As much as Spreckels would hate the comparison, de Young's campaign for the museum was not unlike her determination to establish the Palace of the Legion of Honor. The drive to 'do something for San Francisco', felt by both Spreckels and de Young, was far more intense than any affection for art.

The de Young (the name was changed to honour the founder in 1923) had no clear mission in the beginning and dabbled in European, American, Mediterranean and African art. Curiously some of those early enthusiasms have come back to give the museum a direction and new treasures. **Albert Bierstadt**, for instance, has been resurrected from obscurity as a visionary who brought the unseen American West to wide audiences in his heroic landscapes. The de Young's collection of Bierstadts has consequently become quite significant.

The Visit   American art, both from the US and the Americas as a whole, has become the focal point of the de Young. In 1979, Mr and Mrs John D. Rockefeller III donated their important collection of American art, giving the museum a hyper-boost in its importance. In addition to paintings, which include work by Thomas Eakins, Grant Wood, George Caleb Bingham, Georgia O'Keeffe, Winslow Homer and Mary Cassatt, the de Young also has substantial representations of American sculpture, decorative arts and textiles.

Among the decorative arts and crafts, some of the highlights include replicas of period rooms, such as the 1805 Federal parlour from a Massachusetts house. California art of the nineteenth century is placed nearby Arts and Crafts furniture and ceramics in the galleries.

The de Young collections' time line usually ends in the early twentieth century although there are some exceptions for the sake of coherence.

In recent years the African art collection of bronzes, sculpture and decorative pieces has been given far more consideration in terms of space for display and emphasis by the curators.

Touring shows at the de Young are usually well chosen. This is a prime spot for seeing important exhibitions from the East Coast.

Women are well represented among the collections and on the staff, but there isn't a particular focus on the contributions or achievements of women.

The museum café, the Café de Young, is consistently rated as one of the city's best small cafés – the best place to eat in the entire park.

The California Academy of Sciences

Open daily (even holidays), 10 a.m.–5 p.m.; admission $1–$6 with children under 6 free, tel. 750 7145.

Try not to feel overwhelmed by the Academy's embarrassment of riches. You could easily spend an entire day here and not fully see everything. Like The Smithsonian in Washington, D.C., or the Museum of Natural History in New York, the Academy of Sciences is a feast for not only the scientifically curious, but the garden enthusiast looking for entertainment combined with knowledge.

Founded in 1853, to study and survey the natural world of California and the Pacific Coast, the Academy began as a weekly meeting of naturalists. The first members read papers and compared notes about their forays into the virgin California forests and mountains. In 1891, millionaire James Lick gave the Academy a magnificent six-storey office building on Market Street. By then the work had progressed to the serious and wide-ranging collection, identification and naming of species. Samples of the work were on display for the public in large exhibition rooms devoted to birds, mammals, plants, skeletons and insects. In 1906 the Academy building was badly damaged and soon consumed by fire. Botany curator Alice Eastwood raced there on the morning of the quake and saved many of the most valuable collections, recruiting passersby to help.

ALICE EASTWOOD

When scientist Alice Eastwood looked back on the cataclysmic events of 1906, she always insisted that she was a lucky woman.

'My own destroyed work I do not lament,' she told *Science* magazine after the fire, 'for it was a joy to me while I did it, and I still can have the same joy in starting it again'.

As head botanist for the California Academy of Sciences, Eastwood had amassed a considerable body of work. When the earthquake and fire struck, she hurried from her Russian Hill home to the offices on Market Street. The masonry building was still quivering with aftershocks when Eastwood arrived and drafted a passerby to help her attempt a rescue of priceless scientific samples and papers. The massive marble staircase was rubble, but Eastwood and her helper, a young attorney, climbed to the second floor by grasping the railing and inching upwards by putting their feet between the iron rungs.

Once in her workroom, Eastwood went straight to the most important collections, having kept them separate and ready for evacuation in case of emergency. She also found some of the Academy's earliest records and lowered everything outside with a rope she had improvised from curtains. Eastwood argued with soldiers who told her she couldn't go back into the building when she tried to re-enter. A brisk discussion with the commanding officer cleared her path.

After miraculously finding a man with a horse and wagon who agreed to haul her precious cargo, Eastwood took the records and samples to her home. Worried that even this might not be safe, she orchestrated two more retreats. During all this activity she had no time to move her own possessions from her home and lost everything she owned except her favourite lens and a handsome grey dress. ('It's lucky I did,' she recalled later, 'I was invited out several times after that and it was all I had to wear.')

Eastwood's bravery and quick thinking preserved a priceless botanical collection that is still the centrepiece of the Academy's collection of California plants. Eastwood set about rebuilding the collection almost before the fire was over. She spent several years studying at Harvard, the New York Botanical Garden, London's Kew Gardens, Cambridge University and France's Jardin des Plantes before returning to San Francisco and the Academy.

Eastwood had come to the Academy in 1892 from Denver. Almost entirely self-taught as a botanist, she was a high school graduate teaching high school (a typical arrangement in those days) in Denver when her fevered field work and brilliant papers caught the Academy's attention.

In 1853 the Academy had adopted what passed for an equal opportunity ordinance declaring, 'Be it resolved ... that we highly approve of the aid of females in every department of natural history, and that we earnestly invite their co-operation.' It was the first scientific institution to encourage women and open senior curatorial ranks to them. Eastwood, in fact, replaced a woman as head botanist, the retiring Katherine Brandegee.

Eastwood, who never married, was admired as a scholar and nurturer of young scientists. She was the most published woman botanist of her time and was honoured by a number of organisations and schools. She was prominently featured in the first edition of *American Men of Science*.

A legend in her own time, Eastwood held her position until the age of ninety when she reluctantly retired, but continued to come to her desk at the Academy to work on papers, articles and study her beloved plants. She died four years later, in 1953, full of ideas for new projects and further study.

In 1916, the Academy moved into its new home in Golden Gate Park which has since been enlarged several times. In addition to the natural history museum, the complex includes the Morrison Planetarium and the Steinhart Aquarium. Guided tours are available hourly for the museum and there is a busy programme of lectures, special walk-throughs and hands-on demonstrations. Check at the front desk for the day's activities when you come in.

The Visit   The academy uses dioramas, interactive displays, movement and light to make its displays come alive. The **Wattis Hall of Human Cultures** is a fascinating narrative of human history told in realistic dioramas that include Arctic life and the desert life of Australian aboriginals. The African Safari is a favourite with children who love the life-size reproductions of animals in their natural surroundings.

Wild California brings the state's wild life and eco-system to life, down to the battling sealions. For a giggle there's the **Far Side of Science Gallery** by Gary Larson. The Seattle-based cartoonist whose stock in trade is snakes, lizards and wildlife is an enthusiastic patron of the Academy which displays poster-sized blow-ups of his zany cartoons.

If you have children with you, by all means take them to the **Discovery Room for Children** (see p. 362), a hands-on playroom where children from four to eleven can touch all the displays and make some of their own.

Steinhart Aquarium

Opened in 1923, the Steinhart is the oldest aquarium in North America. There are more than 180 displays in the hall, including seals, dolphins and penguins in almost natural surroundings. A recreated California tidepool is another highlight, both fascinating to see and an on-the-spot learning experience.

The **Fish Roundabout**, however, is the Steinhart's jewel in the crown. You may recognise it from numerous movies which love to use the mysterious water and fish surround for scenes. Hundreds of open ocean fish swirl around you as you walk up a circular ramp. It's dizzying and totally delightful.

Morrison Planetarium

There's an extra charge for the planetarium shows (twice daily, $1.25–$2.50, not recommended for children under six) besides admission to the Academy, but it's definitely worth the extra few dollars. Using state-of-the-art equipment, the night sky is recreated with colour, sound and full-bore planet explosions. It's too intense for little children who often leave in tears but older ones love the loud, colourful show, unknowingly soaking up astronomy lessons.

Japanese Tea Garden

Open 9 a.m.–6.30 p.m., shorter hours during the winter; admission $1–$2, tel. 666 7107.

This is probably the only part of the 1894 fair that the park over-seers truly liked. The five-acre Japanese garden was allowed to remain after the fair closed and became a park within the park. Originally designed by an Australian who had become enamoured of Japanese culture, the garden was eventually taken over by Makoto Hagiwara, one of the gardeners originally imported to work on the garden during the fair. Under the Hagiwara family, the tea garden was one of the park's most popular attractions. Sadly, they lost it when they were interned in 1942. A plaque at the gate commemorates the Hagiwaras' stewardship and devotion to the garden.

Studded with lanterns and statuary, the garden combines Japanese ideas with the American passion for more, bigger, better. If the concept of simplicity isn't fully achieved here, the beauty of the ideas still make a lovely garden. The arched moon bridge and an enormous 1790 bronze Buddha are two of the most popular fix-tures. The garden is planted with flowering trees such as cherries, peach, plum and quince, as well as azaleas, bamboo hedges and dwarf conifers.

Tea and cookies are served by kimono-clad waitresses in the open-air stone tea room. There is also a gift shop.

For another kind of zen-like experience, look for the ad hoc New Age religious shrine in a dell behind the Tea Garden. A four-foot tall concrete post, probably a dumped traffic barrier, has become a magnet for Hindus and free-form spiritual types who see the massive plug as a symbol of devotion to Shiva. Pilgrims burn incense, leave offerings and have even arranged a rock garden out of the stones of a Spanish abbey, donated and forgotten long ago by

William Randolph Hearst. The park administration is uneasy about having a religious site within the park but worshippers claim the shrine inspires inner peace and also cures arthritis. It is also said that it's a good idea to walk around the plug three times, counter-clockwise, and make a wish.

Strybing Arboretum and Botanical Gardens

Open daily, 8 a.m.–4.30 p.m. weekdays, 10 a.m.–5 p.m., weekends; free, tel. 661 1316.

During her first visit to this seventy-acre garden complex one visitor was overheard to say with a happy sigh, 'Well, if I don't make it to Heaven, at least I've been to Strybing Arboretum.'

This is a typical reaction among devoted gardeners and even novice plant fanciers who find the range and depth of the gardens awe-inspiring. This is one of America's best gardens in almost every category. If you are a gardener you'll want to budget plenty of time to explore the many offerings of the Arboretum. Call the education office (tel. 661 0668) to check on lectures, walking tours and demonstrations scheduled during your visit.

The gardens are a gift of the late Helene Strybing, a wealthy San Franciscan who wanted to share her love of gardening with the city. Opened in 1940, the Strybing Arboretum has been in constant motion, experimenting with foreign and local plants, adding new dimensions while maintaining an excellent balance between the demands of tourists, the needs of the plants and maintaining a coherent, intelligent garden.

Among the Strybing's delights are the Japanese Moon-viewing Garden, Garden of Fragrance, the California Collection of Native Plants, the Home Demonstration Gardens, the Walther Succulent Garden and the Nobel Conifer Garden. Several guided tours, all free, are given daily through the gardens.

Conservatory of Flowers

Open daily, 9 a.m.–6 p.m., shorter hours in winter; $1.50, tel. 666 7107.

Separate from the Strybing Arboretum, the Conservatory is another gardener's delight. The graceful Victorian conservatory is perhaps Golden Gate Park's most recognisable building – certainly it is the oldest, erected in 1879. Modelled on the glass palace in Kew Gardens, the conservatory was built in England and shipped to San Francisco around Cape Horn to real estate tycoon, James Lick. He intended it for his San José estate, but died before the conservatory arrived. In 1877 it was sold to a citizens' group led by Leland

Stanford and Charles Crocker who donated it to Golden Gate Park.

The dome accommodates the enormous palms that rise up in the middle of the building. Spectacular tropical flowers flourish in the muggy atmosphere.

The sweeping grounds that preface the conservatory add to the grand scale. The flowerbeds are formal and often used to spell out messages, such as welcomes to dignitaries and cheers for the football Forty-Niners or baseball Giants.

Mary B. Connolly Children's Playground

Open daily; free.

A wonderful place for little children with sandpits, slides, tunnels, playhouses, seesaws and forts. Most exciting of all, however, is the restored 1912 carousel that looks like a children's fairytale come to life. The carousel is open daily during the summer 10 a.m.–5 p.m., and Thurs–Sun, 10 a.m.–4.30 p.m. in winter.

The Rest of the Park

Beyond the museum loop and upper park there are still two miles of woodlands and amusements before the park ends at the Great Highway and Ocean Beach. Stow Lake offers paddle boats, rowboats and electric boats for rent for rides around the man-made lake. There is also an attractive footpath around the lake for close-up looks at the ducks, turtles and geese that live there.

At the Buffalo Paddock you can see genuine American bison grazing and shaking off flies like bovines everywhere. In 1984, Wyoming buffalo were imported to replace the final remnants of the original 1894 herd which had ceased to replace itself.

To take advantage of the twelve miles of bridle paths, check with the Golden Gate Park Stables (opposite 35th Avenue gate) about rentals and lessons, tel. 668 7360. Other sports areas include a fly-casting pool (tel. 386 2630), model yacht sailing on Spreckels Lake (opposite 36th Avenue), public tennis courts (tel. 753 7027) and a nine-hole golf course (tel. 751 8987).

At the very end of the park are two towering windmills, the Murphy Windmill and the Dutch Windmill. Originally installed as part of the irrigation system, they are merely ornamental now. The Dutch Windmill is surrounded by the Queen Wilhelmina Tulip Gardens, a lovely little garden that becomes a riot of colour in early spring.

Despite 'Uncle John' McLaren's best efforts, the park does have a substantial number of statues and monuments. Of the two dozen or so, only one is devoted to women, the 'Pioneer Mother' tucked away below Stow Lake. Unmarked and unremarkable, a stoic young woman clad in pilgrim dress looks out at the middle distance instead of down at her two naked children. The statue seems to be an orphan of the 1915 World's Fair, consigned to the park.

HAIGHT-ASHBURY

Haight-Ashbury (Muni buses 6, 7, 33, 37, 43, 71) has just about come full circle. A middle- and upper middle-class neighbourhood in its earliest days, the Haight (ironically pronounced as 'hate') has been working class, bohemian, marginal and is now a district of middle-class homeowners.

But the neighbourhood's life cycles haven't disappeared without a trace. The Haight is a lively street-oriented area with a large population of under-thirties who fuel the coffee house and club scene. Many of the blacks who moved into the Haight when it was in its decline have held on to their property, giving the area a racial diversity.

The Haight is quite a small neighbourhood, bordered by the Golden Gate Park Panhandle to the north, Golden Gate Park to the west, Twin Peaks to the south and Divisadero Street, more or less, to the east. Hilly, green and intimate, it is rich in parklands from the Panhandle, Golden Gate and Buena Vista Park.

Untouched by the 1906 fires, the Haight was flooded with the homeless in the catastrophe's aftermath. Many of the people living in the refugee camps in Golden Gate Park and the Panhandle decided to stay in the area. A huge building boom put more Queen Anne houses in the Haight than in any part of the city. When the area lost some of its lustre, the big houses were split up into apartments, attractive to North Beach bohemians in the early sixties who were tiring of the increased tourism in their quarter. By the mid-sixties the Haight was a prime student housing area. The Beats, amused at these baby hipsters' new-found nonconformity and rebelliousness, playfully called them 'hippies'. The name stuck and exploded in 1967 when the antiwar-drugs-sexual liberation-rock'n'roll youth culture coalesced in the Human Be-In Gathering of the Tribes in Golden Gate Park in January of 1967.

The counterculture captured the American imagination, especially those still in high school and college. Thousands of young people headed for San Francisco to be part of it all, swelling the Haight during the summer of 1967, the fabled Summer of Love. Like all utopias, the Haight's mellow reign as hippie haven had a brief life, but the resonance from that sweet, young time was powerful and longlasting.

People still come to the Haight looking for hippies. Most go away disappointed as the district does little to capitalise on its famous past. What you will find here is an interesting neighbourhood scene with good cafés, coffee houses, bookstores, tons of

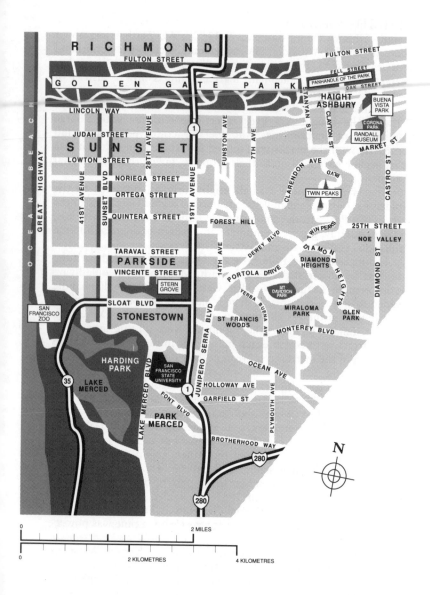

second-hand shops and an endless parade of characters. San Franciscans make a sharp differentiation between the Upper Haight (gentrified) and the Lower Haight (below Divisadero Street, heavily boho). Both sections have their charms, but it sometimes breaks down along generational lines with under-thirties making a beeline for the grunge clubs, dim coffee houses and second-hand shops of the Lower Haight while their older sisters prefer the clean-scrubbed ambience of the Upper Haight's comfortable cafés, well-stocked bookstores and nice shops.

GRACE SLICK

In singers Janis Joplin and Grace Slick, San Francisco produced two of the very, very few women rock'n'roll stars to come out of the sixties. Aside from the 'girl groups' epitomised by the Supremes, rock was almost totally a male form. Women were groupies, occasionally back-up singers but rarely in the spotlight on their own. Joplin and Slick were both integral parts of their bands, with Joplin going on to solo stardom before her death.

Grace Slick, the daughter of an affluent Palo Alto banker and a student at prissy Finch College (now defunct) in New York City, where Tricia Nixon was a classmate, was a surprise candidate for rock stardom. Returning to California after her brief fling at college, she became involved with the rock scene and hit the bigtime with Jefferson Airplane. Slick's piercing soprano spelled out a new consciousness in 'White Rabbit' ('Feed your head') while she happily dispensed with all known rules about what girls should and should not do. Slick embraced all the sixties' adventures – sexual, hallucinogenic and otherwise. She became famous for a series of crashes in fast cars that left her only minimally damaged, including a spectacular bang-up on the Golden Gate Bridge.

In the early 1980s Slick gave up drinking after one of her famous crashes. It was said that Alcoholics Anonymous meetings saw a sudden rise in attendance as people rushed from one meeting to another looking for Slick. Her fans were incredulous that the famous wild woman was actually going to AA and wanted to see for themselves.

Slick has since become a vegetarian as well, devoting herself to animal causes. She has mostly retired from the music business, but still pops up at fundraisers and reunions of the various segments of the band that became the Jefferson Starship, Starship and several other incarnations. Slick's only child, China Kantner, from her longtime liaison with Jefferson Airplane guitarist Paul Kantner, is off in Hollywood to be an actress, while her marriage to rock manager Skip Johnson is in its second decade. The woman who once tried to attend a college reunion at the Nixon White House so she could dump LSD in the punch now lives a sedate life in Marin County. Slick still indulges in her taste for fast cars, but she hasn't banged one into a bridge in quite a while.

As for historic sites, there are the former homes of sixties' rock stars when bands lived communally to cut down on expenses and to play music all the time. The houses are unmarked and visitors are unwelcome, but you can still take a peak at the Jefferson Airplane's old house at 130 Delmar St, the Grateful Dead's crash pad at 710 Ashbury St and even the place where gonzo journalist Dr Hunter S. Thompson entertained the Hell's Angels, 318 Parnassus St.

JANIS JOPLIN

Janis Joplin always described herself as a 'chick singer', but nobody made the mistake of treating her like a bimbo. Small, determined, childlike and explosive, Joplin became one of the first acid rock stars and one of its first martyrs. She burst into the national scene like a comet with an electrifying blues performance at the 1967 Monterey Pop Festival and died of a heroin overdose in 1970.

In between she became a rock'n'roll metaphor. Every obituary written about her quoted Edna St Vincent Millay's poem, 'My candle burns at both ends …'. Joplin lived in the Haight during the mid-sixties, but was living in her own woodsy retreat in Marin when she died. Still, the Haight remained her home in everything but name. She hung out in the clubs, drifted over Golden Gate Park, visited her friends in their communal houses. Involved with a legion of lovers, male and female, Joplin's legend always threatened to overshadow her music, a raw, dark blues that no one could believe a white girl could sing – until they heard Joplin.

Janis Joplin was one of the very few women musicians to make it on her own terms during the sixties. She got into her breakthrough band, Big Brother and the Holding Company, because of her huge voice, not because she was somebody's girlfriend. Although she had friends who helped her and was influenced by business people, Joplin's story wasn't a Pygmalion tale. Her mistakes – and triumphs – were her own. She was never guided nor hindered by a Svengali-type manager as in the Bette Midler film *The Rose*, loosely based on her life.

Born and raised in Texas, Joplin was a natural rebel, never fitting in and yearning for the wider world. She drifted into folk singing and finally into rock'n'roll.

'My gig is just feeling things,' she said of her approach to music. It was also her only rule for her short, fully lived life.

The Randall Museum

199 Museum Way (in Corona Heights Park), tel. 554 9600. Open Tues–Sat 10 a.m.–5 p.m. Free.

This one-time elementary school with a sweeping view of the city has been transformed into a hands-on museum and workshop for children. Josephine D. Randall, who became San Francisco's first superintendent of recreation in 1926, thought learning should be fun for children and envisaged a place that would combine science and art in a cheerful, unpressured atmosphere.

Her ideas have been given form in this busy child-centred museum which is more like a kids' playhouse than an institution. The animal room with birds, snakes, spiders and other creatures is a great favourite with tots who are allowed to handle some of the animals (with supervision).

The Randall places heavy emphasis on developing classes and programmes that families can enjoy together; the Saturday programmes for children also give visitors a chance to mingle with the locals. The drop-in classes (modest fees) are easy to join and offer projects such as mask-making, nature walks and creating sculpture from scraps.

TWIN PEAKS

Towering over the Castro and Noe Valley, these two sharp hills (903 feet and 913 feet) are often obscured by fog. A native legend said the peaks were originally one, representing a bickering couple whom the gods separated with a bolt of lightning. The Spanish called the hills *Los Pechos de la Choca* (Breasts of the Indian Maiden). On the whole, Twin Peaks is much the better name.

The top of Twin Peaks offers the view of views with the whole city, the far reaches of the East Bay and Marin visible on a clear day. Tour buses make this a regular stop or you can take Muni 36 Teresita, which will drop you off near the top. A short walk (one-fifth of a mile) takes you to view wonderful. Be sure to carry a jacket or sweater however you go up. It is always cold and windy on Twin Peaks.

The science fiction towers at the top are television relays that smooth the way for clear TV reception in San Francisco's hilly districts.

THE OUTER LIMITS

The residential southwest quadrant of San Francisco holds little for the casual visitor. There are two spots here, however, that do merit a visit, Stern Grove and the San Francisco Zoo.

Stern Grove

Sloat Boulevard and 19th Avenue, tel. 252 6252; Muni buses 10, Monterey, and 28, 19th Avenue.

Tucked under a hill near a busy intersection, Stern Grove is a sylvan retreat where beautiful music is heard all through the summer. Underneath a hillside eucalyptus grove is a natural amphitheatre, discreetly honed by human hands. From June to August free Sunday afternoon concerts feature first-rate music, usually classical, with performers such as the San Francisco Symphony and the San Francisco Opera Chorus. Sometimes a big star is signed up for the series, but that's not the attraction. San Franciscans make Stern Grove a major event in their lives. Friends plan elaborate picnics, pack up the kids and blankets and spend lazy Sunday afternoons on the soft green lawn.

This was all made possible by Rosalie Meyer Stern, a member of the Levi Strauss denim fortune family. She bought the property, once an infamous gambling resort, as a gift for the city in the 1930s and established the music series as a memorial to her late husband, Sigmund Stern, a nephew of Levi Strauss. The old roadhouse, the Trocadero, still stands in the glade, a lovely 1892 Victorian building that now serves the needs of the big crowds (20,000 is average) who come to the concerts.

You will notice many of the concert-goers in Levi's jeans. It's a tradition among regulars to wear the product that provided the wealth to make Stern Grove possible. Whether you choose jeans or not, make sure you take something warm to wear. When the afternoon shade replaces the sun Stern Grove is very chilly.

San Francisco Zoological Gardens

In the Parkside district at Sloat Boulevard and 24th Avenue, tel. 753 7083. Open daily 10 a.m.–5 p.m. Admission $1–$6.50, free for children under six. Muni buses 10, Monterey, and 18, L-Taraval streetcar.

Lions and tigers and bears, oh my. The San Francisco Zoo is very big, ecologically sensitive and home to more than 250 species of mammals, reptiles, birds and even insects. The zoo is located in the city's farthest southwestern corner, near the ocean and requires a special trip; it isn't on the way to anywhere else. For animal lovers the San Francisco Zoo will be a high point of your trip. For animal likers, it is a pleasant diversion.

A good way to orient yourself around the 125-acre park is to take the Zebra Train. The 30-minute open-air ride ($1.50–$2.50) will show you almost everything in the zoo and allow you to decide how to spend your time.

Founded in 1925, the zoo was significantly enlarged and upgraded during the 1930s by the Depression make-work agency, the Works Progress Administration. Beginning with the 1970s, the zoo began to tune into the environmental movement. Now rated one of the best in the US, the San Francisco Zoo has a state-of-the-art primate centre, near natural settings for most of the big cats, an open, green space for gorillas and an endangered species programme that breeds vanishing birds of prey such as bald eagles, hawks, owls and peregrine falcons and returns them to the wild.

The **Doelger Primate Discovery Center**, opened in 1985, is a multi-level playground for fifteen species of monkeys, most of them endangered. The soaring outdoor atriums are a fun window on monkey life. The gorillas live a couple of habitats away in a green canyon with strategically placed overlooks. The gorillas, those anthropids that so fascinate humans, have a nasty habit of pelting zookeepers and onlookers with their droppings so be prepared to beat a hasty retreat.

Other zoo residents include rare Siberian and Sumatran tigers and snow leopards. The elephants, giraffes, rhinos and penguins are big hits with visitors. The biggest event at the zoo is the 2 p.m. feeding of the lions and tigers in the Lion House. No charge, but people start lining up as much as an hour beforehand to get a good look.

Because there is no vacation for the animals, the zoo has the advantage of being open every day of the year, even major holidays – very handy if you are in a city without holiday plans.

The **Children's Zoo** is a five-acre mini-zoo that features barnyard animals such as sheep and donkeys, an **Insect Zoo** and encourages petting and hands-on activities. There is an additional charge ($1) to the zoo admission. Also a great child-pleaser is the beautiful 1921 **Carousel** with hand-carved animals, mirrors and beautiful detailing. The ride ($1) may be a bit tame for children over nine or ten, but anyone with an eye for design and colour will enjoy looking at this wonderful bit of frivolous art.

ACROSS THE BAY

San Francisco's pleasures don't end at the city limits, but keep right on going across the bay to Marin County and the East Bay. Unlike most central cities, San Francisco has suburbs that are as richly textured as the city itself.

Across the Golden Gate Bridge to the north Marin is a distillation of the best of California, where progressive and goofy ideas are lived out in a pastoral setting of redwoods, hills, coves and charming little towns. To the east, over the Bay Bridge, Berkeley, Oakland and Emeryville form an interlocking series of communities of intellectuals, artists, activists and happy middle-class burghers who are unusual only in their racial diversity.

Bridges, ferries and mindset make the East Bay and North Bay easily accessible from San Francisco. The commuting patterns are geared to accommodate the tens of thousands of workers who make the daily trip from Mill Valley, San Rafael, Sausalito, Berkeley, Oakland and Emeryville to jobs in San Francisco. Consequently, it is an easy matter for visitors to hop across the bay to spend a day visiting the little shops of Sausalito, hiking up Mount Tamalpais or touring the University of California campus in Berkeley.

MARIN

While the rest of the country tells San Francisco jokes (Q: How many San Franciscans does it take to screw in a lightbulb? A: Two, one to screw the bulb and one to share the experience) in San Francisco they tell only-in-Marin tales; for instance where high school football teams limber up with yoga, kindergarten children have their own beepers and business owners don't make a move without their psychics.

The kookiness makes for funny stories, but the underpinnings of a free-spirited community that puts a high premium on tolerance, individuality and creativity makes for a very interesting place to live and to visit. Just the physical beauty of Marin is bracing, from Mount Tamalpais and the Marin Headlands overlooking the Pacific. The towns are very attractive, too, charming in their human-scale and brave efforts to resist total commercialisation.

ISABEL ALLENDE

It really isn't surprising to find Chilean writer Isabel Allende living in Marin. It's actually quite a good match of Latin American magical realism with a California version of the same. Allende herself says Northern California and Chile are very similar. 'It has the same abrupt Pacific coast, the same weather, the same fruits and wines and trees. I feel like I'm back home for the first time.'

The physical similarity and the warm welcome given to Allende by her Marin neighbours and Bay Area fans have not softened the writer's famous cutting edge. Marin, she says, is 'a bubble' in a troubled world. She has been known to call California 'a crazy place'. But her adopted home has clearly begun to work its way into her heart and intellect. Allende is a familiar figure around the Bay Area, where she counts sister writers Amy Tan and Bharati Mukherjee as two of her closest friends. She calls Book Passage, a bookstore-café in Corte Madera, her office and is often seen sharing a pot of tea with fans who approach her. However, the most telling evidence of Allende's feelings for her new home was her fourth novel, The Infinite Plan (1993). A voyage through the US odyssey, the novel is a sprawling tale of post World War II California based on the life of her second husband, San Francisco attorney William Gordon.

Allende left her native Chile after a 1973 CIA-backed coup d'état toppled the Marxist government of her uncle, Salvador Allende. She began writing fiction while living in Venezuela and produced the phenomenally popular The House of the Spirits in 1985. Allende, divorced from her first husband, moved to Marin in 1988 after a chance meeting with Gordon during a book tour.

Allende's two grown children, a son and daughter, soon followed her to crazy California. Her daughter died in 1993 from a rare genetic disease, but her son, his wife and their two children live nearby in Sausalito.

Chile has changed dramatically in the last few years, the generals who deposed Allende having retired. The current middle-of-the-road regime has lifted all the bans on her books and Allende herself has visited many times. Yet she has no plans to live there again. 'Since I left Chile I have always felt a foreigner,' she says. 'That's good for a writer. A writer should always live in exile.'

Sausalito and Tiburon

Both off Highway 101 North. Golden Gate ferry service to Sausalito, tel. 332 6600; Red & White Fleet ferries to Sausalito and Tiburon, tel. 546 2628; Golden Gate Transit bus service from the Transbay Bus Terminal, tel. 332 6600.

These two bayside towns are usually the most of Marin that the casual visitor sees. Easily reached by ferry from San Francisco, Sausalito and Tiburon cater to tourists, but their charms extend beyond T-shirts.

Sausalito's main street is Bridgeway, crowded with colourful little shops. Nice, but not that different from the boutiques and galleries on San Francisco's primo shopping streets. Some people think the best thing about Bridgeway is the annual Fourth of July parade, a hometown extravaganza that mixes cute children in homemade red, white and blue costumes with Marin's zany sense of humour.

MADAM MAYOR: SALLY STANFORD

In 1950 San Francisco's best-known madam ever, Sally Stanford, retired to Sausalito. Actually, Stanford didn't so much retire as begin a new career. She opened a restaurant in a century-old saloon, the Valhalla, on the waterfront and was every bit as successful with food as she had been with sex.

During her career as a madam, Stanford had won the admiration of many powerful San Francisco men for her business acumen. Her houses, located in various spots around the city, were famous for beautiful women, well-stocked bars and absolute honesty. *Life* magazine once called her 'San Francisco's No. 1 businesswoman'.

Stanford was born Mabel Janice Busby in Oregon. She grew up poor and uneducated, marrying many times. She picked the name Sally Stanford when she moved to San Francisco, which happened to be the day of The Big Game, the annual University of California-Stanford football game. Stanford became San Francisco's biggest secret. Her houses were even pointed out on Gray Line tours. Stanford's agility at keeping the law at arm's length was legendary. One young police officer was finally put off the trail when he pushed his way into her famous house at 1144 Pine St and Sally hauled his father – a high-ranking police official – out of an upstairs room to confront him. With friends all over the city, raiding parties were often met at the door by a butler who showed the gentlemen into Stanford's sitting room where she would be sipping tea, surrounded by her adored lap dogs and expensive French and Chinese antiques.

In Sausalito, Stanford didn't stay out of the limelight long. She almost immediately clashed with the city council over the matter of her gaudy neon signs. Stanford lost the fight, but got in the habit of going to the weekly city council meetings, taking it all in and often volunteering her views. In 1962 she ran for a council seat as a reform candidate. Like many of the old-timers, she wanted to keep development and industry out of Sausalito. Stanford lost the first round but was later elected to the council and went on to become mayor.

Stanford was proud of her stint in government and found the avid interest in her prior business unseemly. She was discretion itself as a madam. She never denied her old profession, but found discussing it in mixed company vulgar. She was as horrified as a Victorian matron that complete strangers wanted her to spill everything in casual conversation. Sally Stanford had standards. She died in 1978, aged seventy-five.

Follow Bridgeway west to the former World War II shipbuilding centre, Marinship. Now a yacht harbour, you will see as many funky houseboats as spit-and-polish yachts. The Marin houseboat culture is a world unto itself, a spinoff from Sausalito's long art colony history. On Marinship Way look for the Industrial Center Building, now converted to sixty-five artists' studios. Impromptu studio visits are possible for the genuinely interested passerby.

Also on Marinship Way is another warehouse that houses the marvellous Bay Model, a scale replica of San Francisco Bay that covers an acre and a half. Built in 1956 by the US Army Corps of Engineers to test a series of barriers and water quality proposals, it has a hydraulic system to simulate tides and water conditions. Unfortunately for visitors, the Bay Model isn't operated solely for their benefit. It is used for scientific study and is only filled with water and operated when needed for tests. But even if you don't happen to come on a test day (call 332 3871 to ask) the Bay Model gives you a fantastically clear picture of the Bay Area and how the ecological system works.

Also here is a good historical review of Marinship's history and the role played by women in the war effort. It's all free, but donations are gratefully accepted.

Walking tours of Sausalito are sometimes available through the city. Call 281 3210 for information.

Tiburon

A few minutes away by ferry, Tiburon is a smaller, less clogged Sausalito. Houses cling to the steep hills above the waterfront which is lined with cafés, bars and shops. The year-round Angel Island ferry leaves from Tiburon which is the reason that most non-residents find their way here. Tiburon is the place to go for a totally relaxed day in a bayside village.

Old St Hilary's in the Wildflowers, a former Catholic Church now used for community activities, is a gorgeous sight in the spring, engulfed by rioting wildflowers, many of them quite rare (tel. 435 1853). About three miles out of town is the Audubon Center and Lyford Victorian House. The Audubon Center is a bird sanctuary with self-guided tour and the Lyford House, a lovely 1874 residence, is open for tours on Sundays (tel. 388 2524).

Bay Area Discovery Museum

557 East Fort Baker (outside of Sausalito), tel. 332 7674. Open Wed–Sun 10 a.m.– 5 p.m. Admission, $4 children and adults.

Practically underneath the Golden Gate Bridge, this children-oriented museum has an enthusiastic following among Bay Area kids who love the interactive approach. Geared for children from ages two to twelve, at the Discovery Museum they crew on a fishing boat, drive a Model T Ford, create their own animated stories on computers, record a song in the studio or make a painting or sculpture. Of course, the cars, boats and oceans are recreated models, but they're a wonderful playground for the imagination.

The museum is on the grounds of Fort Baker, a one-time army base now part of the sprawling Golden Gate National Recreation Area.

Marin Headlands

Visitors' Center, Fort Barry, tel. 331 1450.

The beautiful hills that drop off at the Golden Gate are almost all public lands under the auspices of the GGNRA. The military installations that dot the coastside have been allowed to stand and, like Fort Mason in the city, gently turned to different and undreamed of uses.

The headlands encompass hiking paths, camping sites, spectacular views, dense backcountry, rugged beaches and even art centres. If you are looking for relatively quick access to the great outdoors, the headlands is an excellent answer. Start with the Marin Headlands Visitors' Center at Fort Barry, west of the Golden Gate Bridge. Unfortunately, the sole easy public transport is a bus that runs from San Francisco only on Sundays (Muni 76). Driving from San Francisco, take the Alexander Avenue exit off Highway 101 and follow the signs to Fort Barry.

In addition to the Bay Area Discovery Museum, other places to consider within the Marin Headlands include the Headlands Center for the Arts, the California Marine Mammal Center, the Golden Gate Raptor Observatory and Miwok Stables which offers horseback rides through the hills (tel. 383 8048).

Headlands Center for the Arts

Fort Barry, tel. 331 2887 or 331 2787. Open daily 12 noon–5 p.m. Free.

This unusual art centre brings in a variety of creative people to be artists in residence every year. The centre installs them in studios in the vintage army buildings and generally leaves them alone. Periodic programmes bring the artists and the public together for talks, exhibitions and free-form events that have included rituals on the beach and breadmaking.

The Headlands isn't well known – even among San Franciscans – but it is one of the most imaginative public art centres in America. Women artists have been particularly sought out and showcased by the centre, well worth a visit for anyone with an interest in the arts.

Muir Woods National Monument

Muir Woods Road, tel. 388 2070 (off Highway 1, west of Mill Valley). Open daily 8 a.m.–sundown. Free; Golden Gate Transit bus 63, weekends only.

When you see the soaring old redwood trees of Muir Woods, you understand what all the environmentalist screaming is about. This is one of the last untouched remnants of the redwood forests that once covered Northern California. To walk through the paths of Muir Woods is to walk through one of nature's grandest cathedrals. The trees are a hundred and two hundred feet tall, many of them four hundred to eight hundred years old.

There are over 25 miles of trails within Muir Woods, ranging from very easy to strenuous. If at all possible, try to come to the grove on a weekday. This is a major, major tourist stop with caravans of touring buses huffing down the canyon roads. On weekends the place is jammed. While this sounds very off-putting, it only takes a few minutes to walk past most of the visitors and into the deep, quiet forest.

Consider taking a ferry-van tour to Muir Woods. Red & White Fleet takes visitors from Pier 43 1/2 on Fisherman's Wharf to Tiburon and then by van into Muir Woods. It's a full day's outing (five hours), but with plenty of time in the redwoods and an hour or so in Tiburon. The great advantage is having someone else doing all the driving, parking and looking for tricky turn-offs. Tickets are $24 adults, $12 children, tel. 546 2700.

Stinson Beach

Highway 1, public beach, tel. 868 1922 for surf reports; Muni 63 bus, weekends only.

When San Franciscans absolutely, positively, have to go to a beach where they can swim and don't have the time or money to fly to Hawaii they go to Stinson Beach. The three-mile sandbar is an anomaly along the rocky, dangerous coastline. Swimming is permitted and encouraged here, although the beach is sometimes closed when the undertow is too strong. Lifeguards are on duty during the summer months.

As pleasant as it is, the Northern California beach warning prevails and this is not a white-sand tropical beach. The water is rarely above 60°F and a fog often covers the beach in summer. That said, Stinson is a pleasant seaside outing and the little town is very agreeable with unfussy shops and reliable cafés and picnic supply stores.

Green Gulch Farm and Zen Center

1601 Shoreline Highway (Highway 1), north of Sausalito, tel. 383 3134.

Since 1967 San Francisco Buddhists have been coming up to Green Gulch Farm to meditate, raise vegetables and, as the masters say, 'negotiate the Way'. Visible from Highway 1, the one-time horse farm occupies a narrow valley opening in the shoreline hills that runs down to Muir Beach.

Green Gulch is part of the San Francisco Zen Center, followers of the Japanese Soto Zen tradition. The Zen Center is a thoroughly

American group which developed from a fascination among Bay Area intellectuals in the forties and fifties about Eastern religions. Their curiosity led them to Japan and China rather than the immigrant temples of Chinatown and Japantown. Poets Allen Ginsberg and Gary Snyder are the most famous of the early Zen enthusiasts. The Zen Center is made of followers who are mostly white and middle class, but it is a very serious and rather touching attempt to find spiritual solace using the ancient tools of the East in a completely American, contemporary context. Green Gulch Farm is a retreat, not a sealed-off monastery.

Visitors are welcome at Green Gulch for the Sunday meditations and lectures, to take lessons in the weekly tea ceremonies or see the organic gardening beds. If you have a serious interest in Buddhism write ahead for information about residential classes (Green Gulch Farm and Zen Center, Star Route, Sausalito, Calif. 94965). If your interest is less long-term, it is a good idea to call ahead and find out what the weekly schedule holds. Green Gulch has several guest rooms available to overnight and short-term visitors. Rates run from $55–$105 a night and include meals.

EAST BAY

Oakland and Berkeley are more like San Francisco districts than separate suburban towns. For genuine American suburbs you have to go east over the Oakland–Berkeley Hills to Contra Costa County's middle-class housing development or south to the ranchhouse sprawl that surrounds San José or the old money-country club suburban estates of the Peninsula. In the East Bay you find the same kind of fizzy chemistry of beautiful landscape, diverse lifestyles, cultural adventurousness and political activism that characterises San Francisco.

The East Bay's museums, music clubs, bookstores, restaurants and easy accessibility make the east-west connection attractive and continuous. BART is the primary reason for this fluidity, making a trip to Berkeley or Oakland an easy visit.

OAKLAND

Most outsiders are not prepared for the lovely town they discover Oakland to be. More famous for its industries (now declining as in most American cities) and its mean street ghettos, many people who live outside of the Bay Area never hear about the Edwardian residential neighbourhoods, downtown lakes and gardens, lively espresso and bookstore districts and the huge prosperous middle class that is equal parts white, black, Asian and Latino.

While Oaklanders resent the hayseed image of a second city, a doom sealed by Gertrude Stein's famous epigram that 'there's no there there', they also appreciate the dividends of second-class

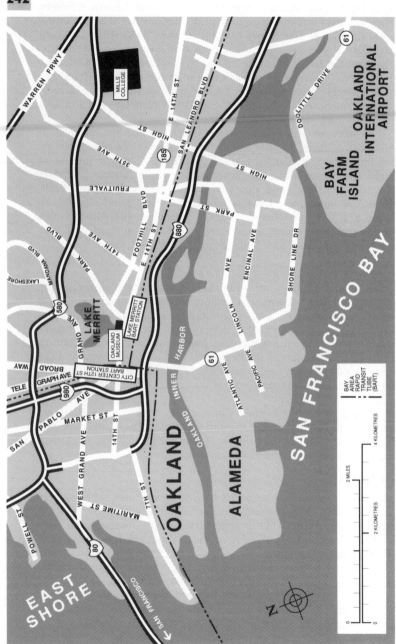

citizenship. The city's attractions are by and for the citizens instead of tourists, and prime Oakland spots such as its Chinatown, Lake Merritt, the hilltop parks and the waterfront are relatively easy to get to, find a parking place and use.

GERTRUDE STEIN

Bête noir is perhaps too kind a term for Oakland's feelings about sort-of native daughter Gertrude Stein (1874–1946). The writer's typically convoluted comments about her childhood home has caused Oakland no end of trouble. Other less than glamorous cities have jokes made about them, but no one has the deadly tag line that Stein saddled on Oakland: 'There's no there there.'

What Stein actually said in her 1937 book, *Everybody's Autobiography* was: 'what was the use of my having come from Oakland it was not natural to have come from there yes write about it if I like or anything I like but not there, there is no there there.'

What she meant, as Oaklanders painstakingly explain every time Herb Caen or some visiting pundit deploys the 'there' missile, was that her Austrian Jewish family had moved to Oakland by a fluke ('it was not natural'). Further, the Stein family estate in East Oakland with flower and vegetable gardens, animals and carriage house, was torn down after the family moved and subdivided into small lots for working-class houses. There was literally no place for Gertrude to return to live ('and write about it if I like … but not there') – no there for her to visit, see?

Stein had practically no interest in Oakland or San Francisco after she left at the age of eighteen. Almost completely devoid of sentiment, Stein looked back on her California years as a tiresome childhood era. Stein's father had moved his family to Oakland in the wake of an acrimonious break with the family textile business in Baltimore. After a nomadic period in Vienna and Paris, Daniel Stein brought his wife Amelia and their five children to Oakland. He had investments on the West Coast and was deeply involved in the new cable car transport business.

Stein's parents died while she was a teenager and her oldest brother, Michael, became head of the family, moving all his younger siblings to San Francisco. Also involved in the cable car lines, Mike Stein was a talented businessman who soon increased the family fortune and assured all the Stein children a comfortable lifelong income.

Gertrude attended Oakland High School and was fondly remembered by friends. She didn't bother to get a diploma, but had no trouble entering Radcliffe College in Massachusetts (to be near brother Leo at Harvard). She left Radcliffe without a degree but again, entered the Johns Hopkins medical school in Baltimore fairly easily. Growing bored, it looked as if Stein would not get a degree there either. Friends urged her to press on, invoking feminist arguments that her cavalier attitude would set back the cause of women. Stein was unmoved. She wanted to live in Europe and write. And so she did.

California bestowed an undeniable blessing on Stein in the person of Alice B. Toklas. Another gently reared, upper-class San Francisco Jewish girl with no plans for marriage, Toklas travelled to Europe and met Stein through mutual California friends. Pleased with the life she saw Stein living in Paris, Toklas settled in and never left.

'As Alice does know how to make everything something we get along fine,' said Stein of her lifelong companion who typed her manuscripts, managed her affairs, ran their household and cooked their meals.

Oakland has tried to leaven Stein's unerasable *bon mot* with a bit of humour. Smack in the centre of downtown is a tall, spiralling sculpture of gaily-coloured rods. It is called 'There'.

Oakland is home to two particularly impressive and often over-looked institutions. The Oakland Museum is an architectural show-piece with a brilliant approach to exhibiting its subject, the state of California. Mills College is the oldest women's college in the American West which a campus revolution catapulted into a land-mark of US feminism.

Oakland Museum

Oak and 10th streets (downtown Oakland), tel. (510) 834 2413. Open Wed–Sat 10 a.m.–5 p.m., Sun 12 noon–7 p.m. Admission charged; BART to Lake Merritt station, walk two blocks to the museum.

Officially named the Museum of California, this innovative institu-tion showcases the state's natural history, art and history on three levels. The museum was a radical concept when it was first unveiled in 1969. Architect Kevin Roche and landscape architect Dan Kiley wrapped the museum in a walled, terraced garden that gives the sense of entering a secret world.

Construction   The city of Oakland had supported a series of small museums almost since its founding in 1852. After a vote to build a city museum in the sixties, a series of accidents gave the city the most original museum building in America. Hitherto unknown, Kevin Roche took over the commission when his mentor Eero Saarinen died during the negotiations. Working with architect John Dinkeloo and Dan Kiley, Roche designed a multi-level museum that flowed easily from level to level, outdoors to indoors.

Oakland, always eager to show up San Francisco, was won over to the design with the argument that it would overshadow any-thing in San Francisco. Among architects, museum administrators, art collectors and urban planners the Oakland Museum was a fantastic hit, inspiring articles, accolades and awards. Among Oaklanders there was a little bit of confusion. They had voted for a huge civic bond act to pay for a big-time museum. Most citizens were expecting something along the palatial lines of Alma Spreckels' Palace of the Legion of Honor, a big, heavy building that spelled out its mission of big, heavy art (see p. 211).

The fabulous design leaked like mad for the first few years, but eventually the problems were cleared up. Likewise, Oaklanders have come to see their museum for the innovative treasure that it is.

The Visit   The museum has invested heavily in an educational approach to its work. With 90 per cent of its support coming from the City of Oakland, where the politics of the haves and have-nots take on religious fervour, the museum has been pressed to demonstrate its so-called 'relevance' to a community that is predominantly black, Asian, Latino and heavily immigrant. In response, the Oakland Museum has walked a fine line between creating programmes that serve its multicultural community and pandering to political correctness. On the whole the museum has acquitted itself very well and the visitor will find a broad range of festivals, performances, lectures, hands-on art workshops and other activities happening almost any day.

For the first-time visitor to the Oakland Museum, the most useful route is the one laid down by the building's organisers. Begin on the first level with the Natural History Gallery. The dioramas show the geographic zones of California. From here, walk up to the **Hall of California History** on the second level. The rich story of California, from pre-Columbian times to the present is traced through wonderfully intelligent groupings of artefacts, paintings, photos and documents. The Gold Rush is recalled in a recreated cabin while the fussy Victorian era is evoked in a San Francisco parlour setting. Big items such as a hand-pumping fire wagon and an ox-cart used by Mexican settlers give the smaller displays a valuable context. The history gallery is equally adept at modern times. Twentieth-century California is represented by its own room where a Mickey Mouse figure holds court with wooden surfboards, a World War II defence worker's apartment, customised cars and hippie memorabilia, plus an impressive gallery of statuary, featuring realistic, lifestyle portraits of Californians.

The third level, Art, is more of a historical survey than a purely artistically-driven exhibition. Within the museum's context, this is perfect. The swashbuckling canvases of the early California painters convey just as much about the state's development as the political posters in the history gallery. The museum has quite properly devoted one of the small art galleries to photography, an art form that has always had a special resonance with Californians. Photographers Dorothea Lange and Imogen Cunningham, both of whom did important work in California, are strongly represented in the permanent collection. The museum's survey of California's infatuation with the Arts and Crafts movement is excellent, including furniture, paintings and crafts.

Guided tours are available daily in the different galleries. The museum has an excellent bookstore and gift shop, and the café, with outdoor dining in good weather, is one of the best small cafés in Oakland.

6536 Telegraph Ave, tel. (510) 428 9684. Open daily 10 a.m.–7 p.m.

Mama Bear's is a time tunnel back to the days of Woymn and Wimmin. A bookstore, coffee house, art gallery and performance space on a dull stretch of Telegraph Avenue near the Oakland Berkeley line, Mama Bear's is a lesbian clubhouse that admits men on a probationary basis. Men are welcome as long as they are 'respectful of this as a woman's place', says the staff. Evening performances, however, which offer music, comedy and readings, are for women only.

The shop publishes its own newspaper, filled with book reviews and community news. Also in the way of community service, Mama Bear's keeps updated notebooks of housing, services and jobs. Along with Old Wives' Tales in the city (see p. 354), Mama Bear's is one of the few woman-centred public places still to be found in the Bay Area.

JESSICA MITFORD

Writer Jessica Mitford likes to say that she and her husband moved to Oakland in the 1940s because he was making too much money in San Francisco. As dedicated Communists, Mitford and her brilliant attorney husband had to accommodate their lives to the party line.

An English aristocrat who bonded with left-wing causes as a teenager, Mitford became one of America's most famous authors with her 1963 blockbuster, *The American Way of Death*. Her exposure of the funeral industry's shameless manipulation of grief-stricken families was a best seller and sparked the consumer rights movement in the US. Mitford also produced important books about the prison system, the anti-war movement of the sixties and most recently, an indictment of the medical establishment's treatment of midwifery, *The American Way of Birth*.

Muckraking reporter was an unlikely destiny for Mitford, one of the famous 'Mitford girls' who thrilled English society and headline writers with their legendary wit, beauty, political intrigues and love affairs. In addition to Jessica who eloped as a teenager with another aristocratic rebel, Esmond Romilly, nephew of Winston Churchill, there was novelist Nancy, Duchess of Devonshire Deborah and Hitler gal pals Unity and Diana. It made for quite a family.

Jessica and Esmond decamped for the US in the late thirties and thrived in the new world. Esmond was killed in World War II and 'Decca' married Robert Treuhaft, a Harvard-trained Jewish labour lawyer. They settled in San Francisco after the war and when life was too easy, resettled in Oakland. Passionate about social justice, they were drawn to the Communist Party's fearless civil rights work. Decca, with her commanding upper-class accent (or 'U', as her sister Nancy would say) and relish for life's absurdities, mystified middle-class Oaklanders. When Treuhaft was summoned before a Congressional committee to be grilled about his leftist activities, Mitford was incensed that she wasn't ordered to appear as well. She made up for it by creating a scene at the hearing.

Denounced as a Communist agitator by a Republican mayor of Oakland in the fifties, Mitford could barely contain her glee when he was charged with embezzlement from a Catholic trust fund and sent to jail. 'Nuns!' she crowed, 'He swindled nuns!'

Mitford and Treuhaft left the CP in the fifties, unhappy with revelations about the Soviet Union and chafing under the heavy hand of party discipline. Not that they have any regrets. Celebrating their fiftieth wedding anniversary in 1993, the couple happily recalled their salad days as radicals. Even the prospect of prison didn't bother them. 'Oh! It was secretly considered quite a vacation by party members,' explained Mitford. 'None of those tiresome meetings, you see.'

Mills College

5000 MacArthur Blvd, tel. (510) 430 2255, fax (510) 430 3314.

Until 1990 Mills College was mostly known as the oldest women's college west of the Rocky Mountains. While its reputation for academics was strong, Mills had only a vague public profile as a dullish place where young women with serious career goals went to college.

Then came the 1990 bombshell when the college announced it was closing the door on the woman's college era and would begin accepting men as students. The Board of Trustees, anxious about skyrocketing costs for a private college education, said there just didn't seem to be very many women interested in attending an all-woman's school.

The Mills student body was enraged over the plan to admit men. Mills students, supposedly placid would-be careerists, sprang into action. The angry talk soon exploded into a campus wide strike, complete with pickets, demos, angry confrontations and T-shirts that screamed, 'BETTER DEAD THAN COED!'

The Mills strike was front page news all over the US. Droves of television crews and newspaper reporters descended on the small, rustic campus in East Oakland to interview the radicalised baby feminists. Mills was such a big story that it even created a backlash. Ever ready to take the retro-male position, *Esquire* magazine ran photos of campus women in tears, nominating the entire Mills student body as the woman the magazine most disliked in 1990.

Impressed by the students' impassioned protest to 'let Mills be Mills', the administration and trustees dumped the coed plans and reaffirmed the commitment for the school to remain all-female (although men have long been admitted as visiting undergraduates and fully credentialled graduate students). There are now fewer than a hundred women's colleges left in the US, many having closed or merged with men's schools in the last two decades. Mills, with its grassroots commitment to a women's agenda, has emerged as a potent symbol for feminism and women's self-determination.

History Mills claims 1852 as its founding date, tracing its roots to a young ladies' seminary that opened in the East Bay town of Benicia that year. Briefly the state capital, Benicia was home to a number of prosperous Californians who could afford to educate their daughters.

Attending the seminary soon became a symbol of achievement for the raw Californians who were eager for badges of status. Writer Bret Harte gently satirised the school in several stories featuring upwardly mobile young women who spoke French 'with a perfect Benicia accent'.

Mark Twain is said to have attended graduation ceremonies in the 1860s and asked headmistress Susan Mills, 'May I kiss one of those pretty girls?' Annoyed at his impertinence she gave him a frosty 'No'.

In 1865 former missionaries Cyrus and Susan Mills bought the academy and moved it to Oakland in 1870. Easterners and college graduates, the Mills wanted to establish a woman's college on the Pacific Coast to equal Susan Mills' *alma mater* Mount Holyoke in Massachusetts or the other outstanding women's colleges such as Smith, Barnard, Vassar, Wellesley and Radcliffe.

Like its Eastern sisters, Mills did develop into a very fine liberal arts school despite some resistance to the need for educating women beyond reading and writing. Susan Mills was particularly amused by one argument that over-educating women would result in such crimes as wives forging their husbands' signatures and bankrupting the family through frivolous, unchecked spending sprees. After her husband's death in 1884, Susan Mills assumed full leadership of the college, remaining president until her death in 1909.

Mills has always stressed academic achievement over the social graces, unlike many early women's schools which put equal emphasis on tea pouring and algebra. Mills students have gone on to graduate school and positions of leadership in much higher proportions than female graduates of co-educational schools. Among the well-known alumnae are painters Jennifer Bartlett and Elizabeth Murray, dancer-choreographers Trisha Brown and Molissa Fenley, former Washington governor Dixy Lee Ray, and an impressive number of diplomats, professors, politicians, attorneys and, increasingly, businesswomen.

The Visit The campus is a 135-acre oasis of parklands in down-at-heel East Oakland. While not located in the truly dangerous ghetto streets, the neighbourhood approaches marginal. Instead of ignoring its surroundings, Mills has built strong ties to the neighbourhood with children's programmes and an effective strategy for recruiting older students, many of them black and Latina, who had never considered college before Mills convinced them to try.

With its thick covering of eucalyptus trees punctuated with Victorian and red-tile roofed mission revival buildings, Mills is almost a dream version of what a Western college campus should look like. Walking tours of the campus are available most weekdays during the school term or upon request from the Admissions Office (tel. 430 2135).

The school grew up around Mills Hall, an imposing 1871 Second Empire/Italianate structure that once was classrooms, offices, dining hall, dormitory and the president's home as well. The Mediterranean look that now defines the campus originated with Julia Morgan, one of the Bay Area's most influential architects and the first woman to complete the architectural course at Paris's Ecole des Beaux-Arts. Morgan's first known major commission was the El Campanil bell tower for Mills (1904). Mills was very supportive of Morgan's career and she contributed several other buildings to the campus, including the magnificent old library (1906), on the oval near Mills Hall.

In addition to its architecture, Mills has a very good art gallery, housed in a 1925 mission revival building. The exhibitions often focus on women artists. Alums Jennifer Bartlett and Elizabeth Murray have been given shows here, as well as artists such as Faith Ringgold, photographer Catherine Wagner (a faculty member) and a sweeping survey of California quilts. The Mills shows aren't very well publicised, unfortunately, so make a point of calling the gallery for its schedule, tel. 430 2164.

ANGELA DAVIS

The Black Panthers were Oakland's dominant symbol of the sixties, the beret and leather-clad urban guerrillas led by Huey Newton and Eldridge Cleaver.

Angela Davis, a fiery intellectual and professor was an equally potent Panther symbol, crowned by a huge Afro and pronouncing the party's radical agenda in the precise theoretical language she had learned from her mentor, Herbert Marcuse.

Implicated in a bloody attempt to free black radicals being tried in Marin, Davis went underground in the early seventies. She was thought to be on the Panther circuit, following the steps of Newton and Cleaver through Cuba and Algeria. Recaptured in the US she was tried and freed in the Marin case and, after extended legal manoeuvres, able to teach again in California public universities.

Currently, America's one-time most wanted radical lives quietly in the Oakland Hills and teaches women's studies at San Francisco State University and at the University of California at Santa Cruz. Unapologetic about her radical and Communist Party politics (she has run for the US senate and vice president under the CP banner), Davis is much in demand on the college lecture circuit where she talks to laid-back nineties' undergraduates about the causes that have defined her life, anti-racism and women's rights.

Music is another forte of Mills. The emphasis on experimental music has attracted faculty such as Darius Milhaud, Anthony Braxton, Pauline Oliveros, Steve Reich, Philip Glass and Charles Shere. Jazz master Dave Brubeck and members of the Grateful Dead have attended their famous classes, eager to be on the New Music cutting edge. Campus performances feature well known composers and performers trying out new works, confident they will get an intelligent hearing at Mills.

BERKELEY

The 1960s are still alive in Berkeley – the good, the bad and the ugly. The counterculture idealists who grew up and stayed in town are variously credited with creating a new American cuisine and approach to food, earnest attempts at genuine, top-to-bottom democracy and a cultural climate that allows an intellectual life to flourish. The downside of the sixties has emerged in an unpleasant rigidity in matters such as rent control and parking tickets and a reluctance to set boundaries that creates constant bickering and pandering to leftist sacred cows.

Berkeley is so completely sensitised to feminist issues that it is hardly remarked upon. A few years ago a waitress at a popular café asked a customer to put away his *Playboy* magazine as she found it offensive. The ensuing controversy thrilled the rest of the country while the burning question in Berkeley was, '*Playboy?* Is it still published? And they sell it in Berkeley, really!'

Getting to Berkeley is fairly simple. BART has several Berkeley stops and connects with local AC Transit buses making most of the town quite easy to visit from San Francisco. Another nice bonus is the weather. On a foggy summer day you can get on BART in the city and in less than half an hour pop out of an East Bay BART stop into cheerful Berkeley sunshine.

WHOOPI GOLDBERG

Like many people who come to Berkeley, Whoopi Goldberg was looking for some-thing. Unlike most of them, she found it. Goldberg popped up in Berkeley in 1983 as a member of the Blake Street Hawkeyes, an irreverent fringe theatre troupe that worked out of a downtown garage.

Goldberg had done stand-up comedy and theatre in San Diego, where she had moved from New York. Searching for a way to blend her political edge with her bent for mimicry and earthy comedy, Goldberg was drawn to the Hawkeyes' theatre of political farce. Within a year she had developed her first one-woman show, the hyster-ically funny *Spook Show*. The show made her name in the Bay Area and caught the eye of producers who took it to New York for a successful Off Broadway run. By 1985 she was in the movies, filming *The Color Purple* with Steven Spielberg.

When she came to Berkeley, virtually penniless, Goldberg scraped by on food stamps, welfare and the Hawkeyes' share-the-wealth generosity. She had her eight-

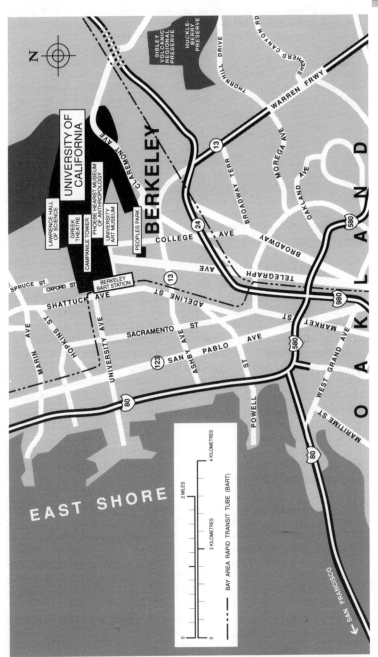

year-old daughter in tow and frequently traded off childcare with other actors and performers. After Goldberg hit the big time with her HBO specials and the movies, she bought a house in the Berkeley Hills and brought her mother out from New York to live there and take care of her daughter. Goldberg tried to keep Berkeley as her home, but her involvement in the movie-comedy-celebrity business was too encompassing. Gradually she became an occasional visitor instead of a resident who left to make movies. Goldberg's mother and daughter followed her south to Los Angeles.

Among her old guerrilla theatre friends, Goldberg is fondly remembered and celebrated for making it, not selling out. Goldberg's colleagues feel Berkeley was an important part of her success, pushing her beyond the aimlessness of stand-up comedy and calling her glibness into question.

Goldberg has returned several times to make films in the Bay Area, including her early flops, *Jumpin' Jack Flash* and *Burglar*. She had better luck with *Sister Act*, then with *Made in America* when she clicked with co-star Ted Danson, showing him around Oakland, Berkeley and San Francisco on their days off. The romance ended elsewhere, but Goldberg seems to get lucky when she's in Berkeley.

University of California

Main gate, Telegraph Avenue and Bancroft Way. Tel. (510) 642 6000.

The outside world calls this university 'Berkeley'. Anyone who has any personal contact calls it 'Cal'. With more than 30,000 students and covering 1200 acres, the university is a major element in Bay Area life and the defining fact of life for Berkeley, a city of 112,000.

The university is a relatively new institution, even for American colleges, opened in 1870. Yet in little over a century Cal has become not just one of America's great universities, but one of the world's leading academic institutions. Until recently, the university liked to point out that it had the same number of Nobel Prize winners as the Soviet Union – fifteen. The university is particularly strong in the sciences, but has made its public reputation on the fervent political activism of the student body on behalf of human rights.

The campus is interesting architecturally and is home to several museums. It is an open campus, easy to navigate and an amusing window on youth culture.

History   California's 1849 state constitution called for the establishment of a state university, but it was 1870 before the University of California opened its doors. Two smaller schools dating from 1855 and 1866 were merged into the new school at Berkeley. When the university was established the regents, apparently without fanfare, adopted a resolution that admitted women as full students, which had not been the case at the two smaller colleges. The regents unanimously resolved that 'young ladies be admitted into the university on equal terms in all respects with young men'. Eight women enrolled in the new school, making up nine per cent of the small student body.

PHOEBE HEARST

Growing up in rural Missouri, Phoebe Apperson Hearst yearned to see far-away places. She particularly longed to visit St Louis. Just becoming a school teacher was quite an achievement for a young woman living on the ragged edges of the frontier with her farm family.

In 1862 Phoebe married a family friend, George Hearst. Almost twenty years her senior, he had returned from California newly rich from the Nevada mines. Phoebe was thrilled with her new life and as her husband's fortunes skyrocketed, she busied herself with good works. George Hearst went to Washington as a US senator and Phoebe Hearst became the town's best hostess and charity benefactor. When her husband died in 1891, Phoebe returned to California and turned her hand to improving the lot of her adopted home state.

She was very big on education and self-improvement and was quickly drawn to the University of California. Impressed with Jane Stanford's commitment to Stanford University, Phoebe Hearst began her long reign as queen bee of the UC campus. Until her death in 1919, Hearst gave more than $15 million to the school, far more than the state. She took a particular interest in the women students, establishing scholarships for them (which still exist and are called 'Phoebes'), inviting them to tea, taking up their causes with administrators and raising their esteem and importance in the eyes of others just by the fact of her interest.

Hearst was appointed to the Board of Regents in 1897, the first woman member, where she was deferential but very powerful.

Hearst adored her only child, William Randolph, but was constantly exasperated by his childish pranks well into his twenties and his playboy life. She could deny him nothing, however, and was always brought around to whatever scheme he embarked upon, including buying newspapers. Phoebe Hearst's great achievement, the nurturing of the University of California, has been vastly overshadowed by her seeming blind indulgence of her son. It is a problem that most mothers will understand.

During most of its nineteenth-century history, Cal was the only public university in California. Other California colleges were primarily church related. Stanford was non-sectarian but private. Inevitably some of the state's riches were settled on the state school. The university's subsequent eminence, however, can be credited in part to its first great champion, Phoebe Apperson Hearst.

Hearst has been unfortunately relegated to footnote status in the decades since her death in 1919, identifying her as the wife and widow of George, mining magnate and senator, mother of William Randolph, publishing behemoth and playboy, and great-grandmother of Patty, kidnap victim, *faux* terrorist and rehabilitated socialite.

Until Phoebe Hearst began taking an interest in the school in the 1890s, Cal was strictly a hick school in the hinterlands. The campus had been situated as far as possible from the temptations of city life (Oakland and San Francisco) without making access to goods and services unduly difficult. The university opposed the establishment of Stanford, fearing that the new school would cut into its pool of students and dilute support for the state university. Without Phoebe Hearst and her millions, it is entirely possible that Stanford would have become the pre-eminent university of the West and UC would never have moved beyond the status of respectable state school.

PATTY HEARST

Great-granddaughter of the founders of the dynasty, granddaughter of the newspaper magnate and daughter of his negligible son, Patty Hearst was just another unremarkable rich girl going to college when she was kidnapped from her Berkeley apartment in 1974.

Hearst was twenty, majoring in art history at UC and living quietly with her graduate student boyfriend Steven Weed, who was her former high school maths teacher. Hearst had put some distance between herself and her overbearing parents, refusing to become a debutante and living openly with her boyfriend. Her kidnappers were a radical fringe group called the Symbionese Liberation Army with no following besides themselves. In a bizarre series of events, Hearst's family agreed to the SLA's demands to feed the poor as ransom, but the young woman announced her intention to stay underground with her captors. She took part in a bank robbery and stayed on the run for nineteen months before being caught with her cohorts by the FBI.

At her trial and in a later book, Hearst argued that the SLA crazies would have killed her if she had demanded her freedom as promised. Once she was underground Hearst accepted the credo that the FBI would kill on sight, not hard to believe after several SLA 'soldiers' died in a massive overkill operation in Los Angeles.

Despite her protestations of brainwashing, sexual abuse and chaotic times, Hearst was convicted of bank robbery and served three years before receiving a presidential pardon from Jimmy Carter. She married her former police bodyguard and now lives in Connecticut with her husband and two daughters. Hearst has re-entered the social life that she was bred for, but with minimal interest. Her adolescent rebellions seemed to resurface a few years ago when she agreed to appear in a John Waters (of *Pink Flamingos* fame) film. Called *Cry Baby* and starring Johnny Depp, Hearst played what else? a society matron.

Hearst's first financial gift to the University of California was the sponsorship of an international competition for a unified campus design in 1896 (see p. 257). Her involvement with the school and enthusiastic support for women students encouraged other rich Californians to take an interest in Cal and added a further legitimisation to co-education.

Although women were slow to advance into the ranks of the faculty, women students have been a visible and active part of the university community.

Buoyed by California's burgeoning population and dedication to civic improvement, the state university system became California's greatest ornament. Other campuses have been added, beginning with Los Angeles in 1919 (UCLA) and now include Santa Cruz, Davis, San Diego, Irvine, Riverside, Santa Barbara and San

Francisco (medical school and research), but Berkeley remains the jewel in the crown of the UC system.

Student activism beyond campus politics began in the 1930s when students plunged into political debates sparked by the crisis of the Depression. The socialists had a big following in Berkeley and the Communist Party made small inroads. Students flocked to San Francisco to join ranks with workers in the waterfront strike of 1934 that became a general strike. The Spanish Civil War struck a chord in Berkeley and more than a few students left to fight in Spain.

In the 1960s, however, the Cal campus came into its own. Always a centre for bohemians, Berkeley students were early and dedicated supporters of the civil rights struggle by black Americans. A regular path was soon beaten down between Berkeley and dusty little towns in Alabama and Mississippi where students went to demonstrate, register voters and teach in freedom schools. When the students continued their political work at home, UC balked at the explosion of speakers, petitioners and pamphleteers who gathered on Sproul Plaza. The university cited priggish state laws banning partisan political campaigning on publically-supported college campuses. In the autumn of 1964 the simmering resentment among students exploded into the Free Speech Movement. The campus erupted when police tried to arrest a young man named Jack Weinberg who had set up a small table on Sproul Plaza to hand out political material. Thousands of students surrounded the police car trying to take Weinberg away. Speeches, singing, chanting and negotiations went on all night.

The Free Speech Movement triumphed, and the university lifted all bans on campus political activity. Berkeley students continued their political commitment, defining and leading the New Left. Berkeley held the first anti-Vietnam demonstration and teach-ins and preached 'bring the war home' policies. But even as the word Berkeley became an epithet among conservatives and complacent Middle America, the university and town were almost spent.

Although much of the country was just getting into the swing of the anti-war movement in 1969, the Berkeley Left was exhausted by then, having been fully engaged since 1964. The last act in the great Berkeley drama was People's Park in the spring of 1969. Essentially a couple of vacant lots off Telegraph Avenue, hippies took over the area and declared it liberated for the people. Flowers and grass were planted, children's play areas were set up and bands showed up to play. UC's imperial expansions beyond the core campus area were an ongoing source of irritation. Whole neighbourhoods would be condemned, houses (often student homes) razed and ugly, impersonal dormitories and parking garages erected in their place. The block between Dwight and Haste was earmarked for more university building until the student-hippie-political takeover. Instead of waiting them out, the university ripped up the park. Riots followed. Governor Ronald Reagan was incensed over what was happening in Berkeley and sent in the National Guard, helicopters spewing teargas and armed tanks. Berkeley was a war zone for weeks. Almost every college and university in California shut down in a sympathy strike with the draconian treatment of the Berkeley demonstrators.

Anti-war demonstrations and organising continued until the US pull-out of Vietnam, but People's Park was a watershed for Berkeley. The town and campus had been bled dry by years of tension and demonstrations. Looking back, many mark the 'back to the country' move among students, hippies and counterculturists from this point.

FACULTY WIVES

One of Berkeley's most potent resources has been the women married to UC faculty members. Well-educated, intelligent, interested in the larger world, generations of these women have followed their husbands to the University of California, usually the crowning achievement of an academic career, and settled in to live their lives and raise their families. Many of the wives were excellent faculty material themselves, but the combined effects of the family/career dichotomy, policies against nepotism and the slow acceptance of first-rank universities to hire women kept most of them out of academia.

Instead of teaching, faculty wives poured their energies into other pursuits. Their impact has been almost invisible but powerful. 'The tea ladies' who are credited with saving San Francisco Bay are a good example. In 1961 Esther Guelick, Kay Kerr and Sylvia McLaughlin were aghast when they saw a US Army Corps of Engineers map of the bay in the year 2020. By then the proud engineers planned to have the marshy areas drained, rivers dammed and acres more of the bay filled in. The three friends, all married to UC faculty members, were further upset at the plans for golf courses, malls and condos. Guelick, Kerr and McLaughlin couldn't believe that they were alone in understanding that the bay was a living, breathing organism that made life possible. They began a modest campaign by mail to alert first their friends, then the public about the lunatic plans for the bay. Their Save The Bay coalition eventually put a stop to filling in the bay and sparked a public awareness of the bay's ecology. Now in their eighties the 'tea ladies', as their opponents sneeringly labelled them, have remained dedicated to the bay. 'The price of saving the bay will always be eternal vigilance,' said McLaughlin.

Theodora Kroeber had studied anthropology under her husband, Alfred Kroeber, an academic superstar. After they married in the 1920s, she put away her degrees to raise their four children. Alfred Kroeber had worked with Ishi, the last member of his tribe, who had walked out of the Stone Age into the twentieth century in 1911. Theodora Kroeber never met Ishi, but she absorbed her husband's experience and ideas and turned it into the successful *Ishi: In Two Worlds*, a bestseller when it was published in 1961 and never out of print since. She became far more famous than her illustrious husband. The Kroebers' daughter, the popular science fiction writer Ursula Le Guin, declined to follow her mother's example of putting family and husband before her own career.

"In her late 70s, my mother said she wished she hadn't waited [to write]," Le Guin has said of Theodora Kroeber. "'I don't have time to do what I want,' she said. And she didn't."

Construction The site selected for the new university was a commanding hillside exactly opposite the Golden Gate. The beautiful vistas inspired one of the regents to quote a poem by George Berkeley, Bishop of Cloyne, 'Westward, the course of empire takes its way ...' The planners decided to call the university town Berkeley (which the Americans pronounced burk-lee instead of the English bark-lee).

While the first builders were impressed by the university's beautiful natural setting, they did little to enhance it. The first buildings were hideous Second Empire piles, terribly out of place on the open hills. The Berkeley founders, probably the most educated people in California at the time, were far more influenced by their sense of themselves as the vanguard of Western Civilisation than blending in with their new world. The mansard roofs of North Hall and South Hall were visible reminders of French culture which most nineteenth-century Americans regarded as the apex of human achievement.

South Hall, built in 1873, has survived and sits at the centre of campus, a grand old party now mellowed with age and ivy. It is the sole remnant of the early days.

In 1899 French architect Emile Benard's master plan of a classical city on a hill was selected as the winner in the Phoebe Hearst sponsored international design competition. Benard happily collected his $10,000 prize, but had no intention of staying in the US to supervise the campus. A runner-up, John Galen Howard, was asked to become the campus architect and ruled Berkeley like a small duchy for the next two decades. Howard modified and rethought Benard's high classicism to recreate a handsome core campus. He worked with Julia Morgan and Bernard Maybeck, two of Phoebe Hearst's favourite architects, in some of the school's most outstanding buildings.

The Hearst Mining Building (1907) is not just Howard's masterpiece, but one of California's great buildings. Its beaux arts splendour is worth the hike across campus. Other buildings from Howard's reign (until 1927) include Julia Morgan's magnificent Hearst Greek Theater (1903), the Doe Library (1907), Sather Gate (1910), Phoebe Hearst Memorial Gymnasium for Women (1925) and the Campanile (1914).

The high standard of building and design declined after Howard, but took a terrible nosedive after World War II when the worst kind of Modernist brutalism became the norm for UC buildings. During the 1960s the buildings became a symbol for the faceless 'multiversity', in Chancellor Clark Kerr's famous and unfortuante phrase that became a rallying cry (as in 'death to') to the Free Speech Movement.

In the 1980s a new trend towards smaller, human-scale buildings emerged with emphasis on the Bay Tradition of architecture.

The Foothill Residence Halls at the northeast corner of campus, Gayley Road and Hearst Avenue, is the best example of this with its brown shingle exterior and rustic detailing.

The Visit   The best time to visit campus is a weekday when you can see it in full flight. Free campus tours are given twice daily at 10 a.m. and 1 p.m. three days a week, Monday, Wednesday and Friday, but you may request your own tour from the Visitor Center, call (510) 642 5215. Cars are banned from the central campus, so you will be doing all your sightseeing on foot.

Architectural must-sees on campus are almost all the largess of Phoebe Hearst: the beautiful Hearst Mining Building, the Hearst Gymnasium with its black marble swimming pool on the roof and Julia Morgan's impressive Hearst Greek Theater.

JULIA MORGAN

Julia Morgan's reputation has been as hotly debated as a politician's. She's a feminist trailblazer, she's a mindless minion of the autocracy, she's a closet lesbian, she's a brilliant designer, she's a no-brainer reactionary.

The debate has been mostly genteel as befits Morgan's own retiring personality but the Morgan stock has definitely gone blue chip in the last decade. At the time of her death in 1957 she was respected for her dedication to her work but written off as hopelessly out of date in her architectural vision.

Morgan enrolled at UC in 1890, the first woman in the mechanical engineering programme and on graduating (with honours), became one of the first American women to graduate in the field. Encouraged by her professors, especially architect Bernard Maybeck, Morgan headed for Paris and the Ecole des Beaux-Arts where she became the first woman of any nationality to complete the architectural course. Returning to the Bay Area, Morgan opened her own office in 1905 and slowly built a major practice. Her first patron was Phoebe Hearst who wanted Morgan to work on UC buildings. Morgan was later taken up by William Randolph Hearst and became his architect in the ongoing construction of San Simeon, the unbelievably opulent castle Hearst built in Southern California, beginning in 1919.

A prime practitioner of the Bay Tradition of redwood shingled rusticity, Morgan's 600-odd houses, offices, churches and community buildings are all over the Bay Area. Her richly textured, romantic buildings are in stark contrast to her monastic life. Morgan, who didn't marry, doesn't seem to have had any intimate relationships. Unlike many women of her generation, Morgan didn't form an attachment with another educated woman to set up a household. Perhaps her most important connection outside her family was her sorority at UC, Kappa Alpha Theta. Morgan's friends in later life tended to be her old sorority sisters, many of whom helped her get architectural commissions at the beginning of her career.

Morgan retired at seventy-one, closed her office, travelled a bit and died at home in Berkeley in 1957. Her obituaries were all but patronising, the old girl never having caught on to Modernism, highrises, the post-war look. In the end, of course, Julia Morgan's faith in beautiful, well-constructed buildings is being vindicated. Her houses sell for millions of dollars and to own 'a Julia Morgan' is the ultimate Bay Area status symbol. Her structures have often escaped the wrecker's ball because they were so sturdily built that they have functioned worry-free since they were put up.

Julia Morgan's work is a statement of optimism and seriousness leavened by flights of fancy.

Sproul Plaza

This plaza is UC's own Hyde Park corner where Christian fundamentalists, anarchists, socialists, feminists, vegetarians and believers of almost every persuasion still talk their talk and walk their walk. Pick up a copy of the student newspaper, *The Daily Californian* (although budget problems have rendered it no longer daily) to see if there are any events happening the day of your visit.

The campus Visitor Center is an inconvenient half mile away at University Hall (Oxford Street and University Avenue, across from the West Gate to campus), but you will be able to get a free campus map at the Student Center on Sproul Plaza.

Downstairs in the Student Center is the ASUC Store (Associated Students of the University of California) where you will find a mini-mall of bookstores, clothing, cards, souvenirs and food. Continuing through the ASUC Store outside to Lower Sproul Plaza you come to one of Berkeley's major gathering spots. Impromptu concerts share the space with regular noontime gigs which feature well-known local bands.

Campanile

Open daily, except university holidays, 10 a.m.–4.15 p.m., 25c for non-students.

Officially Sather Tower, it was modelled after St Mark's bell tower in Venice. The tower is 307 feet tall, the third tallest bell tower in the world, and equipped with 61 bells. A musician plays a programme three times a day, 7.50 p.m., 12 noon and 6 p.m. in addition to hourly chiming. The view from the top of the tower is fabulous. Be careful not to go up, however, at bell time. The noise is beyond deafening.

Phoebe Apperson Hearst Museum of Anthropology

In Kroeber Hall (Bancroft Way at College Avenue), tel. (510) 642 3681. Open Tues–Fri 10 a.m.–4.30 p.m., Sat–Sun 12 noon–4.30 p.m., 25c–$1.50.

With more than 400,000 catalogued items from around the world, this anthropology treasure house is never short of ideas for exhibitions. The museum (until recently called the Lowie Museum) hosts travelling shows as well. The exhibitions often deal with the culture of women, examining artefacts and tools used in domestic life.

Lawrence Hall of Science

In the hills above campus, Centennial Drive, tel. 642 5132. Open daily 10 a.m.–4.30 p.m. (to 5 p.m. Sat–Sun). Admission $2–$5; weekdays there is a free shuttle bus up the hill from Hearst Mining Circle, call 642 5149.

Dinosaurs, telescopes, computers, spaceships and dozens of other delights are to be found in this hilltop science museum, a place Bay Area children love.

The Hall of Science is not to be confused with the famous Lawrence Livermore Lab, the nuclear research facility 45 miles east of Berkeley that is regularly picketed by anti-nuke activists. Both are named for Cal faculty man and Nobel Prize winner Ernest O. Lawrence. Along with J. Robert Oppenheimer, Lawrence was part of a dazzling concentration of scientific brainpower at Berkeley in the 1930s. The Berkeley crowd was the nucleus of the group that built the atomic bomb in New Mexico during World War II. Lawrence's widow has campaigned to have her husband's name removed from the Livermore lab which has been deeply involved in weapons research. The association with the Hall of Science is a much happier connection.

Guilt-free, you can bring your children here for planetarium shows, dream up your own experiments in the Wizard's Lab and walk through a sculpture of a DNA molecule.

University Art Museum and Pacific Film Archive

2626 Bancroft Way, tel. (510) 642 0808. Open Wed–Sun 11 a.m.–5 p.m. Admission $4–$5, children under six free.

A 1970 cubist structure by Mario Ciampi, the University Art Museum is alone among UC's Modernist period buildings with any genuine style or attractiveness. The exterior is tamed Brutalism and the interior is open, airy and well-thought-out.

The museum is primarily interested in twentieth-century art, but some older schools are included in the permanent collection. The museum had its beginnings in a large bequest from Abstract Expressionist painter Hans Hofmann (1880–1966). A native of Germany, Hofmann first came to Berkeley in the early thirties to teach. He revisited regularly and gave a major group of his paintings to the university in the early sixties. Hofmann also made significant cash donations to the museum.

University Art Museum is the largest university-related museum in the US. Its funding, unfortunately, has been only sporadic from UC, but the museum has been adventurous in its programming and collecting. This museum is careful in its selection of travelling shows and has mounted some major exhibitions of its own, such as the 1991 retrospective on the Surrealists. The Matrix Gallery, on the ground floor, is one of the best places in the Bay Area for emerging artists and themes.

The Pacific Film Archive

2625 Durant Ave (in the same building as the museum but approached from the other side of the block), tel. 642 1124.

The university's Pacific Film Archive is one of the nation's best scholarly film archives, as well as one of the best repertory film houses to be found anywhere. PFA is the West Coast sister of the film programme at New York's Museum of Modern Art with an extensive library and more than 6000 films on hand.

Serious film scholars and students are given access to the library but anyone may attend the daily film programmes, usually a double feature, sometimes with the director or a knowledgeable critic speaking before or after in the 200-seat screening room. Tickets to the film screenings are usually $3. A detailed schedule is available in the free bimonthly University Art Museum/Pacific Film Archive newsletter distributed in cafés, bookstores and shops all over the East Bay.

The film programmes are usually tied to an ongoing theme and PFA has been diligent in addressing the issues and personalities of women in film.

Telegraph Avenue

Telegraph is among the world's most famous streets, courtesy of endless demonstrations it hosted in the sixties and seventies. The heart of the street is the four blocks between Dwight Way and Bancroft Way where it deadends into the campus. Since its bohemian heyday of the sixties, Telegraph has got pretty grubby around the edges with the homeless, professional street people and a permanent set of street pedlars who set up their jewellery, pottery, T-shirts and hippie memorabilia wares on blankets and folding tables.

The street is jammed with bars and cafés. Most notable is Larry Blake's, a student hangout now in its fourth decade. The blues club downstairs (see p. 326) is one of the best music spots in town.

Cody's Books, 2454 Telegraph, is one of the great independent bookstores. With more than 250,000 titles as well as a huge inventory of American, European and Asian magazines, Cody's is a book paradise. The store has several author readings a week, usually big names. Check the schedule posted at the front door. Founded in the 1950s by free spirits Fred and Pat Cody, the store was practically the only place around the campus that didn't have its windows smashed during demos. As other shops on Telegraph bricked over their windows and took on the appearance of bunkers, the Codys remodelled, adding bigger plate glass windows.

People's Park

Half a block east of Telegraph Avenue, bounded by Haste Street, Bowditch Street, Dwight Way.

Here it is. The life and death issue of Berkeley. Covering about two-thirds of the block, the park is unappealing to most passersby, with the look of an over-grown haven for street people. Yes, but. Quite respectable gardens have been planted here and there's a sense of housekeeping among the park habitués. A small platform stage accommodates speakers and the occasional performance. A few years ago the university made another claim on its land, installing volleyball courts for students. There were demonstrations, but not riots. Many of the ageing student demonstrators who defended the park would never go there now, but find the idea of UC simply taking it over and building something concrete and bureaucratic unacceptable. The park is too imbued with the past to pass into the present.

The Gourmet Ghetto

Upper Shattuck Avenue, Virginia to Rose streets; AC Transit buses 7, 9, 43.

It's legend now, how Alice Waters decided it would be fun to open a restaurant and run it like her own kitchen, cooking meals for friends.

In 1971 she made the rounds of banks looking for start-up money. Asked for experience and a business plan, she could only point to her UC degree in French culture and her idea of recreating the lovely meals she had eaten while travelling around France. The bankers were too polite to laugh outright, but Waters got the idea. With friends, she raised some money from people she had gone to school with at Berkeley and from family. Chez Panisse opened in a renovated brown shingle on upper Shattuck Avenue serving *prix fixe* meals with a menu that changed every day.

No one, least of all Waters, had big expectations of the little café, but it was the crystallisation of several pressing themes in American culture. Waters's idea of combining classic French and Italian cooking methods with the freshest possible local produce and meats was an unplanned improvement on the health food movement which at that time meant unappetising, unseasoned food in drab surroundings. Waters worked collaboratively and consensually with her staff. The restaurant was always a for-profit endeavour, but Chez Panisse was an attempt to apply co-operative principles to a business.

As Chez Panisse began to catch the eye of critics and writers, the food that Waters and her staff were serving came to be called California Cuisine. While it is an imprecise phrase at best it is still useful as a benchmark in American food.

Waters and Chez Panisse set a new standard for American restaurants, from service to food. There have been other benefits. Chez Panisse not only trained an entire generation of chefs and restaurateurs, but its emphasis on fresh, in-season ingredients sparked a revival in truck farming in Northern California. The popular street farmers' markets that are now daily occurrences in San Francisco, Marin and the East Bay where a direct outgrowth of the California Cuisine trend.

Gourmet Ghetto is another imprecise and generally disliked term, but is usually meant to mean the blocks between Virginia and Rose streets on Shattuck. Chez Panisse (see p. 309) is the only important restaurant in the area now, but in the early seventies there was a clustering of food shops and cafés that generated the name. The other important foodie landmark here is the Cheese Board, 1504 Shattuck. It's across the street from Chez Panisse, but almost invisible behind a small sign and low-key interior. It's the premiere cheese shop in the East Bay and the oldest collective still in business in California.

Organised in 1967, the business is run co-operatively and on the kind of principles that made Berkeley famous. In addition to senior citizen discounts (ten per cent) the shop gives five per cent discounts 'to anyone who needs it'. Profits are shared by the workers and invested in projects and causes that the collective votes on. Of course, none of this good deed stuff would mean anything if the Cheese Board wasn't a well-run, reliable business. And it is. You will see more than two hundred cheeses listed on the blackboard. The shop also bakes and sells wonderful breads and at noontime offers yummy pizzas for takeout.

Black Oak Books, another of Berkeley's landmark bookstores, is in the neighbourhood, 1491 Shattuck. Not quite as large as Cody's but equal in depth and breadth, Black Oak also has a lively readings programme. Cody's and Black Oak have a mostly friendly rivalry over their bookings and the biggest names in literature are careful to alternate visits to the two stores.

Peet's Coffee (see p. 358), a block east of Shattuck at Walnut and Vine, is the Bay Area's mother church of coffee. Unlike the North Beach coffee houses which were established for food and camaraderie, Peet's grew out of an obsession for good coffee. Regulars bring their own cups and fill up the benches outside on warm days, discussing post-structuralism and the Oakland A's chances for the World Series.

ACCOMMODATION

HOTELS

Hotels are a San Francisco art form. Luxury hotels, fun hotels, cute hotels, budget hotels, Euroteen hostels, outdoorsy hostels and more are all to be found in the city and nearby. From its first days, hotels have been a crucial part of San Francisco life. San Franciscans think of the Palace, the Fairmont, the St Francis and a few other places as fondly as their own homes. While you may not be able to afford the grand old places, you will benefit from the spillover of well-trained staff and the particular sense of pride that hoteliers invest in their establishments.

The only reason not to get the hotel room of your dreams is to be remiss in booking a place to stay. Remember that tourism and conventions are the city's number one industry and keeping the hotels full is the key to keeping the economy on track. Consequently there are no truly off seasons. Conferences and conventions are held year-round in San Francisco, frequently keeping the best hotel rooms booked ninety per cent of the year.

It is crucial to book a room as soon as you decide when you plan a visit. You can do this by telephoning or faxing. Of course, you may write a proper letter if you wish, but speed-addicted Americans tend to look at letters as somewhat off-kilter. The universal practice for reserving a hotel room is through credit cards. Some places will hold rooms with a reservation without some kind of prepayment, but that is becoming increasingly rare. If you don't have a credit card, offer to send payment for the first night.

Most of the city's hotels are concentrated in the downtown area, around the Financial District and Union Square. Other concentrations are at Fisherman's Wharf, usually undistinguished chains, and along Lombard Street, which is thick with fifties-style motels (very good if you have a car as parking is guaranteed and free). The downtown hotels, which come in a variety of sizes and prices, are almost always the best choice of places to stay. Their central location and seasoned staff combine for an easy experience in and out of the hotel.

There has been a recent spurt of hotels and motels going up South of Market, but these are still best avoided. While not exactly unsafe, the neighbourhoods are often empty at night, requiring that you drive or take a taxi almost everywhere. Many younger women travellers stay at the freewheeling youth hostels South of Market, but it is easy to come and go since many of the residents stick together. The hostels also tend to be close to the club scene.

The average San Francisco hotel room runs around $100 a night. For that price you may expect a private room with bath, a telephone, sometimes two beds, a desk, at least one sitting chair, television and a clock. Most hotels will cheerfully supply a crib or small folding bed for children. Sometimes there is a charge, usually $10 a night, for the extra bed. In general, the policy is for children under eighteen to stay free if they share their parents' room and no additional bedding or beds are required. Tuck the kids in on the couch or double up in the beds and you'll make a considerable saving. Many of the hotels and chains are developing family packages, recognising that most families travel together these days instead of leaving the kids with grandmother. When you make your reservation, quiz the reservations clerk closely about packages and special deals. Like the airlines, you will be given the highest room price with the other possibilities slowly revealed to you under questioning. One good resource to keep in mind is the centralised San Francisco Reservations, a free service that books rooms by phone. It lists more than 200 Bay Area hotels, 150 of them in San Francisco. The service is especially helpful if you are coming on short notice. The switchboard is open from 7 a.m. to 10 p.m. (California time), tel. 227 1500. There is also a toll-free number within the US, 1 800 677 1550.

In the upscale hotels you will find rooms loaded with extras. The bars, stocked with goodies ranging from candy bars to champagne, are astonishingly expensive. A steward comes around on check-out day and tallies up your expenses. Unless money means nothing to you, avoid using anything in the bar and buy your own treats at the corner grocery. But the four-star hotels are quite cognisant that the guests do expect extra flourishes for the bucks. All kinds of free services are available if you ask, such as having your shoes cleaned overnight, extra pillows and comforts, iron and ironing board set up for you in your room and so on. Most of the bigs now have 'club floors' which serve buffets three or four times a day, provide the daily papers and have a fridge full of free beer and soft drinks day and night.

On the whole the greatest boon of staying in the expensive hotels is service. Everyone you see is friendly, helpful and polite.

Americans, who have always equated service with servile, are not generally adept at the service industry although the country runs on it. San Francisco hotels, especially the expensive ones, have spent a great deal of time, money and thought on training their employees in how to provide good service. The Clift, Ritz-Carlton, Fairmont and Huntington are known around the world for their beautiful manners. For people with money to spend, it's worth it.

If you can't afford the $250 a day and up rates of the elite hotels, don't worry. You will be well treated and well served at most San Francisco inns. The new trend towards smaller, cosier hotels has been a great boon for the traveller. Places such as the Phoenix, the Juliana, the Triton and Inn at the Opera are modelled on small European hotels with nicely decorated rooms and attentive staffs.

Whatever sort of hotels you choose, watch out for the extras that can double or even triple your expected bill. The universally-loathed telephone surcharges are the worst offenders, with hotels tacking on as much as $1 for local calls you dial yourself. Ask carefully about the phone rates before you make even one call. Room service meals are horribly overpriced at every level, as are some business services such as faxing (see p. 17), which can run as much as $5 a page to send or receive. Consider the local copy shop as an alternative. An unavoidable charge is local taxes which, at twelve per cent, can make a serious addition to your bill.

OTHER THAN HOTELS

San Francisco has a number of very attractive alternatives to hotels. Bed and breakfast arrangements in private homes are easy to come by, as well as renting or subletting an apartment for a short stay. Hostels are very popular with the under-thirty travellers.

Sharene Klein's bed and breakfast reservation service is one of the best sources for finding comfortable rooms in San Francisco and the Bay Area. She lists more than 450 places in California and specialises in historic houses. Klein fits clients to rooms like a matchmaker searches for brides and grooms. Children are welcome at almost all her clients' B&Bs. The booking service is free, with Klein's company making its money by commission. Contact Bed & Breakfast International, P.O. Box 282910, San Francisco 94128, tel. 696 1690 or fax 696 1699.

Renting an apartment is fairly easy once you are in San Francisco. The young, travel-loving population ensures a big market for sublets. The best method is looking for ads in the weekly papers, the *Bay Guardian, SF Weekly* and the *Pacific Sun* in Marin and the *East Bay Express* in the East Bay. Look under short-term rentals and sublets, but also consider 'Shared Housing'. The high cost of housing in the Bay Area means that a large percentage of the population lives with one or more roommates. While most people want a year or more commitment, many are open to short-term roomies.

If you want an apartment to yourself, American Property Exchange, a woman-owned business, will do all the finding and renting for you. While the firm is geared towards corporate visitors and does quite a bit of movie-related work, they also handle the needs of average travellers looking for a short-term rental in the city. Prices begin in the range of $85 a night and $450 a month. The company handles apartments, houses, condos and cottages. Contact American Property Exchange, 170 Page St, San Francisco 94102, tel. 863 8484 or fax 255 8865.

Hostels are plentiful, but be aware of the difference between privately-owned places and the hostels that are chartered by the American Youth Hostel organisation, part of the international hostel movement. Age is no longer a requirement at either. AYH places run towards clean-scrubbed summer camp ambience while the private places are more twentysomething clubs. At most hostels you will have to supply your own sleeping bag, towels and padlock for your storage unit. These places are great for meeting people and having an instant group to hang out with. There are givebacks, of course, especially the lack of privacy and conforming to house rules. There is usually a period every day when the hostel is closed for the daily cleaning which means you will be put out no matter what.

Many budget travellers look to schools, universities and religious organisations such as convents for inexpensive rooms, but they are rare in the Bay Area. The University of California, Mills College and the University of San Francisco (a Catholic school) all make room for visitors, but these are either guests of the school, ex-students or faculty. If you have some professional or personal tie with a college, by all means inquire.

On Your Own

Women travelling alone, several women travelling together or a woman with children are in no way unusual in San Francisco. Businesswomen, in fact, are aggressively courted by city hotels. San Francisco hotels are frantic to avoid the kind of tourist 'incidents' that make headlines and keep people at home, so you will find quite good security at most places, from the top of the line down to budget motels. Still, it is important to remain alert as tourists are seen as prime cash cows by criminals and crazies. Never open your hotel room door to anyone you are not expecting. Don't bring any irreplaceable valuables with you on your trip and put your most important items in the hotel safe.

There are plenty of disreputable hotels in San Francisco. If you find yourself booked into a place that makes you the tiniest bit uncomfortable, leave immediately.

A small hotel is usually better for a woman on her own. It's easier to become familiar with the smaller number of staff who will often take an interest in you and check on your welfare. Make yourself known to the desk clerks, and other employees, even the manager. They will provide tons of good advice, tips and directions on how to go about having a good San Francisco vacation. The staff will be invaluable in guiding you around the neighbourhood, suggesting what is safe and what is questionable for a woman alone.

HOTEL FACILITIES

Unless noted, all hotels recommended will have private rooms, private baths, air-conditioning and central heating, telephones, televisions, daily maid service, 24-hour desk, hotel security and a restaurant or bar.

Many hotels are departing from the traditional practice of charging for rooms as singles (one person) or doubles (two people) and charging a flat rate for a room – sometimes a per person surcharge if it is more than two adults. A suite usually means a sitting room and at least one bedroom.

Businesswomen in San Francisco

As a major centre of commerce, banking and conventions, San Francisco sees a lot of businesswomen. The expense account hotels have added hairdryers and pricey women's toiletries, and emphasise services such as aerobics classes that are particularly attractive to women guests. In a poll by *Working Women* magazine, four San Francisco hotels (Stanford Court, Campton Place, Clift and Prescott) were rated as among the best in the country for women business travellers, more than any other city except New York, which also had four.

Big hotels like the four listed above, the Fairmont, the Mark Hopkins and the St Francis, have business centres on the premises and offer other amenities such as morning shuttles to the Financial Center, free. If you are going to be putting in some serious work time in your hotel room it is an excellent idea to compare various hotel services. Prod them a little bit with the data as in, 'I see here you charge for faxes but I understand the Fairmont puts one in your room and one only pays the phone charges.' In-hotel business centres typically offer computers, printers, copying and will help you find secretarial help, translators or messenger services.

Financial District/Union Square

Downtown is the prime hotel district in the city. Many of the hotels are San Francisco institutions with decades of long, illustrious histories. Be assured that they are not getting by on their reputations. The San Francisco market is too competitive for any hotel to last for more than a few hours on its past track record. Although several are at the top of the line, there are many charming places that are very affordable.

Expensive

CAMPTON PLACE KEMPINSKI HOTEL
340 Stockton St, San Francisco, CA 94108. Tel. 781 5555. Fax 955 8536.

Adored by privacy-seeking celebrities, high-powered businesswomen and lovers of luxury of every stripe, the Campton Place is one of San Francisco's very best hotels. Now owned by Germany's Kempinski company, the Campton Place opened in 1983 after a multi-million dollar renovation had completely rebuilt the interior of two small post-1906 hotels. Anchored by a top-rated restaurant, also called Campton Place, the hotel is only a block from Union Square and hard by Maiden Lane, the shopper's nirvana. Campton Place offers every luxury, including thick, terrycloth bathrobes to marble bathrooms, maids who will pack and unpack your bags, morning newspapers from the US and Europe and tea in the lovely roof garden. Room service and a concierge are available 24-hours a day. The hotel is done up in pale colours to give a sense of space and light. The rooms are spacious and well-furnished without being crowded. Campton Place offers some business services, otherwise the concierges will cheerfully and competently arrange whatever you need. There are no special services for children. They are welcome, of course, but this isn't a good kids' hotel. Rooms $185–$320, suites, $395–550, penthouse suites $550–$800.

FOUR SEASONS CLIFT HOTEL
495 Geary St, San Francisco, CA 94102. Tel. 775 4700. Fax 441 4621.

The Clift (nobody in San Francisco calls it the Four Seasons) doesn't have the Old San Francisco notoriety of the St Francis, the Palace or the Fairmont, but it is in many ways the city's most famous hotel – regularly ranked among the top hotels in the world, not just the US. Subdued, soft-spoken and firmly unflamboyant, the Clift sits on the corner of Taylor and Geary amidst the Geary Street theatres and on the edge of the Upper Tenderloin. Like a grande dame who doesn't feel the need to wear her diamonds in public, the Clift's jewels are only for the initiated. It's a full-service hotel without being an enormous place. There is an on-site fitness centre, a very good business centre and special considerations for families with children. But the glory of the Clift is the understated, effortless, seamless service. The lobby is a popular meeting place for friends before the theatre or after a shopping trip. A low-key bar operates in one of the sitting nooks or there is the romantic Redwood Room for serious drinks. The hotel restaurant is the French Room, a Louis XV temple, which serves excellent traditional French food. Guest rooms are country house chic with Brunschwig & Fils fabrics, Georgian reproduction furniture, marble bathrooms, fresh flowers and architectural detailing. If you need work space, emphasise this when booking a room as some of the Clift

rooms can be on the small size.
Rooms $190–$310, suites $355–$820.

SHERATON PALACE HOTEL
2 New Montgomery St, at Market,
San Francisco, CA 94105–3402.
Tel. 392 8600. Fax 543 0671.

Now part of the Sheraton chain, the
Palace Hotel is as San Francisco as
you can get. It was the great dream of
financier William Ralston who built
an opulent palace in 1875. The first
hotel burned in 1906 but another,
equally grand, was built on the
foundations. The hotel today has been
returned to its former elegance after a
two-year shutdown. The public rooms
are some of the city's most impressive.
The Garden Court with its glass-
domed ceiling, crystal chandeliers and
palms is one of the most gorgeous
hotel rooms in the world. Maxfield's,
a bar decorated with a mural by
Maxfield Parrish, is another famous
room. But the important thing, of
course, is where you sleep. The
Palace's rooms are furnished in the
rich, *faux* antiques of most four-star
hotels, with attractive accessories,
mini-bars, safes, marble bathrooms
and plenty of room. Unlike many of
the older hotels, the Palace has
spacious roomy bedrooms. The
business centre has full facilities and
there's a good fitness centre. It fills up
fast, so go early for your workout.
Don't miss the glassed-in rooftop lap
pool; pure bliss swimming laps as the
sun fades over the city. Children
under eighteen stay free (in the same
room with parents). Rates run single
with bath $205–$265, doubles
$225–$315, suites (one and two
bedrooms) $400–$2000.

THE WESTIN ST FRANCIS
Facing Union Square, 335 Powell St,
San Francisco, CA 94102.
Tel. 774 0176. Fax 774 0200.

When Queen Elizabeth II was visiting
California in 1983 and suddenly
needed a place to stay, she and her
entourage checked into the St Francis.
The Queen was scheduled to stay
aboard the yacht Britannia, but rough
seas delayed its arrival from the
Southern California coast. The St
Francis, which has hosted heads of
state, movie stars, diplomats and
garden-variety billionaires almost
since the day of its opening in 1903,
was excited but unperturbed. The
hotel knew the drill.

Walking into the St Francis with cable
car bells and the hustle and bustle of
Union Square still ringing in your
ears, is a delightful sense of being in
the centre of it all. The hotel is of the
grand hotel tradition, quite like a little
village with its own barbershop,
hairdresser, clothing and jewellery
shops, laundry, florist, post office and
art gallery. And, of course, its famous
clean money. In the 1930s socialites
mentioned to the manager that their
white gloves were dirtied by handling
change. He ordered all coins to be
washed and the custom continues
today, even though white gloves have
vanished. The St Francis burned in
1906 and was quickly rebuilt. In the
1970s a tower was added behind the
old hotel. The tower rooms are more
expensive, being bigger and more
modern, but many regulars (who still
call it The Frantic) prefer the old
building for its ambience. The St
Francis has three restaurants and
three bars within the building. The
Compass Rose in the lobby is pleasant
for afternoon tea and for evening

drinks. Victor's, the main restaurant, serves very fine French food.

Children of eighteen and under staying in their parents' room are free. Family packages are also available. In the main building, singles are $160–$245, doubles $195–$280; suites begin at $300 and go up to $1500. Tower rates for singles $250–$280, doubles $285–$315 and suites $525 to $1450.

Moderate

JULIANA HOTEL
590 Bush St, San Francisco, CA 94108. Tel. 392 2540. Fax 391 8447.

Located at the far edge of the Financial District, the Juliana is on a very interesting stretch of Bush Street, a few steps away from the Chinatown Gate. Without intending to, the Juliana ended up with an almost all-woman staff, from general manager on down. They take a lively interest in guests and have a wealth of information to share about the city. The hotel serves coffee and tea in the lobby throughout the day where a wood-burning fireplace, masses of fresh flowers and a plentiful supply of daily newspapers makes for a cosy setting. Businesswomen like the morning shuttle service to the Financial District. The Juliana has some business services, but is very good about helping visitors find what they need. The rooms are airy and comfortable, decorated in pastels and furnished with sturdy, vaguely French furniture. Room service is for breakfast only. Vinoteca, an excellent Italian restaurant is in the hotel. Rooms, double or single occupancy, $119, suites $135–$155. The Juliana is a Kimco hotel and offers many specials throughout the year.

PRESCOTT HOTEL
545 Post St (between Taylor and Mason, two blocks from Union Square), San Francisco, CA 94102. Tel. 563 0303. Fax 563 6831.

One of the best small hotels in the US. Even though the Prescott has limited fitness and business facilities, businesswomen voted it one of their favourite hotels in the country. What the business travellers love, as do other clients, is the wonderful attention to detail and exhaustive personal service. The hotel serves a complimentary breakfast with really good food, not just coffee and mass-market sweet rolls. In the evening guests are invited to a nightly drinks party in the lobby. Other amenities include limousine service to the Financial District, newspapers and mineral water delivered to every room (free) and best of all, special access to the house restaurant, chef Wolfgang Puck's hot Postrio. Like the Juliana (above), the Prescott is a project of Kimco Hotels, a small San Francisco-based company that specialises in redoing old hotels into comfortable new accommodation with hot restaurants. The formula so far seems to be unbeatable. Banker-turned-hotelier Bill Kimpton buys (never builds) run-down hotels and renovates them with an eye towards comfort, ease and accessibility. He doesn't believe in offering tons of extras. 'We sell sleep,' he likes to say. The other important part of the Kimco formula is a restaurant that is not just for the hotel guests, but will bring in local diners. Postrio, which is Puck's first venture out of Los Angeles (he owns the fabulously successful Wolfgang's and Spago), is easily one of SF's top five restaurants. Prescott guests stay in beautifully decorated rooms. The vaguely Biedermeier furniture, all cherry, was made expressly for the hotel. Rooms are $160–$180; suites begin at $210 and the penthouse is $600.

HARBOR COURT HOTEL
165 Steuart [correct spelling] St (facing the Embarcadero), San Francisco, CA 94105. Tel. 882 1300. Fax 415 882 1313.

San Francisco's Cinderella hotel. It's another Kimco inn, but even the Kimco people had no idea of their luck when they decided to buy the 1924 YMCA building on the Embarcadero and turn it into a hotel. The building faced a two-level freeway, but it was still a good spot on the gentrifying South of Market side of the Embarcadero. The hotel, then being renovated, survived the 1989 earthquake quite well but the freeway was torn down. Eureka – the Harbor Court was suddenly presented with the best waterfront views in San Francisco. Other positives include the new YMCA building next door where guests have membership privileges, a business centre, complimentary morning coffee and afternoon wine and the proximity to the Financial District. The Harbor Court is beautifully decorated inside, but some guests have felt a little cramped. There's no room service and visitors are also disappointed when they can't get a bayside room, even when they are willing to pay the extra bucks. There are only thirty rooms with that killer view (out of 130) and they go very fast. The hotel doesn't ban children, but has no special interest in attracting them. This is a place for grown-ups. The hotel restaurant is

Harry Denton's, a wildly popular café and bar. Non-view rooms are $140–$150, bayview $150–$160; the penthouse suite is a very, very good deal for $250.

GALLERIA PARK HOTEL
191 Sutter St, San Francisco, CA 94104–4595. Tel. 781 3060. Fax 433 4409

Tucked into a busy side street off Market at the edge of the Financial District, the Galleria Park is a nifty small hotel with a big city attitude. Which doesn't mean bad attitude. The atmosphere is brisk, cheerful, full of gotta-go-gotta-see-gotta-shop energy. The hotel is closely associated with the Crocker Galleria, an elegant three-level shopping centre next door. Ladies of leisure from slightly out of town (the Peninsula, Contra Costa) enjoy checking in, putting in a full day of shopping, getting a good night's rest and driving home the next day. The management is very savvy about the city streets and is unusually forthright with guests about the problems they might find outside the hotel doors. The concierge staff is especially good and very attuned to women travellers. The rooms are comfortable and tastefully designed with lots of floral prints and blond furniture. No special efforts made for children. The hotel is connected to two restaurants, independently run but on the premises, the Chambord, a French brasserie, and Bentley's, a respectful seafood restaurant. Rooms are $145–$175, suites $175–$325.

HOTEL TRITON
342 Grant Ave (across the street from the Chinatown Gate), San Francisco, CA 94108. Tel. 394 0500. Fax 394 0555.

Imagine Andy Warhol designing a hotel. Imagine the hotel owner insisting on reworking some of his plans, 'But Andy people have to have a place to sleep! We have to put beds in the rooms!' Welcome to the Hotel Triton, a zany, high concept place that doesn't ignore the essentials of hotel comfort for mere style. But what style. The hotel's furnishings were especially designed; chairs that look like squiggly arrows, upholstered in plush velvet, share the lobby with surrealistic lamps and bold colours. The guest rooms, some on the smallish side, echo the lobby with bold furniture, hand-painted wall finishes and unusual colour combinations. The hotel is popular with celebrities (Sharon Stone is said to have recovered from some plastic surgery here) and under-thirty Europeans. The location is very good, right across the street from the Chinatown Gate and on a stretch of Bush Street being called the Euro Corner for its concentration of cafés and foreign consulates. The Triton isn't attuned to children or families. Women, travelling alone or with friends, will be very comfortable here if they are on the same wavelength of the hotel. The Café de la Presse, a European newsstand and café, is part of the hotel as well as Café Aioli, a full-service restaurant. Rooms are $129, suites $169.

Hotel Vintage Court
650 Bush St (off Powell Street, three blocks from Union Square), San Francisco 94108. Tel. 392 4666.

Vintage Court is a favourite with French tourists who enjoy the convenience of a multi-lingual staff. Perhaps the studied indifference of the staff also makes them feel at home. With or without perky employees, the

Vintage Court is a good mid-priced downtown hotel with easy access to Union Square, the Financial District and Chinatown. The rooms are painted quiet colours and furnished with simply designed, sturdy beds, chairs, desks and (in the suites) couches and drinks tables. The hotel is overshadowed by its restaurant, Masa's – another of the great San Francisco restaurants. Dining at Masa's is an event that some San Franciscans save up for all year. It is a superb restaurant, but not the kind of place to drop in on every day. There are many small cafés and other eateries close at hand. Rooms $119–$129, suites $250.

The Inn at Union Square
440 Post St (half a block from Union Square), San Francisco, CA 94102. Tel. 397 3510, Fax 989 0529.

The name is a little misleading, the Inn being across Powell Street and down Post from Union Square, but that is the only flaw in this gem of a hotel. The intimate scale (there are only thirty rooms) make it feel more like a pied-à-terre than a hotel. Service and security are the articles of faith for the staff. The main lobby is tiny, but each floor has its own lobby for guests. Breakfast, afternoon tea and before dinner wine is served every day in the lobbies. The food and drinks are fresh and nicely presented. The rooms are decorated with chintz, pillows, canopies and soft colours. The Inn is romantic and cosy, giving a sense of retreating to an inner sanctum removed from the hustle and bustle of the city outside. This is the perfect place for quietude and rest. The Inn excels at what it does, but there are none of the extras such as fitness facilities or room service. The entire hotel is non-smoking. Children don't fit in particularly well here because of the scale and sophistication. The Inn at Washington Square (see below) is under the same management. Singles $110, doubles $120–$180, suites $145–$400.

THE WARWICK REGIS
490 Geary St, San Francisco, CA 94102. Tel. 928 7900. Fax 441 8788.

This was once the Maryland Hotel, built in 1913 by San Francisco widow Emily Benedict from the $1 million inherited from her husband after he was shot to death in a card game. Typically for San Francisco, the wife was suspected of having her alcoholic husband done in to get her hands on the money. Her father-in-law contested the will, but Emily Benedict prevailed and used her windfall to build an elegant hotel to capitalise on the tourist trade expected for the 1915 Panama Pacific International Exposition. The Maryland declined after World War II and in 1984 was sold to investors who shut it down, combined it with an adjacent hotel and, after an $8 million renovation, reopened it as the Regis in 1988. Now part of the Paris-based Warwick chain, the hotel has the languid feel of a small French hotel. The Louis XVI decor of the lobby and halls enhances the Parisian connection. On the small side, with only eighty rooms, the hotel staff is attentive and friendly without being intrusive. The Regis has a woman manager and has applied itself to attracting businesswomen and

women travellers. The bar-restaurant, La Scène, is nicely dim and romantic. Theatre-goers like to stop by here before or after taking in shows nearby. Some even dash over at intermission, finding it easier to get a drink at La Scène than the mobbed theatre bar. Singles $95–$130, doubles $105–$150, suites $130–$205. Several rooms with wood-burning fireplaces are available; these run $105–$200.

THE CARTWRIGHT HOTEL
524 Sutter St (two blocks from Union Square), San Francisco, CA 94102. Tel. 421 2865. Fax 421 2865.

The Cartwright has the comfortable feel of a boarding house at a genteel resort. The same people come year after year, drawn by the friendly atmosphere, antique-furnished rooms and excellent value. Another hotel from the post-1906 era, built to house earthquake victims and then tourists to the 1915 World Fair, the Cartwright has been owned by the same family for the last twenty years. The lobby has a lived-in look, reassuring, like your favourite aunt's house. The afternoon tea in the lobby is well-attended and very congenial. The Cartwright is light on luxuries, but it is safe, charming and personable. The hotel restaurant has been closed for a while, but may reopen for breakfast in 1994. Singles $99–$109, doubles $109–$119, parlour suites $160–$170. Ask about special 'Workingwomen' packages.

Inexpensive

ANDREWS HOTEL
624 Post St (at Taylor Street, three blocks from Union Square), San Francisco, CA 94109. Tel. 563 6877. Fax 928 6919.

The Andrews is a good choice for the traveller who wants to be near downtown, but is watching her pennies. The hotel has a cosy atmosphere, reinforced by chintz, lace

ACCOMMODATION

and many comfortable chairs. The rooms are plain in the best sort of way with good furniture and fixtures – very clean, very neat and no flashy accessories to try and jazz the place up. A continental breakfast is set out for guests every morning outside their door, another sign of the Andrews' unfussy, but careful service. Good tea and coffee that you pour yourself into sturdy ceramic mugs – nothing styrofoam or cheap. Croissants and fresh fruit complete the tray. Fina, an Italian restaurant and bar, is part of the hotel. Very small, unremarkable but convenient. Rooms $82–$106, suites $119.

CORNELL HOTEL
715 Bush St (off Powell Street), San Francisco, CA 94108. Tel. 421 3154. Fax 399 1442.

This little French hotel really is a little French hotel. The owners are French, the ambience is French and in the small restaurant, the food is most definitely French. The Cornell is a quiet, reserved inn where people speak softly and nod in the halls. It has a loyal following among Europeans and Southern Californians, particularly, who come to stay year after year. Guest rooms are on the small side, but attractively decorated and maintained. Many visitors like to sign up for the meal plan which includes breakfast and dinner from the on-site Restaurant Jeanne D'Arc. Families like to come here, but children are expected to be well-behaved. Some rooms are without baths, but the managers are year by year remodelling to add private baths to every room. Meanwhile the cost is $50–$65, other rooms $75–$85. Inquire about the meal plan prices.

THE PACIFIC BAY INN
520 Jones St, San Francisco, CA 94102. Tel. 673 0234. Fax 673 4781.

No restaurant, no bar, no fitness centre, no business centre, no sherry by the fireplace, no turned down beds at night. The Pacific Bay Inn gets by without almost all of the little extras because it offers just about the best price in town for safe, clean, centrally-located rooms. The hotel is near the edge of the Tenderloin, but still a good spot. The lobby is generic hotel; the rooms will remind you of a Holiday Inn before the chain went upmarket, but they are comfortable to sleep in and easy to pay for. Rooms are $55–$75 a night, with a weekly rate of $159–$199. The hotel often offers specials or seasonal rates.

BRADY ACRES
649 Jones St, San Francisco, CA 94102. Tel. 929 8033. Fax 696 1699.

Deborah Brady offers a no-nonsense, down-to-the-basics housing service which amounts to one of San Francisco's best deals for the traveller who doesn't mind taking care of herself. A white-washed brick building on Jones, edging into the Tenderloin, Brady Acres is more of an apartment building for out-of-towners than a typical hotel. The majority of guests are people relocating to the city or experienced visitors who come again and again. All 25 units have private baths and are equipped with mini-kitchens that include a microwave oven, sinks, refrigerator, coffeemaker, toaster and dishes, cutlery and glasses. Linens are supplied weekly. There is a laundry room in the building and if you want clean sheets every day, you can have them as long as you wash them yourself. There's no central desk.

Guests are given a key and an answering machine in your room takes messages. Brady and her staff are helpful, interested in their guests and full of great advice and info about the city and trips beyond San Francisco. Units are $50–$55 for one person, $60–$65 for two. Weekly and monthly rates are also available.

SAN FRANCISCO CARLTON HOTEL

1075 Sutter St (at Larkin Street), San Francisco, CA 94109. Tel. 673 0242. Fax 673 4904.

The Carlton describes itself as Union Square, but actually stands on the farther reaches, closer to Van Ness than the square. The hotel's budget price makes up for its out-of-the-way location. Situated in an early 1900s building, the Carlton has no dominant motif or theme. The lobby and guest rooms are decorated in low-key colours and furnished with hotel furniture of the tasteful sort. Ask for a room as high up as possible in the nine-storey building. The views are terrific at the top. Wine is served in the evening by the lobby fireplace and coffee and tea are available throughout the day. The restaurant, the Oak Room Grille, is all right at a pinch, but you can do better for the same money outside the hotel (Brother Jupiter's down the block, for instance). Rooms $65–$94. The hotel offers many specials and seasonal deals.

SHEEHAN HOTEL

620 Sutter St, San Francisco, CA 94102. Tel. 775 6500. Fax 775 3271.

A former YWCA, in its transformation to a small hotel, the Sheehan has retained all the grand touches of a girls' club of old. Some of the bonuses of the past include the impressive, high-ceilinged lobby, a theatre that is often used by some of the city's small companies and a pristine, heated Olympic-size pool in the basement gym. Rooms are mostly small, lightly decorated and furnished with standard hotel pieces. Families with children like the hotel because of its informality and prices. There is a friendly wine bar-tea room, called The Bridge in the lobby. No room service. Single without bath $45, single with bath $60–$80; double without bath $55, double with bath $70–$95. Children until twelve stay free in the parents' room.

HOTEL BEDFORD

761 Post St (three blocks from Union Square), San Francisco, CA 94109. Tel. 673 6040. Fax 563 6739.

Guests actually look forward to the Bedford's 5–6 p.m. wine party. Instead of strangers furtively getting their drinks and avoiding eye contact, there is good conversation, pleasant mingling and gentle laughter. The bright young staff sets a tone of congeniality that seems to spread effortlessly throughout the hotel. Located among rows of apartments, the Bedford feels very at home in the city. Another Kimco hotel, its decor is a bit too heavy handed with florals and semi-canopies in the quest for that country house look. The Wedgwood Bar is very clubby and comfortable; the in-house café, the Canvas Café, is still finding its way. The hotel is quite good value in the budget class with its emphasis on personal service. Rooms $99–$109, suites $155, with many seasonal special rates.

ACCOMMODATION

Robert Louis Stevenson called it the 'hill of palaces' and a century later it still is. Nob Hill hotels are renowned for their luxury. Travellers benefit not just from the services, but the intense competition among the hotels. Budget-minded visitors can manage to stay in these palaces with a bit of planning. The hotels keep their thousands of rooms filled any way they can, which means tons of special deals.

Expensive

RITZ-CARLTON SAN FRANCISCO
600 Stockton St (between California Street and Bush Street, two blocks from the top of Nob Hill), San Francisco, CA 94108. Tel. 296 7465. Fax 986 1268.

A relative newcomer to the San Francisco hotel sweepstakes, the Ritz-Carlton has zoomed to the shortlist of the city's very best luxury hotels since opening in 1991. The hotel took over a magnificent 1909 Roman revival stucco building that was first an insurance company's western headquarters, then a business college. A complete renovation has turned the stucco palace into a fantasy of what a four-star hotel should be. The Ritz-Carlton knows that first impressions can be everything. The marble and polish lobby is set off by the attractive people who inhabit it. The Ritz keeps the clientele looking good through a discreetly enforced dress code. No faded denims, no sweats, no tank tops, no cut-offs, or other 'inappropriate' dress in the lobby, please. Rooms are spacious and well equipped with all the amenities. There is also a fitness centre and pool, excellent full-service business centre, tons of attentive staff and good restaurants and bars. San Franciscans like to drop by for the afternoon tea in the lobby lounge and the hotel's

two restaurants – simply called the Ritz-Carlton Dining Room (big time) and the Ritz-Carlton Terrace (casual) – have been highly reviewed. Rooms $205–$400, suites $450–$500.

STOUFFER STANFORD COURT HOTEL
905 California St (at Powell Street), San Francisco, CA 94108. Tel. 989 3500. Fax 955 5536.

After Jane and Leland Stanford's elaborate mansion burned in 1906, a luxury apartment building was erected on the corner of California and Powell. You can still see the old retaining wall on the backside of the block (Pine Street) with the demarcation between the Stanford and Hopkins properties. The Stanford Court Hotel (Stouffer is the chain owner) opened in 1972 and has been continually upgraded to four-star status since then. In some ways the Stanford Court is the wallflower among the city's luxury hotels. It has the marble, gloss, concierges, haute cuisine and cuddly terrycloth robes of the other plush hotels, but somehow never quite gets the same level of attention. Evidently, that's how the Stanford Court's loyal guests like it. While the hotel regularly racks up good ratings from the professionals, the most telling number one rating comes from *Working Women* magazine which did a careful survey of its readers (no mail-ins but controlled sampling) on good hotels for businesswomen. The Stanford Court fans zeroed in on the hotel's pampering of guests and practical benefits, such as no hotel surcharge on credit card or direct dial phone calls, free receipt of faxes, dictionary in every room, automatic delivery of the morning paper and coffee or tea within fifteen minutes of the wake-up call. For fitness, the hotel uses the Nob Hill Club across the street, but has the full range of business services in-house. Children are welcomed (under 18 stay free with parents) and catered to. This is a spectacular hotel. Rooms $195–$325, suites $450–$2000. The hotel has a continual programme of specials and discounts, especially for weekends when the business travel drops off.

FAIRMONT HOTEL

950 Mason St (at the summit of Nob Hill), San Francisco, CA 94108. Tel. 772 5000. Fax 772 5013.

Thanks to the TV series 'Hotel', millions of people around the world envision the Fairmont when they think of San Francisco. The Fairmont is up to the challenge of being the city's poster child. Its rich and rakish history (see p. 90) makes it an excellent symbol for the city and its ongoing life as a world class hotel fits SF's image of itself. One of the intangibles about staying at the Fairmont is the buzz. It isn't unusual to find President Clinton giving a speech in the ballroom while a Saudi sheik and his entourage of a hundred sweep through the lobby, all of which is extraneous to the jazz worshippers in the New Orleans Room being mesmerised by this week's legendary performer. No SF hotel has a lock on celebrities, politicians or billionaires, but somehow the Fairmont gets more than its share of excitement. Part of this stems from the setting. The Fairmont has never worried about undesirables hanging out in its majestic lobby and removing the seating, as many big hotels did over the last decade. The Fairmont lobby is like a great train station from the old days of tour groups, entourages, stray guests and armies of employees sweep in and out. In the overall luxury hotel sweepstakes, the Fairmont staff may be just a bit less adoring of its guests than the Ritz-Carlton and Stanford Court, but the hotel has all the right stuff. Guests have a fitness centre, business services, valet service, shops, restaurants and bars. Women travellers feel comfortable here and the staff is practised at giving good advice on getting around and the safety factor. The doormen in particular are very sharp about the city. The Fairmont has that dread accessory of all old hotels: the new addition. Rooms in the tower are a bit more expensive and on the bay side have killer views. The older rooms have more character. Main building rooms $175–$205, suites from $450; tower rooms $235–$350, suites from $500.

WHITE SWAN INN

845 Bush St (on lower Nob Hill), San Francisco, CA 94108. Tel. 775 1755. Fax 775 5717.

The White Swan is part of a very small family-owned group of inns called the Four Sisters. Located in a quiet 1908 building on the edge of Nob Hill, the White Swan has modelled itself after the better London hotels with English antique furnishings, hunting prints, warm colours, polished wood detailing and wood-burning fireplaces. There are only 26 rooms in the hotel, giving it both intimacy and privacy. Women travellers like the unobtrusive security and personal service.

Inexpensive

THE LELAND HOTEL
1315 Polk St (one block from Van Ness), San Francisco, CA 94109. Tel. 441 5141. Fax 775 8322.

The Leland is actually down the hill on Polk Gulch, but it is fun to associate this funky place with Nob Hill. Not officially or entirely a gay hotel, the Leland attracts a large gay clientele and about forty per cent of its guests are women. It's a 1950s kind of potted plant place with a cavernous lobby, bantering desk clerk and seedy carpets. The rooms are strictly average with laminated wood furniture and polyester bedspreads. The hotel has a zany charm, especially for travellers who are gay, adventurous and/or enjoy hanging out with a gay crowd. The guests are about fifty per cent foreign (primarily European) and overwhelmingly young. The Leland is clean, safe and full of personality. If it's the kind of personality you like, the hotel is a very good deal. About 25 per cent of the 108 rooms are without baths. Singles $40–$48, doubles $48–$55.

SAN FRANCISCO RESIDENCE CLUB
851 California St (one block below Nob Hill summit at Powell), San Francisco, CA 94108. Tel. 421 2220.

This is the kind of place that most Americans think only exists in old Rosalind Russell movies – a gracious, old-style residential hotel where messages are taken at the front desk,

Almost next door is Petite Auberge, the other San Francisco inn under the same ownership – equally comfortable, beautifully decorated and oozing with personal service. Petite Auberge is slightly less expensive. Rooms in both of these are $145–$250.

overnight guests are banned and sit-down meals are served in the dining room. Once a plush apartment building, the Residence Club is an unhurried, comfortable place to settle for a week or a year in San Francisco. The club caters to short-termers such as foreign students learning English, executives on temporary stays and tourists of the more conservative type. Children are accepted and even welcomed, but there are no special services for them, or anyone for that matter. The office staff take messages between 9 a.m. and 7 p.m., an answering machine the rest of the time. Your phone messages are posted on a bulletin board. If you need twentieth-century communication, you are welcome to have a phone installed in your room. Mealtimes are strictly observed (a full American breakfast and light supper) and appropriate dress (no bathrobes, haircurlers, bare feet) is required. There is maid service, but no fitness facilities, lobby bar or most of the other usuals. The Residence Club, however, is a wonderful place to stay if you like a slow pace and genteel formality. All dealings are in cash or travellers cheques, the hotel does not accept credit cards of any kind. Many rooms have shared baths. Prices for one person $38–$90/day; $230–$600/week; $675–$1600/month; two people $55–$95/day; $300–$600/week; $950–$1600/month.

Fisherman's Wharf is home to more chain hotels per square foot than anywhere else in San Francisco – maybe anywhere else in Northern California. A couple are mentioned here, but on the whole you can get better service, nicer rooms and more of the real San Francisco in hotels that were designed for San Francisco. Surprisingly, North Beach doesn't have very many hotels. The innkeeping business never matched the district's passion for restaurants.

Moderate

RAMADA HOTEL AT FISHERMAN'S WHARF
590 Bay St, San Francisco, CA 94133.
Tel. 885 4700. Fax 771 8945.

Reliable, predictable, well-run. If you have been in a Ramada hotel anywhere in the world you have been in the Ramada at Fisherman's Wharf. The advantage in staying here is almost exclusively for families. The rooms are larger than most in San Francisco and the hotel offers specials and packages for families. The hotel is also completely and effortlessly accessible for the disabled. Rooms are $69–$140; there is an enormous range according to season, day of the week, whether you have children with you, etc. Ask a lot of questions when booking.

TUSCAN INN
425 North Point (two blocks from Fisherman's Wharf), San Francisco, CA 94133. Tel. 561 1100. Fax 561 1199.

The Tuscan Inn is a good attempt at creating a country inn in the Wharf area. There's a lovely garden, quietly elegant lobby with a wood-burning fireplace and guestrooms done up in chintz and subtle accessories. Unlike many boutique hotels, the Tuscan

actively encourages children and offers special activities for them. The hotel has many of the personal service touches of the downtown hotels, such as an evening wine hour in the lobby, a shuttle service to the Financial District and tea and coffee throughout the day. The restaurant doesn't have a bar but the Café Pescatore is a very good Italian fish restaurant next door. Rooms $108–$178, suites $198–$208.

WASHINGTON SQUARE INN
1660 Stockton St (across from Washington Square in North Beach), San Francisco, CA 94133.
Tel. 981 4220. Fax 397 7242.

The Washington Square Inn sets a standard for small inns that looks easy (do everything right, without any fuss), but is devilishly difficult to deliver in the year-in-year-out way that this place does. Because of its track record, guests come back year after year, making bookings difficult at times as there are only fifteen rooms. Some have shared baths, but all are tastefully decorated with antiques, tranquil colours, fresh flowers and comfortable chairs. The friendly staff creates a congenial, but never pushy atmosphere which turns the continental breakfasts and

ACCOMMODATION

afternoon teas into pleasant socialising among the guests. The inn is right on the street, but has excellent security. Ask for a room on the second floor, as far away from the street as possible. Traffic noise is the only thing that can disturb one's pleasure here. Rooms without baths $85–$95, rooms with private baths $95–$180.

Inexpensive

SAN REMO HOTEL
2237 Mason St (between North Beach and Fisherman's Wharf), San Francisco, CA 94133. Tel. 776 8688. Fax 776 2811.

The San Remo is a little charmer. The rooms are small and there are no private baths, but this family-owned pensione is comfortable, squeaky clean and safe. The bathrooms, for instance, are old Victorians with tile floors, claw-foot tubs and brass fixtures – all in perfect working order. The San Remo's guestrooms may be the last honest small hotel rooms in America. While they have iron beds they are not buried in frou-frou. The 'penthouse', a cottage on the roof, does have its own bathroom. A continental breakfast, served family style, is part of the deal. The San Remo Restaurant is a pleasant, small-scale Italian restaurant and the hotel bar is a popular neighbourhood hangout. Singles $35–$55, doubles $55–$75, the penthouse (if you can get it) is $85.

Pacific Heights

The neighbourhood doesn't encourage hotels, which makes it even more appealing for the visitors who do take a room here – an easy place to blend into San Francisco life. Staying in Pacific Heights is a bit out of the way, but very pleasant. The Western Addition, south of Pacific Heights has seen a mini-boom of bed and breakfasts as the neighbourhood gentrifies and investors try to make those big Victorian houses profitable in some way.

Expensive

SHERMAN HOUSE
2160 Green St (off Upper Fillmore Street), San Francisco, CA 94123. Tel. 563 3600. Fax 563 1882.

A restored 1876 town house raised to a perfection it perhaps never knew even in its first glory days. A labour of love by Iranian immigrants Manou and Vesta Mobedshahi, the Italianate mansion with terraced gardens is an idyllic spot within the city. Each of the fifteen rooms and suites are decorated individually with very, very good period pieces, elegant accessories and lovely colours. Nothing has been skimped on here where you will find elaborate canopied beds, not the half-canopies or faux canopies of hotels/inns straining for a suggestion of luxury. Expect marble fireplaces, tiled bathrooms, bay views, jacuzzis, 24-hour room service from the first-class kitchen on the premises. Most people come to the Sherman House for a blissful getaway, but businesspeople (with huge expense accounts) often stay and are fully accommodated with secretarial services, a limousine to the Financial District and anything else their little hearts desire. The Sherman House dining room is a restaurant, open to the public, and serves three meals a day. This is a fantasy sort of place, dedicated to making visitors feel that they have stepped into a scenario from 'Dynasty' or 'Masterpiece Theater'. It is expensive, but delivers what it promises. Rooms and suites $235–$750.

Moderate

EL DRISCO
2901 Pacific Ave, San Francisco, CA 94115. Tel. 346 2880.
Fax 567 5537

The El Drisco is so popular that no one but its regulars knows about it. Owned and operated by the same family since the 1920s, the hotel was the preferred stop for Presidents Eisenhower and Truman in the days before a small army and bunker security were required for a presidential trip. The pace is slow here and the atmosphere wonderfully tranquil amidst the deep pile carpets, green leather banquettes, crystal chandeliers and polished mahogany. The views are excellent (be sure to ask for a room with a view) from the hotel's hillside perch. The hotel is in a residential neighbourhood, but a brisk walk takes you to parks, shopping or public transport. Staying at the El Drisco is to become a resident of San Francisco rather than a tourist. Children will do fine here, especially since the quiet neighbourhood setting makes it easy to take them out for walks and play without worrying about traffic. The guestrooms are surprisingly modest compared to the public rooms, but roomy and comfortable. Rooms are $65–$85, suites $175.

Civic Center

Businesswomen who come to San Francisco for assignments with the state, federal and city government or arts-related projects like staying here, where they can walk to work. Visitors who are drawn to the city for the arts likewise enjoy booking rooms near the major performance venues. Civic Center has a good selection of places to stay. At night the area can be questionable. If alone, take a taxi or attach yourself to a group of people.

Moderate

INN AT THE OPERA
333 Fulton St (half a block from the San Francisco Opera House, Davies Symphony Hall, off Van Ness Avenue), San Francisco, CA 94122. Tel. 863 8400. Fax 861 0821.

People in the Bay Area love to check into this gorgeous inn for a special treat. They have a night at the ballet, opera, symphony or a pop concert in one of the Civic Center halls, then stroll back to the luxury of the inn, forgetting about the drive home until tomorrow. Out-of-towners are fond of the hotel, too. It's not unusual to see visiting artists such as Placido Domingo, Twyla Tharp or Mikhail Baryshnikov hurrying through the lobby to rehearsal or winding down afterwards in the bar. Non-arts business travellers also like the hotel, which is equipped with basic business services and a concierge service attuned to business needs. The inn is

situated in a narrow 1927 building, which was completely redone in the 1980s. The decor in the lobby and guestrooms is muted colours, comfortable chairs upholstered in leather or florals, fresh flowers and Chippendale-ish reproductions. The lobby restaurant, called the ACT IV, is as elegant as the hotel and the bar is low-key and sophisticated – very comfortable for women. Rooms $110–$170, suites $165–$220.

Inexpensive

ABIGAIL HOTEL
246 McAllister St, San Francisco, CA 94102. Tel. 861 9728. Fax 866 5848.

The Abigail Hotel is prized by many businesspeople, arts devotees and researchers who come to San Francisco specifically for Civic Center. City Hall, the US Federal Building, the State of California's main SF office building, the Main Library, the opera, ballet, symphony and Museum of Modern Art are all within a five-minute walk. A cosy, European-style hotel, the Abigail is light on business traveller features (on-site copying, PC, printer and other services), but the attorneys, state officials, researchers and arts business people find the hushed atmosphere and comfy rooms are more than adequate compensation. The hotel serves a continental breakfast and evening wine in the lobby. The Portico Restaurant, off the lobby, has very good Mediterranean inspired food and a pleasant pub. Rooms are $50–$75, suites $100–$125; weekly and monthly rates available.

PHOENIX INN
601 Eddy St (middle of the Tenderloin, at Larkin Street), San

Francisco, CA 94109. Tel. 776 1380. Fax 885 3109.

The Phoenix used to be a scuzzy motel frequented by hookers, drug dealers and crazies. This fact is widely known because it is lavishly illustrated in the motel's colouring book, passed out to guests with their keys. The Phoenix is the David Letterman of hotels. Letterman's late night TV show is a parody of late night TV, even as it performs brilliantly. The Phoenix revels in perfecting its imitation of an old-fashioned 'no-tell motel', delivering one of the most memorable hotel experiences in San Francisco. Even its location at the centre of the seedy Tenderloin hasn't impeded the motel's popularity. Musicians love the place. Sinead O'Connor, the Red Hot Chili Peppers, k.d. lang, Nirvana, Jesus Jones, Arlo Guthrie, Billy Idol and Ten Thousand Maniacs have all bunked here, as well as John F. Kennedy Jr and other out-of-towners with a taste for the madcap and unpredictable. The pool, decorated by artists, is surrounded by sculpture and other artworks. The hotel's bent for goofiness doesn't interfere with its focus on comfort. The rooms are decorated in an amusing Key Westian tropical, wildly out of place in San Francisco but part of the Phoenix karma. The hotel has its own cable system for TVs, playing all made-in-San Francisco movies. In addition to your own Phoenix colouring book, guests are given brochures about how to tour the city 'Beyond Fisherman's Wharf'. There is also an on-site massage therapist and a friendly, helpful staff. The hotel café is Miss Pearl's Jam House, an excellent neo-Caribbean restaurant. Some vigilance is called for in moving around the neighbourhood, but the Phoenix has very good security. Rooms $80–$89, suites $119–$139.

ALBION HOUSE INN

135 Gough St (off Market Street, at Page Street), San Francisco, CA 94102. Tel. 621 0896.

The Albion House is a very small bed and breakfast, with only nine rooms. It is everything one wants in a modest inn, with comfortable, clean, pleasant rooms, fresh flowers and a friendly staff. The full breakfast is the inn's outstanding feature, served family style in the dining room. No room service, but wine in the evenings. Children are accepted with a bit of reluctance. The inn is very popular with artsy types who are in town to attend opera, symphony, ballet or have some professional (but low-paying) connection to the arts. There are two rooms without baths and one suite. Prices are $85–$145.

Other Neighbourhoods

For most travellers, the benefits of taking a room in one of the downtown or above Market neighbourhoods far outweighs any special deals or extras offered by hotels in the city's outer reaches. There are, however, some hotels and inns that are worth going out of your way for, depending on your needs.

Oakland

Expensive

CLAREMONT HOTEL AND RESORT

Ashby and Domingo Avenues, Oakland, CA 94623. Tel. (510) 843 3000. Fax (510) 848 6208.

The huge white Claremont Hotel dominates the Oakland Hills skyline. A sprawling Edwardian building of multiple wings and grounds covering 22 acres, the Claremont is a genuine resort within a city. It has pools, tennis courts, steambaths, a luxurious spa and (nearby) a golf course. Families love coming here for the children's programming and many local Bay Area women check in for a night or a weekend for a stress-relieving rest and relaxation. Many packages available, with minimal to maxed-out spa programmes. Rooms $149–$209, suites $295–$720.

ACCOMMODATION

Moderate

SAUSALITO HOTEL
16 El Portal, Sausalito, CA 94965.
Tel. 332 4155. Fax 332 3542.

In downtown Sausalito (if that doesn't sound too inflated for this little toy town), the hotel is a Victorian dreamhouse with the big, heavy furniture that the era loved, softened with cheery fabrics, fireplaces and attractive knick-knacks. The hotel is only 15 rooms, the upstairs of a Mediterranean-style block of shops. Pleasant views and you can take the ferry to the city whenever you want. Some shared bathrooms. Rooms $75–$160, suites $180–$210.

BUDGET: HOSTELS, MOTELS, B&Bs AND WOMEN-ONLY INNS
Budget places, often with their own cooking facilities, can be ideal for staying with children.

Financial District/Union Square

MARY ELIZABETH INN
1040 Bush St (between Jones and Leavenworth), San Francisco, CA 94109. Tel. 673 6768. Fax 441 7451.

Only for the woman who enjoys a very quiet, semi-religious atmosphere. Built by Methodist philanthropist Lizzie Glide (the benefactor of Glide Church) as a residence for wayward women in 1914, the Edwardian building is now a non-profit residence for students, tourists and 'women in transition'. The Mary Elizabeth Inn is for women only. Children are accepted on a case-by-case basis. Amenities include a laundry, library and two meals a day. Some rooms have shared bathrooms. Daily rates begin at $45 single, $60 double. Weekly rates are $147–$189, monthly $624–$803.

Near Fisherman's Wharf

SAN FRANCISCO INTERNATIONAL AYH-HOSTEL
Located in Upper Fort Mason (enter at the Bay Street and Franklin Street gate), Building 240, San Francisco, CA 94123. Tel. 771 7277.

Situated in a renovated Civil War barracks, this hostel has one of the most gorgeous settings in the world. Perched on one of the high points above the bay, hostel guests have drop-dead views at their front door and the cultural and amusement facilities of Fort Mason a few steps away. This is an extremely popular hostel, as you might imagine. While some visitors luck out by simply showing up, the best idea is to make a reservation with your credit card. You can become a hostel member (no age requirements anymore) on the spot or write for info to AYH, P.O. Box

37613, Washington, D.C. 20013.
Visitors sleep six to a room and bring
their own sleeping bag. A communal
kitchen (former Army mess) is
available to anyone who wants to fix

meals. There are also vending
machines, locked storage spaces, coin-
operated washers and dryers and
several community rooms. The nightly
charge is $12.

The Marina

MARINA MOTEL
*2576 Lombard St (between Divisadero
and Broderick), San Francisco, CA
94123. Tel. 921 9406. Fax 921 0364.*

When the Golden Gate Bridge opened
in the 1930s, everyone prepared for
the expected deluge of tourist and
commuter traffic by building modern
motels on Lombard Street, the main
artery to the bridge. The Marina
Motel dates from that time. A mission
revival compound of stucco buildings
with red tile, flowerbeds and arched
doorways, it is a pleasantly nostalgic
return to the days before motels
became concrete bunkers. The Marina
is newly renovated with fresh paint,
new plumbing, new furnishings and
new management. If you are travelling
by car the great bonus is free parking.
Many of the units have kitchenettes,
making this an even better deal,
especially for families. Ask for one of
the buildings in the back to get away
from the continuous traffic noises on
Lombard. The staff is cheerful and
welcoming. Singles $36–$60, doubles
$40–$65, suites $60–$85.

THE LANGTRY
BED AND BREAKFAST
*637 Steiner St (in the Western
Addition, near Alamo Square), San
Francisco, CA 94117. Tel. 863 0538.*

The Langtry is a romantic Victorian
inn by, for and about women. The inn
has a primarily lesbian clientele, but
straight women and yes, even men,
are welcome. It is a small place – only

five rooms and two suites – and heavily
booked but it is definitely worth the
trouble to stay here. Hidden behind a
mass of trees and surrounded by a
garden, the Langtry has a delightful
sense of isolation. The public rooms
and bedrooms have been quietly
returned to their nineteenth-century
grandeur with the marble fireplaces,
beautiful dark wood panelling, high
ceilings and architectural detailing
making the house's statement instead
of over-decorated rooms. Amenities
include a hot tub, jacuzzis in the
rooms, sun deck, full American
breakfasts, daily maid service and
private phones. The inn will prepare
gourmet dinners upon request. No
credit cards are accepted; all payment
is in cash or travellers cheques.
Rooms are $75–$100 (some shared
baths), suites $170.

PLANTATION INN
*3100 Webster St (at Greenwich, lower
Pacific Heights), San Francisco, CA
94123. Tel. 921 5520.*

A classic fifties' motel: two levels of
unimaginative rooms on top of
parking spaces, all centred around a
small swimming pool with a chainlink
fence. It sounds pretty dreary, but this
anonymous motel is clean, quiet and
an easy walk to the shops on Fillmore,
the Marina Green and Fort Mason.
Some of the rooms have kitchenettes.
This is a good, inexpensive place to
stay if you're driving (free parking),
have active kids and/or want a little

distance from the density of
downtown. Rooms are $65–$85.

SAPPHO'S
*859 Fulton St (in the Western
Addition at Fillmore Street), San
Francisco, CA 94117. Tel. 775 3243.*

Sappho's, 'a residence for women', is
a shabby old Victorian in a so-so
neighbourhood (safe during the day,
questionable at night). Run as a non-
profit by a group of women, staying
here is like crashing with college
friends in a group house. Perpetually
being improved and remodelled, the
house has twelve guest rooms, none
with private bathrooms, some with
beds, some with mattresses. A
continental breakfast is set out in the
morning for guests, who are welcome
to use the kitchen on their own.
Sappho's is strictly for the traveller
who isn't interested in creature
comforts. Many of the guests are
students travelling through the US,
particularly Australians and Germans.
All dealings are cash or travellers'
cheques; $15 a night – weekly and
monthly rates on request.

South of Market

INTERCLUB GLOBAL HOSTEL
*10 Hallam Place (off Folsom Street,
between 7th and 8th streets), San
Francisco, CA 94103. Tel. 431 0540.
Fax 252 1498.*

Club is the key word here. This laid-
back hostel is a clubhouse for the
globe-trotting under 25s who are
usually in transition between school
and work. Luxuries are non-existent
but the Interclub provides a safe,
pleasant atmosphere and supplies the
basic needs of bedroom and
bathroom. Don't expect privacy, and
the bunkbed dorm rooms are unisex.
Managers and guests say it's no
problem, no hassle, but women
sometimes request an all-female room
which can be arranged. This hostel
isn't connected with the youth hostel
movement. There are no curfews and
few rules, but the staff does keep an
eye on the guests. Amenities include a
high level of cleanliness, an excellent
rooftop sundeck and an inexpensive
café for breakfast and supper. The
Interclub is perfect for travellers who
are looking to make friends, find
touring companions and plug into the
worldwide travel network. The hostel
is located on a very hip stretch of
Folsom Street. Most guests come and
go in groups, which is wise at night.
No credit cards, all dealings are in
cash or travellers' cheques. Rooms are
$13 a night, no maximum stay, $80 a
week. During slow periods guests may
have a private room for $30 a night.

Haight-Ashbury

THE RED VICTORIAN INN
*1665 Haight St (two blocks from
Golden Gate Park), San Francisco,
CA 94117. Tel. 864 1978.*

The Summer of Love haunts this
sweet, silly bed and breakfast like a
gentle ghost. Artist and dreamer Sami
Sunchild presides over the Red Vic inn
and Global Village Center on the first
floor, a coffee house cum gallery.
Each of the 18 rooms on the two
floors above street level is decorated

around a theme. 'Cat's Cradle' is the house cat's room which she shares with paying guests. There is also 'Summer of Love', 'Teddy Bear Room', 'Redwood Forest Room' and 'The Rainbow Room'. Some have shared baths and some have futons. Inquire closely about the furnishings beyond the fanciful descriptions if you stay here. What makes the inn so pleasant is Sunchild's genuine devotion to her world view. She's not a parody of a sixties veteran – she truly is a woman whose reality revolves around world peace, meditation, outlandish art projects and a cultivated childlike attitude. Genuine children, however, are accepted on a limited basis (one per adult). The Red Vic is clean and well cared-for though it has a kind of patched together feel about it. An amusing place to stay for atmosphere and immersion into the neighbourhood. Rooms, some with shared bath, $55–$135.

Ocean Beach

SEAL ROCK INN
545 Point Lobos Ave (close to the Cliff House and Sutro Heights Park), San Francisco, CA 94121.
Tel. 752 8000. Fax 752 6034.

The Seal Rock Inn is far, far from the madding crowds. It is ordinary in looks, both outside and inside, but a marvellous place to be near the ocean. Enigmatic Sutro Heights Park is right across the street and Land's End, the Cliff House, Ocean Beach and miles of coast are a brisk walk away. The motel is frequently enveloped in fog, adding to the *Wuthering Heights* feel of the place. Many of the Seal Rock's rooms are equipped with wood-burning fireplaces (extra) which makes for a cosy evening at home with the fog. The motel has an enclosed patio with a pool and table tennis games. Some rooms are equipped with kitchenettes. This is a very good place for families travelling by car. If you're without a car, Muni buses stop practically at the front door. Singles $70–$94, doubles $74–$98. Be sure to ask for a room with a fireplace and ocean view.

Marin

GOLDEN GATE AYH HOSTEL
Building 941, Fort Barry, Sausalito, CA 94965. Tel. 331 2777.

Up in the Marin Headlands, a couple of miles from Sausalito, this is another of the hostels making brilliant use of a converted army base. This one is rather isolated – you have to wait for a bus or hike into town to catch the ferry to San Francisco – but for outdoorsy types this is a perfect place to launch yourself to mountain or beach trails every morning. A kitchen is available for do-it-yourself meals; rooms are dormitory style. Beds $8 a night.

EATING AND DRINKING

Food and drink are to San Francisco what politics is to Washington, D.C., or the Church is to Rome. The city is obsessed with food and wine, supporting more restaurants, bars, cafés, eateries, kitchen stores and liquor shops than it could possibly need. There is a frenetic turnover in the restaurant and bar business, but for every place that closes two seem to spring up in its spot. The only problem you will have in excellent dining and enjoyable drinking is making choices.

EATING

A recent poll says that the average San Franciscan eats out six times a week. If anything, the number is probably low. Like most Americans, San Franciscans are spending less time at home and with two-career couples, homemade meals are becoming a luxury. But in addition to the urban life zeitgeist, San Francisco has a history of being in love with restaurants. In the late nineteenth century there were popular songs about the most famous restaurants and everyone, whether they could afford to dine out or not, knew the cafés and restaurants like they knew the names of vaudeville stars.

In a way, not much has changed in a century. Restaurants are still celebrities and their strengths and weaknesses are debated as passionately as the fortunes of the Giants and the Forty-Niners. Entering in the dining out fervour is to enter into one of the liveliest parts of San Francisco life.

The biggest problem for women dining alone is being shunted off to the worst table in the house. The table for two beside the kitchen, near the draughty front door, beside the waiters' station, all far from the view, is inevitably given to a woman. Look carefully around the room before the maître d' or waiter leads you to a table. Politely decline the table next to the ladies room and point out another you would rather have. Most restaurant people give in readily if you are pleasant and firm. Point out you need room to read your book spread out the newspaper, or you want a good view. Don't apologise for your choice, but let the people you are dealing with know what you want. 'Oh, that'll be a ten-minute wait for a table by the window,' the waiter will say and try and change your mind. Tell him or her, 'Fine,' you will wait.

Menu writing has hit the ridiculous stage in California with even the simplest dishes wildly over-described. Ask your waiter whatever you don't understand. Waiters are also quite reliable about suggesting dishes. Most of them are opinionated foodies and will steer you towards the house speciality or the day's best dish. They are also helpful on wine, but all too often will cite the highest priced vintage when a more modest bottle would do equally well.

The hot restaurants are always difficult to get into – if you go at peak hours. As a traveller, you're free to dine whenever you want which puts you at a great advantage, especially for Financial District eateries and the chic lunch places such as Postrio and Stars. Go before noon or after 2 p.m. for a stress-free lunch. The tippy-top restaurants, such as Masa's and Chez Panisse, are booked weeks in advance, but you can often get in at the last minute when they have cancellations. Call around and you'll almost surely come up with a table.

Businesswomen will find that restaurants are extensively used for making deals and socialising. San Francisco businesspeople are as workaholic as the rest of the country, but they don't see any reason to eat bad food at their desks when they can conduct business at Jack's, Ernie's, One Market, Square One or any of the other good downtown restaurants. If you're taking clients out, try to speak to the maître d' or waiter before the meal to identify yourself as the host so the bill will be given to you. Actually, most restaurants are quite good about recognising women as businesswomen rather than dates. When a waiter isn't sure who gets the bill, he or she will place it centrally or hover for a minute waiting for a signal. When choosing a restaurant for a business meal it's best to ask a local friend or contact about the suitability. Some of the most popular restaurants are hideously noisy with crowded tables. On your own, select two or three and ask your guests beforehand if they would prefer one over the others. Most San Franciscans love talking about restaurants and giving advice. This will only endear you to your colleagues rather than causing you to lose face for not picking the perfect place single-handed.

Dining out with children is an up and down experience. Most of the upscale restaurants will make only minimal concessions for children, although almost all places do have booster seats and highchairs, even if they are stored in the manager's office, covered with dust. When you consider taking children under fifteen along for a special meal, it doesn't hurt to call ahead and ask a few questions about children's menus and so on. Even if you're not concerned about the expense, the attitude of the person you speak to will tell you what you need to know about the restaurant's position on children. Loud children and crying babies may be asked to leave the room and quieten down in the more rarefied restaurants.

The city does provide excellent resources for feeding children in the way of take-outs, markets and delis. This is ideal for restless children, as you can buy delicious, moderately priced food and dine in a nearby park or back in your hotel. There are fast food places, McDonald's, Burger King and so on, but fewer than in other American cities. Neighbourhoods and restaurateurs fight furiously to keep the chains out. They haven't been completely successful, but they have certainly cut into the proliferation of fast food chains in San Francisco.

You won't have any problem tuning into the foodie hotline when you arrive. The local press, including the daily newspapers, alternative weeklies and magazines, give hearty if not saturation coverage to restaurants and food. The Wednesday food sections in both the *Examiner* and *Chronicle* have restaurant reviews and news along with recaps of the most recent reviews. There is also a monthly free food magazine called *BayFood*. Look for it in restaurants, coffee houses and shops.

Finally, all San Francisco restaurants have non-smoking sections and a great many have banned smoking altogether. If you are a smoker always ask before lighting up. San Franciscans have become very censorious about smoking over the last decade.

PRICES

Cafés and restaurants listed are rated by the price of entrées. Some dishes may be more, some less but the majority fall into the price range indicated. Lunches are usually a bit less for the same dishes. Remember that this is only one factor in your final bill. Tax plus extras such as wine, dessert and side dishes can almost double your bill.

Inexpensive: Under $9
Moderate: $9–$14
Expensive: $15–$20
Very Expensive: Over $20

Financial District

Lunch and breakfast spots are as thick on the ground here as stockbrokers. The Financial District is home to many pricey restaurants because this is where the people with big expense accounts hang out. Big bucks don't necessarily mean an unforgettable meal, but there are some spectacular restaurants around here.

Breakfast and Snacks

CARNELIAN ROOM
555 California St (in the Bank of America building), 52nd Floor, tel. 433 7500.

Sunday brunch in the Carnelian Room is a tremendous treat. The food is heavy-handed French, but fitting for the room. The view from here is marvellous. Best of all is watching the fog roll in below you. Also open for supper every night. Expensive.

Restaurants: American

BISTRO ROTI
In Hotel Griffon, 155 Steuart St, tel. 495 6500.

Star chef Cindy Pawlcyn has masterminded another star restaurant. Impossible to get into after it opened in mid-1993, things have calmed down a bit. Simple main dishes such as grilled chicken and salmon are served with interesting light sauces and gorgeous vegetables. Good wine list. Expensive.

FOG CITY DINER
1300 Battery St (along the Embarcadero), tel. 982 2000.

Classic American food in a recreated diner. Another Cindy Pawlcyn eatery, tough to get into but try on off hours. Try the 'small plates' menus, which are more than appetisers, less than entrées. Moderate.

JACK'S
615 Sacramento St (at Montgomery), tel. 986 9854.

One of the great old San Francisco restaurants, a traditional male grill kind of place. Women are comfortable here but it's still a kind of

HARRY'S HOT DOGS
240 Kearny St, tel. 399 9432.

San Francisco has never developed a food cart culture. You will see a few outdoor hot dog carts around the Financial District, but the city prefers a restaurant, even for fast food. Harry's is fast food, but its loyal followers swear this is the haute cuisine of hot dogs. Inexpensive.

boys' club. Distinguished, unfussy food with the city's best Hollandaise sauce. Expensive.

ONE MARKET RESTAURANT
1 Market St (across from Justin Herman Plaza), tel. 777 5577.

A huge new power breakfast-lunch-dinner restaurant from star chef Bradley Ogden. When Jane Fonda and Ted Turner were in town for a TV convention they took over the whole restaurant, which seats 170, for a dinner party of 40. They didn't want to be overheard or ogled as they dined on Ogden's born-in-the-USA dishes, reimagined with new spices, combinations and presentations. This eagerly awaited restaurant by SF foodies has mostly lived up to expectations. Ogden's other restaurants, Campton Place and Lark Creek Inn, are classics. The menu at One Market borders on overwhelming and service is a shade on the arch side, but the food is marvellous. Expensive.

SQUARE ONE
190 Pacific (at Front Street), tel. 788 1110.

EATING AND DRINKING

Joyce Goldstein was one of the first Chez Panisse alumnae to make a big splash on her own. Square One is her restaurant, where you will find flavours from around the world. On any given day, you might find classic Italian pasta dishes sharing the menu with Greek lamb kebabs, Moroccan couscous and grilled fish in a Yucatanean marinade with black beans. Yet all of this adventurousness doesn't seem at all jumbled or confused. The restaurant is attractive and very well run. Expensive.

TADICH GRILL
240 California St, tel. 391 1849.

San Francisco's oldest continuously operated restaurant. Tadich's has moved a couple of times, but the chops and fish always come up perfectly grilled. If you want a genuine old-time San Francisco dining experience (as opposed to the recontextualised Victorian eateries all over town) come to Tadich's which really hasn't changed all that much since 1849. They don't take credit cards or reservations. Expensive.

A DECENT TEA

Americans love the idea of afternoon tea, but rarely carry it off. Most American teas are big on ruffles and flourishes such as gooey pastries and silver spoons, but miss the point: brewed tea and a light meal. Fortunately, a handful of places in San Francisco get it right. You may order a pot of tea or a full tea service; prices range from $2 (tea only) to $15 (high tea).

Acorn Tea and Griddle – a genuine blending of English tea and California cuisine, excellent black teas served with quiche and sandwiches on crusty baguettes. South of Market, 1256 Folsom St, tel. 863 2469.

Bread and Honey Tea Room – located upstairs from the lobby in the King George Hotel, this dowdy little room is comfortable and homey. The food is plain, the tea well brewed. Near Union Square, 334 Mason St, tel. 781 5050.

Fairmont Hotel – taking tea here is rather like being on the Orient Express, watching the clamorous comings and goings of a changing set of characters. The tea is strong and the food is of the cream tea variety. Nob Hill, California and Mason streets, tel. 772 5211.

Neiman Marcus Rotunda – the dining room is directly beneath the beautiful 1909 stained-glass ceiling, all that remains of the famous City of Paris department store. Happily the food and tea compliment the setting. Union Square, 150 Stockton St, tel. 362 4777.

Ritz-Carlton – a grand tea with a harpist and pianist on the side. Pricey, but the tiny sandwiches are carefully assembled and the tea is brewed in nice big pots. Nob Hill, 600 Stockton St, tel. 296 7465.

St Francis – the Compass Rose Room, a few steps up from the main lobby, serves a respectable tea in lush surroundings. Union Square, Powell and Geary, tel. 397 7000.

Chinese

WU KONG
*101 Spear St (in the Rincon Center),
tel. 957 9300.*

Drawing on the Shanghai tradition, this elegant Chinese restaurant presents spicey, creative dishes prepared with a light touch and ultra-fresh ingredients. Attractive setting, although dining in the central plaza near the Rincon's famous 'water column' can be distracting. Moderate.

Italian

IL FORNAIO
*1265 Battery St (in Levi's Plaza),
tel. 986 0100.*

This is like some very grand café/restaurant you might find in Rome or Florence. The interior is beautiful, lots of marble and mahogany, and a wall of windows looking out on the plaza. Dine on

pasta, stuffed artichoke, grilled veal chop, risotto, or bean soup. Perfect for morning coffee and one of the delicious fresh breads or pastries. The takeout shop is great for a quick, inexpensive meal of panini and antipasto. Moderate.

Seafood

AQUA
252 California St, tel. 956 9662.

Perhaps in a hundred years Aqua will be the quintessential San Francisco fish house. Seafood isn't just beautifully cooked, but prepared with unusual combinations of sauces, spices and vegetables. While the restaurant is so carefully designed as to border on contrived, it is a beautiful room, from the 32-foot white maple bar to the serene high-ceilinged dining room. Aside from fish, Aqua is known for its killer *crème brulée*. Expensive.

295

UNION SQUARE

Union Square

Absolutely bursting with restaurants, coffee shops, cookie counters and even old-fashioned unadorned hamburger joints. For a quick, uncomplicated lunch with unlimited selections, try the food halls in the basement of Macy's and Emporium Capwell, the department stores. Many of the city's top restaurants are in the Union Square area.

Breakfast and Snacks

SEARS FINE FOODS
439 Powell St, tel. 986 1160.

The cable car runs right by the front door of Sears, which is also a San Francisco fixture. This is an old-line breakfast house that believes in the bigger the better. Scrambled eggs,

waffles and the famous Sears' Swedish pancakes are dished up by friendly waitresses in fifties-style uniforms. They are the real thing; this isn't a recreation of an *Alice Doesn't Live Here Anymore* kind of café; Sears just never changed. No reservations, no credit cards. Inexpensive.

Restaurants: American

POSTRIO
*545 Post St (in the Prescott Hotel),
tel. 776 7825.*

Always packed, always on the short list of the city's best restaurants. Owner-inspiration Wolfgang Puck lives in Los Angeles, but is closely involved with the restaurant which is under the direction of husband-and-wife chef team Anne and Gingrass. Their food is pure California with unexpected Asian interpretations. Roasted Chinese duck with mango sauce is one of their specialities. The food is delightful for anyone, but the traveller with a highly evolved palate will probably think she has gone to heaven. Very expensive.

Chinese

CHINA MOON
639 Post St, tel. 775 4789.

Chef Barbara Tropp's 'Chinese bistro' was a sensation when it opened a decade ago, combining Chinese cooking with the California cuisine philosophy. Dismissed in the beginning as San Francisco trendiness run amuck, China Moon has proved its talent and appeal through its longevity. You will find good noodle dishes, great Dungeness crab in season, ginger ice cream with hot chocolate sauce, 'Peking antipasto', stir-fry served over pan-fried noodle 'pillows'. Absolutely *sui generis*. Expensive.

French

MASA'S
In the Hotel Vintage Court, 648 Bush St, tel. 989 7154.

Masa's isn't just a great San Francisco restaurant, it is one of the world's greatest. The food is refined, elegant and always surprising. Masa's food, from soup to salad to entrée to dessert, is even better than you think it can be. The restaurant serves only dinner and reservations, as far in advance as possible, are mandatory. Very expensive.

Nob Hill/Polk Gulch

The Nob Hill hotels all have famous restaurants. As a rule of thumb it is the top-of-the-line room that is worth the money. The big hotels just don't do coffee shops and snacks very well. Downhill in Polk Gulch there are many small cafés, ice cream shops and cookie counters.

Restaurants: American

BIG FOUR RESTAURANT
In the Huntington Hotel, 1075 California St, tel. 771 1140.

Like the Huntington, the Big Four is the least known of the Nob Hill potentates, but again like the hotel itself, it is a lovely experience. The Big Four is as close as you can come to visiting one of the old SF clubs without actually going to the Olympic or the Pacific Union. The dining room is dim, comfortable and rich with leather and mahogany. Excellent for quiet business lunches. Moderate.

Italian

ACQUERELLO
*1722 Sacramento St (between Polk
and Van Ness), tel. 567 5432.*

Small, quiet, relaxing café with
elegant and imaginative Italian food.
The comfortable dining room is hung
with water-colours (hence the name).
The restaurant serves dinner only and
has one of the best wine lists of any
small restaurants in the city.
Expensive.

Seafood

SWAN OYSTER DEPOT
1517 Polk St, tel. 673 1101.

Breakfast, but especially lunch, at this
countertop café is the great SF
equaliser. Truck drivers, politicians,
secretaries and socialites all jostle for
one of the few precious places at
Swan's. It's a retail fish market run by
a family and all the guys behind the
counter are brothers. The marble
counter accommodates twelve people
at a time for the clamchowder, fresh
oysters, great smoked salmon sliced to
order, and cocktails or salads of
prawns or Dungeness crab. Add a
glass of white wine, sourdough bread
– it doesn't get any better than this.
Moderate.

Chinatown

Many of the Bay Area's best and most interesting Chinese restaurants aren't in Chinatown; the rents are too high and the traffic is
too congested. But Chinatown is a sea of restaurants. Unless you
can't cope at all, skip the fixed price meals and order off the menu.
The bill will be less (especially if you are sharing) and the fare will
more clearly reflect your tastes. Ask for rice and then order vegetable and meat dishes. A good rule of thumb is to order one dish
per person at the table (in addition to the rice). Most San Francisco
restaurants are Cantonese which is a blander cuisine than northern
Chinese. Hunan translates for the diner as spicy, very spicy and
maximum spicy. Shanghai tends to be a more sophisticated sort of
cooking, reflecting the city's European influences. Dim sum is a
moving cafeteria; waiters come through with food on carts or trays
and you point at what you want. The bill is tallied by counting your
dishes. The restaurants in Chinatown range from OK to pretty
good, with terrible and outstanding being rare. You are just as well
off picking a place by its looks as by reading the menu. Avoid anything too dressed up or too seedy.

Breakfast and Snacks

PING YUEN BAKERY AND
RESTAURANT
650 Jackson St, tel. 986 6830.

A favourite with Chinatown residents

who like to meet here for morning
coffee and chats. The meat-filled buns
make a tasty quick lunch; have one
now and wrap up one for a fall-back
meal. The Chinese bakeries tend to
have a heavy hand with white sugar in

pastries and cakes. Ping Yuen isn't an exception, but they are so pretty you can't resist.

Restaurants

PEARL CITY
641 Jackson St (near Grant Avenue), tel. 898 8383.

Very homey as befits a popular Chinatown meeting place. Rustic cooking with big portions. A good place to learn the dim sum ropes. Inexpensive.

SUN HUNG HEUNG
744 Washington St (near Portsmouth Square), tel. 982 2319.

Another favourite with locals, but of the non-Chinatown type. Sun Hung Heung topped a Bay Area poll for where residents like to go for an inexpensive meal when they are in Chinatown proper. Now seventy years old, the café is on the dowdy side but the Cantonese food remains very good and very cheap. The stuffed chicken wings are a speciality of the house. Inexpensive.

North Beach

This is the place for coffee, pastry and bread. The eating adventure in North Beach is moving from coffee house to coffee house to find your favourite. And you will. Like music, the North Beach coffee house is an intensely personal choice. You hate one and love another while your mate or best friend has the opposite reaction. North Beach, as one might expect, has a zillion Italian restaurants. Unfortunately, many are aimed at the tourist trade as opposed to the neighbourhood which has a very discriminating palate. Follow the North Beachians in your dining.

Breakfast and Snacks

CAFFE ROMA
414 Columbus Ave, tel. 391 8584.

The prettiest Italian café in San Francisco. Wonderful murals of angels baking bread, brought in decades ago from Italy. They know how to make espresso and cappuccino here and they don't care if you sit forever. One of the window tables is a prized seat on a sunny Sunday afternoon, looking out on always interesting Columbus Avenue. Inexpensive.

CAFFE TRIESTE
601 Vallejo St (at Grant Avenue), tel. 392 6739.

The real thing. Caffe Trieste is North

Beach's oldest coffee house, opened in 1956, still in the era of genuine beatniks. Owned by the opera-loving Giotta family, the café blends bohemian and Italian with flair. The Saturday opera musicales are the stuff of legend. Inexpensive.

DIANDA'S ITALIAN BAKERY
565 Green St (at Grant Avenue), tel. 989 7745.

Mouth-watering traditional Italian sweets, rolls, breads. Inexpensive.

MARIO'S BOHEMIAN CIGAR STORE
566 Columbus Ave (at Union Street), tel. 362 0536.

Mario's isn't a cigar store, it's not

particularly smoky and it is somewhere between a coffee house and café. There is so much about Mario's that is quintessentially San Franciscan. It's a narrow little space with a European flavour. All kinds of people drop in for the meatball and eggplant sandwiches on focaccia. In the evening young people gather here to drink cappuccino and talk. Inexpensive.

STELLA'S PASTRY
446 Columbus Ave (at Vallejo), tel. 986 2914.

One of the handful of old-style Italian bakeries remaining in North Beach. Wonderful pastries that make you feel like a child again and delight any children you might have in tow.

Restaurants: American

ALFRED'S
886 Broadway (next to the Broadway Tunnel), tel. 781 7058.

This is the place for steak. Alfred's ages its own corn-fed beef and it is excellent. The porterhouse steaks are a speciality among the specialities. It's an old-style steak house with red leather banquettes and waiters in tuxedos. There's a very good wine list. Begin with antipasto, a large platter (meant for two) of Italian American food like bean salad, mortadella, ripe olives, pickled pig's feet. Expensive.

MOOSE'S
1652 Stockton St (across from Washington Square), tel. 989 7800.

To walk into Moose's is to breathe the rarefied air of San Francisco's in-crowd. The conversation at lunch is quoted in the newspaper columns the next day; the people you see huddled together at a corner table are setting the course of the city and the state. Ed Moose, the former captain of the Washington Square Bar & Grill, decided to go back into business and Moose's is the pleasing result. Happily the food is quite good or you might just settle for a drink at the bar and take it all in. Expensive.

WASHINGTON SQUARE BAR & GRILL
1707 Powell St (across from Washington Square), tel. 982 8123.

Once the premiere media-literary-politico hangout (of the star vintage, not the foot soldiers) of San Francisco, the 'Washbag' has found itself called to do battle for the hearts and minds of its clientele with Moose's. Loyalties go back and forth across Washington Square, with the older restaurant as crowded and noisy as ever. 'This is like being inside Sylvia Plath's mind during her last year,' one shell-shocked patron has said of the café at its height. Like Moose's, the food is good, but secondary. The pasta is always a safe bet. Moderate.

Basque

DES ALPES
732 Broadway, tel. 391 4249 or 788 9900.

San Francisco still has a few holdover Basque restaurants from the days when it was a way station for immigrant Basque sheepherders on holiday. These places are kind of fun – the food isn't memorable but it is solid, generously served and low-priced. Des Alpes has a five-course dinner for a set price: tureen of soup, salad, two meat courses with French fries, salad and ice cream. Is that six courses? Moderate.

Italian

BUCA GIOVANNI
800 Greenwich St, tel. 776 7766.

Buca is Italian for 'cave' and this basement café is satisfyingly cloistered downstairs in a kind of wine cellar. Giovanni's is a wonderfully straightforward Italian place with fresh pasta, good salads, perfectly cooked chicken with beef. Owned and staffed by Italians. Dinner only, expensive.

IL POLLAIO
555 Columbus Ave, tel. 362 7727.

Quick, affordable and geared to families. Il Pollaio ('the chicken coop')

turns out a variety of dishes built around perfectly grilled chicken. The salads are good and the non-chicken dishes are definitely up to par. No credit cards, inexpensive.

TOMMASO'S
1042 Kearney St, tel. 398 9696.

The once and future North Beach pizza joint. Tommaso's aged check tableclothes, faded Italian murals, dim interior and slow service do nothing to keep the crowds away. The pizza and calzone are just too marvellous. Don't stray from the pizza menu – with the exception of the salads, everything else that comes out of the kitchen is a disaster. Moderate.

Fisherman's Wharf/The Marina

One widely accepted definition of a 'real San Franciscan' (an ongoing dialogue that totally captivates locals) is someone who has never eaten at Fisherman's Wharf. In a city with more good restaurants per capita than any place in America, it is unfortunate, to say the least, that so many visitors insist on taking their meals at Fisherman's Wharf. The Marina has much better cafés, but it isn't very densely populated with places to eat.

Breakfast and Snacks

BUENA VISTA CAFÉ
2765 Hyde St, tel. 474 5044.

Breakfast is as indifferent as the rest of the food served here, but you can have a Bloody Mary with your scrambled eggs. It's also pleasant very early in the morning before the crowds grow into unwieldy numbers. Ride the cable cars before 8 a.m. for a tranquil, early morning experience, finish up on the Hyde Street line at Aquatic Park and have breakfast at the Buena Vista. Inexpensive.

VILLAGE PIZZERIA
3348 Steiner St, tel. 931 2470.

Part of a four-store chain, the VP is a great favourite with expatriate New Yorkers who find the delicious pizzas and pizza parlour atmosphere just like home. Inexpensive.

Restaurants: American

BALBOA CAFÉ
Lower Pacific Heights-Marina, 3199 Fillmore St, tel. 921 3944.

Famed as a singles place, the Balboa is also quite a good restaurant. The hamburgers are the best in town, especially the 'bar burger'. The rest of the menu is creative California cooking. Shoppers from Union Street like to come by for lunch. To avoid the heated-up singles scene come early in the evening; to plunge into the scene, come late (after 9 or 10 p.m.). Moderate.

Italian

PANE E VINO
Cow Hollow neighbourhood, 3011 Steiner St, tel. 346 2111.

Pane e Vino is very, very popular which almost always means a wait, but it is a delightful, high-spirited Italian restaurant. The food is simply prepared trattoria staples, nothing fancy. The pasta, grilled whole fish and grilled veal chops are perfect. The café's truly outstanding dish is an appetiser of marinated cold shrimp with feta cheese and mint. Moderate.

Seafood

SCOTT'S SEAFOOD GRILL & BAR
2400 Lombard St, tel. 563 8988.

Everybody's favourite seafood restaurant in San Francisco. Scott's food is simple and uncomplicated, but always as fresh as possible and well prepared. Locals prize the restaurant for its consistency. You won't have the meal of your life at Scott's, but you will never be disappointed. Expensive.

Vegetarian

GREENS
Building A, Fort Mason, tel. 771 6222.

The restaurant, which began as a project of the Zen Center, is absolutely and completely meatless (although dairy products are used). This is a vegetarian restaurant that even the most dedicated meat-eater will love. The food is imaginative without being silly. Black bean chili, pizza, pastas, vegetable stews and luscious desserts banish stereotypes of tasteless tofu-burgers. The water-level view is marvellous and the restaurant's mellow interior adds to the satisfaction. Expensive.

Pacific Heights/Japantown

Pacific Heights tends towards small neighbourhood cafés rather than big-time restaurants. Even the rich want simple little drop-in places in their neighbourhoods. Japantown has numerous restaurants in the mall and for blocks around.

Breakfast and Snacks

SPINELLI'S
2455 Fillmore St, tel. 929 8808.

Popular with the arty crowd and Financial District crowds (before and after work). In a coffee-mad city, Spinelli's coffee drinks are rated at the top. Only a few places to sit; this is a tank-up spot rather than a linger and read all morning kind of place. Inexpensive.

VIVANDE
2125 Fillmore St (at California), tel. 346 4430.

Open for lunch only, but consider the fabulous take-out counter. You can pick up a pastry or some cheese and bread or an entire meal. Moderate.

Restaurants: American

ELITE CAFÉ
2049 Fillmore St, tel. 346 8668.

Many diners have become gun-shy about New Orleans cuisine after the sudden mania for gumbo and blackened redfish swept through the US in the 1980s. Overnight every restaurant in the country was serving terrible food, calling it cajun or creole (two different traditions). The Elite, despite being 1500 miles from New Orleans, serves the real thing. From the delicious jambalaya to the spicy shrimp remoulade and flaky pecan pie, this is genuine New Orleans food. Dinner and Sunday brunch only, moderate.

Japanese

ELKA
In the Miyako Hotel, 1611 Post St, tel. 922 7788.

Chef Elka Gilmore has masterfully joined French and Japanese cooking for one of the city's best new restaurants. The service and the food is delicate and elegant, with touches such as the tiered wooden box that carries your appetiser plates. Each course is served on a piece of china designed for just that purpose. Very expensive.

Civic Center/Hayes Valley

A good restaurant neighbourhood. The government offices bring breakfast and lunch places, the arts events support the elegant dinner clubs.

Breakfast and Snacks

MAX'S OPERA CAFÉ
601 Van Ness Ave, tel. 771 7300.

Max's serves up diner food deluxe. Great sandwiches, bagels, salads and desserts that use half of the world's sugar-cane crop. And the cheerful waiters are all aspiring opera singers who take turns belting out their best stuff. A great place for the kids. Moderate.

VICOLO PIZZERIA
201 Ivy St (off Gough Street), tel. 863 2382.

Tucked into a tiny one-way street behind Davies Symphony Hall, Vicolo is a fun neo-geo kind of place, where the pizzas are sophisticated but not silly. Light salads, great desserts and

cafeteria service make this a good place to take kids. Inexpensive.

Restaurants: American

CALIFORNIA CULINARY ACADEMY
625 Polk St, tel. 771 3500, ext. 233.

The culinary Harvard. The academy has two restaurants which feature that day's lessons, and they are all A+. Well, sometimes a little off but an amusing place to eat, often with very good results. Moderate.

MISS PEARL'S JAM HOUSE
In the Phoenix Inn motel, 601 Eddy St, tel. 775 5267.

Caribbean-American is a fuller description. The food is spicy and rich with strong Mexican influences. The

Sunday brunch is always pleasant, popular but not so crowded as to spoil your day. Moderate.

STARS
150 Redwood Alley (off Van Ness Avenue), tel. 861 7827;
Stars Café, 555 Golden Gate Ave, tel. 861 4344.

Jeremiah Tower, a Chez Panisse alum, has established a veritable kingdom with Stars, the restaurant, Stars, the café, and Stars, the market. They are all located within the same block, but with different entrances. The restaurant, a high-gloss place that regularly racks up top local and national reviews, is a beautiful room populated by glamorous people. It isn't a snooty place – you can even get a hot dog at the bar. The menu changes daily but is always good, Tower's exciting combination of French and Californian bringing back people for meal after meal. Emily Luchetti, the pastry chef, is equally renowned. Very expensive. Stars Café is more intimate, more manageable and more affordable. The food is scaled down in ambition, but every bit as good as the restaurant. Moderate. The Stars Market sells wine, foods, kitchen stuff.

ZUNI CAFÉ
1658 Market St, tel. 552 2522 or 552 2525.

Most evenings Zuni Café looks like a movie set for a romantic story about city life. Despite sitting on a dreary stretch of Market Street, the café looks exciting and lively, its expanse of windows steamed up from all the people and activity, softened by the interior lights. The restaurant, happily, is as good as it looks. Chez Panisse graduate, Judy Rodgers, presides over the kitchen, infusing Mediterranean flavours in the superbly cooked food. Zuni is a pleasant but overlooked spot for breakfast. Light streams in those big windows, Market Street shakes itself to life and the steaming coffee, Zuni-made jams and fresh-baked pastries make a very pretty morning picture too. Expensive.

Seafood

HAYES STREET GRILL
320 Hayes St, tel. 863 5545.

Probably the city's best fish restaurant. You can always count on it having a good assortment of whatever fish are best that day. Hayes Street truly goes out of its way to buy the best. Once this first-rate fish is in the Hayes Street kitchen, it is cooked simply with the diner's choice of several sauces, usually accompanied by French fries (excellent). Ethnic influences have been introduced in the last few years, especially Thai and Chinese. This is a fave pre-concert dinner spot so schedule your visit around the traffic jams. Late lunches are always pleasant here.

South Beach

The area is in transition between old waterfront dives and upscale condo buildings. Cafés are few but interesting.

Breakfast and Snacks

RED'S JAVA HOUSE
Pier 28 (at Bryant and Spear streets), no phone.

In the midst of South Beach gentrification, Red's is a welcome anachronism, an untouched waterfront eatery which offers no quarter to diet, health or fitness innovations of the last fifty years. The food is greasy, unrefined, tasty and very cheap. Eggs, toast and coffee in the morning, burgers and beers until mid-afternoon closing. Located right on the bay, many patrons take their food outside, sharing their leftovers with the gulls. Very cheap.

Restaurants: American

DELANCEY STREET
600 The Embarcadero, tel. 512 5179 (see p. 183).

Operated by the Delancey Street Foundation, the restaurant is a pleasant waterfront room with a wide-ranging menu and superb service. Moderate.

South of Market

SoMa is rich with cafés and coffee houses, but they tend to come and go. Some simply change their names when the crowds begin to drift away to the new hot spot. Trendiness is being transformed into something more substantial as the gravity shift towards South of Market begins to bring more money, more residents and more serious eaters, no longer afraid to venture into darkest SoMa.

Breakfast and Snacks

ACORN & GRIDDLE TEA ROOM
1256 Folsom St, tel. 863 2369.

A nineties version of Ye Olde Tearoom. Chintz and portraits of the Queen have been replaced with a bright yellow colour scheme and stylish prints. The café serves lunch, tea and dinner, as well as Sunday brunch. The fare is intelligent California cuisine of baguette sandwiches, quiche, soups and salads. There is a very good California wine list and fabulous desserts. Moderate.

SOUTH PARK CAFÉ
108 South Park Ave, tel. 495 7275.

A small, appealing French café set down on the South Park oval (see pp. 178–9). The café's lunch and dinner menus are very nice (salads, roast duck and chicken), but the South Park is often overlooked for breakfast. Espresso and pastries or perhaps the blinis. Moderate.

Restaurants: American

HAMBURGER MARY'S
1582 Folsom St (at 12th Street), tel. 626 1985.

Once a hippie hangout, Mary's has been around long enough to become a San Francisco institution. Located near the club ground zero of Folsom and 11th, the café is the *real* Hard Rock café. A full bar, pinball machines, people in strange clothes and a menu that mixes red meat hamburgers and vegetarian sandwiches all combine to make

Mary's a sensual and visual experience. Inexpensive.

LuLu
816 Folsom St, tel. 495 5775.

How many restaurants can be described as 'hot' at any one time? In San Francisco that particular time-space conundrum doesn't apply. This food-mad city has the time and space for as many great restaurants as chefs can set up. LuLu, the creation of chef Reed Hearon and restaurateur Louise (Lulu) Clement, is very hot. A converted warehouse, the restaurant takes its text from French Riviera drop-in cafés. There's a strong Mediterranean flavour to the food which is served family style. LuLu's grilled dishes are perfection and the rest of the menu comes close. Expensive.

French

FRINGALE
570 Fourth St, tel. 543 0573.

Chef Gerald Hirogoyen accurately read the San Francisco map in opening his chic, upscale Parisian café South of Market. Crowded, popular and surprisingly affordable, Fringale has proved attractive to the growing white collar population of SoMa, the discerning residents and arts folk drawn to the new Yerba Buena arts district. The mussels are considered the best in San Francisco and the rest of the entirely French menu rates raves. Moderate.

RITORANTE ECCO
101 South Park St, tel. 495 3291.

Drop-dead elegant with a peach-coloured interior that suggests ancient Italian walls inexplicably moved to San Francisco and tastefully done up by a modern decorator. Northern Italian cuisine with superb pastas. Expensive.

Mexican

CHEVY'S
150 4th St (across from Moscone Center), tel. 543 8060.

Chevy's is a chain restaurant, but the kind that almost gives the institution a good name. Cheerful to the point of perkiness with pinatas, tortilla-making machines and a young staff, Chevy's makes all this worthwhile with good food that is accessible to the non-adventurous diner without ignoring the precepts of Mexican cuisine. The *frajitas* are first-rate. Moderate.

Thai

MANORA'S THAI CUISINE
1600 Folsom St (at 12th Street), tel. 861 6224.

Popular with Thai emigrés, Manora's is one of two cafés owned and operated by Manora Srisopa and her family, late of Thailand. The South of Market Manora's is known for its delicately spiced dishes which come in generous proportions. The le mongrass soup is the city's best. Inexpensive.

The Mission is, of course, heavily Latino with Mexican and Latin American cafés and restaurants. But the cross-seeding of the Mission has brought in many other cuisines, from vegetarian to French. With the *tacquerias* you mostly can't go wrong; bad food doesn't last in the Mission very long. The Castro is a different case. There are many bars and quite a few restaurants here but none of the cafés are particularly known for their food – more for the type of clientele they attract. When dining in the Castro read the posted menu and peek in at the café to make your choice.

Breakfast and Snacks

COUNTER CULTURE CAFÉ
2073 Market St, tel. 621 7488.

At the edge of the Castro, this little café is renowned for its take-out. Sandwiches, salads, desserts and an excellent selection of vegetarian dishes. Inexpensive.

NEW DAWN
3174 16th St (between Albion and Guerrero streets), tel. 553 8888.

Big, heavy breakfasts served all day in this hole-in-the wall café. A favourite meeting place for Mission rock'n'rollers (they don't bring their instruments), New Dawn serves sandwiches, home fries (thickly sliced potatoes, fried and served with sour cream), sautéd vegetables and a changing selection of other moderately fast food. No charge for the sneering attitude that comes with it. Great for people watching. Very cheap.

PAULINE'S PIZZA PIE
260 Valencia St, tel. 552 2050.

Pizza to die for. The pesto pizza is the house star, but you can't go wrong here. Pauline's has a wacky sort of ambience (don't miss the shrine to

garlic in the bathroom). The only other thing they do besides pizza is a green salad made with organic baby lettuces and served with a breadstick made from pizza dough. Good jukebox (Patsy Cline lives!) and children are very welcome. Moderate.

RORY'S TWISTED SCOOP
4101 24th St (at Castro), tel. 648 2837.

An ice cream shop with a twist. Literally. Rory's (which has a second shop in Pacific Heights) mixes toppings into the ice cream before dishing it up in waffle cones. This is really fun stuff with creative flavours and first-class ice cream.

Restaurants: French

TI-COUZ
3108 16th St (at Valencia Street), tel. 252 7373.

Delightful crêperie run by a young couple from Brittany. The menu has a couple of salads, but an extensive list of savoury and sweet crêpes. Some of the combinations are unusual (egg, cheese and almonds, shrimps and scallops), but they are excellent. The place is small but kids fit in quite well. Cheap.

Mexican

LA CUMBRE
515 Valencia St, tel. 863 8205.

The house speciality, steak burritos
(*carne asada*), are so good you have to
get in a separate line to order them.
La Cumbre is a Mission institution –
loud, cheerful, good food. No credit
cards, cheap.

LA RONDALLA
*901 Valencia St (at 21st Street),
tel. 647 7474.*

The year-round Christmas decorations
tell you a lot about La Rondalla, a
cheerfully tacky neighbourhood café.
The Mexican cuisine is hearty,
unselfconscious and tasty. The
margaritas are delicious but lethal.
Along the same stretch of Valencia
with Old Wives' Tales and Modern
Times Bookstore, a good mixture of
immigrant and intellectual cultures.
No credit cards. Cheap.

West of Divisadero

Restaurants thin out in the residential areas, both in quality and
quantity. You will see coffee shops (as opposed to coffee houses)
and fast food places with much greater frequency here.

Breakfast and Snacks

DOUBLE RAINBOW ICE CREAM
1724 Haight St, tel. 668 6690.

Double Rainbow is SF's number one
gourmet ice cream, but that bourgeois
designation doesn't keep the bohos
and punks from coming to this coffee
house cum ice cream parlour. Also
serves strong coffee, pastries, bagels.
Cheap.

JAMMIN' JAVA COFFEEHOUSE
*701 Cole St (at Waller Street),
tel. 668 5828 (or 668 JAVA).*

Simply put, a great coffee house.
A mixed crowd of bohos, upscale
neighbourhood types (houses in the
Haight are very expensive now), kids
and artists congregate here for the
coffee, art shows, poetry readings and
ambience. Cheap.

TASSAJARA CAFÉ & BAKERY
*1000 Cole St (at Parnassus),
tel. 664 8947.*

Originally part of the Zen Center's
café endeavours (as was Greens in
Fort Mason), this is a serene spot in
the further reaches of the Haight. The
handmade breads, pies, cakes, rolls
and scones of the Tassajara bakers are
on sale or you can eat here. Soups and
sandwiches also available. Cheap.

Restaurants: American

IRONWOOD CAFÉ
901 Cole St, tel. 664 0224.

A small café in the Haight, inspired by
Midwestern American cuisine: pot
roast, chicken pie, biscuits, apple pie.
The cosy, rustic atmosphere is a
perfect compliment to the handmade
comfort food. Moderate. (Check out
the 101 Carl Bakery Café almost next
door, also owned by the Ironwood
people; good for desserts and coffee.)

Chinese

CHINA HOUSE BISTRO
501 Balboa Ave (at 6th Avenue),
tel. 752 2802.

In China House, Joseph and Cecelia
Chang have recreated the
sophisticated, European-influenced
cuisine they experienced growing up
in pre-World War II Shanghai. Their
airy, evocative bistro serves up
beautiful food, carefully prepared and
presented. The Changs, one or both,
are almost always present, working
the room, happy to talk about their
food in minute detail if asked. The pot
stickers, bits of succulent pork in
dainty dough shells, are the best in
San Francisco. Vegetarians will find a
very friendly menu here. Moderate.

French

ALAIN RONDELLI
126 Clement St, tel. 387 0408.

French chef Alain Rondelli came to
San Francisco on vacation in 1989
and liked it so much he stayed. After
working for others, he opened his
own restaurant in 1993 in the
Richmond. This was an instant hit,
even though some San Franciscans
had to consult maps to find their way
into the Richmond. The menu and
wine list are small but exquisite.
Rondelli has a light, imaginative
touch with food, investing his French
dishes with California ideas.
Expensive.

Across The Bay

Marin and the East Bay have wonderful restaurants, from small
unsung neighbourhood cafés to world-class dining superstars.
Several places in the North Bay and East Bay are worth a trip just to
have a meal there. Some places are important not just for their food,
but their community standing.

GUAYMAS
5 Main St, Tiburon, Marin,
tel. 435 6300.

Tapas heaven. Guaymas popularised
the idea of tapas – small tasty dishes –
and has continued to cook wonderful
Mexican-infused food. In good
weather you can dine on the waterside
deck. Moderate.

LARK CREEK INN
234 Magnolia Ave, Marin,
tel. 924 7766.

Bradley Ogden, one of the city's
culinary superstars, opened this
charming woodsy restaurant to fully
express his ideas about American

food. Set in a renovated Victorian
farmhouse, Lark Creek Inn serves
dishes that recall childhood through a
California filter. Mashed potatoes are
perfect with the addition of garlic,
while roasted chicken, pork chops and
even liver are raised to a level of
refinement that seemed impossible
before Ogden's inspired cooking took
the Bay Area by storm. Expensive.

MILLY'S
1613 Fourth St, San Rafael, Marin,
tel. 459 1601.

Along with Greens, Milly's is the
premiere vegetarian restaurant in the
Bay Area. Talented, elegant cooking
turns the all-vegetarian menu (eggs

and dairy products are used) into not just good vegetarian dishes, but good food by any measure. Moderate.

BETTE'S OCEANVIEW DINER
1807 4th St, Berkeley,
tel. (510) 644 3230.

Bette's was already famous in the Bay Area as an excellent breakfast spot when it became nationally known (for about 15 minutes) as the anti-*Playboy* café. The café also serves lunch and has a full-service take-out counter. Moderate.

BLUE NILE CAFÉ
2525 Telegraph Ave, Berkeley,
tel. (510) 540 6777.

The best Ethiopian restaurant in the Bay Area. The Blue Nile's spicy food is especially relished by students, who appreciate the big portions and low prices, and vegetarians, who always find good, delicious dishes on the menu. Cheap.

BRICK HUT CAFÉ
3222 Adeline St (near Ashby BART),
tel. (510) 658 5555.

Begun as a lesbian collective, the Brick Hut is sought out for its robust breakfasts. Women, straight and gay, predominate, but men come here too, often and unselfconsciously. Lunch is also served – usually hamburgers for the regulars. No credit cards, cash only. Cheap.

CHEZ PANISSE
1517 Shattuck Ave, Berkeley,
tel. (510) 548 5525.

The mother church. Alice Waters still presides over the restaurant she and some friends opened in 1971. The downstairs restaurant is for dinner only, with reservations made well in

advance. The downstairs restaurant's fixed-price meals are symphonies of food – three courses on Monday nights ($35) and four and five courses the rest of the week ($45–$65). Dining is far more informal in the upstairs café, which serves lunch and dinner. The changing café menu features simply cooked fish and meats, pizza and calzone and salads. The delicious desserts, upstairs and downstairs, are lighter than most gourmet restaurants'. Renowned pastry chef Lindsey Shere (she was one of the founders, with Waters) has a preference for fruit in desserts and is amazingly creative in her baking. If you are on a tight budget, make Chez Panisse your splurge meal. You can dine at the café for under $10 if you are careful. Chez Panisse, created by women (mostly), intuitively organised along familial, cooperative lines, is in its own way a women's landmark. It is also a quintessential Bay Area place. Prices in the café are moderate.

LOIS THE PIE QUEEN
851 60th St, Oakland,
tel. (510) 658 5616.

Queen Lois died a few years ago, but her Louisiana-bred family continues the tradition of this Southern café with enormous breakfasts (pork chops, eggs, potatoes, grits, biscuits and coffee), meringue pies and fried chicken. Lois's is a major gathering place for the black community, but the clientele is at least half white, Asian and Latino. Cash only. Cheap.

THE TEA SPOT CAFÉ
2072 San Pablo Ave, Berkeley,
tel. (510) 848 7376.

Owned and staffed by women, the Tea Spot is becoming a central meeting place for women. Housed in a big, warehouse storefront, the café serves hearty breakfasts and lunches and makes the place as child-friendly as possible. Cash only. Cheap.

DRINKING

Carmen MacRae sings a wonderful old jazz tune called 'I'm Always Drunk in San Francisco', which has a certain docu-drama accuracy. San Francisco is not a town of drunks, but it is a town of drinkers, even in this age of saturation twelve-step programmes. It's widely believed that it has more bars per capita than any city in the US. New Orleans stiffly takes issue with this, but with more than 10,000 drinking establishments, San Francisco is clearly a place that likes its liquor.

The city loves bars and the bar culture; popular bartenders become local celebrities, often opening their own places after building a following. Bars are usually well integrated into a café or restaurant setting. Places like 'Cheers', without food or entertainment, are very rare and tend to be very male neighbourhood preserves.

Women alone or with other women aren't at all odd in SF bars. You will have as much or as little company as you want. On the rare occasion when you do feel harassed turn to the bartender for help, but usually it's just a matter of a firm and unequivocal, 'No, I do not want to talk to you'. Women's bars are a rare breed. Since Amelia's closed several years ago there isn't one exclusively lesbian bar in the city. The Café (formerly the Café San Marcos) in the Castro is a major lesbian hangout, but the old-line lesbian/community centre/working-class bar has disappeared for now.

Despite San Francisco's easy-going attitude towards alcohol, drinking laws are strict and hawkishly enforced. The minimum age for drinking any form of alcohol is 21 and bars and clubs routinely check IDs. It's not unusual for people with grey hair and experienced faces to be 'carded' (asked for identification). Be sure and keep a picture ID with you all the time. If you are under 21, your chances of getting a drink are slim to none. Liquor licences can be revoked for a few infringements; bars do not look the other way when it comes to liquor licence problems.

Mixed drinks run at about $3.50, beer $2–$3.50 and wine $3–$5. Expect to pay fifty cents to a dollar more in hotel bars and upscale places. Bars that depend on the tourist trade, such as the highrise penthouse bars and those around Fisherman's Wharf, will charge much more: $4–$5 for beers, $6–$8 for drinks. Most bars advertise their prices based on 'well drinks' which means that your drink is made from the most inexpensive liquor on hand. If you 'call' (name your brand) when ordering your drinks, they will be $4–$5. Likewise the house wine is likely to be a cheap Chardonnay or bland red table wine (California mixed varietals) and is quite cheap – around $2. Name your wine and the price shoots up.

Bartenders and cocktail waitresses are tipped the same as restaurants, 15 to 20 per cent.

The new trend among bars is microbreweries and brewpubs – small, boutique breweries that produce serious beers down in the basement and serve them upstairs. The works are usually on view, either through a tour or a window where you can see the brewmakers at work. The terms are beginning to blur, but generally a brewpub makes only enough beer to be sold on site while a microbrewery produces beers that are sold at its bar and marketed elsewhere.

ANCHOR STEAM

Anchor Steam beer has a special place in the San Francisco pantheon of drinking. In 1965 it was the last operating steam brewery in the city. Where once there had been dozens of small breweries, dating from Gold Rush times, Prohibition and the great maw of American homogenisation had pushed the little guys out of business one by one. Fritz Maytag, a footloose scion of the Maytag appliance manufacturing fortune, heard about Anchor Steam and was intrigued. He bought the brewery and devoted himself to learning about the science of beermaking and incidentally, how to keep a small business afloat. Slowly Anchor Steam began to rebuild a following and edged into success. Maytag's work inspired others and he is seen as the father of the microbrewing industry. Anchor Steam is on tap in many SF bars, clubs and restaurants.

The brewery, located on Potrero Hill, 1705 Mariposa St, does have a limited number of tours (free) on weekdays. Call ahead to make a reservation, tel. 863 8350.

Wine offerings will vary, but many of the upscale bars offer quite good wines by the glass (usually California vintages). If you're planning to have more than a glass, it's usually cheaper to buy the whole bottle.

Financial District

Almost all Financial District restaurants have bars, essential for after work wheeling and dealing. Everyone, men and women, is dressed in suits.

GORDON BIERSCH
2 Harrison St (facing the Embarcadero), tel. 243 8246.

This is Gordon Biersch No. 3, a microbrewery that perfected its beer and atmosphere near the Stanford University campus. No. 3 is a kind of grad school outpost, a watering hole for the young and still single professionals toiling in the Financial District. GB is also famous for its fine Germanic beers.

LONDON WINE BAR
415 Sansome St, tel. 788 4811.

Very big for after-work drinks with the Financial District crowd. The wine bar concept hasn't generated much interest in the US, but this bar has developed a following.

MAXFIELD'S BAR & GRILL
Palace Hotel, Market and New Montgomery streets, tel. 392 8600.

A dark and beautiful bar where Carole Lombard or Rosalind Russell would look very at home. Dominated by a mural of the Pied Piper by Maxfield Parrish, the bar is a favourite with Financial District types and conventioneers. Excellent martinis and free caviare on Monday, Wednesday and Friday happy hours.

Union Square

Aside from the hotel places, not very many bars.

CAFÉ CLAUDE
7 Claude Lane (off Bush Street), tel. 392 3505.

A little bit of Paris transported to San Francisco, this cosy little lunch spot stays open in the evening. Some nights there's live jazz, but always an easy-going atmosphere for early evening drinks.

REDWOOD ROOM
In the Clift Hotel, 495 Geary St, tel. 775 4700.

Like most of the old-line SF hotels, the Clift has a grand bar, the dim and sophisticated Redwood Room off the lobby. Sometimes there is a pianist playing Cole Porter on the grand piano, but there is always the tinkle of glasses and the easy, relaxed conversation of people who know they're where they want to be.

Nob Hill

TONGA ROOM
Fairmont Hotel, California at Mason, tel. 772 5131.

True to San Franciscans' ability to turn anything into camp, the Fairmont's Tonga Room has become somewhat of a kitsch favourite among the younger set. An upscale island-themed bar that resembles a Polynesian wet dream – waterfall and all – this is the place to go for drinks with umbrellas and fruit chunks. Dancing to big band music on weekends.

TOP OF THE MARK
Mark Hopkins Hotel, California and Mason streets, tel. 392 3434.

The drinks are expensive and San Franciscans make fun of it, but the original penthouse view bar still has fabulous views of the bay and hills. Avoid cute drinks and have a glass of wine or a beer and soak up the view. Sunset can be magical.

Chinatown

GRASSLAND COCKTAIL LOUNGE
905 Kearny St, tel. 362 9570.

Recently voted the city's favourite 'dive' bar. The friendly folks at Grassland don't quite seem to get the joke – they think their jukebox with Chinese pop music and tired Christmas decor is pretty cool.

LI PO BAR
916 Grant Ave, tel. 982 0072.

Site of the interior bar shots of now-famous director Wayne Wang's early

feature film *Dim Sum*. Good atmosphere, funky Chinese decor, stiff drinks.

North Beach

ENRICO'S
504 Broadway, tel. 982 6223.

This long-time North Beach landmark has died and been brought back to life several times. Avoid the food and order an espresso or a drink, either at the bar or the sidewalk tables which are heated in winter.

SAN FRANCISCO BREWING CO.
155 Columbus Ave (off Broadway), tel. 435 3344.

The city's first brewpub fittingly established in an old Barbary Coast saloon. The interior plays up SF's bent for Victoriana with stained glass, mahogany bar and detailing. One of the brewery's lagers is named for Emperor Norton, another nice touch.

TOSCA CAFÉ
242 Columbus Ave, tel. 986 9651.

Bartenders wear white jackets, the jukebox plays opera and regular patrons include Mikhail Baryshnikov, Sam Shepard, Jessica Lange and Francis Ford Coppola. There's a private poolroom for the celebs, admitted at the discretion of owner Jeannett Etheridge, a kind of bar diva. If you're not admitted, you can still

have a good time taking in the scene and sipping the famous Irish coffees.

VESUVIO'S
255 Columbus Ave (off Broadway), tel. 362 3370.

Untouched by the decades, this classic '50s hipster bar is as much a museum as a good place to get a drink. Henri Lenoir opened this bar in the 1940s and while it is still a popular late-night hangout, it's frozen somewhere in the early 1960s, after the invention of the birth control pill and before women's liberation. The collage decor of paintings, posters, graffiti and newspaper headlines has a saucy tone that was ribald thirty years ago, but is sweetly nostalgic now. One of the few new additions to Vesuvio's wall is a stark poster from the state of California warning that alcohol can cause brain damage to unborn children. An even bigger PS adds, 'Consuming alcoholic beverages before or during intercourse can cause pregnancy'. Who could have written that but a genuine hipster? The jazz is soft, the drinks are reasonable and smoking is allowed. Vesuvio, like City Lights, has remained true to its vision.

Marina/Pacific Heights

Little neighbourhood bars, usually on the quiet side. Lower Pacific Heights and the Bermuda Triangle is another story.

The Bermuda Triangle

This is probably the city's most famous bar corner at Fillmore and Greenwich. Hordes of singles, usually college age to late twenties, surge from bar to bar. When there's an attraction, the smitten man and woman disappear, geddit? The Bermuda Triangle? The Balboa Café, 3199 Fillmore, is the centre of the circuit, almost as well known for its excellent food. Actually, four spots make up the Triangle (another mystery); the others are Pierce Street Annex, 3138 Fillmore, Golden Gate Bar & Grill, 3200 Fillmore and Baja Cantina, 3154 Fillmore.

PARAGON
In the Marina, 3251 Scott St, tel. 922 2456.

Cosy and hip, Paragon is an upscale spot where you can feel free to sit at the bar, warm yourself by the fire and relax.

PERRY'S
1944 Union St, tel 922 9022.

For years Perry's was the definitive singles bar. It has ascended to emeritus status, but still draws a respectable crowd of men and women, usually over thirty, checking each other out. There's a café, too, renowned for its hamburgers.

Civic Center

STARS
150 Redwood Alley (off Van Ness Avenue), tel. 861 7827.

Mix with the beautiful people. Make yourself at home at Stars's glitzy bar, have a couple of drinks and even order something to eat. Insiders often slip past the long lines waiting for a table to take a place at the bar where you can drink, order off the menu and watch haute San Francisco come and go.

South of Market

A serious club zone. Most of the bars are part of a music or dance club with a very young orientation.

20 TANK BREWERY
316 11th St (near Folsom), tel. 843 2739.

As a favourite site for bachelor parties and over-exuberant come-ons, the 20 Tank can be a bit much. But approached as a beer lover conducting a science experiment, a night here can be quite entertaining. Order your beer, sit on or hover near a bar stool and check your watch to see how little time passes before some frat boy (or frat boy in a past life) attempts to put the moves on you. Or sit upstairs and peer over the railing, and you'd swear you were watching the behaviour patterns of an ant farm. Amazing.

THE CARIBBEAN ZONE
55 Natoma St (next to Club DV8), tel. 541 9465.

Diners waiting for supper tables at

this restaurant can sip cocktails while sitting inside an aeroplane fuselage. The decor of this under-the-freeway watering hole is designed to look like the aftermath of a non-fatal plane crash.

The Mission

Tons of neighbourhood bars, but there's often a high level of machismo floating around. Stick to the boho watering holes.

THE ALBION
3139 16th St (at Albion), tel. 552 8558.

The Albion has your typical San Francisco bar staples of free-flowing beer, luxurious stools, art on the walls, plenty of attitude – and more. Ladies, the Albion has one of the city's most fabulous bathrooms. OK, so it's only got one stall, but the *trompe l'oeil* columns and tidy fixtures make the Albion's loo one ladies' lounge you won't mind waiting to use. The club's allegedly smoke-free back room hosts live bands and spoken-word performances on some nights.

DOCTOR BOMBAY'S
3192 16th St (at Guerrero), tel. 431 5255.

Faux Tiki masks and mildly Tahitian decor make this cheap bar a cut above the usual dive.

ZEITGEIST
199 Valencia St (at Duboce).

This super serious biker-oriented slacker bar is one place that yupsters looking to make the scene fear to tread. Cheap and good beer. Be sure to park nearby or take a cab, as this part of Valencia Street is not the best.

The Castro

Castro bars are more cruise spots than neighbourhood hangouts but almost all have pool tables. Women are welcome and comfortable here.

THE CAFÉ
2367 Market St (at Castro), tel. 861 3846.

The Café (formerly the Café San Marcos) is probably the city's oldest and most beloved 'mixed' bar, one of the few places in town where hyper-butch gay boys share the pool table with oh-so chic lipstick lesbians, and vice-versa (natch). Since anything goes at the Café, even straight boys mixing with straight girls raises nary an eyebrow. Curl up by the cosy fireplace with a coffee drink, or do some serious cruising, especially Friday night.

THE STUD
399 9th St, tel. 863 6623.

A gay bar for everybody. The Stud is friendly and colourful. Music on weekends.

EATING AND DRINKING

The Haight, especially the Lower Haight, is the premiere bar scene for the under thirties. Anchored to Toronodo, Mad Dog in the Fog and Noc Noc, you can make the circuit rather quickly, and many of the local twentynothings and out-of-town scenesters pop in and out of these bars in attempts to find where it's the most 'happening'. You'll generally find an 'in' looking crowd of tattooed and/or pierced types and grungy long hairs – people who don't seem to be worried about getting up for work in the morning, but each place has its own seedy charm. Further out in the middle-class Avenues/Richmond district, there's a heavy concentration of Irish pubs.

BOOMERANG
1840 Haight St (near Belvedere), tel. 221 1960.

Former site of the fifties-flavoured Rockin' Robins (which itself was the former site of God knows what else), Club Boomerang is currently inhabited by the spirit of the local alternative music scene. Cheap beer and bands flow daily.

IRELAND'S 32
3920 Geary Blvd (at 3rd Avenue), tel. 386 6173.

This stretch of Geary Boulevard, which runs all the way to Ocean Beach, is sometimes called 'County Geary' and 'The Irish Mile' for its concentration of Irish bars. Irish expats hang out on weekdays, a more diverse crowd on weekends. Very political crowd. Expats of the acceptable political persuasion (anti-imperialism) are welcomed with open arms. Other Irish bars nearby include: Pat O'Shea's Mad Hatter (3848 Geary, tel. 752 3148) and The Plough and Stars (116 Clement St, at 2nd Avenue, tel. 751 1122).

MAD DOG IN THE FOG
Lower Haight, 530 Haight St, tel. 626 7279.

Expatriate Brits (and those who just look like them), tend to favour the Mad Dog in the Fog. Aspiring Joni Mitchells and Kurt Cobains fill the rosters for the popular Tuesday night open mikes. Full roster of British beers and ales.

NOC NOC
557 Haight St (at Steiner), tel. 861 5811.

Spiky welded bar chairs and strangely configured couch-like sitting areas make up the dim interior of the very PoMo (post modern) Noc Noc. Surprisingly low-key.

TORONODO
547 Haight St, tel. 863 2276.

This bar established its claim as pop culture leader of the pack by having weekly showings of 'The Simpsons', the cartoon show with an attitude. You don't have to have a bad attitude to drop in at Toronodo, but it helps you to fit in.

There are plenty of good bars across the bay in both directions. Marin tends towards laid-back, adult places, Oakland is the Bay Area centre for black singles and Berkeley, naturally, is covered with student hangouts.

Sausalito

ALTA MIRA HOTEL
125 Bulkley Ave, Sausalito, tel. 332 1350.

The view from the terrace is fabulous. Drink whatever you like best and sink into a reverie. This is the place to let the magic of the Golden Gate do its number on you.

NO NAME BAR
757 Bridgeway, Sausalito, tel. 332 1392.

Jazz some nights, very laid back.

East Bay

CHERIE'S
131 Broadway, Oakland (near Jack London Square), tel. (510) 271 0350.

Until recently known as Geoffrey's, this always packed bar is the number one gathering spot for upscale black singles in the Bay Area. Sometimes called buppies (black urban professionals), the men and women who frequent Cherie's range from pro athletes (local and on tour) to judges to stockbrokers to executives. Don't think of showing up here unless you are dressed to kill.

HENRY'S
Durant Hotel, 2600 Durant Ave, Berkeley, tel. (510) 845 8981.

Whatever else changes in Berkeley, Henry's has remained the Cal fraternity and sorority hangout of choice. Lesser mortals (especially those celebrating their 21st birthdays) have been known to park themselves at the pricey but good-natured bar, if only for the thrill of ordering one of Henry's up-to-the-minute wackily named drinks, such as a 'brain haemorrhage', an 'abortion' and that old stand-by, 'sex on the beach', in all its infinite varieties.

TRIPLE ROCK BREWERY
1920 Shattuck Ave, Berkeley, tel. (510) 843 2739.

One of the East Bay's premiere brewpubs, Triple Rock serves up its amber, golden and chunky-dark brews to townies and university students alike. The pub food is better than usual (fresh salads and sandwiches, an array of nachos), as is the jukebox. The air-hockey table is an extra-added attraction, but the yummy beer is enough to keep most people in the place for a night.

San Francisco knows how to entertain you, whatever your idea of entertainment might be. Rock'n'roll, opera, ballet, jazz, avant garde puppetry, Shake-speare, Broadway musicals and professional sports are all well and fully represented in the Bay Area. While you can see world-class performers and spectacles in every medium (Bruce Springsteen, Ian McKellen, *Guys and Dolls*, championship football, Placido Domingo, k.d. lang, Twyla Tharp) you can also sample a huge range of performance, from garage bands just breaking into the clubs to opera night at an Italian cafeteria in Oakland. It's not just the first-class, absolute best music, dance and performance that makes San Francisco so interesting but the constant bubbling, percolating arts scene that breeds audiences and entertainers.

Entertainment is big news in the Bay Area and thoroughly covered in the daily and weekly press. The Sunday entertainment section of the *Chronicle*, a tabloid called the 'Pink Book', for the hideous paper it is printed on, is the most complete guide to what's going on. The *Friday Examiner* (afternoon paper) has a good weekend guide and the weekly alternative newspapers such as the *Bay Guardian, SF Weekly* and the *Sentinel* are extremely detail-oriented on the club scene and offbeat stuff such as performance art and gay events.

NIGHTLIFE AND GIGS

San Francisco has always been big on nightlife. From the days of the Barbary Coast to the great jazz clubs of the fifties to the psychedelic ballrooms of the sixties, the city has been a pacesetter in Going Out.

Clubs

The contemporary club scene is a valiant attempt to please all the people all the time. The range of nightclubs is both inspiring and daunting. Wonderful to have the choices, but how to get to them all? Jazz clubs have begun to re-emerge in a significant way with Yoshi's and Kimball's East in the East Bay rated as among the top jazz venues in the US. Swank supper club-nightclubs make up another trend that looks like it might really take hold. Club 181 and Harry Denton's are sleek music and dinner clubs where grown-ups can feel at home. Music clubs are the staple of the going-out circuit, both dance clubs and live music, usually fuelled by the endless waves of under thirties who love the sweaty, jam-packed dance floors and the 'mosh pit' (wild body contact slam dancing). Big name musicians, from Prince to Billy Joel, like to show up at SF clubs unannounced and do an informal preview of new material or a revamped show. The stars know no matter how big they are, they will get clear and reliable feedback from an SF audience.

Clubs have distinct personalities and constituencies, but there's an agreeable fluidity about club going. Straight college kids love the hard-core gay bars like the Stud while it isn't at all unusual to see Asians at the salsa/mambo clubs of the Mission and Latinos at rap shows and African Americans at the post-college temple of cool, Johnny Love's. Gays and lesbians frequent clubs other than those that are primarily gay.

CLUB CRUISES

It's a familiar dilemma, you want to have fun, hit the clubs, but don't quite know where to start and how do you find these places anyway? Two words: club tour.

Paula Sabatelli, a seasoned scenester who owns Paula's Clubhouse, came up with the first club tour, Three Babes and a Bus. With her two partners, Sabatelli loads up partyers on a comfortable mini-bus late Friday and Saturday nights and heads for the clubs. The bus hits four places, with the guides carefully counting passengers going in and coming out so as not to lose any along the way. As the bus rattles back and forth across Market Street, the Babes tell raucous jokes, conduct daffy quizzes and keep the fun level high. Occasionally they end up with some tipsy passengers, but the Babes (they prefer the term) know how to keep the fun on track without a heavy hand. While the places on the tour are usually middle-of-the-road, Sabatelli and her partners are extremely tuned into the club scene and dispense excellent advice about where and how to club solo. Even if you are not shy about going about on your own, the bus is a terrific orientation cruise for the city nightlife. Reservations are required, partygoers must be 21 and have an ID (for drinking), $30 a person, tel. 552 2582.

The Mexican Bus is another club tour, concentrating on Latino music and dance clubs. Tour times depend on how many signups they have for the weekend, so call as early as possible to make sure your bus fills up, tel. 648 2979.

Both of these tours are perfect for women alone.

Women, alone or with other women, are a big part of the club scene. The cruising, immediate pick-up scene has slowed considerably in the age of AIDS (among gays and straights), but 'meeting somebody new' remains the big drive for going out. Clubs are hardly the territory of political correctness, but San Francisco's sensitivity to women's issues does extend into club life. Bartenders and bouncers will intercede with men who won't take no for an answer from women patrons. Bouncers and door people are also very good about watching over women leaving clubs, especially if they are alone or have a long walk to their cars.

There's a tremendous amount of overlap among bars, clubs and restaurants, but generally clubs are defined here as the night spots that emphasise entertainment over drinking and eating, while bars are where people come primarily for drinks. Among the clubs, many of the dance clubs rely almost completely on recorded music, bringing in bands only on weekends. The jazz and music bars, however, usually have dancing but the music is centre stage. At Slim's for instance, with its state-of-the-art sound system, dancing usually slows, then stops as the crowd moves towards the stage, swaying together to the music.

Some clubs change personalities and names nightly. One way of coping with the tight economy and declining profits in nightclubs (AA is blamed; sober people drink inexpensive mineral water instead of high-profit liquor and beer) has been to attract as many patrons as possible. Many clubs have different theme nights devoted to reggae, world beat, jazz, lesbians, gays and seventies music. Some big spaces, such as the South of Market warehouse at 650 Howard St, have a different club every night. It can be very confusing, but the people who want a scene always seem to find it sooner or later.

Lesbian Clubs

Lesbians grumble that they don't have a 'real' club to call their own, but the gay women's entertainment circuit is enough to keep any woman busy seven nights a week. Lesbian club nights draw big crowds at Faster Pussycat (the Playhouse, Wednesdays), The Girl Spot (the Endup, Saturdays) and Club Skirts (Club Touche, Sundays). The scene is very sexy (clubs give discounts to women who show up in bustiers and bras) with heavy-breathing music and curvaceous go-go girls that *Playboy* would love to make Playmate of the Month.

The new addition to the women's club scene has been lesbian sex clubs – no holds barred parties extrapolated from the gay male world. Before AIDS a room for anonymous sex was standard equipment at male gay clubs. Women's sex clubs are floating parties that have two levels, the pick-up dance floor and a semi-private upstairs where party-goers pair off (or triple or quadruple off) amidst futons, mattresses and gauzy curtains.

Despite a wave of publicity and fierce debates among lesbians about the propriety/usefulness/need of the sex clubs, they have not been a great success. Some would-be revellers find the no-alcohol policies a drag while the really wild girls complain that there are far too many people watching instead of doing. The sex clubs don't have a fixed place or time but have a habit of popping up about once a month or every six weeks. Club Ecstasy is the longest-running party which maintains a hot line for news about party dates (tel. 267 6915). Word spreads about upcoming dates by word of mouth, handbills and ads in the gay press. The lesbian sex clubs may or may not be more than a passing fad. So far the most excitement has been among straights, thrilled by the voyeuristic stories that have popped up in the daily newspapers.

San Francisco Clubs

BABYLON
Lower Pacific Heights, 2260 Van Ness Ave, tel. 567 1222.

When Johnny Love's opened, everyone held their collective breath to see if the most beautiful people in the world under thirty would desert Babylon for the new club. So far there doesn't seem to be a shortage of beauties, male and female. A DJ spins records for a tiny dance floor, but checking out the crowd is the big entertainment.

BAHIA TROPICAL BRAZILIAN CLUB
Downtown, 1600 Market St, tel. 861 8657.

A Brazilian band pounds out the beat every night, drawing accomplished dancers to fill the floor. Some are Brazilian and Latin American emigrés, some are San Franciscans who learned their sophisticated moves right here at the Bahia. Some cruising, but primarily draws men and women who adore dancing.

BOTTOM OF THE HILL CLUB
Potrero Hill, 1233 17th St, tel. 626 4455.

The hot new music club – for a while. This place is off the club path, deep in Potrero Hill (east of the Mission), but popular for its all-live music programming. New, unusual and favourite local bands play seven nights a week. Small, but the place to see and be seen.

THE CHAMELEON
In the Mission, 853 Valencia St (between 18th and 19th streets), tel. 821 1891.

Formerly one of the city's most raucous and raw live music sweatboxes, the Chameleon has toned down its act in recent months to better comply with the fire marshal's wishes. Opting for a more subdued scene, the owners have opened the Underbelly Lounge to host more sedate coffee-house activities, such as the Monday night 'poetry slams' which are among the city's premiere spoken-word events. Schedule and cover vary.

CAFÉ DU NORD
Edge of the Castro, 2170 Market St, (at Sanchez), tel. 861 5016.

This Upper Market hot spot boasts some form of live entertainment each night of the week. Especially popular are the Sunday night Cabaret du Nord shows which put a San Francisco spin on the New Vaudeville (political clowning) craze. Of course, plenty of locals go to 'The Nerd' simply to hang out and watch the parade of hipsters and Eurotrash and maybe collect a few phone numbers. Cover $5 or under.

JAZZ IN THE CITY

San Francisco, once a great city for jazz where legendary musicians such as Cannonball Adderly, Charles Mingus and even Benny Goodman, were familiar faces around North Beach clubs, has been experiencing a jazz renaissance over the last decade. Yoshi's, an elegant sushi bar in Oakland and Kimball's East, another East Bay club, book the crème de la crème of the jazz world. In the city, the New Orleans Room at the Fairmont, Café du Nord and Pearl's are all lively jazz showcases drawing big, enthusiastic fans of all ages. All this jazz mania coalesces into the two-week San Francisco Jazz Festival every fall. The free-floating carnival of music books performers into clubs, cafés, theatres, classical music halls and even churches for one of the most comprehensive surveys of contemporary jazz possible. In addition to stars such as Joe Henderson, Branford Marsalis, Pat Metheny and the Kronos Quartet, the festival rounds up new and unusual talent, from local teenagers to the Bulgarian Women's Choir to gospel to Afro-Cuban and Brazilian bands. The festival, formerly called Jazz in the City, is usually scheduled for the first two weeks of November. Call 864 5449 or write to SF Jazz Festival, 141 10th St, San Francisco CA 94103 for next year's schedule.

CLUB 181
In the Tenderloin, 181 Eddy St, tel. 673 8181.

Once a famously cool nightspot, Club 181 re-opened recently, no doubt in part to capitalise on the rebirth of the jazz and supper-club scene in San Francisco. Conveniently located in the heart of the city's sleazy Tenderloin District, Club 181 offers DJ music Tuesdays through Saturdays and live, cutting-edge jazz jams on Sundays. Cover varies.

DNA LOUNGE
South of Market, 375 11th St, tel. 626 1409.

One of the brighter spots on the SoMa scene, the DNA hosts both big and large, local and nationally recognised musical acts. Visiting rap artists also make the DNA their San Francisco venue of choice. Within its trippily painted day-glo walls, the DNA is one of the city's only reliably after-hours clubs, with dancing nightly until 4 a.m. Cover runs around $5, sometimes more for big headliners.

ELBO ROOM
In the Mission, 647 Valencia St (near 16th Street), tel. 552 7788.

Most of the twentynothings who nightly crowd into this Mission District watering hole have no idea that it used to be Amelia's, the city's last all-lesbian bar. Only the famous gate remains. Downstairs at Elbo Room, you'll find a photo booth for remembering your visit on film. Upstairs, for a cover under $5, local 'acid jazz' and alternative groups play on weeknights, while weekends are usually reserved for dancing to pre-recorded funk-flavoured flashbacks.

THE ENDUP
South of Market, 401 6th St, tel. 543 7700.

Saturday this gay club is *the* lesbian place to be when it becomes Girl Spot, a huge dance party with DJs and go-

go girls. Mixed gay crowd other nights for techno and tea dances.

JOHNNY LOVE'S
Near Van Ness, 1500 Broadway, tel. 931 6053.

If you can get in, you'll find the premiere young'n'-restless singles club of Northern California. Named for the club's head bartender, Johnny 'Love' Metheny, a near-mythical figure in SF nightlife, the place has the same easy charm and party-hearty reputation of Mr Love. The club is a favourite stop for pro athletes, who usually have to line up like everyone else to get in for the food, music and pick-up scene.

HARRY DENTON'S
Financial District, 161 Steuart St, tel. 882 1333.

This elegant supper club has been compared to Studio 54 in its heyday, but the would-be flatterers seem to have forgotten the absolute abandon of the druggie seventies. Denton's is the haunt of well-dressed and well-heeled lawyers, stockbrokers, deal-makers of the nineties stripe. As in, 'I like fun, I am here to have fun, but fun has its place and remember, I have to meet my trainer at 7 a.m.'

THE KENNEL CLUB
Lower Haight, 628 Divisadero, tel. 864 7040.

The Kennel Club offers a mix of live music and DJ engineered dance nights. Local bands or big-name alternative touring acts are booked at the club Mondays, Wednesdays and Fridays, while the Broun Fellinis, a hot trio at the forefront of the Bay Area's 'acid jazz' movement hold court on Tuesdays. The Box on Thursday nights features high-energy dance music for both genders and all persuasions, while Saturdays and Sundays are World Beat dance nights. Cover rarely exceeds $8, but can go higher for super-hot headliners.

RAVES

San Francisco has been a couple of beats behind on the rave phenomenon, but the semi-secret druggie dance parties have begun popping up all over the city. Word is passed at dance clubs or through handbills: 'Psst, there's a rave tonight in the Haight, South of Market, near Potrero Hill'. Some party givers even organise scavenger hunts to find the rave. Primarily the preserve of college-age kids, a group takes over a large indoor space such as a warehouse, sets up a huge sound system, lasers for light shows and at the more sophisticated raves, even bring in fog machines and a myriad of sound effects. The music is almost always recorded. A San Francisco variation on the international rave staple of techno-house music is a preference for homeboy band the Grateful Dead and rockabilly bands. The high cover charge ($10–$25 a person) only seems to add to the mystique. Drug dealers circulate freely usually dispensing Ecstasy, the designer drug that creates a state of untempered bliss for a couple of hours. To find a rave ask in clubs or scrutinise posters and handbills in Haight Street or around SoMa clubs.

LOU'S PIER 47
Fisherman's Wharf, 300 Jefferson St, tel. 771 0377.

Two sets, every day, with some of the best blues bands around. Motown is heard here, too, in this middle-of-the-road club. Lou's popularity can be measured by the fact that it draws a large local crowd who regularly brave Fisherman's Wharf to hang out at the club. Big pick-up scene, but just say no if you're not interested.

NEW ORLEANS ROOM
Nob Hill, in the Fairmont Hotel, California and Mason streets, tel. 772 5229.

Surprisingly, one of the best jazz rooms in the Bay Area is in the grand old Fairmont Hotel. Reminiscent of a forties jazz club, the New Orleans Room has an easy-going affability which makes it a comfortable place for women. Usually soloists and small combos are booked here.

NICKIE'S BBQ
Lower Haight, 460 Haight St (between Fillmore and Webster), tel. 621 6508.

A barbecue joint-cum-danceteria, Nickie's features some of the city's most beloved multi-culti DJs spinning everything from Zairean tunes to hardcore funk. But watch your purse and don't stray far alone, as the neighbourhood is known to be questionable after dark. Cover $5 or less.

PARADISE LOUNGE
South of Market, 1501 Folsom St, tel. 861 1912.

With two stages downstairs, an upstairs cabaret lounge, three bars, pool tables and plenty of chairs and room to schmooze, the Paradise is the club you can turn to in desperation and walk away feeling entertained. The Paradise is home to a music-loving crowd who turn up for the variety and the low cover – usually $5 or under, $10 max for one of the

frequent superstar 'drop-in' gigs the club is known for by the likes of Chris Isaak or Concrete Blond's Johnette Napolitano.

PAULA'S CLUBHOUSE
In the Mission, 3160 16th St (at Albion), tel. 561 9771.

A different club every night, but always something out there on the edge. Wednesday is girls' night with Faster Pussycat, named after the infamous Russ Meyer cult film about a trio of murderous, sportscar-driving go-go dancers. Those particular girls might not be there, but women DJs (usually Downtown Donna) and all-female bands do show up, along with a wall-to-wall crowd. Call for other night themes, which change.

PEARL'S JAZZ RESTAURANT AND BAR
North Beach, 256 Columbus Ave, tel. 291 8255.

The only jazz club in North Beach is worthy of the mantle it has received. Pearl's is a superb jazz venue, booking top talent both locally and nationally, and running a well-organised, fun bar.

RAWHIDE II
South of Market, 280 7th St, tel. 621 1197.

A Country & Western gay bar that at first seems to be a parody of a macho gay bar, but no it is the real thing. DJs spin Patsy Cline, Billy Ray Cyrus and all the twangers while boy-boy and girl-girl couples dance expert Texas Two-Steps and elaborate line dances. Come for free dance lessons and hang out in the right-hand corner of the dance floor, the 'gal corral'.

SLIM'S
South of Market, 333 11th St,
tel. 621 3330.

Just across the street, within earshot of the Paradise, Slim's features some of the country's biggest names in rock, blues, New Age, hip-hop and alternative music. Owner Boz Scaggs often drops in, but at Slim's the emphasis is on the music, not on Boz-gazing. Cover usually runs $10–$15, but occasional local band showcases are under $5 or even free.

East Bay

Across the Bay Bridge from downtown San Francisco, you'll find the East Bay cities of Oakland, Berkeley and Emeryville. Oakland, in particular, with its history steeped in West Coast Blues, has plenty to offer the music-loving traveller. Here are a few East-Bay hot spots you won't want to miss.

Oakland

ELI'S MILE HIGH CLUB
3629 Martin Luther King Jr Way,
tel. (510) 655 6661.

Widely acknowledged as 'the home of West Coast Blues,' Eli's has long been recognised as a gem of a nightclub, despite the fact that it sits proudly in what is not known as a 'desirable' neighbourhood. A working-class black bar, Eli's was discovered by white UC-Berkeley students who flooded the place. For a while the owners feared the club was going to become a black club for whites, but Eli's has found its balance. Beloved long-time owner Troyce Key (who was white) died from leukaemia last year, but Key's wife Margaret (African American) continues the club's homey and welcoming atmosphere. The superb house band still bears Troyce's name. Friday and Saturday nights, blues legends and up-and-comers sit in with the band, and cover can run up to $7 and $8. A blues experience you won't want to miss.

JIMMIE'S COCKTAIL LOUNGE
1731 San Pablo Ave,
tel. (510) 268 8445.

This blues club is a big favourite with black singles who appreciate the sophisticated, non-rap music and the down home cooking. Jimmie's supplements its live stage shows with recorded music. Call for shows. The club draws white patrons, too, but white women should especially be tactful about appearances. Black men dating white women is a combustible issue among African American women.

YOSHI'S
6030 Claremont Ave,
tel. (510) 652 9200.

An Oakland institution, Yoshi's is likely the only Japanese restaurant/jazz joint you'll come across in your travels. Where else can you stuff your face full of first-rate sushi and tempura while listening to jazz greats on the order of Joe Henderson and Branford Marsalis? Headliners do two shows nightly at 8 and 10 p.m. A night at Yoshi's can run on the expensive side, with tickets as much as $20 apiece and dinner and drinks at restaurant-quality prices.

Emeryville

KIMBALL'S EAST AND KIMBALL'S CARNIVAL
5800 Shellmound, tel. (510) 658 2555, tel. (510) 653 5300.

Just off the Bay Bridge, between the cities of Oakland and Berkeley, is the odd little town of Emeryville. Besides minor league gambling parlours (legal) and converted artists' lofts, Emeryville's main attraction is the EmeryBay Public Market, a post-modern village of speciality stores and restaurants, the centrepiece of which is the elegant jazz club Kimball's East and its newer, Latin-flavoured sister club, Kimball's Carnival. Both supper clubs emphasise food more than you might expect at a nightclub, probably since the owners got into the club business by first running a restaurant near San Francisco's Civic Center. Cover at Kimball's East can run as high as $20–$24, while entrance to the dance-friendly Carnival is generally less.

Berkeley

ASHKENAZ
1317 San Pablo Ave, tel. (510) 525 5054.

This unpretentious northwest Berkeley nightspot (modelled architecturally after an Eastern European community hall) is the place to go if you're in the mood to dance. Groups with roots in New Orleans, West Africa, Nigeria, Latin America and Hawaii regularly play here, and with the very Berkeley do-your-own-thing all-ages atmosphere, apple juice is as likely to flow as beer. With its proximity to the UC Berkeley campus, Ashkenaz tends to draw a multicultural crowd of expatriate students, their friends, and family folks who prefer an ethnic mix to standard dance club fare. Cover $5–$8, can go as high as $10 for occasion World Beat superstars.

LARRY BLAKE'S
2367 Telegraph Ave (at Durant), tel. (510) 848 0886.

Blake's has lately begun to stray from its heretofore strictly blues format into the oh-so lucrative terrain of local alternative rock. Steve Gannon still holds down the Monday Night Blues Jam, but more often than not, Thursdays through Saturdays at Blake's belongs to the kids. Cover not usually more than $5.

Pop Concerts and Gigs

Most of the major players on the local music scene can be found any night of the week playing their heart out in the city's myriad of smaller haunts and clubs. But within the course of a year, practically every big-time rock star or pop act is booked into one of the Bay Area's major concert venues, with surprise après-mega show appearances in smaller dives thrown in for good measure.

Sprinkled about the Bay Area are outdoor amphitheatres, some of them quite massive, which can accommodate concert-goers while taking advantage of the fairly pleasant May-to-October weather. But summers in the Bay Area being as frigid and fog filled as they are (remember what Mark Twain said), you'll want to dress warmly and bring a blanket or two (that spare one in the hotel-room closet should do nicely) to brave the elements.

Since both Shoreline Amphitheater in Mountain View and the Concord Pavilion are booked by Bill Graham Presents, the late impresario's San Francisco-based concert promotion group, the venues tend to present the same artists on different nights as they wend through the area. The Greek Theater, situated just above the U.C. Berkeley campus, is also booked by BGP, but its roster tends to favour more unique and college-oriented acts.

Bigger pop and rock acts also turn up at the city's larger indoor spaces. Don't expect to catch a show at the legendary Fillmore Auditorium just yet, but you can experience some great music in a concert-hall setting. Crowds vary according to who's playing, and it's impossible to generalise about a scene that changes so blatantly from year to year, taste to taste, blockbuster to blockbuster. Size and voraciousness of mosh pits wax and wane with the artist in question. You can't go wrong with sturdy shoes and plenty of attitude, but other than that, you never know what to expect.

TICKETS

Tickets to most major entertainment events are available through a central agency called BASS/TM. With a credit card, you may order tickets over the phone and charge them to your account. Be aware, however, that a handling charge is added by BASS and you will pay up to $2 in addition to the price of each ticket. The central BASS line for the Bay Area is (510) 762 BASS (or 762 2277). BASS also has a number of offices around the city, where you may pick up tickets without paying the phone charge.

Half-price and discounted tickets are often available for dance, classical music and theatre events, but you have to ask for most of them. The symphony, ballet and opera all have standing room and student rush deals, while Berkeley Repertory Theater puts twenty tickets on sale at half price the day of performances for a first-come-first-serve bargain.

The major dispenser of discount tickets is the TIX/Bay Area booth in Union Square. Located on the Stockton Street side of the park, TIX sells half-price and discounted tickets on the day of the show for touring shows, local productions and a variety of other entertainments. TIX is on a cash (or travellers' cheque) basis. No credit cards. The booth is closed Sunday and Monday, tel. 433 7827.

San Francisco

THE WARFIELD
982 Market St, tel. 775 7722.

From the street, this venerable concert hall could be confused easily with the less-than-reputable 'theatres' (actually, porno cinemas and strip-houses) that share its Market Street block. But a closer look reveals that the Warfield regularly includes some of the country's hottest rap, hip-hop, rock and alternative acts, reveals the theatre's true cutting-edge purpose. The club often saves a stash of tickets for the day of the show.

GREAT AMERICAN MUSIC HALL
859 O'Farrell St (near Van Ness), tel. 849 0750.

Another venue in a less-than-desirable location, the GAMH has carved out a formidable niche on the national folk and pop music circuit despite its high-Tenderloin address. You'll want to take a cab or walk quickly to the door, as it shares the block with the notorious Mitchell Bros Theater. The Hall is booked most nights by acts ranging from superstars of the lesbo-folk world (Holly Near, Ferron, Rhiannon, *et al.*), to way out performers the likes of local sound artists Negativland. No matter who's playing, the atmosphere is decidedly friendly, and if you get to the show on time, you can usually have your choice of lower- or upper-level tables. There's also ample floor space.

HOLLY NEAR

The Western headquarters of women's music is in the Bay Area, primarily because of singer-songwriter Holly Near. A Northern California farm girl, Near founded her own label, Redwood Records, in 1973 when she couldn't get a record deal that would allow her to do her kind of music – political, feminist, uncategorisable. A star on the antiwar-feminist circuit with her full voice and witty, moving songs, Near came out as a lesbian in 1976. Redwood, eventually opening offices and studios in Oakland, became a beacon and a symbol for lesbians and feminists, producing records, organising tours, sponsoring music festivals and making women's music visible, important and fun. Near, who had come close to becoming a Hollywood starlet during her student days at UCLA (she co-starred with Don Johnson in his first movie, the cult fave *The Secret Garden of Stanley Sweetheart*), continued to invent her career as she went along. In 1980 she teamed up with fifties folk singer Ronnie Gilbert, of the Weavers, for a concert tour, reviving Gilbert's career. In 1990 Near published her autobiography, *Fire in the Rain … Singer in the Storm*, which shocked her fans by revealing her long-running affair with Berkeley's black male mayor, Gus Newport. The fans recovered as did Near who still defines herself as a lesbian. With her theatre director sister Timothy Near, Holly Near turned *Fire in the Rain* into a stage show that won popular and critical acclaim in Los Angeles, Berkeley and Off Broadway in New York. The only cloud on her horizon has been the troubling financial downturn for Redwood, which has been struggling for several years. Holly Near, who could have been a Hollywood star but happily moulded herself into a feminist 'cultural worker', has left her mark on the music business by forcing it to take notice of women's music. Whatever happens in Redwood's future, its past is a solid gold hit.

BILL GRAHAM CIVIC AUDITORIUM
(Formerly the San Francisco Civic Auditorium)
Grove at Polk St; call BASS for info, tel. 762 2277.

Its renaming being just one more piece of evidence of Bill Graham's effect on the music in this town, the Civic actually reminds one of the basketball court or indoor stadium it was meant to be. Very large acts play here, often those who in warmer weather would be playing stadiums. Civic Center lots provide available parking, but one should exercise caution.

Peninsula

SHORELINE AMPHITHEATER
Amphitheater Parkway, off Highway 101, Mountain View; call BASS for info, tel. 762 2277.

The late Bill Graham himself built this

massive open-air concert theatre on land in the southwest corner of San Francisco Bay, about thirty miles south of San Francisco proper. With seating capacity of 20,000, thanks largely to the Shoreline's enormous lawn (which can turn into a convection oven during the hottest of summer days), this venue showcases some of the nation's hottest and biggest rock and country acts. The Shoreline is not the place to see up-and-comers. The concert season typically runs from Memorial Day (late May) to Halloween.

East Bay

CONCORD PAVILION
2000 Kirker Pass Road, Concord, tel. 762 2277.

Smaller in scale than the Shoreline, but booking many of the same acts, the Concord Pavilion also has the tendency to be a bit less adventurous than one might assume. It is also situated in one of the more conservative areas of the East Bay, as reflected by audiences – especially when country artists appear (they love 'em). The advantage for visitors of

seeing acts here instead of Shoreline is the BART connection. BART runs to Concord where you catch a free Concord Pavilion shuttle bus to the amphitheatre, then take it back after the show.

GREEK THEATER
Piedmont Avenue, above U.C. Berkeley campus; call BASS for ticket info, tel. 762 2277.

Actually patterned after a historical Greek theatre, and smaller in scale than its open-air counterparts throughout the area, the Greek is quite a pleasant place to catch a concert. Concerts include Pearl Jam, Bob Dylan and the Grateful Dead. Particularly wonderful are summer twilight concerts at the Greek, where those in the audience, especially those in the cheapest lawn seats, can experience a gorgeous Bay Area sunset above, while enjoying the show. Or if you'd rather, just park yourself on one of the many embankments outside the Greek's entrance. The sound is almost as good as in the paying seats, and you can come and go as you please.

THE ARTS

Classical Music and Opera

Some San Francisco visitors are surprised at the quality and depth of the city's classical music. The San Francisco Opera and the San Francisco Symphony are world-class organisations that attract star artists, collect sterling reviews in the US and Europe and produce a level of art that easily holds its own in international comparisons. But somehow, aside from music fans, the world isn't completely aware of the city's devotion to classical music.

While the classical tradition in the Bay Area provides a steady audience and pool of performers, the music scene goes far beyond Mozart and Wagner. The Women's Philharmonic, an all-female orchestra, has found critical and popular success playing music by women composers, while the Kronos Quartet has shown the music world an entirely new approach to string quartets. This kind of open, eager atmosphere has made San Francisco a prime centre for the New Music of contemporary composers and encouraged the big institutions to take a few chances. The San Francisco Opera has premiered works such as 'Nixon in China' and 'The Death of Klinghoffer' and commissioned sets and costumes from such artists as David Hockney.

Tickets to events can be difficult to get at short notice and quite expensive. For the big, big events (Placido Domingo at the opera) you can always turn to scalpers who either advertise in the papers or discreetly offer tickets near the performance site. For most concerts, however, you can turn up at the box office a bit in advance and do quite well. San Francisco Opera and Symphony tickets can easily run to $50, but the smaller groups can be seen for under $10. If you are on a budget, consider the inexpensive standing room tickets at the opera or bad seats behind the orchestra at the symphony. There you'll sit with the students and bohemians who make up the popular support for the arts in San Francisco.

The newspaper listings, both daily and weekly, are the best source of surveying what performances are scheduled as well as the touring artists who come through town.

BERKELEY SYMPHONY
Different venues, tel. (510) 841 2800.

Under rising star Kent Nagano this small community orchestra has become one of the most exciting musical groups in the Bay Area. New music is a passion with Nagano, who takes time out from his international duties (Paris Opera) to return to Berkeley regularly.

KRONOS QUARTET
Different venues, tel. 731 3533.

A new kind of string quartet that dresses like members of the *Star Trek* crew and plays only twentieth-century, preferably as late as possible in the twentieth-century, music. Based in San Francisco, the three men and one woman of Kronos travel year round, but you can catch them at home several times a year. Check the

music listings or call the Kronos office.

OAKLAND EAST BAY SYMPHONY
Calvin Simmons Theater, Oakland, tel. (510) 446 1992 or 547 5289.

Michael Morgan, one of the few black conductors of a US symphony, has mixed popular music such as spirituals with the orchestra's classical repertoire. The Oakland Symphony is a reliable, if not always exciting, company that has tried to define itself outside of San Francisco's very long shadow.

POCKET OPERA
Different venues, tel. 989 1855.

A refreshingly low-key approach to opera with professionals accompanied by a pianist (usually company founder and saint, Donald Pippin) on a mostly bare stage, using minimal props and costumes. The emphasis is on the pure joy of music. Programming is usually old favourites such as 'Cosi fan tutte' and 'The Bartered Bride', performed all around the Bay Area in churches, small auditoriums, even nightclubs. March to June.

SAN FRANCISCO OPERA
War Memorial Opera House, 301 Van Ness Ave, tel. 864 3330.

Opera on a grand scale with half a dozen major productions each season. In addition to great stars such as Placido Domingo, Kathleen Battle, Frederica von Stade and Luciano Pavarotti, productions feature rich scenery and costumes and first-rate support from its chorus and orchestra. Under director Lofti Mansouri the opera has put together an approach that balances tradition with new work. The audience is as entertaining as the singers, enthusiastically rewarding great singing with thundering applause and bravos, sitting on its collective hands for lesser work. Even after opening night, the opera is dress-up time, for men and women. If you aren't actually attending a performance you might want to just swing by and take in the crowd. September to May.

SAN FRANCISCO SYMPHONY
Davies Symphony Hall, Van Ness and Grove, tel. 431 5400.

The Symphony's luxurious hall has threatened to become more famous than the orchestra for its acoustical problems. Opened in 1981, the $33-million hall was condemned by musicians and critics as a disaster. A multi-million dollar reworking tried to correct the problems by 'squaring off' the round hall – some improvement but the grumbling continues. The orchestra, however, forges ahead. Scandinavian conductor Herbert Blomstedt will step down after 1994 and Michael Tilson Thomas will take over, the Symphony's first American conductor since 1900. A protégé of Leonard Bernstein, Tilson Thomas is expected to give the orchestra a more modern, American sound and look. September to June.

WOMEN'S PHILHARMONIC
Different venues, tel. 543 2297.

A professional orchestra of women musicians, dedicated to performing the work of women composers, the Women's Philharmonic is a critical and popular success. Under conductor Joann Faletta the orchestra has grown from a small, struggling group to a middle-sized orchestra winning regional and national attention. While critics cite the need for stronger musicianship among the players, anyone can enjoy a Women's Philharmonic performance. These are major women's events in the Bay Area and often take on the feel of a pep rally rather than a concert. October to May.

Theatre

San Francisco has been wild for theatre since its beginnings. 'San Francisco was full of actors,' recorded one Gold Rush visitor. He was astounded at the city's huge appetitie for entertainment, demanding more than just gambling houses and brothels. That excitement about the stage has continued unabated, producing one of the most interesting theatre cities in the US.

Two of America's best regional theatre companies are deeply rooted in the Bay Area. The American Conservatory Theater and Berkeley Repertory Theater combine classics, new work and revivals for a broad range of plays, many more daring than the commercial theatre of New York would produce. Smaller companies, such as the Asian American Theater Co., Theater Rhinoceros, the Magic Theater and the San Francisco Mime Troupe work more experimental veins.

The Bay Area has, or has had, black theatres, gay theatres, Asian theatres, Latino theatres, absurdist theatres and political theatres. Oddly there hasn't been a really well-known women's theatre. Women have, however, moved into the upper ranks of theatre fairly quickly. Both ACT and Berkeley Rep have women artistic directors and Carole Shorenstein Hayes, the theatrical producer who brings the Broadway hits to San Francisco has moved into producing for Broadway.

Unfortunately, there has been some involuntary restructuring of the theatre scene. The tight arts money of the last few years combined with lingering effects of the 1989 earthquake killed off some local companies, including the Eureka, the theatre that developed *Angels in America*, the most important American play of the last few years.

In the realm of pure entertainment, there's *Beach Blanket Babylon*, the longest-running musical revue in US history and touring Broadway shows (see p. 333). Other little revues and gimmick shows often pop up in the small stages around Union Square seeking tourists' entertainment bucks.

A wide spectrum of alternative theatre also exists in San Francisco, from zany comedy to drama (David Mamet and Jean Genet seem to be the favourite playwrights of tiny, underfunded SF companies) to interactive theatre. To take in the fringe productions, look through the alternative newspapers and the theatre listings in the *Chronicle*'s Sunday 'Pink Book', Josie's Juice Joint and the Marsh are prime spots for catching trends in the making and new performers.

Theatre is an affordable pleasure if you do a bit of checking around. Tickets for first-run and major houses can easily be $20–$45 for decent seats while alternative and store-front theatres charge as little as $3. Most theatres have some kind of discount and the half-price ticket booth in Union Square is always a source of good bargains.

AMERICAN CONSERVATORY
THEATER
30 Grant Ave, tel. 749 2200.

ACT, long the good grey lady of West Coast theatre, has taken on a more exciting, if not always successful, attitude since one-time classics scholar Carey Perloff became artistic director.

Perloff has introduced more classics, often with a hip-hop or post-modern approach, to the schedule but hasn't dumped crowd pleasers such as last season's *Pygmalion* and the lavish annual *Christmas Carol*. November to June.

ASIAN AMERICAN THEATER CO.
403 Arguello Blvd, tel. 751 2600.

The Asian came to life in the political ferment of the early seventies and has matured into a theatre company with a wide range. It has nurtured the better part of the new generation of Asian American playwrights and actors, including David Henry Hwang (*M. Butterfly*) and Philip Kan Gotanda (*The Wash*). Offerings include workshop productions and full productions of new and established plays.

BEACH BLANKET BABYLON
Club Fugazi, 687 Green St, tel. 421 4222.

Now beginning its third decade, this rock'n'roll cabaret show has become as familiar as the Golden Gate Bridge. And almost as beloved. Backed by a terrific rock band, an accomplished troupe of singers and dancers present everyone from Michael Jackson to President Clinton to Elvis. Lightly satirical with great singing and tap dancing. Year around.

BERKELEY REPERTORY THEATER
2025 Addison St (off Shattuck Avenue), Berkeley, tel. (510) 845 4700.

A typical Berkeley Rep season might include a Caryl Churchill play, *Volpone*, David Mamet, Ibsen and a work commissioned by the theatre from a new playwright. In many ways, Berkeley Rep delivers the most consistently satisfying theatre in the

Bay Area. The selection of works performed is very sophisticated, but artistic director Sharon Ott delivers a rich, textured package with marvellous sets and costuming, knock-out lighting and, of course, excellent acting. October to June.

CALIFORNIA SHAKESPEARE FESTIVAL
Bruns Amphitheater, Orinda, tel. (510) 548 9666.

Unlike some outdoor 'Shakespeare' festivals, this one is strictly Shakespeare – no guest playwrights at all. Relocated from a Berkeley park to a gorgeous new amphitheatre in a rural patch beyond the Oakland Hills, the California Shakespeare Festival is great fun. Four plays are done every summer, often with modern settings (*The Merchant of Venice* in fascist Italy). Access from San Francisco is by BART with a free shuttle to the amphitheatre. Bring along all your warm clothes, this little valley freezes after the sun goes down – even in July.

CLIMATE THEATER
252 Ninth St (off Folsom), tel. 626 9196.

This South of Market theater has become a kind of underground trademark as in, 'You wanna go see that new show? It's, like, a very Climate kind of piece'. Translated that means anything goes. You will be surprised. Disappointed sometimes, but definitely surprised. Climate bookings tend towards performance art and one-person shows.

JOSIE'S CABARET & JUICE JOINT
In the Castro, 3583 16th St, tel. 861 7933.

Carrot juice, beer, gay and lesbian singers, comedians, actors, singers.

ENTERTAINMENT

And some straight and sexually undeclared performers, too. A major stop for the very hip.

MAGIC THEATER
Building D in the Fort Mason Center, tel. 441 8001.

Once the West Coast stage for Sam Shepard, the Magic has been in a transition period for several seasons, trying to define its mission. Devoted to showcasing new plays and new playwrights, the theatre usually delivers at least one stunning production per season. November to June.

THE MARSH
In the Mission, 968 Valencia St, tel. 641 0235.

This scruffy storefront theatre proudly calls itself 'a breeding ground for new performance', a wonderfully apt description. Big on monologists – the long-winded storytellers who can be magical (Spalding Gray, Josh Kornbluth) or deadly boring.

SAN FRANCISCO MIME TROUPE
Performs at various venues, tel. 285 1717.

The Mime Troupe, which actually never shuts up talking, is the original and still champion American guerrilla theatre company. Founded in the 1960s, the Mime Troupe has been denouncing war, greed, cruelty, deceit and the evils of capitalism without a pause for more than 25 years. The company, a collective, writes and produces a play (usually with a song or two) about topical issues and tours it around Bay Area Parks all summer. Absolutely free, but a hat is passed, of course. Always a fun afternoon. May to October.

SAN FRANCISCO SHAKESPEARE FESTIVAL
Performs at various venues, tel. 666 2222.

During the late summer this festival performs one Shakespeare play in Golden Gate Park during weekends, moving to Oakland and San José parks before Labor Day. Usually a comedy or romance, the professional company gives the play a broad spin but without damage. Free but donations gratefully accepted. July to September.

THEATER RHINOCEROS
In the Mission, 2626 16th St, tel. 861 5079.

A gay-oriented, professional theatre that performs mainstream works (*Boys in the Band*, *Bent*) and seeks out and stages new works by gay and lesbian playwrights. Often the new stuff features attractive young people in their underwear, but every theatre needs to have a broad range.

Comedy

Who killed comedy? One day it was among North America's fifteen largest growth industries, the next day you can't find a comedy club. San Francisco's yeasty comedy circuit bred and nurtured a number of major comedians, including Robin Williams, Paula Poundstone, Dana Carvey and Whoopi Goldberg. The comedy business has slowed down considerably over the last few years, but the city still supports a couple of all-comedy clubs. The annual Comedy

Competition is a major career-booster for US comedians and closely followed by Hollywood.

Women have leapt into stand-up in a big way; it's rare to find a comedy bill without at least one woman. Some music clubs have comedy nights, but there are two full-time comedy clubs left in San Francisco.

COBB'S
In The Cannery, 2801 Leavenworth St, tel. 928 4320.

National comedy headliners, full bar.

PUNCH LINE SAN FRANCISCO
In the Financial District, 444 Battery St, tel. 397 7573.

Big name comedians along with local showcases.

Dance

Isadora Duncan left San Francisco early in the century, annoyed that the provincial Californians weren't more sympathetic to her art. She has since been fervently reclaimed as a native daughter and icon by the Bay Area dance community. It's easy to think that Duncan wouldn't mind and would, in fact, feel very at home around San Francisco these days.

San Francisco ranks only behind New York as America's dance capital. Classical ballet, feminist satire, contact improvisation, modern dance, Indian kathak, African dance-drumming and American Indian tribal dancing are just the beginning of types and schools of dance to be found in San Francisco.

The dance season is roughly divided into two major waves, autumn and spring, with the Christmastime *Nutcrackers* constituting a season unto themselves and a boomlet of contemporary dance performances and festivals in the summer. The San Francisco Ballet, the biggest dance company in San Francisco (or California for that matter), dominates the spring while the smaller, scruffier Oakland Ballet performs in the autumn. The modern dance companies don't have clearly defined seasons and pop up all year round. Watch newspaper listings and South of Market telephone poles for word of their performances.

Tickets range from $70 for an opening night, prime seat at the San Francisco Ballet to $8 and 'whatever you can afford' at alternative venues in the Mission and South of Market.

BAY AREA DANCE SERIES
Laney College Theater, 900 Fallon St (across from the Oakland Museum), Oakland, tel. (510) 464 3540.

The new and different gestate at this yearly festival which runs January through May. A hit-or-miss affair that dips into the current crop of local modern and ethnic dance groups, the festival is prime window on the ideas flowing through the dance world. Two names to look for are the

ENTERTAINMENT

feminist Dance Brigade company which has spoofs of *The Nutcracker* and *Cinderella*, and Terry Sendgraff's Motivity group famous for its members (all women) dancing on trapezes, stilts and bungi cords.

CAL PERFORMANCES
Zellerbach Hall, University of California campus, Berkeley, tel. (510) 642 9988.

Cal Performances is the entertainment branch of UC, bringing in first-rate artists to campus. The dance selections are very strong, very impressive. Twyla Tharp, Merce Cunningham and Les Ballets Africains are a sampling of the schedule. As an extra bonus, Zellerbach is an exceptional theatre for dance, with perfect sightlines and state-of-the-art technical equipment.

OAKLAND BALLET
Paramount Theater, 2025 Broadway, Oakland, tel. (510) 465 6400.

Undeniably the poor cousin of the San Francisco Ballet, the Oakland Ballet doesn't wilt under the SFB's big shadow. National critics have followed the Oakland Ballet closely, intrigued by artistic director Ronn Guidi's imaginative use of dancers who come in various shapes and sizes – an incredible breech of ballet orthodoxy. Guidi's choreography can be lugubrious, but the company has made a brilliant career of reconstructions of ballets by Bronislava Nijinska (Nijinsky's sister) and Leonid Massine, many of which were originally created for Serge Diaghilev's Ballets Russes de Monte Carlo. The company's signature piece is Eugene Loring's *Billy the Kid*, primecut Americana delivered blood rare. From October to February.

SAN FRANCISCO BALLET
San Francisco War Memorial Opera House, 301 Van Ness Ave, tel. 776 1999.

Ever since Helgi Tomasson, a precision classicist from the New York City Ballet, took over this company in 1986, it has risen steadily in the pantheon of American ballet companies. Some say SFB now rivals the best New York troupes for the quality of its dancing, if not the depth of its repertoire. Predictably, son-of-Iceland Tomasson's choreography tends to be on the chilly side, but the company's guest choreographers redress the balance. The Frankfurt Ballet's dynamic William Forsythe and wunderkind Mark Morris have been particularly memorable. If performance tickets are sold out, as happens frequently, join the students and poverty-level balletomanes lining up for standing room tickets, sold an hour before curtain time. SFB's *Nutcracker* is among the world's best, which is fitting as the company retrieved it from oblivion in the 1940s and made it into a modern classic. The Opera House is scheduled to shut down for seismic work in 1996–97. An alternative venue hasn't yet been announced.

SAN FRANCISCO ETHNIC DANCE FESTIVAL
Palace of Fine Arts, Lyon and Bay streets, tel. 474 3914.

Founded in 1978 before the word 'multicultural' broke the surface, this June festival is a smorgasbord of cultures. A typical evening might feature dances from Ghana, Spain, Ireland, Palestine and even Serbia. Most of the dancers are local amateurs, but that's not a problem. This is a quintessential San Francisco event.

SAN FRANCISCO PERFORMANCES
Cowel Theater, Fort Mason Center,
tel. 392 4400 or 398 6449.

Known for its classical music
performances, this long-time series
has recently added a modern dance
segment. This is the place to see
excellent touring performers such as
the Pilobulus dance company or the
Indonesian choreographer Sardono.

THEATER ARTAUD
450 Florida St (at 17th St),
tel. 621 7797.

In a black box theatre named for
French theorist Antonin Artaud, you
can see some of the more
technologically sophisticated work in
the Bay Area, replete with multi-
image projections and, if it's your
lucky night, a robot. Look out for the
national Black Choreographers
Moving Festival (usually in March)
and the young dancers' Summertime
Dance Festival.

YERBA BUENA CENTER FOR THE
ARTS
Mission and Third streets,
tel. 978 2787.

Multiculturalism is the key word at
the city's newest temple to the arts.
The theatre is well-appointed, flexible
and seemingly headed for a career as a
major dance venue after its late 1993
opening.

848 PERFORMANCE SPACE
848 Divisadero St, tel. 885 2003.

Don't expect to find big puffy stories
in the newspapers about 848
performances. Don't even try and find
listings. This impromptu community
performing arts room is so happening
that nobody can predict when or how
the next performance will be. Call the
taped message for info. Not for the
timid, 848 hosts performance art with
themes that push the boundaries of
aesthetics and/or decorum.

Dance Groups to Look Out For

Not all dance companies can afford to maintain a permanent
studio-auditorium or launch a formal season. Check the newspaper
listings for these companies or call their information lines.

Margaret Jenkins Dance Company (tel. 863 1173) has been a
modern dance pacesetter for two decades. ODC/San Francisco (tel.
863 6606) is another established company that is always worth
watching. The Joe Goode Performance Group (tel. 648 4848) and
Contraband (tel. 558 8821) are two of the younger dance companies with avant-garde outlooks. The Dance Brigade, an all-women's
feminist company, has worked at making dance a non-sexist, politically expressive medium, so far with erratic results (tel. 510/652 0752).

Film

San Francisco is a movie-friendly place with hundreds of movie
houses spread all over the city, Marin, the East Bay and the
Peninsula. Happily there are serious movie theatres still in business
in the Bay Area; every big theatre hasn't been reduced to mini-
screeningrooms nor are new theatres all cineplexes.

First-run films are usually $7, but matinees and other off-peak hours can reduce the ticket price. Because the city is considered so sympathetic to offbeat films, many new movies get early openings in San Francisco with the producers hoping that a successful run in the city will boost their chances for a wider success. Check the local newspapers for daily listings and reviews. The weekly papers are very devoted to films, too, running many features and reviews in addition to detailed listings. The Bay Area has several notable revival and art theatres which have close ties to local filmmakers, who range from teenagers with handheld videocameras to major industry players (George Lucas, Francis Ford Coppola) who choose to live far away from Hollywood.

Women's films, including new work by women filmmakers, historic retrospectives and avant-garde films, are a significant part of the cinema offerings locally.

Festivals

San Francisco's film community (makers and fans) support several film festivals. The San Francisco Film Festival, held every April, is the oldest in North America and one of the most respected. It is audience rather than industry oriented and has inevitably launched a few overlooked jewels; *She's Gotta Have It*, *The Baghdad Café* and *Stop Making Sense* all opened at this festival.

The San Francisco International Lesbian and Gay Film Festival (June) is the world's largest gay-themed film festival. The Jewish Film Festival (July), based on Berkeley, and the Mill Valley Film Festival (October) in Marin, are also well known, attracting important films and major filmmakers.

Resources, Revival Houses

CASTRO THEATER
Castro and Market streets,
tel. 621 6120.

The luxury liner of movie palaces; how movies were meant to be seen. Programming leans towards classics and gay films.

FILM ARTS FOUNDATION
346 Ninth St, tel. 552 3456.

Film screenings, conferences, classes, information about the local film and video scene.

PACIFIC FILM ARCHIVE
A department of University Art Museum, 2621 Durant Ave, Berkeley, tel. (510) 642 1124.

With its more scholarly approach PFA shows more obscure stuff than the other revival houses along with ambitious projects (The Complete Works of Michelangelo Antonioni).

RED VIC MOVIE HOUSE
1728 Haight St, tel. 668 3994.

Eclectic programming of classics, new Asian animation, old faves. The audience sits on couches, chairs in the small, friendly theatre.

ROXIE CINEMA
In the Mission, 3117 16th St,
tel. 863 1087.

Heavy emphasis on political, Third
World and feminist films.

UC THEATER
East Bay commercial theatre,
2036 University Ave, Berkeley,
tel. (510) 834 6267.

Home of the most famous 'Rocky
Horror' Saturday night tradition in
the US – a live show at midnight for
the last eighteen years. Asian films,
imaginative double features and
classics on the big screen.

SPORTS
Spectator sports are a prime American pastime and a major diversion in the Bay Area where there are two professional baseball
teams, a pro football team and a pro basketball team as well as college sports, travelling tournaments and annual events such as the
September rodeo and horse show at the Cow Palace just south of
the city limits in Daly City. Even for the avowed non-fans, a visit to
a stadium is a wonderful bit of American life, easily enjoyed. Be
aware that Candlestick Park, the bayside stadium home for the San
Francisco Giants (baseball) and San Francisco Forty-Niners (football) is a freeze zone, winter and summer. Always take several layers
of clothing.

Spectator Sports

BAY MEADOWS RACECOURSE
Highway 101, San Mateo,
tel. 574 7223.

South of San Francisco, near the
airport, Bay Meadows hosts
thoroughbred horseracing. The track
has a steady schedule of events to lure
fans during the season,
September–January.

GOLDEN GATE FIELDS
East Bay, US Highway 80, Albany,
tel. (510) 526 3020.

This racetrack opens its season when
Bay Meadows closes, running
January–June. Neither track is a big
deal on the racing circuit (both are flat
racing), but the afternoon races are a
pleasant getaway. The track is beside
the bay, near Berkeley.

GOLDEN STATE WARRIORS
Oakland Stadium Arena, 66th Avenue
and Hegenberger Road, Oakland,
tel. (510) 638 6300.

The basketball team, claimed by both
San Francisco and Oakland, hasn't
had a championship season in years,
but the fans are not discouraged.
Many come to the games to see the
other teams. Easy to get to on BART,
but tickets ($15–$45) can be hard to
come by.

OAKLAND ATHLETICS
Oakland Coliseum, Oakland,
tel. (510) 638 0500.

The A's play in a sunny, comfortable

stadium easily accessible by BART which makes an A's game an easy day's outing from San Francisco. Most American visitors to Oakland games are amazed by the food counters where fans order pizza, yogurt and even sushi. It's quite a change from the industrial hot dogs of most baseball parks. Tickets are $6–$20; the season is April–October.

SAN FRANCISCO FORTY-NINERS
Candlestick Park, Bayshore Freeway, tel. (510) 762-BASS.

Football games, because there are fewer of them in a season than basketball and baseball, are tougher to get tickets for, especially if the 'Niners are having a good season. Single tickets are $18–$40, available through BASS tickets. The season is August–January.

SAN FRANCISCO GIANTS
Candlestick Park, Bayshore Freeway, tel. 467 8000.

The baseball season is April–October. Tickets range from $5 to $18 a game. You will never have a problem getting into a weekday daytime game. Take a stadium express bus to Candlestick; call Muni, 673 6864.

Participation

Golf

GOLDEN GATE PARK GOLF COURSE
Golden Gate Park, west end near the Great Highway, tel. 751 8987.

This nine-hole course is a good workout in the midst of a great park. Small greens fee, no reservation necessary.

LINCOLN PARK GOLF COURSE
Clement and 34th Ave, tel. 221 9911.

One of the most beautiful views of San Francisco accompanies a game on this public eighteen-hole course. The Palace of the Legion of Honor art museum shares the park, which is situated on a dramatic cliff over the bay, west of Golden Gate bridge. Call for reservations; green fees are $17–$21.

MISSION BAY GOLF CENTER
South of Market, 1200 6th St, tel. 431 7888.

Close to downtown in the desolate reaches of South of Market, this popular golf centre has a two-tier driving range, putting greens, lessons and the St Andrew Café, a discreet singles spot.

Horseback Riding

GOLDEN GATE PARK STABLES
Golden Gate Park, off John F. Kennedy Drive, tel. 668 7360.

Deep in the centre of Golden Gate Park, the stables offer trail rides and lessons.

MIWOK LIVERY
End of Tennessee Valley Road, off US 101, outside of Sausalito, tel. 383 8048.

Stable manager Linda Rubio leads rides through the Marin Headlands. It's sightseeing instead of a serious riding workout, but quite fun and Rubio has unusually good stable horses.

Inline Skating

It may be all over by the time you read this, but for the last few years an informal Friday Night Skate through the city has drawn dozens of inland skaters who roar up and down hills, leap out of the way of traffic and in general take over the streets. It's a 12.5-mile ride, beginning precisely at 8.30 p.m. from the Ferry Building on the Embarcadero, looping along the waterfront, up through Pacific Heights, around Chinatown, Union Square and back to the Ferry Building. The crowd is mostly in their twenties (surprise) and strong on stamina. There are more men than women, but it's not a male bonding thing. You must be able to skate, of course, and helmets and pads are required.

Running and Hiking

Golden Gate Park's miles of trails and the Golden Gate Promenade along the waterfront are favourites for local runners. If you're running alone, stick to populated, open areas such as the main roads in Golden Gate Park.

San Francisco Frontrunners (tel. 206 9312) is a group of gay men and lesbians who run together in Golden Gate Park every day. You don't have to be gay to tag along.

Hikers looking for group and/or guided treks have a myriad of choices. The Sierra Club has dozens of hikes going on every week, all over the Bay Area. The best way to find out about the outings, which are handled by club volunteers rather than the high-powered, eco-warrior chapter office, is to drop by the Sierra Club Bookstore and pick up a current copy of *The Yodeler*, the monthly newspaper. The bookstore is in the Civic Center area, 730 Polk St, between Eddy and Ellis, tel. 923 5600.

Other good sources for hiking are the San Francisco Audubon Society, tel. (510) 843 2222; Friends of Recreation and Parks at Golden Gate Park, tel. 221 1310 and the Golden Gate National Recreation Area (Fort Point, Land's End, Marin Headlands, Point Reyes), tel. 556 0560.

SHOPPING

San Francisco likes to shop. Not loves to shop, likes it. And, as with everything else, the locals want to be amused which means you will find a high degree of whimsy in the items on hand and decorator excess in almost every retail establishment, from department stores to kitchen shops.

Dylan Thomas, during his disastrous, drunken tour of the US in 1957, took time from his carousing in San Francisco to write home to his wife Caitlin, answering her questions about the shops. They are 'full of everything you have ever heard of and also full of everything one has never heard of or seen,' Thomas told her, promising her a great time when they visited San Francisco together.

The Thomases never got to San Francisco, but the poet's assessment of the shopping possibilities is still correct. In addition to the overflowing department stores around Union Square, you will find interesting and even useful shops all over the city. Union Square is the heart of the shopping district and lobbies hard to keep tourists and locals interested and buying with promotions, festivals, in-store decorations and when all else fails, sales.

The Embarcadero Center near the bay and San Francisco Shopping Center on Market Street are two other major downtown concentrations of shops. In the neighbourhoods, Union Street, at the edge of Pacific Heights, is a favourite shopping district with pricey little shops that range from greeting cards to estate jewellery to handmade furniture to clothing. Sacramento Street and the Upper Fillmore are other critical mass areas of the new and different.

Whole Earth Access is perhaps the Bay Area's most original store. It began as a counterculture collective selling items needed for the hippie household and has grown into a regional chain stocking everything from wood-burning stoves to stylish jeans to computers. Whole Earth retains its sixties sensibility (though it is no longer a collective).

Bargains don't come first with San Francisco, a city full of people living on minimum wage jobs who will only drink gourmet coffee and wear natural fibre clothes. Quality and style are more compelling to most shoppers than price. You will, however, find a good range of prices and types of goods. The secondhand stores, both the commercial shops and the places run by volunteers to benefit charities, for instance, are fun and a good value.

Look through the daily papers, especially the Sunday editions, for sales and special deals. The Wednesday Home sections of the *Examiner* and *Chronicle* frequently run stories about new shops and have periodic 'reviews' of shopping areas.

Department Stores

Some visitors have been known to disappear into the big department stores around Union Square and only emerge in time to catch the flight home. These stores, as you would expect, are big, stuffed with zillions of consumer goods and attractive. Being at the centre of a sophisticated shopping world keeps the big stores on their toes as well. They compete with the specialised, designer stores through bigger selection and sales and try to lure mall habitues into the city with more interesting goods and, again, good prices. For out-of-towners, the stores are very good about shipping your purchases home. Not a cheap service, but for those who can afford it, a great simplifier.

EMPORIUM CAPWELL
815 Market St (at 5th Street),
tel. 764 2222.

The grand old lady of San Francisco department stores, the emporium is laid out in the traditional big store design. Experienced shoppers love the basement where bargains often pop up among the slightly damaged and massively marked-down goods. The typical range of department store items, with a smaller upscale range. Look for sales.

I. MAGNIN
Union Square, tel. 362 2100.

One of San Francisco's oldest businesses, dating from 1876, Magnin's is best known for its women's clothes, with all the big-name designers. You'll also find shoes, scarves, cosmetics and some jewellery. If you have serious bucks to spend, ask for one of the store's personal shoppers to help you edit down the choices. Magnin's has men's and children's sections as well as small selections of china, decorative items and gifts.

MACY'S
Union Square, tel. 397 3333.

Department store heaven, the store is the largest in the city with a medium to enormous selection of almost everything. The cosmetics section on the ground floor is a world unto itself and Macy's Cellar, the food hall in the basement, is another highlight. Macy's East, a separate building, is a temple to men's fashion. Children's clothes are at the East store, too, in every price and style range.

NEIMAN MARCUS
Union Square, tel. 362 3900.

'Neiman' is like a frivolous debutante you can't help but like – it elevates shallowness to art. The Texas-based chain makes no apologies for its high-profile, high-style approach. If you want to buy something cheaper and dowdier, that's your business. If you want to have some fun with your money, well then, that's Neiman's business. The Rotunda Café is a favourite lunch place of ladies who make a career of lunching.

NORDSTROM
In the San Francisco Center, 865 Market St, tel. 753 1344.

Fairly new to San Francisco, this Seattle-based chain is renowned for its helpful sales clerks and the customer is *always* right philosophy. Not as quick to mark down as Macy's or

Emporium, Nordstrom has a superb inventory of men's, women's and children's clothes. The shoe selection is the best in the city.

SAKS FIFTH AVENUE
Union Square, tel. 986 4100.

Not as flashy as Neiman, not as old money as Magnin, Saks has a kind of New York single-mindedness. Whatever is the big fashion news, it's all over the store, in every colour. Heavy European influence in the designer labels.

SAN FRANCISCO SHOPPING CENTER
865 Market St (at 5th Street).

Anchored by Nordstrom, the San Francisco Center is a downtown shopping mall. The circular escalator that takes shoppers up through the nine-storey atrium is the only one in the US. The centre provides easy access to Nordstrom, the Emporium, the Powell Street BART station and more than a hundred shops.

DISCOUNT SHOPPING

Over the last decade or so, San Francisco has developed a thriving discount-warehouse shopping area South of Market. Clothing, primarily women's, is the staple but children's clothes, men's clothes, toys, household items, shoes and even appliances can be found here. Bargains undeniably abound, but the problem is getting to them. The stores are spread all over the sprawling South of Market area, to the Mission and Potrero Hill. Consider how much of a time investment you want to make in searching out the bargains. Sally Socolich's *Bargain Hunting in the Bay Area* is an indispensable guide to the semi-hidden stores. Shopping tours are an ideal way to shop until you drop. For a quick visit to discount land, there's the Six-Sixty Center, 660 3rd St, off Townsend. A former auction house showroom/warehouse, Six-Sixty houses several floors of shops, ranging from sweaters to shoes to dresses. If this doesn't exhaust you, then you're ready to do some serious discount shopping.

STONESTOWN GALLERIA
In the Sunset (19th Avenue and Winston Drive)

San Francisco has escaped the malling

that has taken over most American cities and killed the downtown shopping areas, but it does have Stonestown, an enormous, two-level mall with dozens of shops, including the Emporium, Nordstrom, the Pottery Barn and Gap Kids.

WHOLE EARTH ACCESS
In the Bayview district, 401 Bayshore Blvd (off Highway 101), tel. 285 5244. Other branches in Berkeley, Concord, San Mateo, San José and San Rafael.

The sixties' generation's nineties' department store. Beginning as a no-frills collective in Berkeley in the early 1970s, Whole Earth has evolved into a natural fibre-green consciousness-computer-California kitchen cuisine empire. The stores are still unadorned warehouse, but the goods range from basic jeans and flannel shirts to German coffeemakers to top-of-the-line electronics and elaborate gardening tools. The Berkeley store (tel. 510/845 3000) is the largest, but all the Whole Earths are an interesting cultural window.

Second-Hand Clothing

Second-hand stores are plentiful and varied in San Francisco. Period and vintage clothes were a big deal a few years ago, but the interest in them has waned, leaving only a few shops that specialise in fashions from other eras.

AARDVARK'S ODD ARK
1501 Haight St, tel. 621 3141.

Reproductions and vintage clothes at reasonable prices. The staff can hardly be bothered with the customers so forge ahead on your own.

BUFFALO EXCHANGE
1555 Haight St, tel. 431 7731.

Leather jackets, jeans – everything for the young and the hip.

CATHEDRAL SCHOOL SHOP
Nob Hill, 1036 Hyde St, tel. 776 6630.

An old-line ladies' guild kind of place, the shop supports Grace Cathedral's boys' school. Very good for quality children's clothes (girls and boys).

FELINO'S VINTAGE CLOTHING
In the Mission, 3162 16th St, tel. 863 5706.

A favourite of local nostalgia buffs who say the forties', fifties' and sixties' men's and women's clothes are in great shape and have the city's best prices.

LOVE PROJECT
766 Geary St, tel. 928 3773.

Run by old hippies, the shop carries almost everything, from clothes to houseware. The quality changes week to week, but the prices are low and bargaining is expected and good-natured.

REPEAT PERFORMANCE
In Pacific Heights, 2223 Fillmore St, tel. 563 3123.

A project of San Francisco Symphony supporters, this is the place to find previously owned designer dresses and the occasional fur coat.

SPELLBOUND
1670 Haight St, tel. 863 4930.

The best vintage clothing shop in the city with pieces dating back to the 1890s.

THE THIRD HAND
*In Lower Pacific Heights, 1839
Divisadero, tel. 567 7332.*

The oldest vintage clothing store in California, Third Hand has fashions from the last century for sale or rent. This is said to be Catherine Deneuve's favourite shop in all of San Francisco.

Miscellaneous Apparel

GROGER'S WESTERN STORE
1445 Valencia, tel. 647 0700.

Cowboy boots, fringe jackets, Western-tailored clothing, bolo ties, turquoise jewellery and more.

NORTH BEACH LEATHER
190 Geary St, tel. 362 8300 and 1365 Columbus Ave, tel. 441 32308.

Another old hippie business that flourished in spite of itself. Designer leather from fringe jackets to mini-skirts and accessories.

STORMY LEATHER
1158 Howard St, tel. 626 1672.

Not to be confused with North Beach Leather, Stormy's isn't for the faint of heart. S&M and bondage equipment, toys and, ah, fashions are on sale here, either off the shelf or made to order. Owned and staffed by women, the Stormy Leather philosophy is that sex play is normal, healthy and open to women.

VICTORIA'S SECRET
395 Sutter St, tel. 397 0521 and 2245 Union St, tel. 921 5444.

San Francisco's gift to the world, the popularisation of sexy lingerie.

Designer Clothing

New York and European designers are closely followed by the San Francisco fashion cognoscenti. A few designers have their own shops or shops within a larger store, but the largest and most varied top-of-the-line fashions are found in the designer sections in Magnin, Saks and Neiman Marcus.

ADRIENNE VITTADINI
865 Market St, tel. 777 3440.

Sportswear, evening clothes, accessories for the woman sleek enough to wear Vittadini.

CHANEL BOUTIQUE
155 Maiden Lane, tel. 981 1550.

Three floors of Chanel. The air is very rarefied here.

EMPORIO ARMANI
1 Grant Ave, tel. 677 9010.

Whoopi Goldberg loves to buy men's suits here and accessorise them with African fabrics. Expensive, of course, but if you can't afford the clothes, have an espresso at the Armani café.

JEANNE-MARC
262 Sutter St, tel. 362 1121.

The SF husband-and-wife team of Jeanne Allen and Marc Grant produces women's clothes in bold colours and classic lines.

JESSICA MCCLINTOCK
353 Sutter St, tel. 397 0987.

Perhaps San Francisco's best-known designer, McClintock's clothes are unabashedly feminine, with an Edwardian sensibility.

LAISE ADZER
160 Stockton St, tel. 981 3505.

Gauzy, romantic clothes inspired by Adzer's life in Morocco.

NICOLE MILLER BOUTIQUE
50 Post St, tel. 398 3111.

Miller is one of the wittiest designers around. Her scarves are prized for their thematic humour. Day and evening wear.

OBIKO
794 Sutter St, tel. 775 2882.

Clothing and jewellery from dozens of different designers, many of them as yet unknown. Artwear and ethnic designs are a large part of the offerings here. The store is tiny but welcoming.

WILKES BASHFORD
375 Sutter St, tel. 986 4380.

Best known as a men's clothing empire, Bashford (a famous man-about-SF) also carries women's fashions. The sales staff are legendary snobs so don't feel you are being singled out for icy treatment.

Other Women's Clothing

Beyond designer clothing there are many interesting shopping choices, including specialities such as maternity wear and large sizes.

BANANA REPUBLIC
256 Grant Ave, tel. 788 3087.

Founded by two burned-out San Francisco journalists, Banana Republic is now an international boutique with its natural fibre, stylish clothes for the disco or the bush.

ESPRIT FACTORY OUTLET
499 Illinois Ave, tel. 957 2550.

This factory outlet is a major tourist stop in itself. Esprit's comfortable, colourful clothes are here in children's and adult sizes. The markdowns aren't terrific, but the shopping experience is fun.

THE FORGOTTEN WOMAN
550 Sutter St, tel. 788 1452.

Large sizes, from lingerie to rainwear to business suites – many designer labels, no polyester tents.

JAPANESE WEEKEND
Wo Boutique, 864 Post St, tel. 775 1529.

Maternity clothes designed and manufactured in San Francisco. All natural fibre in attractive styles with (most important) comfortable cotton waistbands.

WOMEN'S CLOTHING

LIZ CLAIBORNE
Embarcadero 4 Center, tel. 788 5041.

A new store devoted exclusively to the clothing and accessories of one of America's most popular designers of women's wear.

MAC
812 Post St, tel. 775 2515.

New designers and clothing lines you have never heard of are brilliantly showcased here at 'Modern Appealing Clothing' which is famous for spotting the coming looks.

POLO/RALPH LAUREN
90 Post St, tel. 567 7656.

The Ralph Lauren look, from sweetheart of the rodeo to debutante wannabe, in all available sizes and colours.

ROLO
1301 Howard St, tel. 861 1999.

Rolo has several stores but this South of Market location is seeing the hip-hop, boho, new barbarian styles in their natural eco-zone.

SAN FRANCISCO PENDLETON
464 Sutter St, tel. 788 6383.

Classic Sportswear from the famous Oregon house of (plaid) style.

Shoes

Among the department stores, Macy's and Nordstrom have the largest and most varied shoe departments.

BALLY OF SWITZERLAND
238 Stockton St, tel. 398 7463.

Elegant and comfortable shoes – very expensive.

BIG 5
2159 Chesnut St, tel. 474 8670.

Enormous selection of athletic shoes at very good prices.

BIRKENSTOCK NATURAL FOOTWEAR
1815 Polk St, tel. 776 5225.

The official shoe of Northern California.

JOAN & DAVID
172 Geary St, tel. 397 1985.

The first Joan & David boutique for their young, perky shoes.

KENNETH COLE
2078 Union St, tel. 346 2161.

Beautiful shoes in sleek movie-set shop.

McB'S SHOES FOR WOMEN
715 Market St, tel. 957 9988.

Specialising in hard-to-find sizes from tiny to huge.

TAMING OF THE SHOE
2637 Mission St, tel. 282 2900.

Where do those boho types get those wild shoes? Look no further.

THE WALK SHOP
2120 Vine St, Berkeley, tel. (510) 849 3628.

A wide-ranging stock of shoes from sturdy hiking shoes to evening slippers, all selected for their comfort.

WILD WILD WEST
2193 Market St, tel. 626 1700.

This amusing Castro recreation of the Old West has the biggest selection of Western-style boots in the city.

Luggage and Bags

THE COACH STORE
164 Grant Ave, tel. 392 1772.

Classic handbags, wallets, briefcases.

GLASER DESIGNS
32 Otis St, tel. 552 3188.

Handmade leather pieces that are renowned among travellers for their thoughtful construction and durability.

HERMES
212 Stockton St, tel. 391 7200.

A medium-sized Hermes boutique.

LOUIS VUITTON
317 Sutter St, tel. 391 6200.

Trunks, suitcases, bags for any purpose from the stylish French craftsman.

LUGGAGE CENTER
828 Mission St, tel. 543 3771.

A clearance centre for first-class and budget luggage where savings can be as much as 50 per cent.

MALM LUGGAGE
222 Grant Ave, tel. 392 0417.

In San Francisco for more than a hundred years, carries designer lines and some less expensive bags.

MARK CROSS
170 Post St, tel. 391 7770.

Handbags, suitcases, address books, attaché cases, etc. with all the traditional Cross craftsmanship.

Jewellery

Many of the street vendors around Union Square and on Telegraph Avenue in Berkeley have interesting and inexpensive handmade jewellery. Be suspicious of anything pricey and don't be shy about bargaining. Downtown San Francisco is home to a number of very grand jewellery and gem establishments.

GUMP'S
250 Post St, tel. 982 1616.

A revered San Francisco institution since 1865, especially noted for its fine jade pieces.

JEST JEWELS
2049 Union St, tel. 563 8839.

An entertaining shop full of cheeky imposters.

LAUREL'S
258 Chesnut St, tel. 441 5952.

This sweet little shop is crammed with previously owned treasures including some nice estate jewellery at reasonable prices.

OLD AND NEW ESTATES
2181–A Union St, tel. 346 7525.

Estate jewellery is the face-saving name for sold-off family pieces. Old and New deals in vintage watches, wedding rings, fine old bracelets, necklaces, earrings and some art objects.

SHREVE AND CO.
200 Post St, tel. 421 6500.

Another SF grand old party, dating from 1852. Very expensive, traditional jewellery.

SIDNEY MOBELL FINE JEWELLERY
141 Post St, tel. 986 4747.

A favourite for engagement and wedding rings among the locals, wealthy and trying to be.

TIFFANY AND CO.
252 Grant Ave, tel. 781 7000.

A branch of the renowned New York jeweller.

WASTELAND
1660 Haight St, tel. 863 3150.

Among the second-hand clothes, used furniture and clouds of incense you will find masses of old costume jewellery that will thrill the collector and bore everyone else to tears.

TOM WING AND SONS
190 Post St, tel. 391 2500.

Where San Franciscans buy their pearls. Wing's jade is very fine, too.

Cosmetics

Any drugstore or supermarket has a substantial selection of inexpensive cosmetics and the department stores have over-designed counters for every upscale line. There are also some shops and lines worth looking for.

BENEFIT
2219 Chesnut St, tel. 567 1173 and 2117 Fillmore St, tel. 567 0242.

Locally made cosmetics by a team of identical twins, Jean Ford Danielson and Jane Ford Blackford. Ex-models, the sisters developed their own line of cosmetics, sold in their three shops (two in SF, one in Marin) as well as I. Magnin. Their products have ditzy names such as Boo Boo Zap for blemish coverup, Lemon-Aid for eyelid colour corrective and lipsticks called 'But Officer!' and 'Book 'Em', but come in no-nonsense packaging and at below most designer cream prices. The shops also offer treatments such as facials.

ESTÉE LAUDER SPA
In I. Magnin, Union Square, tel. 765 8046.

Pick up Estée Lauder creams and cosmetics or have the specialists give you a facial, put on your makeup or other beauty rituals.

LANCOME
In Macy's, Union Square,
tel. 296 4242.

The Lancome beauty specialists will
sell you their products or give you the
full salon treatment.

NEW YORK COSMETICS AND
FRAGRANCES
318 Brannan St, tel. 543 3880.

A clearance centre where lipsticks,
eyeshadow, nail polish, blusher and
foundation are not labelled (by brand
names) and sold at big discounts.

PERFUMANIA
125 Ellis St, tel. 981 8590.

A perfume outlet where you will find
gift packages and discontinued lines at
big discounts.

Bookstores

San Francisco is a booklover's paradise. There are bookstores of
every type and variety from the neighbourhood gathering spot to
gay bookstores, black bookstores, architectural bookstores, Asian
bookstores, scholarly bookstores and much, much more.

ALEXANDER BOOK COMPANY
Downtown, 50 2nd St, tel. 495 2992.

Handsome new downtown bookstore
with a wide selection of books. Strong
children's department.

A CLEAN WELL-LIGHTED PLACE
FOR BOOKS
*Civic Center, in Opera Plaza, 601
Van Ness Ave, tel. 441 6670.*

Well-organised and sophisticated,
covering all the major and many
minor categories. Author readings
here and at the Marin store.

BLACK OAK BOOKS
*East Bay, 1491 Shattuck Ave,
Berkeley, tel. (510) 486 0698.*

One of the great bookstores, mixing
bestsellers, scholarly work, used
books, art books in a big, well-
designed store. Probably the best
reading series in the Bay Area.

CITY LIGHTS BOOKSTORE
*North Beach, 261 Columbus Ave,
tel. 362 8193.*

The great, good companion to
Ginsberg, Kerouac and the other Beats
(see p. 115). A varied, interesting stock,
very good for contemporary poetry.

LITERARY LIFE

The Bay Area is one of the top book markets in the US, supporting more bookstores
per capita than any place in the country. And the devotion to books doesn't end with
buying them. All over San Francisco, Marin, Berkeley, Oakland and the Peninsula there
are book clubs, literary circles and library reading groups where writing is discussed,
debated and savoured. Author readings and poetry slams are tremendously popular.

The Bay Area has a long history of excitement over the written word, from the
nineteenth-century salons of Ina Coolbrith (see p. 130) and Gertrude Atherton (see
p. 152) to the jazz and poetry readings of the Beats. While author appearances had
always been a staple in local bookstores, the idea took off in the early eighties when

Black Oak Books in Berkeley began promoting readings as major entertainment events. A popular subscription series in San Francisco, City Arts and Lectures organised about the same time, regularly selling out hundreds of seats in Herbst Auditorium with writers such as Salman Rushdie, Truman Capote, Alice Walker, Doris Lessing and newer, rising stars.

Bookstore readings draw touring writers promoting new books, but the huge pool of local writers is regularly tapped. Women writers attract huge crowds. In addition to the big stars like Alice Walker, Amy Tan, Jessica Mitford and Isabel Allende, Bharati Mukherjee, Sheila Ballantyne, Diane Johnson, Terry McMillan, Susan Griffith, Maxine Hong Kingston, Paule Marshall and Dorothy Allison may be seen on a fairly regular basis at local readings.

An entirely new scene has evolved in the nineties, the 'spoken word' performances of poets and writers, usually in clubs and coffee houses (see below). Annoyed at comparisons with the Beats ('It's like asking the organisers of Woodstock if Bing Crosby and Jack Benny are gonna be there'), the spoken word crowd show up on the appointed night and read, chant and sing their work, usually with a strong political bent. Poetry slams are part of the spoken word scene, where poets compete like athletes, judged either by the audience applause or judges who score them and hold up cards, just like the Olympics.

To find author readings, check the *Sunday Chronicle* or pick up *Poetry Flash*, the free monthly newspaper that follows the local literary scene. The slams and spoken word events are sometimes more difficult to find, advertising often limited to notices posted around South of Market and in the Haight.

CODY'S BOOKS
East Bay, 2454 Telegraph Ave, Berkeley, tel. (510) 845 7852.

A Berkeley landmark and one of the largest bookstores in the Bay Area. All new books, huge magazine and newspaper section, many European and Asian periodicals.

GREEN APPLE BOOKS
The Avenues, 506 Clement St, tel. 387 2272.

Big, jumbled, crowded and full of treasures. A favourite hangout for young urban types.

RICHARD HILKERT BOOKSELLER
Civic Center, 333 Hayes St, tel. 863 3339.

The bookseller is almost always on the premises and cheerfully answers questions and steers you towards what you want. This is the kind of personal bookstore that is becoming a lost art. Very good on art, crafts and history.

MODERN TIMES BOOKS
Mission, 968 Valencia St, tel. 282 9246.

Collectively run, Modern Times has a heavy tilt towards Marxism, Latin America, gay and gender works.

SPOKEN WORD
Clubs and coffee houses with regular spoken word evenings:

Above Paradise Lounge 1501 Folsom St, tel. 861 6906; Sunday nights 8 p.m.

Brainwash Café 1122 Folsom St, tel. 892 0158; Saturday night poetry slams 9 p.m.

Café Babar, 994 Guerrero St, tel. 282 6789; Thursdays 8 p.m.

E'Space 520 Hayes St, tel. 861 4657; Thursdays 8 p.m.

Sacred Grounds Coffeehouse 2095 Hayes St, tel. 387 3859; Wednesdays 7.30 p.m.

Wordland at the Women's Building, 3543 18th St; call for times, 567 6689.

Other poetry readings:

The Poetry Center San Francisco State University. The late Ruth Witt-Diamant initiated concert-like poetry readings in 1953, building into the American Poetry Archives with an unrivalled collection of audio- and videotapes of poets reading and discussing their work. Readings are usually held in the SF State library with famous and emerging poets. Call 338 2227 for information.

Intersection for the Arts 446 Valencia St, tel. 626 2787. Poets and writers in residence give workshops and readings.

STACEY'S
Downtown, 581 Market St,
tel. 421 4687.

Full-service downtown bookstore, very good on computer literature.

TILLMAN PLACE BOOKSTORE
Downtown, 8 Tillman Place (off
Grant Avenue), tel. 392 4668.

An appealing little downtown bookstore that looks unchanged from the 1940s. Except for the books, of course. Personal service and a good selection of current fiction and San Francisco and California books.

Specialist Bookstores

A DIFFERENT LIGHT
Castro, 489 Castro St, tel. 431 0891.

The premiere gay and lesbian bookstore in the Bay Area. A full service bookstore and a busy schedule of author appearances.

BOOK PASSAGE
Marin, 51 Tamal Vista Blvd, Corte
Madera, tel. 927 1503.

One of the most comprehensive selections of travel books available.

There's also a very popular café here.

BUILDERS BOOKSOURCE
Potrero Hill, 300 De Haro St,
tel. 575 3980.

Superb collection of architectural books. Also very good on gardening and interior design.

EAST WIND BOOKS AND ARTS
North Beach, 1435–A Stockton St,
tel. 781 3331.

Chinese and Asian American subjects are the focus at East Wind which also has substantial sections on the martial arts and Asian medicine.

GAIA
East Bay, 1400 Shattuck Ave,
Berkeley, tel. (510) 548 4172.

Goddess, New Age, spirituality books, magazines and programmes. The staff is extremely knowledgeable and helpful.

MARCUS BOOKS
Fillmore, 1712 Fillmore St,
tel. 346 4222.

The oldest and most comprehensive African American bookstore in the

Bay Area. Excellent selection of fiction, non-fiction, children's books, racial politics, biographies and more. Marcus also has a Berkeley store.

SAN FRANCISCO MYSTERY BOOKSTORE
Noe Valley, 746 Diamond St, tel. 282 7444.

A cosy little shop of new and used mysteries of every description. If they haven't got it, the book probably doesn't exist. Only open Fri–Sun.

SIERRA CLUB BOOKSTORE
Civic Center, 730 Polk St, tel. 923 5600.

Environmental books, hiking guides, maps and travel books.

UNIVERSITY PRESS BOOKS
East Bay, 2430 Bancroft Way, Berkeley, tel. (510) 548 0585.

Books from university-related presses all over the US, Canada and Europe.

Arcane and deeply scholarly books you can't find anywhere else.

Women's Bookstores

MAMA BEAR'S
East Bay, 6536 Telegraph Ave, Oakland, tel. (510) 428 9684.

A coffee house-art gallery-bookstore where men are admitted on probation. Some hard-to-find feminist, women's and gender studies books here along with a large selection of pulpy lesbian fiction and the usual range of women's books.

OLD WIVES' TALES
Mission, 1009 Valencia St, tel. 821 4675.

The oldest women's bookstore in the Bay Area. A community centre as well as a business, Old Wives' offers friendly staff, local resource guides and a varied programme of events.

Music

Bay Area record stores are goldmines, especially for nostalgia buffs and collectors. There has been some decline in the total number of titles available as shops have struggled with how to allot their floor-space among records, CDs and cassettes. Generally you will find the major hits in all three media while the newer, more cutting edge music tends to go only into cassettes and CDs.

AMOEBA RECORDS
East Bay, 2455 Telegraph Ave, Berkeley, tel. (510) 549 1125.

Amoeba's huge stock of used CDs and records at excellent prices brings in customers from all around the Bay. The new music stocks are equally impressive. Poster collectors come here for the original music posters from sixties' San Francisco bands.

BPM MUSIC FACTORY
Polk Gulch, 1141 Polk St, tel. 567 0276.

This is where the club DJs buy their records. BPM is very big on imports and hard to find stuff such as acid jazz, techno, foreign and domestic house. The store is adding a line of rave clothing.

DOWN HOME MUSIC
East Bay, 10341 San Pablo Ave,
El Cerrito, tel. (510) 525 2129.

The record collector's nirvana. American roots music, world beat, gospel, imports and wild stuff such as the seminal 1927 Carter Family sessions, the beginning of country music, from a Japanese company that has remastered the ancient tapes. Down Home has the best and most comprehensive women's music section of any store in the Bay Area. (El Cerrito, where Down Home lives, is a small town between Oakland and Berkeley. San Pablo Avenue is a major East Bay highway.)

SAN FRANCISCO OPERA SHOP
Civic Center, 199 Grove St,
tel. 565 6414.

Excellent selection of classical music and, as you might expect, heavy on the San Francisco Symphony and current guest artists with the San Francisco Opera. Also stocks a varied assortment of toys, gifts, books and magazines with opera themes.

STREETLIFE RECORDS
Castro, 3979 24th St, tel. 282 3550.

Used records. Collectors love this place because you never know what you're going to find.

TOWER RECORDS
North Beach, Columbus Avenue and
Bay Street, tel. 885 0500.

The best full-service record store in the Bay Area. Tower is the supermarket of music, but that doesn't mean it's a sterile place. This is one of North Beach's hottest spots on weekend nights.

Crafts, Art and Design

CREATIVE GROWTH GALLERY
355 24th St, downtown Oakland,
tel. (510) 836 2340.

Outsider Art, the new rage among American collectors, has turned this small non-profit art centre for mentally and emotionally disabled men and women into a major art market. Work by the centre's artists, who are given materials but no lessons, is on sale in the adjacent gallery and includes paintings, sculpture and textiles. One of the star artists is obsessed with Elvis, another with squirrels.

FILLAMENTO
Pacific Heights, 2185 Fillmore St,
tel. 931 2224.

If it's trendy, Fillamento had it first and has probably already sold out and gone on to something else. The shop is full of silly objects, but some wonderful items too – china, linens and whatever is hot in the home accessories department.

GUMP'S
250 Post St (near Union Square),
tel. 982 1616.

Expensive and exquisite jewellery, china, crystal, antiques and artwork, much of it from Asia.

LA TIENDA SHOP
Mexican Museum, Building D, Fort
Mason, tel. 441 0404.

The museum shop is equal to spending an hour in Mexico City. The shop has a good range of prices and quality. Toys, books and folk art are the main items.

LIMN COMPANY
South of Market, 290 Townsend St, tel. 543 5466.

It's not exactly the kind of goods you can pack in your suitcase, but LIMN is the cutting edge of the new furniture, home accessories market. For a window on what the architecturally inclined designers are doing to beds, tables, chairs, lamps and even garden gates, drop by the two-storey showroom.

NEEDLEPOINT INC.
251 Post St (near Union Square), tel. 392 1622.

The largest needlepoint shop in the US has everything for the needle artist. One-day classes are a speciality, often led by visiting experts.

OUT OF HAND
1303 Castro St, tel. 826 3885.

Excellent handmade ceramics and other artwork.

SAN FRANCISCO WOMEN ARTISTS GALLERY
Civic Center, 370 Hayes St, tel. 552 7392.

A non-profit women's art center that displays and sells attractive, expert arts and crafts ranging from paintings and sculpture to jewellery and textile art.

VIRGINIA BREIER
Pacific Heights, 1091 Sacramento St, tel. 929 7171.

Virginia Breier is a showcase for contemporary American crafts. The shop is especially known for its art furniture, but also has pottery, jewellery and sculpture.

Stationery and Posters

ARTROCK
South of Market, 1153 Mission St, tel. 235 7390

This unimpressive looking shop has the best collection of historical (antique? collectible? what does one say?) rock'n'roll posters in the city. Posters from the San Francisco acid rock era are the best to be had.

DOWNTOWN STATIONERS
119 New Montgomery St, tel. 392 8085.

Old-line office supply store where you can find everything from sombre business stationery to yellow legal pads, pens and paperclips.

FLAX ART AND DESIGN
Downtown, 1699 Market St, tel. 552 2355.

Flax is basically an art supply store, but has wonderful paper, pens, games and useless but engaging items such as a tiny Zen sand garden. Very unusual wrapping materials from handmade papers to gossamer ribbons. A good place to pick up a sketch book and some simple coloured pencils for the kids as well as the sophisticated stuff.

PAPYRUS
Financial District, 2 Embarcadero Center, tel. 781 8777. Also five other stores in San Francisco.

A small chain of card stores based in San Francisco, Papyrus devotes itself to stocking new and different art cards. Pricey but almost everyone's first choice for a special card.

COST PLUS
Fisherman's Wharf, 2552 Taylor St,
tel. 928 6200.

The original cheap import place, Cost Plus has become a mini-empire of stores with German candy, Filipino linens, Chinese baskets and wicker from everywhere. The large garden shop is heavy on houseplants.

CRATE AND BARREL
Union Square, 125 Grant Ave,
tel. 986 4000.

Deceptively simple, the rough-hewn pottery, unadorned cutlery and bright-coloured linens can turn out to be pretty pricey, but Crate and Barrel is a favourite shop for kitchenware coffee tables and such for the house.

THE GREENERY
Marina, 3227 Pierce St, tel. 567 4991.

A favourite with city gardeners, this little shop is full of surprises, including the garden at the back. In addition to gardening supplies you will find candles, baskets, wreaths and charming little gifts with a green theme.

SOKO HARDWARE
Japantown, 1698 Post St,
tel. 931 5510.

Japanese gardening tools, ikebana vases and flower-arranging supplies make this shop riveting for gardeners.

WILLIAMS SONOMA
Union Square, 150 Post St,
tel. 362 6904.

California's gift to the cook, Williams Sonoma is an upscale but not sniffy shop that carries everything for the kitchen except major appliances. There's a huge fun factor in shopping at Williams Sonoma which always seems stocked with some odd little tray, spoon or new kind of knife that one just can't do without.

Miscellaneous Shops

GAMESCAPE
Marina, 333 Divisadero St,
tel. 621 4263.

Everything from Monopoly to obscene party games to board war games. Especially notable for its used section where you can find long-forgotten board games from childhood.

GOOD VIBRATIONS
Mission, 1210 Valencia St,
tel. 974 8980.

A feminist and lesbian sex store. Good Vibrations is full of couples, gay and straight, earnestly looking at dildos, how-to books, checking through the video library and examining the vibrator museum.

GREENPEACE
Fisherman's Wharf, 890 North Point,
tel. 474 1870.

The retail arm of the watchdog environmental group. Before you get to the books, T-shirts, recycled paper cards, jewellery and toys you will be presented with a battery of petitions to sign. Non-signers are allowed to shop.

THE NATURE COMPANY
*Fisherman's Wharf, 900 North Point,
tel. 776 0724.*

Like Greenpeace, the Nature
Company is a green business,

dedicated to environmental harmony.
This shop is for profit, however, and
has a wider variety of games, toys,
science games, books, etc., often with
a pronounced cuteness.

Food and Drink

California wine is the major souvenir many travellers want to take
home from San Francisco. Foreigners returning to your own country are usually allowed to bring in two litres of wine duty free,
either still (non-champagne) or sparkling (champagne). Any amount
over that must be declared at Customs and will be subject to tax.
The tax can range up to 25 per cent of the cost of the wine, or less.
If you are interested in more than a few bottles, it would be worthwhile to make inquiries before leaving home. Wineshops will ship
wine for you, but it will be expensive. Usually a case is the minimum that will be sent and will cost at least $60 to send by air.
Winestores are very helpful about packing the wine for you; styrofoam boxes fitted to two or three wine bottles make carry-on an
easy matter.

Wine and beer are sold at most grocery stores; the larger supermarkets have liquor as well. You must be 21 to purchase alcohol
and IDs will be checked.

San Francisco is awash in foodshops, from corner delis to
gourmet take-out shops to all kinds of speciality foods. Good bread
is a passion with San Franciscans; you will even find fresh, handmade breads at the supermarket, extremely unusual in North
America.

Wine, Liquor, Coffee and Tea

COST PLUS WINE SHOP
*Fisherman's Wharf, 2598 Taylor St,
tel. 928 2030.*

Large selection of low- and medium-
priced wines.

NAPA VALLEY WINERY
EXCHANGE
*415 Taylor St (near Union Square),
tel. 771 2887.*

The experts on how to take wine

home with you. The wine choices are
solid if somewhat conservative.

PEET'S COFFEE AND TEA
*Marina, 2156 Chesnut St,
tel. 931 8302.*

Peet's is an institution in the Bay
Area. Locals wake up on Peet's soul-
stirring coffee, either at home or in
one of the coffee shops. The Marina
Peet's is the small chain's first SF
location. Sample the different coffees
(and teas) and order a few ounces to
take home.

PLUMP JACK WINES
Cow Hollow, 3201 Fillmore St,
tel. 346 9870.

A sleek, trendy wineshop, but the
society proprietors of Plump Jack's
(sons of Ann and Gordon Getty) have
done their homework and have a very
good selection of California wines
with competitive prices.

Food

IL FORNAIO
Levi Plaza, 1265 Battery St,
tel. 391 4622.

An Italian bakery that turns out
baguettes, rolls, rounds in addition to
small pizzas, tarts and cookies. Very
good bread.

JUST DESSERTS
Castro, 248 Church St, tel. 626 5774.
Other stores in the Bay Area.

The champagne of pastry shops.
Cakes, pies, cookies, cheesecake and
other sugar-dripping treats are served
up with espresso or may be taken out
for later.

LUCCA DELICATESSEN
Marina, 2120 Chesnut St,
tel. 921 7873.

A classic Italian deli with rich food
ranging from roast chicken to lasagne.

SEE'S CANDIES
Downtown, 542 Market St,
tel. 362 1593.

Homemade American favourites such
as fudge (chocolate candy) and
divinity (vanilla and nut candy) are
the staples at See's, a modest chain of
confectionery shops.

SNOOKIE'S COOKIES
Financial District, 560 Sacramento St,
tel. 788 1878.

Downtown businesspeople love
Snookie's, either for a stress-relieving
treat or their much-prized gift baskets
as expense account gifts.

VIVANDE PORTA VIA
Pacific Heights, 2125 Fillmore St,
tel. 346 4430.

The take-out counter of the popular
lunch spot Vivande is stocked with
food, glorious food, that can be
devoured immediately or taken along
for later meals, either al fresco or
warmed up at home.

CHILDREN

Years ago Frank Sinatra admiringly said of San Francisco, 'Now there's a grown-up swinging town'.

What he meant by 'swinging' is open to debate, but Sinatra effectively caught the adult playground quality of San Francisco. The US Census counts San Francisco as having a disportionate number of residents between eighteen and thirty-five. Like New York, Los Angeles and Chicago, San Francisco is where young people come to begin their 'real' lives, to find adventure and to live out their dreams. When they marry and have children (or just have children) they move to the suburbs or back home, somewhere with good schools and affordable houses. All of which makes children a bit of an oddity in San Francisco. The city isn't quite clear what to do with them. For instance, the Tenderloin, with its heavy population of immigrant families from Southeast Asia, has more than twice the school-age population of any neighbourhood in the city, but there is no local grammar school. Build a new school? The city can't seem to absorb the concept so the Tenderloin kids are bussed to schools all over the city.

Despite this general air of befuddlement about children, you will find plenty of ways to entertain kids and accommodate them in San Francisco. The attitude towards children isn't hostile, just not much interested. Breast-feeding in public isn't a problem. People stare out of curiosity rather than censure. Over the last few years nappy-changing stations have begun appearing in department stores, stadiums and auditoriums. New mothers raised on feminism have asked for children's facilities and usually they have been quickly added in a tone of 'Oh, sorry, never thought of that'.

As a major tourist city, San Francisco has snapped to the increasing emphasis on bringing the kids along which fuels special programmes and entertainments. There is also the hyper-organised populace which swiftly rallies to any real or perceived quality of life deficiency in San Francisco and busies itself with finding remedies. The baby boom among gay men and lesbians (through adoption and artificial insemination) has contributed to a child-awareness in the city. Many of the programmes and entertainments for children strike outsiders as over-organised and perhaps more geared to what adults think children should like rather than children's own tastes but, as one San Francisco mother said with some exasperation, 'These kids have seen it all! You can't keep them happy with just a walk in the park and a simple movie.' Visitors reap the rewards of San Francisco parents' endless struggle to keep their children entertained.

Restaurants, one of the major city preoccupations, don't make a big effort for children. Cafés at Fisherman's Wharf and other tourist-heavy spots feature kids' menus and specialities, but these ideas are largely unknown in most of the first-class restaurants. Ask waiters and dining room managers for help if you don't see anything on the menu – they will almost always respond cheerfully and quickly. However, fussy, loud children, especially crying babies are looked on with undisguised irritation. Parents are expected to take the noisy ones outside if a reasonable quiet can't be maintained.

Strict regulation of liquor sales means that children are not welcome in bars where the minimum age is 21. The easy atmosphere of the neighbourhood pub where the whole family gathers around is almost unknown in the US. Drinking establishments are adult only.

San Francisco parents are obsessive about children's safety in the city. Unfortunately, it is for good reason. There have been a number of cases of children of twelve and under simply disappearing off city streets. Crime experts debate how common the snatched child syndrome really is (after the elimination of custody disputes), but that talk does little to comfort parents. Children under fifteen should never be out of your sight unless they are with someone you know.

Pier 39 and Fisherman's Wharf are, of course, packed with kid-oriented cafés, entertainments and shops. The Cannery, Ghiradelli Square and The Anchorage, the nearby shopping centres, are also packaged for family shopping. And shopping is the point here, where everything has a price tag. There is some free entertainment by jugglers and the sealions, but on the whole you have to spend money to take part in the fun. Even if you are not on a tight budget, the spend-spend-spend mindset of the Wharf area can be annoying. Many families like to limit their time with a one-day or two half-day quickie visits through the area.

Babysitting
(See Directory p. 41)

CHILDREN

The museums and historic sites listed here are places that children respond to without coaxing. There are a number of musical shows specifically for children throughout the year. Check newspaper listings for kids' shows and special performances of the symphony and ballet aimed at young people.

BARBIE DOLL HALL OF FAME
460 Waverly St, Palo Alto,
tel. 326 5841.

It's difficult to call a museum with more than 16,000 Barbie Dolls 'culture', but this little museum near Stanford University is regarded as a sacred site by some girls under eleven. You can see Barbie in almost all her decades of glory, from bride to astronaut to careerist with a briefcase. Maybe it is culture.

CALIFORNIA ACADEMY OF SCIENCE
Golden Gate Park, tel. 750 7145.

(see p. 221) The Academy is a wonder-land for kids and not just the scientifically curious. The Discovery Room is a great place deep within the building where everything is hands-on. The Steinhart Aquarium and Morrison Planetarium, both part of the Academy, are sure winners with children.

BAY AREA DISCOVERY MUSEUM FOR CHILDREN
East Fort Baker, Sausalito,
tel. 332 9646.

(see p. 238) Marvellous hands-on fun for children.

EXPLORATORIUM
Bay and Lyon streets, tel. 561 0360.

(see p. 148) The Exploratorium is a must see. This do-it-yourself museum

makes science more fun than Disneyland.

FORT POINT
Underneath the Golden Gate Bridge,
tel. 556 1693.

A Civil War-era fort where children may help with the daily cannon drill and explore the restored fort's spiral stairways, tunnels, hallways, jail block and the trails around the fort.

LAWRENCE HALL OF SCIENCE
University of California campus,
Berkeley, tel. (510) 642 5132.

(see p. 260) High above the UC campus, children find out about dinosaurs and other marvels in this popular science museum.

MAKE-A-CIRCUS
Fort Mason Center, tel. 776 8477.

Clowns, acrobats and performers literally create a circus during their summertime park shows, pulling in kids from the audience to walk on stilts, do simple tricks and join in the fun. Call for the schedule or check newspaper listings. It's free and very entertaining, even for the adults.

JOSEPHINE D. RANDALL MUSEUM
199 Museum Way, tel. 554 9600.

(see p. 230) Drop-in art classes, petting zoo, interesting projects.

SAN FRANCISCO MARITIME NATIONAL HISTORICAL PARK AND AQUATIC PARK
Across from Ghiradelli Square, Beach and Polk streets, tel. 556 3002.

The museum is a treasure trove of history and elaborate ship models. On the Hyde Street Pier children may board and explore four historic ships. Aquatic Park is a pleasant green place with benches and a small beach.

Food

Many of the upscale SF restaurants are not particularly child friendly. A quick peep will tell you whether you think your children will fit in. A good solution, and an economical one, is to take advantage of the city's profusion of take-out counters and delis. Picnic in the parks or in your hotel room.

BURGER KING
The Presidio. No phone.

If your children are determined to have fast food, no matter how many simple pastas and grilled chickens you push at them, try this completely ordinary Burger King with one of the city's most beautiful views.

GHIRADELLI CHOCOLATE MANUFACTORY
Under the Clock Tower, Ghiradelli Square, tel. 474 3938.

A recreated old-fashioned ice cream shop featuring Ghiradelli chocolate as ice cream, poured over ice cream, in milkshakes and every other way you can imagine.

GOLDEN GATE FORTUNE COOKIE FACTORY
In Chinatown, 56 Ross Alley. No phone.

The real thing; see these funny little cookies made and have some to eat.

HARD ROCK CAFÉ
1699 Van Ness Ave, tel. 885 1699.

Kids love this ersatz rock'n'roll eatery.

MCDONALD'S
Chinatown, corner of California and Grant. No phone.

An absolutely ordinary McDonald's, but children love seeing their favourites written up in Chinese characters.

SWENSEN'S ICE CREAM
1999 Hyde St (on the Powell-Hyde cable car line), tel. 775 6618.

The mother ship of the Swensen ice cream empire. A pleasant old ice cream parlour.

Zoos, Parks and Playgrounds

The best outings for kids are the easiest ones – riding the ferries and cable cars. In either case the ride can take you somewhere or you can just ride. Wide open spaces are surprisingly plentiful around San Francisco. For letting off steam, places where the children are free to run and scream without disturbing anyone, there are the expanses of Golden Gate Park, the Presidio, Ocean Beach and Golden Gate Promenade, the 4.5-mile walkway from Aquatic Park to Golden Gate Bridge.

CHILDREN'S FAIRYLAND
Lakeside Park, Oakland,
tel. (510) 452 2259.

The model for Disneyland, a sweet fairytale-inspired, low-tech park for children.

GOLDEN GATE BRIDGE
Highway 101

Walking across the bridge is one of the great pleasures of a San Francisco visit. It's free, lives up to everything you have heard and even young children can manage the 1.2-mile walk each way.

GOLDEN GATE PARK

In addition to the museums, the park has a children's playground and huge expanses of wide-open space for running, jumping, rolling around and yelling at the top of one's lungs. Children especially like the little boats on Stow Lake and seeing the windmills at the western edge of the park, near Ocean Beach.

THE JUNGLE
South of Market, 555 9th St,
tel. 552 4386.

An indoor play park that covers 15,000 feet. Kids can jump, run, climb and play on a labyrinth of tubes, slides, cargo nets and three-level structures. Parents or adults must accompany the kids, but once there you may turn them over to counsellors and retreat to the 'peace & quiet room' reserved for grown-ups.

MARINA GREEN
Along Marina Boulevard, from
Laguna to Lyon.

The city's number one kite-flying site. A favourite with runners, rollerbladers, sun-seekers and strollers.

MARINE WORLD AND AFRICA USA
Marine World Parkway, Vallejo,
tel. (707) 644 6722.

Located at the northern edge of the bay in the industrial town of Vallejo, Marine World is a 160-acre wildlife park that combines slick showmanship with environmental awareness. The park's tigers, lions, chimpanzees, birds, whales and dolphins all earn their keep through daily performances while mechanised dinosaurs rotate and growl away in their own mini-park. An aquarium is another of its major attractions. Marine World has a ferry service from Pier 39 which makes it an easy, pleasurable trip.

PARAMOUNT'S GREAT AMERICA
2401 Agnew Road, Santa Clara,
tel. (408) 988 1776.

Great America, near San José, is the only major theme park in Northern California. It's a hundred acres of rides, amusements, stage shows and cartoon characters. It doesn't have the history or panache of Disneyland, but children love the place.

SAN FRANCISCO ZOO
Sloat Boulevard and 45th Avenue,
tel. 753 7061.

One of the most child-conscious institutions in San Francisco, the zoo has many features that appeal to children. The Children's Zoo and the Insect Zoo are big favourites with older children and younger ones love the old-fashioned carousel.

SLIDE RANCH
2025 Shoreline Highway, Muir Beach,
tel. 381 6155.

Children learn about life in the country through half-day and longer programmes at this rustic ranch in Marin. They can milk goats, collect eggs from hens, card wool, pick vegetables in the garden, feed the chickens and get to know the Angora rabbits. Bread-making, hiking and special projects are also offered. Reservations are required. Write ahead for a ranch schedule (zip code 94965).

Shops

BASIC BROWN BEAR FACTORY AND STORE
South of Market, 444 De Haro St,
tel. 626 0781.

'The place where teddy bears are born' shows you and your children how the little creatures come to life in the workrooms. Tours are available at different times (call for the schedule), but be prepared to buy something when it's over; the shop isn't hard sell in any way. It doesn't have to be, being around all the cuddly toys for an hour or so does the work for them.

DOTTIE DOOLITTLE'S
1680 Sacramento St, tel. 563 3244.

The kiddie Brooks Brothers. The children's fashions here run strongly towards traditional, tailored clothes such as Florence Eiseman.

GAP KIDS AND BABY GAP
Downtown, 100 Post St,
tel. 421 4906.

Gap's popular sports clothes, heavy on jeans and T-shirts, scaled down for babies, children and young teens.

MACY'S
Union Square, tel. 397 3333.

Huge selection of children's clothes, shoes and accessories in Macy's East, which also includes the men's departments. Five floors of shopping – and this is an 'annexe'.

MUDPIE
Lower Pacific Heights, 1699 Union St, tel. 563 7140.

Chic clothes, shoes and accessories for children, up to about age eleven or twelve. A favourite with the Pacific Heights mothers such as Linda Rondstadt and Danielle Steel.

NORDSTROM
865 Market St, tel. 243 8500.

Excellent children's department, clothes, shoes and accessories but the great draw here is the mother's room, a rest room separate from the regular women's rest room. Nursing mothers and mothers with small children find this place a haven.

F.A.O. SCHWARZ
Downtown, 48 Stockton St,
tel. 394 8700.

The Rolls Royce of toy stores. The toys here are the result of combining unfettered imagination and unlimited money. Indulgence doesn't even begin to describe the human-sized stuffed animals, gasoline-powered tiny sports cars and elaborate train sets. The shop is surprisingly child friendly, allowing plenty of touching, playing and poking the merchandise. Often there are more adults than children here.

Women love to come to San
Francisco on business trips.
And the city loves for them
to come. Hotels compete for
their business, refining the
ordinary business deals into
'Workingwomen's Specials' while
shops and services address their
advertisements to 'Businesswomen!'.

As a major financial nerve centre for the western US and,
increasingly, for Asia, San Francisco sees hordes of attorneys,
accountants, executives, deal-makers, investors, developers and
their minions. The city is attuned to big-time business people, in the
city for a day or a week, focused on getting as much done as possible.
In this business-friendly travel atmosphere, women find the added
bonus of a manageable, woman-friendly city where it's possible to
fit in a bit of shopping or sightseeing without losing any work time.

The downtown hotels are hugely popular with businesswomen
because they are only minutes away from the Financial District, the
shops on Union Square, first-class restaurants and even the cable
cars. Hard-driving financial analysts have been known to use the
thirty-minute break between sessions in mega-million dollar negotiations to zip over to I. Magnin, Saks or Macy's to buy a pair of
shoes or a new raincoat. Refreshed from shopping, the analyst re-
enters the fray with renewed enthusiasm while the men try to clear
their heads from a visit to a nearby bar.

Women are welcomed into business settings with a friendly sort
of civility that stops short of chumminess. The heated-up debate
about sexual harassment in the US has made American businessmen
incredibly nervous, even the normally easy-going San Franciscans.
Many women find this state of affairs quite amusing as men moan
and groan about the implications of the new emphasis on conduct
in the workplace.

'Does this mean if I tell a colleague I like her dress I'll be sued?'
they cry. And it's not just the unreconstructed male supremacists;
men of exceptional good will seem shaken by the idea that they no

longer define what constitutes sexual harassment. A 1993 Supreme Court decision that ruled a Tennessee company's most productive saleswoman was entitled to damages from her boss, a nonstop sexual jokester, has had almost as much impact as the Anita Hill-Clarence Thomas hearings. The saleswoman's victory established that a woman doesn't have to have a nervous breakdown before unpleasantness can be called sexual harassment.

If you are travelling on your own, without an office to work out of in San Francisco, you will find an array of services and businesses to help you. Your best resource is the hotel concierge. The larger hotels such as the Clift, Palace and the big chain hotels, have on-site business centres. The smaller hotels have some business services and well-informed concierges who can direct you to what you need or line up the services for you. Occasionally, you will come across a dud concierge, of course, but try the hotel resources first. Then turn to the telephone Yellow Pages, a very thorough listing of every service available.

Try and have fun in San Francisco. You are here to work, of course, but the city's fun-loving nature and the compactness of the place make adding some pleasurable moments very possible. Have a massage in your hotel room, ride the cable cars, walk the Embarcadero to Golden Gate Bridge, drop into a club for the late show. No one should go home from San Francisco with only a memory of the beige walls of a hotel conference room.

Helpful Services

(Also refer to the Directory, p. 41).

SECRETARIAL SERVICES
Tempositions, 150 Post St, tel. 392 5856, and **Robert B. Hermonon**, 742 14th St, tel. 742 9494.

FOREIGN NEWSPAPERS AND PERIODICALS
Café de la Presse, 342 Grant Ave, tel. 398 2680. Look for **Eastern News-stands**, sprinkled around downtown, Embarcadero Center 1 (tel. 433 4007) and Embarcadero 3 (tel. 982 4425) and in 1 Market Plaza (tel. 546 1488). Call ahead if you are looking for a particular publication or specific day.

CAR RENTAL AND LIMOUSINE SERVICES
Rentals: **Alamo**, tel. 673 9696; **Budget Rent-A-Car**, tel. 775 5800; **Hertz**, tel. 771 2200. Reliable car and drivers, **Associated Limousines**, tel. 563 1000; **Ishi Limousine**, tel. 567 4700.

SPAS
Full-service spas in downtown: **Mister Lee**, 834 Jones St, tel. 474 6002 – half-day, full-day or blitzkrieg pampering, with massage, haircut, facials, manicures, water massage, even lunch; **Spa Nordstrom**, Nordstrom's in the San Francisco Center, tel. 978 5102 – go for a day or just a pedicure, relaxing, luxurious surroundings with massage, hair, manicure, facials and other treats.

GETAWAYS

San Francisco is the centre of a vast tourist empire, stretching south to the magnificent rugged coast of Big Sur, inland to Yosemite National Park and north to the Wine Country and the funky North Coast. There are wonderful places to see beyond the Bay Area, but these sights are easily a vacation in themselves. The most popular day trip from the city is Napa Valley, the cradle of the California wine industry. There are a number of tour companies solely devoted to the Wine Country, which makes this a very easy trip to do.

Many of the side trips require a car – either renting one or having friends drive you. Public transport exists in the form of buses in almost every place, but making connections from San Francisco is usually cumbersome and time-consuming. Easy-to-use mass public transport outside of the urban core is still a strange idea to most Americans.

Getting out of the city is about seeing the natural wonders of California. There are some attractive small cities in Northern California and charming villages, but nothing more varied and interesting than San Francisco itself in the way of towns. Los Angeles, of course, is an entirely different world. It is four hundred miles south, a long drive or forty minutes by air, not an easily manageable side trip.

Getting Around   The simplest and most relaxing way to visit the farther reaches, especially Napa and Yosemite, is by tour. Grayline is always reliable and there are a number of other good tour companies that package one-day visits from the city to popular places in Northern California. Your hotel concierge can book a tour for you or you can do it yourself. You will have several choices of when to go, but always try for a weekday.

Renting a car is the other option for getting away, way out of town. You will need a valid driver's licence and a credit card to rent a car. While in theory cash is acceptable for both a deposit and full payment, rental car companies can't relate to anything but credit cards (see recommended companies, p. 42). They are also distrustful of drivers under 25 and anyone under 21 is ineligible to rent a car. If you have a concierge who can help you, very good, as charges are as complicated as algebra. Charges for mileage and insurance can pile up a huge bill very fast so doing some research is worth the trouble. Use any coupons, credit card specials or other deals that come your way. You can also rent a car with a driver if you have a generous budget.

The Wine Country

Napa and Sonoma counties, 60 miles north of San Francisco: by car to Sonoma take 101 North across the Golden Gate Bridge, east on Route 37, then north on Route 121; to Napa take I–80 east across the Bay Bridge, north to Vallejo, north on Route 121, then onto Route 29 at the city of Napa. Numerous bus tours take day trips from San Francisco to the Wine Country. Grayline covers both Napa and Sonoma in its daylong tour (tel. 558 9400), while Tower Tours takes smaller buses and will accommodate requests for particular wineries (tel. 434 8687). Quality Tours (tel. 994 5054) will custom-design an entire day in the Wine Country for clients.

The first European settlers immediately snapped to the idea that Northern California was ideal for grape growing. First the Spanish padres, then nineteenth-century Italian immigrants planted vines and established rudimentary wineries. It took another century for anything to come of it, but in the 1970s American wineries swept into a new era, producing wines as good as anything in Europe and turning the sleepy agricultural valleys of Napa and Sonoma into sophisticated enclaves drawing hundreds of thousands of tourists every year. These areas are green and lovely but edging towards overkill, despite the furious efforts of residents to curb and control development.

Wineries aren't merely 'open to the public' – most are completely geared to pulling in as many visitors as possible. Typically, a visit includes a guided tour of the winery and a wine tasting afterwards. Buying wine, of course, is the idea. The prices are not any better than what you will find in most winestores. The wineries will also insist that you can't find most of the wines in winestores; what you are tasting today is 'reserve' or 'special reserve' or only sold at the winery, blah, blah, blah. Be sceptical and only buy if you are in love with the wine.

Be careful, too, about drinking and driving. The Highway Patrol gives more traffic tickets in Napa County than anywhere else in California – that's total numbers, not per capita. The car's driver should not drink at all or limit herself or himself to one or two glasses of wine.

These aren't particularly interesting trips for children unless you are skipping the wineries and only sightseeing.

You will hear a lot about the Wine Train, but it isn't really a mode of transport. The Wine Train is more clearly described as a three-hour moving restaurant. Running along the Napa Valley floor, it avoids the traffic snarls but doesn't stop anywhere! You get aboard in Napa, ride through the countryside to St Helena, turn around and return to Napa. Train buffs enjoy the restored 1917 elegance of the train cars and the meals served are quite good. There are ongoing wine tastings, too. It's expensive (tickets are $60 for lunch, $70 for dinner, no children's rates), but simple, tel. (707) 253 2111 or 1 800 427 4124.

Napa

The Napa Valley is a long, narrow tunnel between rounded green and golden hills. Beginning at the city of Napa to the south, the valley runs north to the hot springs resort town of Calistoga. Route 29 and the two-lane Silverado Trail follow the valley floor and together pass almost every winery in the area. Most visitors, especially those driving themselves, find that three wineries is the max that they can absorb in one day. For a big overview of Napa and the wine business, Christian Brothers Winery, 2555 Main St, St Helena, is a good stop. Founded by the Christian Brothers order, the winery is one of the few in California with an unbroken history. The wine industry was all but destroyed in the 1920s during Prohibition when an amendment to the US Constitution outlawed the manufacture and consumption of alcohol. The only exception was sacramental wines which allowed Christian Brothers to continue its winemaking (open Saturday and Sunday, 10 a.m. – 4.30 p.m., tel. 707/963 0765). Interesting small wineries are Merryvale, 1000 Main St, St Helena (daily, 10 a.m. – 5.30 p.m., tel. 707/963 7777) and Rutherford Hill, in Rutherford on the Silverado Trail (daily, 10 a.m. – 4.30 p.m., tel. 707/963 7194). Domanine Chandon is a champagne winery with quite an elaborate visitors' centre, 1 California Drive, Yountville (daily May to October, 11 a.m. – 6 p.m., Wed–Sun November to April, tel. 707/944 2892).

Calistoga

At the northern end of the valley, Calistoga is known for not just its bottled mineral water but its popular mud baths. Hot springs ooze heated, mineral-rich mud which is carefully packed over spa clients, reclining in bathtub-like vats. It all sounds ghastly but is a wonderful, rejuvenating treatment. People with arthritic problems swear by Calistoga mud baths. Hot air balloon and glider rides are also booked from here. If you can do an overnight, Calistoga makes an excellent base camp for doing Napa Valley and nearby Sonoma. For the mud baths and overnight, try Nance's Hot Springs, an old-line spa and motel that is frill free and affordable (1614 Lincoln Ave, Calistoga, tel. 707/942 6211). Outside of town the Mountain Home Ranch is a wonderfully old-fashioned paying guests kind of place with a rustic lodge and cabins. Perfect for families, the modest rates include meals in the ranch dining hall (3400 Mountain Home Ranch Road, Calistoga, tel. 707/942 6616).

Sonoma

Sonoma County, immediately to the west of Napa, is its rival in wine production and more recently, competitor for visitors. Sonoma doesn't have quite the simplicity of Napa's valley layout, but it is a user-friendly region studded with wineries. Like Napa, the county and a key town have the same name and are used interchangeably. The town of Sonoma is a pleasant place with many visible traces of its Spanish colonial past. Viansa Winery, off Highway 121, 25200 Arnold Drive, south of Sonoma, is a good place to start in Sonoma, a mid-sized winery with sweeping views, picnic tables and a good take-out café (daily 10 a.m. – 5 p.m., tel. 707/935 4700). Ravenswood, a small winery, is noted for its zinfandel, California's only native wine, and weekend barbecues during the summer months, 18701 Gehricke Road, Sonoma (daily 10 a.m. – 4.30 p.m., tel. 707/938 1960). Buena Vista, an older winery with its own art gallery, is the kind of rustic, low-key spot most people have in mind when they visualise a Northern California winery, 18000 Old Winery Road, Sonoma (open daily, 10 a.m. – 5 p.m., tel. 707/938 1266).

The Sonoma Plaza, with its 1823 mission and other Spanish and Mexican colonial buildings, is a pleasant walk-about place. This was the home of the short-lived Bear Flag Revolt, the bridge between California's history as a Mexican province to American territory in 1846. Nearby Glen Ellen was Jack London's last home where he built a ranch and his dream home, Wolf House, which burned just days before he was to move in. London continued to live in his old ranchhouse which is now part of Jack London State Park. The park is north of Sonoma; take Arnold Drive and follow the signs to London Ranch Road (open daily, 9.30 a.m. to sunset, tel. 707/938 5216).

Point Reyes

North of the Golden Gate, Point Reyes peninsula is part of a national park, the Point Reyes National Seashore. Take the Golden Gate Bridge to US Highway 1. Enter the park turning west onto Bear Valley Road or Sir Francis Drake Highway (they eventually merge into one); free and always open. Golden Gate Transit bus service from San Francisco and San Rafael (tel. 453 2100).

The Point Reyes peninsula is a rugged landscape that has both clear views of the dreaded San Andreas Fault and the Pacific Ocean. The peninsula is a geologic quirk, the furthest point of the continental drift, moving the coastline north, two inches a year. Point Reyes is an easy day trip from the city (38 miles) and offers absolutely pristine beaches. There is no swimming, but the wading, walking, birdwatching, picnicking and meditating are first-rate. The beaches are easily reached from convenient parking lots. Check in at the Visitor Center on Bear Valley Road for maps, ranger tips and orientation. Serious hikers love Point Reyes for its 70,000 acres of undisturbed back country. For a first trip, make the Point Reyes Lighthouse your goal. To get there, one drives the narrow, curling Sir Francis Drake Highway through the heart of the park along Inverness Ridge. You pass through the lovely village of Inverness, go by several working dairy farms then down to the sea. The lighthouse is starkly beautiful and often surrounded by visiting sealions on nearby rocks. From here you can explore Point Reyes Beach to the north – fifteen miles of prime wild beach. South from the lighthouse is Drake's Bay, almost certainly the protected inlet where Sir Francis beached the *Golden Hinde* in 1579 to make repairs during his voyage of discovery. Drake claimed the coast for Elizabeth I, but wasn't really sure where he was. The suit for new Albion, as he called California, was never pressed. Drake's Beach is another lovely walk, the site of an annual Labor Day sandcastle contest that draws deadly serious teams from SF architectural firms. Often the beach will be wreathed in a soft fog while the sand is still warm from the sun.

Big Sur

On US Highway 1, 140 miles south of San Francisco.

Big Sur is an imprecise place, but you will know it when you get there. It is one of the most beautiful places in the world, the green, powerful mountains dropping off into the boiling Pacific Ocean. Big Sur begins about thirty miles south of Monterey and it is accessible only by a twisting, turning, two-lane highway along the coast. The difficult landscape has proved almost impossible to develop so has remained a mostly undisturbed bit of natural perfection. Once the preserve of cattle ranches and bohemians (led by writer Henry Miller who moved to Big Sur in 1947), the rough country of rivers, hills, beaches and wildflowers developed a reputation as a tolerant stretch of coastline. Esalen Institute, the place that popularised hot tubs, gestalt therapy and encounter groups is here. Endlessly satirised, Esalen is still in business but open only to people attending workshops (call 408/667 3000). There are several state parks along the way and a number of resorts, ranging from extremely expensive to primitive. You will almost surely have to drive to Big Sur. It is possible to take a Greyhound bus to Monterey and connect with the Monterey-Salinas Transit authority for a local bus to Big Sur (tel. 408/899 2555), but it isn't an easy or quick connection. Try to avoid summer weekends when the roads back up with sightseers and campers in their RVs (recreational vehicles). Drive slowly and look as much as you can after passing Point Lobos. Pull over often and just let California wash over you. You can easily camp at Andrew Molera State Park ($3 per person, no showers or reservations, tel. 408/667 2315) or Pheiffer Big Sur State Park (showers, store, reservations sometimes, tel. 408/667 2315). Slightly more comfortable is Deetjen's Big Sur Inn, a ramshackle collection of cottages that is wildly popular (reservations are crucial, $38–$75, tel. 408/667 2377) or for the ultimate in eco-correct luxury, Ventana Inn ($170–$775, tel. 408/667 2311; children discouraged).

Yosemite National Park

The park is 183 miles south east of San Francisco: by car from across the Bay Bridge to I–580, south then west to Route 120 to Yosemite; Amtrak (from Oakland, tel. 1 800 872 7245) has daily service to Merced, where bus connections may be made for the 50-mile trip to the park; Grayline offers one-day guided tours to Yosemite from SF, tel. 588 9400.

Yosemite is a stretch for a quick visit from San Francisco, but this stunning valley never fails to disappoint anyone who sets foot in it. The one-day Grayline tour is the simplest way to visit and hits all the high spots. If you can manage an overnight, it will be worth it even if you are the sort who only likes nature with a motel in it. Yosemite, 1200 square miles of rugged forest, valleys, rivers, waterfalls, mountains and meadows, is one of America's great treasures, barely saved from ruinous ranching and logging in the late nineteenth century. Engraved on the popular imagination through Ansel Adams' elegant photographs, the park annually draws millions of visitors. If you can avoid summer weekends, your visit will be ever so much better. A first-time trip should concentrate on Yosemite Valley, the glacier-carved canyon that is the heart of the park. Rock formations such as Half Dome and El Capitan, the waterfalls and redwood groves are stirring sights and may be seen from a car window or in fairly easy walks. Yosemite can provide hikes as tough as you want, or as simple. Its grandeur is easily sampled. The park has accommodation ranging from campsites and modest cabins to the super luxurious Ahwahnee Hotel. Reservations are a must during the summer high season and may be arranged through a central number (209) 373 4171. Write to Yosemite ahead of time for information about the park, Yosemite Park and Curry Co., Yosemite National Park, CA 95389.

BACKGROUND

RECOMMENDED BOOKS

Women in History

Jacqueline Baker Barnhart, *The Fair but Frail: Prostitution in San Francisco 1849–1900* (University of Nevada Press, 1986). A thoughtful, scholarly study that separates the economic and social reality faced by women of the West from the swooning sentimentality attached to 'dance hall girls'.

Sara Davison, *Loose Change* (1975, out of print). Three Berkeley sorority sisters come of age during the Free Speech Movement. Their stories illumine an age.

Curt Gentry, *The Madams of San Francisco: An Irreverent History of the City by the Golden Gate* (Doubleday, 1964). An archly male view of prostitution. Despite Gentry's snide patronisation, his facts are generally sound and the stories are told in context.

Jo Ann Levy, *They Saw the Elephant: Women in the California Gold Rush* (University of Oklahoma Press, 1992). Clear-eyed and well-researched, Levy's narrative of the female Gold Rush experience redresses the male-oriented imbalance of most Gold Rush histories.

Jessica Mitford, *A Fine Old Conflict* (Alfred A. Knopf, 1977). A rollicking and insightful account of Mitford's move to San Francisco in World War II as a young widow and her subsequent remarriage, Americanisation and careers as a Communist and writer.

Dame Shirley, *The Shirley Letters* (Peregrine Smith Books, 1970). The bright-eyed and biting letters of Louise Amelia Knapp Smith Clappe written during 1851–52 from the California frontier to her sister back East. A wonderful first-hand account of an early California woman.

Walton Bean and James J. Rawls, *California: An Interpretive History* (McGraw-Hill, 1988). Intended as a textbook on state history, this is the best single volume survey of California, from pre-Columbian to contemporary times.

David Darlington, *Angels' Visits: An Inquiry into the Mystery of Zinfandel* (Henry Holt, 1991). The wine culture of Northern California and incidentally the San Francisco preoccupation with fine food and dining is explored in this illuminating account of California's mystery wine, zinfandel.

J.S. Holliday, *The World Rushed In* (Simon & Schuster, 1981). The classic story of the 1849 California Gold Rush, the impetus for the development of San Francisco.

Kevin J. Mullen, *Let Justice Be Done: Crime and Politics in Early San Francisco* (University of Nevada Press, 1989). A revisionist history of the post-Gold Rush Vigilante era of the 1850s by a former San Francisco Police Department deputy chief turned historian.

Charles Perry, *The Haight-Ashbury: A History* (Vintage Books, 1985). We were so much older then, we're younger than that now.

Carol Pogash, *As Real as it Gets: The Life of a Hospital at the Center of the AIDS Epidemic* (Birch Lane Press, 1992). A year in the life of San Francisco General Hospital, a key MASH unit in the war against AIDS.

Randy Shilts, *The Mayor of Castro Street* (St Martin's Press, 1982). Biography of Harvey Milk, the first openly gay San Francisco supervisor; traces Milk's life and the growth of the city's gay community.

Ronald Takaki, *Strangers From a Different Shore: A History of Asian Americans* (Penguin, 1989). A survey of Asian immigration and communities in North America. San Francisco, as a focal point for early arrivals, figures heavily in this story.

Evelyn Wells, *Champagne Days of San Francisco* (Doubleday, 1939). The romanticised history of San Francisco of the Gilded Age which fondly remembers madams with hearts of gold and a town populated by sweetly naughty misogynists.

Women, Arts and Letters

Sarah Holmes Boutelle, *Julia Morgan, Architect* (Abbeville Press, 1988). A lavishly illustrated study of Morgan's work and life.

John Malcolm Brinnin, *The Third Rose: Gertrude Stein and Her World* (Addison-Wesley, 1959). A genial appraisal of Stein, who grew up in Oakland and San Francisco, and her companion, San Francisco-born Alice B. Toklas.

David Dempsey with Raymond P. Baldwin, *The Triumphs and Trials of Lotta Crabtree* (William Morrow, 1968). The incredibly dramatic life of America's first theatrical sweetheart.

Carolyn Cassady, *Off the Road: My Years with Cassady, Kerouac and Ginsberg* (William Morrow, 1990). A woman's Beat experience which translated into a bizarre combination of housewife, lover and all-forgiving den mommy for the wild boys Neal Cassady and Jack Kerouac.

Isadora Duncan, *Isadora Speaks* (City Lights Books, 1981). In her own words.

Emily Wortis Leider, *California's Daughter: Gertrude Atherton* (Stanford University Press, 1991). Atherton's novels of spunky Western heroines finding true love with English lords are unreadable now, but her life in San Francisco, New York and London is illuminating.

Josephine DeWitt Rhodehamel and Raymund Francis Wood, *Ina Coolbrith* (Brigham Young University Press, 1973). Comprehensive if dullish biography of Ina Coolbrith, California's first poet laureate and inspiration of Jack London, Mark Twain and Bret Harte.

General Arts and Architecture

Thomas Albright, *Art in the San Francisco Bay Area 1945 to 1980* (University of California Press, 1985). A comprehensive and readable study of the Bay Area's generally overlooked modern art movement.

Misha Berson, *The San Francisco Stage: From Gold Rush to Golden Spike, 1849–1869* (San Francisco Performing Arts Library & Museum, 1989), and *The San Francisco Stage: From Golden Spike to the Earthquake, 1869–1906* (SF PALM, 1992). A lively and insightful history of San Francisco's love affair with the theatre. Berson pays careful attention to women performers such as Isadora Duncan, Lola Montez and Adah Issacs Menken.

Pat and Fred Cody, *The Life and Times of Cody's Books: A Berkeley Bookstore 1956–1977* (Chronicle Books, 1992). Cody's was – and is – a Berkeley intellectual landmark. Pat Cody tells how she and her late husband weathered student riots, McCarthyism and the vagaries of the book trade.

Lawrence Ferlinghetti and Nancy J. Peters, *Literary San Francisco* (Harper & Row, 1980). Profusely illustrated with photographs and drawings, particularly good on the late nineteenth century and Beat eras.

Douglas Frantz, *From the Ground Up: The Business of Building in the Age of Money* (Henry Holt & Co., 1991). The drama of the American urban landscape distilled into the story of Rincon Center, an eighties development in downtown San Francisco.

Caroline A. Jones, *Bay Area Figurative Art 1950–1965* (University of California Press, 1990). When New York was still proclaiming Ab Ex the only true religion, San Francisco artists were blazing new trails.

George Martin, *Verdi at the Golden Gate: Opera and San Francisco in the Gold Rush* (University of California Press, 1993). An examination of early San Francisco's love affair with opera.

Sally B. Woodbridge, John M. Woodbridge, Chuck Byrne, *San Francisco Architecture* (Chronicle Books, 1992). A usable and useful guide to San Francisco and Bay Area buildings and neighbourhoods.

Novels Set in San Francisco

Dashiell Hammett, *The Maltese Falcon* (Knopf, 1930). Still the greatest detective novel after all these years, set within a few foggy blocks of San Francisco.

Jack Kerouac, *Desolation Angels* (Perigee reprint, 1990) and *The Dharma Bums* (Signet, 1958). Both have the same characters (different names) careening around San Francisco, Marin, Berkeley and incidentally, Mexico, Europe and Tangier, looking for enlightenment, good cheap wine and sex.

Gus Lee, *China Boy* (Penguin, 1991). Autobiographical coming of age story of a Chinese American boy growing up in 1950s San Francisco who finds himself through boxing.

Oscar Lewis, *I Remember Christine* (Alfred A. Knopf, 1942). In this fictional biography of a San Francisco millionaire, Lewis, the city's historian laureate, gives full rein to his encyclopaedic knowledge of San Francisco history. It is also a surprisingly sympathetic and insightful portrait of an 1890s woman who stumbles into the role of mistress.

Armistead Maupin, *Tales of the City, More Tales of the City, Further Tales of the City.* (Harper Collins, 1978–1983). Maupin is the impish Dickens of San Francisco, chronicling the lives and loves of a tangled group of friends and lovers, gay and straight, who start out in a zany Russian Hill boarding house in the early 1970s.

Ruthanne Lum McCunn, *Thousand Pieces of Gold* (Beacon Press, 1981). The fictionalised account of one of McCunn's relatives, a Chinese girl sold into slavery in nineteenth-century California who eventually finds freedom and her own life.

Maxine Hong Kingston, *The Woman Warrior* (Viking). Powerful and brilliant retellings of Chinese legends in a woman's voice. Hong Kingston now lives in Oakland, after losing her Berkeley Hills home in the disastrous 1991 fires.

John Miller (ed.) *San Francisco Stories: Great Writers on the City* (Chronicle Books, 1990). Fiction and travel writing set in San Francisco from a remarkable group of writers, including Anthony Trollope, Dylan Thomas, Alice B. Toklas, Jack London, Amy Tan, Mark Twain and many more.

Marcia Muller, *Edwin of the Iron Shoes* (Mysterious Press paperback, 1978). Sharon McCone, the archetypal hard-boiled woman detective makes her debut, sorting out a murder in the Tenderloin.

Diana O'Hehir, *I Wish This War Were Over* (Pocket Books paperback, 1984). The funny and poignant coming-of-age of teenage Helen during World War II Oakland and Berkeley.

Danielle Steel, *Fine Things* (Dell, 1987). The plot doesn't really matter – a variation on a beautiful and kind woman in a terrible mess who eventually finds a beautiful and kind man. Steel's vision of San Francisco, her hometown, is probably the most widely disseminated in the world given her tens of millions of readers.

Amy Tan, *The Joy Luck Club* (Putnam, 1989). Approaching the status of a modern classic, the interlocking stories of Chinese immigrant mothers and their thoroughly (or so they think) American daughters.

Travel Books

Adah Bakalinsky, *Stairway Walks in San Francisco* (Lexikos Press, 1984). Easy-to-use guide to SF's hidden stairway streets and lanes.

Shirley Fong-Torres, *San Francisco Chinatown: A Walking Tour* (China Books, 1991). Author and culinary expert Fong-Torres's popular walking tours transferred to guidebook form.

James M. Forbes, *Café San Francisco* (self-published, 1993). A habitué's guide to the city's lively café life.

Don Herron, *The Dashiell Hammett Tour* (City Lights Books,

1991). Herron has been leading this walking tour since 1977, making it the longest standing such tour in the US. He put it all in a book because he keeps saying, 'This is the last year I'm going to do this.' His legion of fans refuse to take him seriously.

Don Herron, *The Literary World of San Franciso & Its Environs* (City Lights, 1990). Walk tourmeister Herron's encyclopaedic knowledge of San Francisco scribblers is entertaining reading and expert guidance.

Ariel Rubissow, *Golden Gate National Recreation Area Park Guide* (Golden Gate National Park Assn, 1990). Easy to use, easy to carry guide to the sprawling parklands tended by the GGNRA, from Aquatic Park to the Golden Gate, along Ocean Beach in San Francisco and the Marin Areas.

Sharon Silva and Frank Viviano, *Exploring the Best Ethnic Restaurants of the Bay Area* (San Francisco Focus Books, 1990). The insider's guide to the plethora of Vietnamese, Burmese, Thai, Mexican, Cuban, Slavic, Chinese, Caribbean, African, etc. restaurants in San Francisco and beyond.

Carey Simon and Charlene Marmer Solomon, *Frommer's San Francisco With Kids* (Prentice Hall Travel, 1992). The best in the San Francisco division of the growing genre-within-a-genre of travelling with children guidebooks. While the writers rely heavily on chain hotels and cafés, they are very skilful in zeroing in on kids' needs and preferences.

Sally Socolich, *Bargain Hunting in the Bay Area* (Wingbow Press, 1993). The definitive shopper's guide to San Francisco and environs. Updated yearly and covers everything from toys to designer dresses.

Patricia Unterman (ed.), *Best Restaurants of San Francisco* (Chronicle Books, 1991). Compilation of reviews and tips from the formidable *San Francisco Chronicle* foodie corps. Updated regularly.

Richard Saul Wurman *et al.*, *San Francisco Access* (AccessPress, 1992). One of the first now-famous Access guidebooks. Justifiably a classic with updated, comprehensive information – a very heavy emphasis on architecture.

Women and Lesbian Writers

Alice Adams, *Almost Perfect* (Knopf, 1993). Novelist Adams has lived in San Francisco almost two decades, writing finely tuned fiction about women trying to come to terms with youthful dreams and middle-age reality. This is her finest novel.

Isabel Allende, *The Infinite Plan* (Harper Collins, 1993). Allende writes about her adopted home, California, for the first time in this story of one man's journey from childhood to manhood in post World War II California.

Dorothy Allison, *Bastard Out of Carolina* (Plume paperback, 1993). Allison, a lesbian activist who lives in San Francisco, had mainstream success with her autobiographical novel of growing up poor and white in Appalachia.

Maya Angelou, *I Know Why the Caged Bird Sings* (Virago, 1993). Angelou's 1969 autobiography has become a classic, tracing her life as a bright young black girl from segregated Arkansas to covertly segregated San Francisco.

Phyllis Burke, *Family Values: Two Moms and Their Son* (Random House, 1993). Burke, a San Francisco lesbian, tells the story of how she and her lover became the legal and emotional parents of her partner's biological son.

Terry McMillan, *Waiting to Exhale* (Pocket Books paperback, 1993). McMillan who moved to the East Bay from Arizona to raise her son in a multicultural environment, has become the fiction laureate of middle-class African American women.

Gertrude Stein, *The Autobiography of Alice B. Toklas* (Harcourt, Brace, 1933). Stein's most accessible book, combining her own and Toklas's views of growing up in San Francisco.

Alice Walker, *Possessing the Secret of Joy* (Pocket Books paperback, 1993). Author of *The Color Purple*, Walker has lived in the Bay Area for twenty years but still writes out of her experience growing up black, proud and poor in Georgia. *Joy* seeks out some minor characters from *The Color Purple* to explore the ritual mutilation of African girls.

Feminism

Susan Faludi, *Backlash: The Undeclared War Against Women* (Chatto & Windus, 1993). Faludi, a Wall Street Journal reporter based in San Francisco, defined the second front of feminism with her breakthrough book.

Susan Griffith, *A Chorus of Stones: The Private Life of War* (Doubleday, 1992). Berkeley feminist, author activist Griffith put forth a dazzling new interpretation of conflict. Griffith's other books, *Pornography and Silence: Culture's Revenge Against Nature* and *Rape: The Power of Consciousness* have established her as a leading American feminist philosopher.

Arlie Hochschild, *The Second Shift* (Avon, 1990). Hochschild

FEMINISM

teaches sociology at Berkeley and pays close attention to women's lives. *Second Shift* documented what women already knew: they do all the housework.

Jessica Mitford, *The American Way of Birth* (Plume reprint, 1993). The grand old Anglo-American muckraker takes on the medical establishment.

Diana E.H. Russell (ed.), *Making Violence Sexy: Feminist Views on Pornography* (Open University Press, 1993). Russell, a Mills College professor of sociology, was a leader rallying feminists against pornography. This anthology is a window on current thinking and themes among anti-porn feminists.

Children

Alice Waters, *Fanny at Chez Panisse* (Harper Collins, 1992). A child's eye view of the famous restaurant. A kind of 'as-told-to' book in the words of founder Alice Waters's seven-year-old daughter, the Eloise of Berkeley.

Tricia Brown, *The City by the Bay: A Magical Journey Around San Francisco* (Chronicle Books, 1993). A large-format picture book with enchanting illustrations by Elisa Kleven, this child's guide to San Francisco is a fun read even for adults. History, culture and amusing facts are effortlessly woven into the text.

CHRONOLOGY

1500 B.C.– 500 A.D.	First Indian tribes settle in San Francisco and around the Bay.
500–1776	Tribes later called Coastanoan and Miwok by Europeans supplant earlier Indian groups; they are hunters and gatherers of semi-nomadic traditions.
1542	Spanish explorer Cabrillo sails past San Francisco Bay, but charts most of the California coast.
1579	Sir Francis Drake comes ashore at either Point Reyes or Monterey and claims the coast for Queen Elizabeth I.
1769	Gaspar de Portola overland expedition comes upon San Francisco Bay; probably the first Europeans to see the Bay.
1775	Juan Manuel de Ayala sails through the Golden Gate and makes the first chart of San Francisco Bay.
1776	A Spanish colony is officially founded by a party of soldiers and priests. The first Mass is held on 29 June at Mission Dolores. On 17 September the military base or presidio, is dedicated.
1791	Mission Dolores is finally completed and dedicated.
1821	Mexico declares independence from Spain and California becomes a province of Mexico.
1834	Mexican government secularises the missions and throws Indians and land ownership into chaos.
1835	English whaling mate turned Californio William A. Richardson builds a 'rough board shanty' on Yerba Buena cove for his shipping business; it's the first permanent structure of what becomes the village Yerba Buena and later the city of San Francisco.
1839	French grocer Jean Vioget, who once studied surveying, is commissioned by Alcade Francisco de Haro to lay out streets for the growing town.
1846	American occupation; San Francisco and California ceded to the US during the Mexican-American War.
1848	Discovery of gold in the Sierra foothills, east of San Francisco.
1849	Gold Rush begins with arrival of first '49ers' on 28 February in San Francisco Bay. On 24 December first of San Francisco's great fires devastates the city.
1850	California is admitted to the union as a free (non-slave) state. The state constitution, adopted the year before, is the first in the US to make provisions for married women to own their own property.

1851	First Committee of Vigilance is formed.
1852	A school for young women is founded in nearby Benicia; it will become Mills College, the first women's college west of the Rocky Mountains.
1855	California's first anti-Chinese laws are enacted by the state legislature.
1856	Second Committee of Vigilance formed.
1859	Comstock Lode discovered near Virginia City, Nevada. This silver seam will eventually yield $400,000,000 making several San Francisco fortunes.
1865	Susan Mills, a graduate of Mount Holyoke in Massachusetts, and her husband Cyrus purchase the Benicia Female Seminary and move it to Oakland. The school is renamed Mills College and introduces a rigorous intellectual curriculum.
1868	University of California chartered.
	Golden Gate Park officially initiated when the City of San Francisco purchases 1017 acres – mostly sand dunes for a park.
1869	Transcontinental railroad is completed at Promontory Point in Utah linking San Francisco to the East Coast.
1870	University of California begins classes in Berkeley; women admitted as full students.
1873	Cable cars introduced; they conquer San Francisco's steep hills.
1877	Anti-Chinese riots led by Denis Kearney; federal troops and finally called in.
	California law prohibiting women from practising law is repealed by the legislature and Clara Shortridge Foltz and Laura DeForce Gordon join the California Bar.
1890	San Francisco Medical Association admits its first woman member, Lucy Maria Field Wanzer.
1891	Stanford University opens; women are enrolled on an equal basis with men.
1893	Sierra Club founded.
1894	The California Midwinter Exposition is held in Golden Gate Park.
1896	Third Cliff House and Sutro Baths open to the public.
1906	An 8.3 earthquake shakes San Francisco; fires that follow level most of the city.
	Later that year, graft investigations shake the city.
1910	Immigration station opens on Angel Island.
1911	California women win the right to vote in a statewide election.

1915	The Panama Pacific International Exposition celebrates the opening of the Panama Canal and the rebuilding of San Francisco.
1916	Rebuilt City Hall, a Beaux Arts palace, opens.
1917	Redlight abatement law puts most bordellos and parlour houses out of business, forcing prostitutes onto the street. It is also the end of the infamous Barbary Coast.
1917–18	US enters World War I; San Francisco mobilises for war effort but the direct impact on the city is minimal.
1924	The Palace of the Legion of Honor, an art museum founded by socialite Alma deBretteville Spreckels and given to the city, dedicated.
1933	Construction begins on Golden Gate and Oakland Bay Bridges.
1934	Waterfront strike spreads all through San Francisco, escalating into a General Strike. Longshoreman Harry Bridges emerges as labour spokesman.
1936	San Francisco-Oakland Bay Bridge opens.
1937	Golden Gate Bridge opens.
1939	Golden Gate International Exposition held on Treasure Island.
1941–45	World War II: San Francisco is primary staging area for war in the Pacific. Thousands of civilians pour into the Bay Area to work in war industries, particularly ship-building.
1942	Japanese-Americans evacuated to inland camps.
1945	V-J Day; celebrants jam downtown and spark a riot.
1953	City Lights Bookstore opens in North Beach.
1955	Del Martin and Phyllis Lyon found Daughters of Bilitis, a lesbian social club, the first lesbian organisation in the US.
1957	Lawrence Ferlinghetti arrested on obscenity charges for selling copies of Allen Ginsberg's poem, 'Howl'.
1964	Free Speech Movement, Berkeley.
1967	'Summer of Love' catapults Haight Ashbury neighbour-hood into international prominence as hippie world headquarters.
1969	People's Park riots, Berkeley.
1971	Alice Waters opens Chez Panisse in Berkeley, unknow-ingly founding 'California Cuisine' and marking the entry of women into the higher realms of haute cuisine.
1972	San Francisco becomes the first American city to enact an anti-discrimination law for homosexuals.
1977	Gay activist Harvey Milk is elected to the SF Board of Supervisors, the first openly homosexual city official in America.

1978	Dianne Feinstein becomes SF's first woman mayor when Mayor George Moscone and gay city supervisor Harvey Milk are gunned down by a disgruntled cop-turned-politician, supervisor Dan White. Feinstein is twice elected mayor on her own, stepping down in 1988.
1981	AIDS surfaces.
1989	Loma Prieta earthquake strikes on 17 October.
1990	Students of Mills College, the last all-women's college in the West, go on strike when the Board of Trustees announces the school will go co-ed. Students force the administration to reverse the decision.
1991	Fires devas.ate the Oakland-Berkeley hills, killing 25 people and destroying 3000 homes.
1992	San Francisco-based journalist Susan Faludi publishes *Backlash: The Undeclared War Against American Women* and a new era of American feminism is declared.
1992	Barbara Boxer and Dianne Feinstein make American and California history by winning both US Senate seats; first time in US history that two women have been elected to the Senate from the same state.

GLOSSARY

AC Transit: Alameda County Transit Authority, the bus system for the East Bay.

Alta California: Northern California, which the Spanish defined as all land that was not the peninsula, beginning roughly at San Diego. Baja California (the peninsula) remained part of Mexico.

BART: Subway system, Bay Area Rapid Transit.

Bathroom/ladies room/rest room: Toilet.

Bay Bridge: San Francisco-Oakland Bay Bridge.

Bohos: Bohemians of the nineties, usually college age or just past.

Brown Shingle: Bay Area variation of Arts and Crafts architecture, characterised by the use of redwood shingles.

Cal: Nickname for the University of California at Berkeley, sometimes also called UC.

California Cuisine: Classic French and Italian style cooking using fresh, in-season local produce, fish and game.

Californios: Spanish and Mexican settlers of California, all non-Indian Californians before the American annexation of 1846.

City Beautiful Movement: Late nineteenth-century school of thought that believed in moral uplift through creating beautiful urban environments with neo-classical architecture and elaborate gardens.

Condo: An apartment or townhouse that is individually owned.

Elevator: Lift.

First floor: Ground floor of a building.

GGNRA: Golden Gate National Recreation Area, US National Park body that administers historic sites and parklands from San Francisco's Aquatic Park to Point Reyes.

Hip-Hop: Youth culture heavily influenced by rap, street fashions and black stars such as Spike Lee and Queen Latifah.

Latte: Café Latte, San Francisco's most popular drink. Steamed milk with a shot of espresso coffee mixed in.

Loma Prieta: Spot in central California where the 1989 earthquake originated; the earthquake is called by that name rather than the date, as with the 1906 earthquake.

Muni: San Francisco Municipal Railway system, Muni usually refers to the buses.

Sex-positive feminists: Feminists who reject most anti-pornography arguments as an abridgement of freedom of speech. By celebrating sexuality, these feminists say, it is redeemed from male possessiveness. Lesbian 'sexologist' Susie Bright is San Francisco's biggest contribution to the movement.

The Avenues: The numbered streets north to south on the western side of the city, from the Presidio to Lake Merced. Primarily small, detached houses originally built for working-class and middle-class residents.

Twentysomethings: The post-baby boom generation, also called 'slackers' and 'generation x'.

WPA: Works Progress Administration, a Depression era agency that hired the jobless and created projects to be carried out. Much of the work was done in national parks, historic sites and civic improvements.

Zip code: Postal code.

INDEX

INDEX